Models of Modals

Topics in English Linguistics

Editors
Susan M. Fitzmaurice
Bernd Kortmann

Volume 110

Ilse Depraetere, Bert Cappelle, Martin Hilpert, Ludovic De Cuypere,
Mathieu Dehouck, Pascal Denis, Susanne Flach, Natalia Grabar, Cyril Grandin,
Thierry Hamon, Clemens Hufeld, Benoît Leclercq, Hans-Jörg Schmid

Models of Modals

From Pragmatics and Corpus Linguistics
to Machine Learning

DE GRUYTER
MOUTON

ISBN 978-3-11-162072-5
e-ISBN (PDF) 978-3-11-073415-7
e-ISBN (EPUB) 978-3-11-073425-6
ISSN 1434-3452

Library of Congress Control Number: 2022948631

Bibliographic information published by the Deutsche Nationalbibliothek
The Deutsche Nationalbibliothek lists this publication in the Deutsche Nationalbibliografie;
detailed bibliographic data are available on the Internet at http://dnb.dnb.de.

© 2024 Walter de Gruyter GmbH, Berlin/Boston
This volume is text- and page-identical with the hardback published in 2023.
Cover image: Brian Stablyk / Photographer's Choice RF / Getty Images
Typesetting: Integra Software Services Pvt. Ltd.

www.degruyter.com

Preface

This book considerably builds on the results of a funded Franco-Swiss project (2017-2021), *Rethinking English Modal Constructions (REM): from feature-based paradigms to usage-based probabilistic representations*, and we gratefully acknowledge the financial support we received from ANR (ANR-16-CE93-0009) and FNS (100012L/169490/1).

The rich literature on modality notwithstanding, it was our aim to investigate how a combination of empirical methods and theoretical insights could result in a deeper understanding of the factors that drive a speaker's choice of modals. A team of linguists from the University of Lille and the University of Neuchâtel joined forces. In Lille, the team involved Ilse Depraetere, Bert Cappelle, Mathieu Dehouck (currently at Lattice, CNRS – École Normale Supérieure – Sorbonne Nouvelle), Pascal Denis, Natalia Grabar, Cyril Grandin, Benoît Leclercq (now at the University of Paris 8) and Bo Li (subsequently at Baidu Research). In Neuchâtel, the researchers were Martin Hilpert and Susanne Flach (who is now at the University of Zürich). The project was characterized by a wish to move beyond the pairwise comparison of modals, to build a rich empirical database (the REM dataset, used in several chapters of this book), and to check in what ways the lexico-grammatical premises of Construction Grammar, approaches to meaning in lexical pragmatics, and methodologies from natural language processing and machine learning could complement each other. We called upon the additional expertise of Ludovic De Cuypere (University of Ghent and Free University of Brussels), Thierry Hamon (Université Paris-Nord), Clemens Hufeld and Hans-Jörg Schmid (both at Ludwig Maximilian University of Munich) while designing the general rationale of the book and working on some of the analyses. This volume as a whole is co-authored by all people mentioned. While not all chapters in it are written by all the authors, several authors have been involved in the co-authoring of multiple chapters, which, we hope, adds to overall coherence of the book to an extent not always achieved by edited volumes. We have described in detail in the introduction how our aims have shaped the general organisation of the chapters.

In a way, our book complements volume 1 of Declerck's (2006) *The Grammar of the English Verb Phrase*, which provided a detailed account of English tenses (Declerck, in coop. with Reed and Cappelle, 2006) and which also appeared in this series. However, unlike *The Grammar of the English Tense System: A Comprehensive Analysis*, the present book is not a full, descriptive and 'traditional' grammar of English modality. While there is a lot of attention to the key descriptive issues in the field, it has method triangulation in the foreground and adopts a broader scope involving individual variation as well as facets pertaining to acquisition. An earlier offshoot of the project dealt with modality (not exclusively in English) from the perspective of diachronic Construction Grammar (Hilpert, Cappelle and Depraetere 2021).

The REM dataset and the annotation guidelines have been made available on the companion website of the book (https://www.degruyter.com/document/isbn/9783110734157/html). This website also provides access to supplementary material for individual chapters: additional datasets used, open R markdown documents, and more.

We would like to thank Bernd Kortmann, the series editor, for his engagement throughout this project, as well as Nathalie Fecher, Barbara Karlsson, and Birgit Sievert from De Gruyter Mouton, for their editorial support. We are also grateful to the external reviewers of chapters, listed here in alphabetical order: Ronny Boogaart, Robert Daugs, Israel de la Fuente, Holger Diessel, Dagmar Divjak, Katrin Erk, Gaëtanelle Gilquin, Stefan Hartmann, Jan-Ola Östman and Naoaki Wada. Their feedback has greatly helped us in making this book as accessible and accurate as we could, but any remaining shortcomings are, of course, ours.

References

Declerck, Renaat, in cooperation with Susan Reed & Bert Cappelle. 2006. *The Grammar of the English Verb Phrase. Volume 1: The Grammar of the English Tense System: A Comprehensive Analysis* (Topics in English Linguistics 60–1). Berlin/New York: Mouton de Gruyter.

Hilpert, Martin, Bert Cappelle & Ilse Depraetere (eds.), 2021. *Modality and Diachronic Construction Grammar* (Constructional Approaches to Language 32). Amsterdam/Philadelphia: John Benjamins.

Contents

Preface —— V

Introduction —— 1
Ilse Depraetere, Bert Cappelle and Martin Hilpert

1 English modals: An outline of their forms, meanings and uses —— 14
  Ilse Depraetere and Bert Cappelle

2 Modality revisited: Combining insights from Construction Grammar and Relevance Theory —— 60
  Benoît Leclercq

3 Possibility modals: Which conditions make them possible? —— 93
  Bert Cappelle, Ludovic De Cuypere, Ilse Depraetere, Cyril Grandin and Benoît Leclercq

4 Necessity modals and the role of source as a predictive factor —— 118
  Benoît Leclercq, Bert Cappelle, Ilse Depraetere and Cyril Grandin

5 You *must*/*have to* choose: Experimenting with choices between near-synonymous modals —— 149
  Susanne Flach, Bert Cappelle and Martin Hilpert

6 Does the intersubjectivity of modal verbs boost inter-individual differences? —— 177
  Clemens Hufeld and Hans-Jörg Schmid

7 Modals as a predictive factor for L2 proficiency level —— 199
  Natalia Grabar, Thierry Hamon and Benoît Leclercq

8 Revisiting modal sense classification with contextual word embeddings —— 225
  Mathieu Dehouck and Pascal Denis

9 Modals in the network model of Construction Grammar —— 254
  Martin Hilpert and Susanne Flach

Index —— 271

Introduction

Ilse Depraetere, Bert Cappelle and Martin Hilpert

1 Modal verbs and why they have attracted a lot of attention

This volume applies different approaches to an area of English linguistics that is particularly challenging, that of the meaning of English modals. Our aim is to arrive at a better and richer understanding by combining insights from methods and theories among which there has as yet not been much interaction. In the course of doing so, we test their relative strengths and potential shortcomings, and show in what ways they complement each other and can shed new light on the topic at stake.

Modality, the linguistic expression of possibility and necessity, is a topic that has inspired a lot of research. This is hardly surprising for a lexical-grammatical area that pertains to an indispensable aspect of human cognition. As Narrog (2012: 1) puts it, "[h]uman beings constantly imagine things that are not real but still possible or even contrary to facts. They continually evaluate the reality status of states-of-affairs, or urge or allow interlocutors to bring about states-of-affairs in reality." Take any moderate-sized stretch of spoken or written text and you will find that as people, we cannot help but communicate our natural interest in what is possible and what is necessary. A common way of expressing this pervasive concern is by means of modal verbs. To illustrate this, we provide in (1a-d) just some of the sentences with modal verbs that appeared on the website of a conference on English linguistics:[1]

(1) a. ISLE6 preliminary program summary 31 August 2020 – subject to change
Wednesday, 3 June 2020 9/10–12 Workshops, Part 1 (individual workshops **may** start later)
b. The session chair will introduce the speaker(s) and you **may** begin your presentation.
c. In total, around five minutes of kneading **should** be fine. [from a page devoted to the host country of the conference, with recipes of some local food]
d. The length of your abstract **should** not exceed 500 words (excluding references).

---

[1] These sentences are taken from https://sites.uef.fi/isle6/ and underlying pages (accessed 8 August 2021; boldface added – ID, BC, MH).

https://doi.org/10.1515/9783110734157-001

In (1a-b), the modal verb *may* expresses shades of possibility; in (1c-d), the modal verb *should* expresses kinds of necessity. 'Modality' is an important, possibly universal, functional concept; it has been defined not only in terms of forms that represent situations as possible or necessary, but also, in more general terms, as forms that represent a situation as less than factual. Following Van der Auwera and Plungian (1998), we subscribe to the former, more restrictive approach. This implies that volition, which does not enter, in a straightforward way, into the possibility-necessity paradigm, will not be in the foreground in the chapters of this book. In any case, given the ubiquity of modal verbs in discourse, there is little wonder that they have been of prominent interest in linguistic research. Two more specific reasons can explain why linguists have been fascinated by them.

A first main reason for linguists' attention to modal verbs is their semantic versatility. In (1a) and (1c), the modal verbs *may* and *should* both express epistemic modality, reflecting on the speaker's perceived likelihood of the situation being the case (moderately likely in the case of *may* and very likely in the case of *should*), based on some knowledge of reality the speaker has.[2] In (1b) and (1d), the same two modals express root, or non-epistemic, modality: the utterer is not concerned here with any degree of certainty as to the truth of the non-modalized proposition, but more directly with factors that impact on the actualization of the situation expressed. The existence of permission makes the situation of beginning a presentation possible in (1b); the existence of a formal requirement makes it necessary for participants' abstracts not to exceed a word limit in (1d). Again, possibility and necessity are involved, but it should be clear that root interpretations of these two modals differ substantially from the same two modals' epistemic readings. How to deal insightfully with the availability of these two radically different semantic notions of modal verbs has, understandably, been a major analytical challenge. There is some controversy, for example, as to how distinct these notions are. In the same recipe from which (1c) was drawn, we find this example:

(2) Use your hands to knead the dough in the bowl. It **should** become elastic.

Is this use of *should* epistemic (the writer considering it quite likely that the dough will become elastic when kneading it), non-epistemic (the writer pointing out that it is important for the dough to become elastic), or some kind of mixture? While the exact interpretation may not matter a great deal in this specific context,

---

[2] Here and elsewhere in this book, we use 'speaker' and 'hearer' to refer to the sender and receiver, respectively, of any type of communication, whether it is spoken or written.

the question is whether such an example suggests that epistemic and root (or non-epistemic) meanings can coexist. Coates (1983: 17) has discussed such cases under the heading of 'merger'. The context here simply does not allow us to decide with absolute certainty which of the two interpretations, which really *are* conceptually different, was intended by the writer. (In this case, it was probably the non-epistemic reading, as recipes are essentially sets of instructions.) We shall have more to say about the notion of merger in Chapter 1.

A second important reason for the popularity of modal verbs in linguistic research is that for any single intended modal meaning, broadly defined (e.g., epistemic possibility; non-epistemic necessity), there are typically several modal verbs that can be used, with often little discernible semantic difference. Thus, in the examples given above in (1a-d), we could substitute other modal verbs and thereby hardly change the meaning of the sentences:

(3) a. ISLE6 preliminary program summary 31 August 2020 – subject to change
Wednesday, 3 June 2020
9/10–12 Workshops, Part 1 (individual workshops **may / might / could** start later)
b. The session chair will introduce the speaker(s) and you **may / can** begin your presentation.
c. In total, around five minutes of kneading **should / will / ought to** be fine.
d. The length of your abstract **should** not / **must** not / **ought** not **to** / **may** not / **can**not exceed 500 words (excluding references).

The availability of multiple expressions for a single meaning raises familiar linguistic questions relating to variation and competition. In this respect, note that while the focus in this book is on modal verbs (sometimes just called 'modals') in the English language, there are various other formal realizations of modality. Consider the following sentence, in which the main clause, which does not have a finite verb, expresses non-epistemic necessity thanks to *best (to)*:

(4) If you think a concept like white privilege has some validity, **best to** explain carefully what you mean by it, and what you don't. (*The Economist*, 1 July 2021; boldface added – ID, BC, MH)

For an overview of the kinds of markers that have been addressed under the heading of modality, see, for example, Portner (2009: 2–8). Modal adverbs and adjectives, specifically, have been studied by Hoye (1997), Simon-Vandenbergen and Aijmer (2007) and Van Linden (2012).

Modality, and modal verbs in particular, thus constitute the classic double problem of (i) single forms having multiple meanings and (ii) single meanings being expressible with multiple forms. This, and their centrality in thought and language, make them an ideal testing ground for fundamental semasiological and onomasiological research into variation in meaning and form. Accordingly, modality has been studied within various theoretical models, both linguistic and philosophical in nature, and from various research perspectives. In linguistics, modality has been dealt with from a formal semantic approach (e.g. Kratzer 2012, Portner 2009, 2018), within Relevance Theory (e.g. Papafragou 2000), and within cognitive linguistics and Construction Grammar (e.g. Talmy 1988, Sweetser 1990, Langacker 2003, Mortelmans 2007, Boogaart 2009, Boogaart and Fortuin 2016). Different research practices and concerns can be distinguished as well. For instance, the diachrony of modal verbs has been a major focus of attention (e.g. Traugott and Dasher 2002, Hilpert 2008, 2013a, 2013b, Furmaniak 2011, Narrog 2012, Gregersen 2020) and modal verbs have been studied within the field of natural language processing (e.g. Ruppenhofer and Rehbein 2012, Marasović and Frank 2016). Corpora, right from their emergence, have served to describe the form and functions of modal verbs (e.g. Coates 1983, Palmer 1979, 1990, Westney 1995), with proper attention to geographical variation (e.g. Hundt and Gut 2012, Collins 2009, 2015) and sociolinguistic variation (e.g. Williams and Korhonen 2020). Apart from the use of corpora, other empirical approaches have been adopted, notably in language acquisition studies (e.g. Ozturk and Papafragou 2014).

With such a fecund literature on modality, what justifies yet another book on what can be considered the core markers of modality, that is, modal verbs? Isn't it the case that most has been said and written about English modals? We do feel there is a need for another book-length treatment. In the next section, we will spell out our motivation for this book, and our basic methodological stance.

2 Why we still need another book on modal verbs

The very rich body of modality research notwithstanding, there are various ways in which the state of the art, on modal verbs specifically, can be advanced. To begin with, we aim to address the double problem (variation in meaning and in form) mentioned in Section 1 more thoroughly and more systematically.

With respect to variation in meaning, we aim to supply some theoretical concepts with which we can understand the different interpretations that a modal verb may have in context. A modal verb comes with a set of conventionalized meanings, such as 'ability', 'permission', 'opportunity' and a few others in the case of *can*, but it is the context in which it appears that determines which specific meaning is recovered. Some of these contexts can themselves also take the form of linguistic routines or formulas, such as *I can't help but* VP (see e.g. Leclercq 2022) and *Why can't you just* VP?, which are associated with rich content, including not just semantic aspects but typically also pragmatic ones, such as speech-act information (cf. also Cappelle and Depraetere 2016). The linguistic contexts around modals are thus less free and variable than could be assumed; rather, many recurrent 'chunks' around modals lend themselves to being seen as linguistic units in their own right. In other words, we shouldn't restrict the form side of modals to just the modal verb itself, but we may have to extend that form to some of its surrounding lexical elements and/or syntactic categories. This has serious implications for the semantics-pragmatics interface, making it untenable to claim that only and all semantic content is encoded in a (non-complex) linguistic form while all pragmatic information remains to be purely inferred from the linguistic and situational co(n)text. In short, considerable attention will be given in this book to the semantics-pragmatics interface (as understood by e.g. Finkbeiner 2019, Leclercq and Depraetere 2022) and the ways in which the context-dependent meaning of modal verbs can be captured adequately. Chapter 1, in particular, is devoted to this, as is Chapter 2, which explores hypotheses about the interpretation of English modals within Relevance Theory and Construction Grammar, two theories of cognition between which there has been little interaction. One of the aims of our book, then, is to see whether there can be cross-fertilization between different theories, as well as between different methodologies – which we now come to.

As regards variation in form, we are interested to find out what makes speakers of English choose one verb among the full range of available modal verbs of possibility and necessity. What linguistic knowledge plays a role in this selection process? Which methodologies can be used to lay bare the factors that drive the selection at work? We would like to go beyond analyses that focus on pairs of verbs, such as *can* and *be able to*, *must* and *have to*, or *should* and *ought to*, and instead consider discriminating factors governing the choice of a modal within larger groups, such as all those that express possibility. In terms of the combination of methodologies and research practices, how can hand-annotated corpus findings be enriched with insights from machine-learning techniques that can handle 'big data'? To what extent do results from psycholinguistic experiments confirm the corpus findings? How do modals feature in the output of language learners at different proficiency levels? And more in general, to what extent is individuals' use of modals determined by factors like age, education and gender? In other words, we will take a multi-model, multi-method approach in this book, as we:

- explore the semantics-pragmatics interface for modal meaning (Chapters 1 and 2);
- use a lexico-grammatical approach typical of Construction Grammar (Chapters 1, 2, 9 and passim);
- apply relevance-theoretic notions, specifically the distinction between 'conceptual' and 'procedural' meaning (Sperber and Wilson 1995), to the interpretation of modals in context (Chapter 2);
- use statistical methods that test and measure the significance of proposed syntactic, semantic and pragmatic features typical of the mainly qualitative, corpus-based, descriptive approaches to modal verbs in English (Chapters 3, 4, 5 and passim);

and in addition:
- seek convergent evidence via psycholinguistic data or, at least, determine to what extent there is psycholinguistic evidence that can back up the cognitive reality of the discriminating factors identified via a corpus-linguistic investigation (Chapter 5);
- explore variation in the use of modals across speakers (Chapter 6);
- harness learners' use of modals to predict their L2 proficiency (Chapter 7);
- use data-driven approaches typical of computational sciences (Chapters 6 to 8).

Finally, based on our insights and on new data from machine-learning analyses, we will
- propose a rethink of the network model within which modal verb constructions, perceived as form-meaning pairings, are linked to each other (Chapter 9).

The theoretical model based on the reassessment of the semantics-pragmatics interface outlined in Chapter 2 reserves due place for the respective contributions that can be made by Relevance Theory and Construction Grammar. In a similar way, the last chapter of the book makes explicit the ways in which we believe the state of contemporary usage-based linguistics can be advanced. In sum, our approach is both theoretical and empirical. The generalizations made in the other chapters all build on empirical data, be they data sets extracted from corpora or results of experiments, to which various quantitative methods are applied in order to get a better grip on the semantic and pragmatic profile of modal verbs.

Summing up, we will move from reflections on how pragmatics interfaces with semantics (as well as with lexico-grammatical structure) and from corpus linguistics involving manual annotation to machine learning and beyond – to novel linguistic ways of conceptualising modal verbs as nodes in a network. The uniqueness of this new book on English modals, motivating its addition to the rich existing literature on them, is therefore at least twofold. The different theoretical and empirical perspectives taken in this work are not presented alongside each other, as is often the case in an edited volume (as opposed to a co-authored one like ours), but jointly help us build a coherent picture of modal verb constructions, used by both native speakers and learners of the English language. At the same time, by dealing with a single, well-known topic in English linguistics, the book demonstrates that not a single one of these approaches is sufficient by itself but that their strengths lie in their mutual compatibility and complementarity.

3 Overview of the chapters

Chapter 1, English modals: An outline of their forms, meanings and uses (Ilse Depraetere and Bert Cappelle), addresses some of the long-standing questions in research on modal verbs in English. After a brief presentation of the formal properties of modal verbs, the chapter turns to taxonomic issues and critically reviews the distinctions that have been made in the literature. This discussion informs a taxonomy that is based on explicit criteria that are systematically applied to the set of English possibility and necessity modals. Our proposal leads us to reflect on what is semantic/pragmatic about the meaning of modals and on the monosemy/polysemy question. In this chapter, we also describe the data sets that are used in the book and we briefly present the main methods used to analyze them.

Chapter 2, Modality revisited: Combining insights Construction Grammar and Relevance Theory (Benoît Leclercq), looks at the benefits of combining insights from Construction Grammar (Hoffmann and Trousdale 2013; Hilpert 2019) and Relevance Theory (Sperber and Wilson 1995; Clark 2013), and it addresses the theoretical issues introduced in Chapter 1 from this combined perspective: it presents a new model for the analysis of modal meaning, with appropriate consideration of the main contextual and co-textual factors that shape the meaning of modal sentences. First, the morphosyntax of modality in English is revisited, and it is proposed that modals are best understood in terms of a complex network of related constructions, each of which contribute in their own way to the interpretation of a modal sentence. Then, the category of modality is defined and it is argued that the complexity of pinning down the meaning of modal constructions comes from the dual nature of their semantic content, both conceptual (i.e. possibility/necessity) and procedural (i.e. the speaker's attitude, root or epistemic), a distinction central to Relevance Theory (cf. Escandell-Vidal, Leonetti and Ahern 2011). Finally, it is claimed that while modal constructions are semantically polysemous (as assumed in Construction Grammar), the interpretation of modal sentences remains essentially a pragmatic affair guided by general cognitive principles (as assumed in Relevance Theory). In particular, the interpretation of modal constructions primarily involves 'lexically regulated saturation' (Depraetere 2010, 2014, Leclercq 2019), an inferential process of meaning reconstruction.

Chapter 3, Possibility modals: Which conditions make them possible? (Bert Cappelle, Ludovic De Cuypere, Ilse Depraetere, Cyril Grandin and Benoît Lerclercq), is the first of a number of empirical chapters. It reports on the findings from an extensive corpus-based study that aims to pin down the subtle syntactic, semantic and pragmatic differences between five possibility modals: *can, could, may, might* and *be able to*. In the REM project a sample of 2,500 tokens from the Corpus of Contemporary American English (Davies 2008) were manually annotated in terms of 36 variables that previous smaller-scale theoretical and empirical studies have argued to be relevant to modal verb selection.[3] Some of these variables are mainly semantic in nature, for example, whether the subject of the modal expression is generic or not (e.g., *Potatoes can be planted anytime in summer* vs. *Once the leaves turn pale yellow and wilt I can harvest potatoes*). Others are syntactic (e.g. presence of negation, inversion, etc.). Yet other variables are pragmatic (relating, for instance, to speech acts). In this chapter, logistic regression techniques are used to determine which of the potentially relevant variables are significant for the speaker's selection of a particular possibility modal expression.

In **Chapter 4, Necessity modals and the role of source as a predictive factor** (Benoît Leclercq, Bert Cappelle, Ilse Depraetere and Cyril Grandin), we turn to necessity modals, more in particular to *should, must, ought to, need to* and *have to* when they express root meaning. The concept of source is central here, understood as the person or circumstance that makes it necessary for a situation to actualize or that makes it necessary for someone to do something. Five types of sources are distinguished: subject-internal, discourse-internal, circumstantial, conditional, and 'rules and regulations'. On the basis of the REM data set annotation, we try to determine to what extent specific modals are typically attracted or repelled by specific types of sources. We find that *must* is often used for 'rules and regulations' and *have to* for circumstantial sources, compared to the other modal verbs in our data set. These observations are in conformity with what is often claimed in the linguistic literature, but some of our findings also lead us to modify previously made claims.

---

[3] As explained in the preface, this book considerably builds on the results of a Franco-Swiss funded project, *Rethinking English Modal Constructions (REM): From feature-based paradigms to usage-based probabilistic representations*, in the context of which a database was compiled and annotated. The REM dataset will be described in more detail in Chapter 1.

Starting from the findings in the previous chapter, and taking into account three further factors annotated in the REM dataset (person, agentivity, and genericity), **Chapter 5, *You must/have to choose*: Experimenting with the choice between near-synonymous modals** (Susanne Flach, Bert Cappelle and Martin Hilpert), checks to what extent results from corpus analysis and psycholinguistic experiments converge. It is to be situated against the common, more general question of whether and in how far corpus findings are psychologically real. This question is addressed by asking to what extent explanatory factors from corpus analyses also underlie speakers' preferences between the near-synonymous modals *must* and *have to*. The results indicate that preferences for either *must* and *have to* are primarily explained by source (i.e., rule-based stimuli favor *must*), as well as by verb association (i.e., whether the post-modal infinitive is more strongly associated with either *must* or *have to*), included in the study as a control variable. In terms of theoretical implications, the results are compatible with dynamic network model approaches of link strength and link activation (cf. Chapter 9 on network models).

Having examined the impact of linguistic features on the choice of modal on the basis of corpus analyses (Chapters 3, 4 and 5) and having used experimental methods to probe into the cognitive mechanisms that drive the choice between two necessity modals (Chapter 5), the next chapter investigates external factors that potentially determine speakers' use of modals: the discussion now turns to individual variation in the use of modals across speakers and the potential effects of social variables like gender, age, education and social class, this time making use of computational methods. **Chapter 6, Does the intersubjectivity of modal verbs boost inter-individual differences?** (Clemens Hufeld and Hans-Jörg Schmid), investigates whether the degree of inter-individual variation in the use of n-grams is conditioned by the presence of modal verbs. This research question is motivated by the expectation that linguistic elements and expressions that convey highly intersubjective meanings, such as modals, should be more subject to inter-individual variation than less loaded elements. Controlling for frequency of occurrence, 22 modal and non-modal uni-grams (e.g. *can* vs. *get*), bi-grams (e.g. *you can* vs *you think*) and tri-grams (e.g. *'ll have to* vs. *I went to*) are extracted from the spoken part of the British National Corpus (BNC) 2014 and compared in their frequency distribution. The two groups are first compared with regard to their normalized frequencies of occurrence and variation in usage frequency across individual speakers (using the coefficient of variation). Then regression models including social markers such as age, gender and educational quality as covariables are fitted. The model results are inspected for effects of these social variables, and the dispersion values are used as indicators of the degree of inter-individual differences. It turns out, surprisingly, that none of the analyses yields results that indicate that n-grams containing modal verbs show stronger individual differences than other n-grams. Although the null-hypothesis cannot be rejected, the chapter provides thought-provoking insights into inter-individual variation in the use of spoken language and opens up exciting alleys of research for quantitative corpus studies.

Chapter 7, Modals as a predictive factor for L2 proficiency level (Natalia Grabar, Thierry Hamon and Benoît Leclercq), investigates yet another facet of speaker variation, again on the basis of corpus data: it deals with English modals from the perspective of second-language production. That is, this chapter aims to find out to what extent the use of modal verbs is indicative of L2 level of proficiency. More in general, what is investigated here is the automatic prediction of the proficiency level of English learners on the basis of various linguistic features, modal verbs and expressions being one type of predictor, next to readability scores and learner n-grams (as identified via a comparison with reference n-grams from the BNC and COCA corpora). The EFCamDat corpus, which contains texts produced by speakers belonging to six different proficiency levels (see Chapter 1, Section 4), serves as the main database. Different supervised learning algorithms are exploited; when all features are used, they result in a high predictive power of L2 proficiency level in English. Modal verbs and expressions alone predict the right category for almost a third of productions.

Chapter 8, Revisiting modal sense classification with contextual word embeddings (Mathieu Dehouck and Pascal Denis), addresses the question of modal sense classification (MSC), using the most up-to-date word representation techniques. In Chapter 1 we were concerned with the delineation of semantic categories of modal meaning and we offered a critical analysis of previous taxonomies. Here, the aim is to predict modal meanings, starting from specific taxonomies that have been applied to datasets and making use of machine-learning methods. While often overlooked in research on computational linguistics, MSC is an interesting task in many regards. It complements its bigger sibling, word sense disambiguation, in being interested in words with more 'abstract', 'grammatical' meanings. Language models such as BERT (Devlin et al. 2019) have proven very useful for a number of challenging natural language processing tasks, and MSC poses its own specific difficulties because of the small size of the annotated datasets that are available and the skewedness of the data distributions. This chapter thus investigates the potential of using contextualized word representations to see how modals overlap in terms of their meaning and contextual profiles. This approach is compared with previously published results for existing datasets and the method is applied to the REM dataset.

Chapter 9, Modals in the network model of Construction Grammar (Martin Hilpert and Susanne Flach), explores how modal constructions can be understood in terms of the network model of Construction Grammar (Goldberg 1995, 2006, Hilpert 2019). More specifically, the chapter proposes a re-conceptualization of modal constructions as networks of associative connections, thus placing a major emphasis on the role of links in the organization of linguistic knowledge. Following recent work in Construction Grammar that distinguishes between different connection types (Diessel 2019, Schmid 2020, Sommerer and Smirnova 2020), it is examined how these ideas apply to modal constructions. The central argument of the chapter is that speakers' knowledge of modal constructions can be captured in terms of symbolic, paradigmatic, syntagmatic, and pragmatic associations. The general claim is illustrated on the basis of empirical evidence from psycholinguistic work and corpus studies.

References

Boogaart, Ronny. 2009. Semantics and pragmatics in Construction Grammar: The case of modal verbs. In Alex Bergs & Gabriela Diewald (eds.), *Contexts and constructions*, 213–241. Amsterdam & Philadelphia, PA: John Benjamins.

Boogaart, Ronny, & Egbert Fortuin. 2016. Modality and mood in cognitive linguistics and construction grammars. In Johan van der Auwera & Jan Nuyts (eds.), *The Oxford Handbook of Mood and Modality*, 514–533. Oxford: Oxford University Press.

Cappelle, Bert & Ilse Depraetere. 2016. Short-circuited interpretations of modal verb constructions: Some evidence from *The Simpsons*. *Constructions and Frames* 8 (1). 7–39.

Clark, Billy. 2013. *Relevance Theory*. Cambridge: Cambridge University Press.

Coates, Jennifer. 1983. *The Semantics of the Modal Auxiliaries*. London & Canberra: Croom Helm.

Collins, Peter. 2009. *Modals and Quasi-Modals in English*. Amsterdam & New York: Rodopi.

Collins, Peter (ed.). 2015. *Grammatical Change in English World-Wide*. Amsterdam: John Benjamins Publishing Company.

Davies, Mark. 2008–. The Corpus of Contemporary American English (COCA): 560 million words, 1990-present. Available online at https://www.english-corpora.org/coca/

Depraetere, Ilse. 2010. Some observations on the meaning of modals. In Bert Cappelle & Naoaki Wada (eds.), *Distinctions in English Grammar, Offered to Renaat Declerck*, 72–91. Tokyo: Kaitakusha.

Depraetere, Ilse. 2014. Modals and lexically-regulated saturation. *Journal of Pragmatics* 7. 160–177.

Devlin, Jacob, Ming-Wei Chang, Kenton Lee & Kristina Toutanova. 2019. BERT: Pre-training of deep bidirectional transformers for language understanding. In *Proceedings of NAACL-HLT*, 4171–4186.

Diessel, Holger. 2019. *The Grammar Network: How Linguistic Structure is Shaped by Language Use*. Cambridge: Cambridge University Press.

Escandell-Vidal, Victoria, Manuel Leonetti & Aoife Ahern (eds.), 2011. *Procedural Meaning: Problems and Perspectives*. Bingley: Emerald Group Publishing.

Finkbeiner, Rita. 2019. Reflections on the role of pragmatics in Construction Grammar, *Constructions and Frames* 11(2): 171–192.

Furmaniak, Gregory. 2011. On the emergence of the epistemic use of *must*. *Sky Journal of Linguistics* 24. 41–73.
Goldberg, Adele. 1995. *Constructions: A Construction Grammar Approach to Argument Structure*. Chicago: University of Chicago Press.
Goldberg, Adele. 2006. *Constructions at Work: The Nature of Generalization in Language*. Oxford: Oxford University Press.
Gregersen, Sune. 2020. *Early English Modals: Form, Function and Analogy*. PhD Dissertation. University of Amsterdam.
Hilpert, Martin. 2008. *Germanic Future Constructions: A Usage-Based Approach to Grammaticalization*. Amsterdam & Philadelphia: John Benjamins.
Hilpert, Martin. 2013a. *Constructional Change in English: Developments in allomorphy, word formation, and syntax*. Cambridge: Cambridge University Press.
Hilpert, Martin. 2013b. Die englischen Modalverben im Daumenkino: Zur dynamischen Visualisierung von Phänomenen des Sprachwandels. *Zeitschrift für Literaturwissenschaft und Linguistik* 42. 67–82.
Hilpert, Martin. 2019 [2014]. *Construction Grammar and its Application to English*, 2nd edn. Edinburgh: Edinburgh University Press.
Hoffmann, Thomas & Graeme Trousdale (eds.), 2013. *The Oxford Handbook of Construction Grammar*, Oxford: Oxford University Press.
Hoye, Leo. 1997. *Adverbs and Modality in English*. London & New York, NY: Longman
Hundt, Marianne & Ulrike Gut (eds.), 2012. *Mapping Unity and Diversity World-Wide: Corpus-Based Studies of New Englishes*. Amsterdam: John Benjamins.
Kratzer, Angelika. 2012, *Modals and Conditionals: New and Revised Perspectives*. Oxford: Oxford University Press.
Langacker, Ronald W. 2003. Extreme subjectification: English tense and modals, In Hubert Cuyckens, Thomas Berg, René Driven & Karl-Uwe Panther (eds.), *Motivation in Language: Studies in Honor of Günter Radden*, 3–26. Amsterdam: John Benjamins.
Leclercq, Benoît. 2019. *On the Semantics-Pragmatics interface: A Theoretical Bridge between Construction Grammar and Relevance Theory*. PhD thesis. University of Lille.
Leclercq, Benoît. 2022. From modals to modal constructions: an n-gram analysis of *can*, *could* and *be able to*, *Constructions and Frames* 14(2). 226–261.
Leclercq, Benoît & Ilse Depraetere. 2022. Making meaning with *be able to*: modality and actualization. *English Language and Linguistics*, 26(1). 27–48.
Marasović, Anna & Anette Frank. 2016. *Multilingual Modal Sense Classification Using a Convolutional Neural Network*. Proceedings of the 1st Workshop on Representation Learning for NLP, Berlin, Germany.
Mortelmans, Tania. 2007. Modality in Cognitive linguistics. In Dirk Geeraerts & Hubert Cuyckens (eds.), *The Oxford Handbook of Cognitive linguistics*, 869–889, Oxford: Oxford University Press.
Narrog, Heiko. 2012. *Modality, Subjectivity, and Semantic Change. A Cross-Linguistic Perspective*. Oxford: Oxford University Press.
Ozturk, Ozge & Anna Papafragou. 2014. The acquisition of epistemic modality: From semantic meaning to pragmatic interpretation. *Language Learning and Development* 11(3). 1–24.
Palmer, Frank R. 1979. *Modality and the English modals*. London: Longman.
Palmer, Frank. R. 1990 [1979]. *Modality and the English Modals*. 2nd edn. London: Longman.
Papafragou, Anna. 2000. *Modality: Issues in the Semantics-Pragmatics Interface*. Amsterdam: Elsevier.

Portner, Paul. 2009. *Modality*. Oxford: Oxford University Press.
Portner, Paul 2018. *Mood*. Oxford: Oxford University Press.
Ruppenhofer, Josef & Ines Rehbein. 2012. Yes we can!? annotating English modal verbs. In *Proceedings of the Eighth International Conference on Language Resources and Evaluation (LREC'12)*, 1538–1545. Istanbul, Turkey, May 2012. European Language Resources Association (ELRA).
Schmid, Hans-Jörg. 2020. *The Dynamics of the Linguistic System. Usage, Conventionalization, and Entrenchment*, Oxford: Oxford University Press.
Simon-Vandenbergen, Anne-Marie & Karen Aijmer. 2007. *The Semantic Field of Modal Certainty. A Corpus-Based Study of English Adverbs*. Berlin: Mouton de Gruyter.
Sommerer, Lotte & Elena Smirnova (eds.), 2020. *Nodes and Networks in Diachronic Construction Grammar*. Amsterdam: John Benjamins Publishing Company.
Sperber, Dan & Deidre Wilson. 1995. [1985] *Relevance: Communication and Cognition*. 2nd ed. Oxford: Blackwell.
Sweetser, Eve. 1990. *From Etymology to Pragmatics*. Cambridge: Cambridge University Press.
Talmy, Leonard. 1988. Force dynamics in language and cognition. *Cognitive Science* 12(1). 49–100.
Traugott, Elizabeth C. & Robert B. Dasher. 2002. *Regularity in Semantic Change*. Cambridge: Cambridge University Press.
van der Auwera, Johan & Vladimir A. Plungian. 1998. Modality's semantic map. *Linguistic Typology* 2. 79–124.
Van Linden, An. 2012. *Modal Adjectives. English Deontic and Evaluative Constructions in a Synchronic and Diachronic Perspective*. Berlin: Mouton de Gruyter.
Westney, Paul. 1995. *Modals and Periphrastics in English*. Tübingen: Niemeyer.
Williams, Cara Penry & Minna Korhonen. 2020. A sociolinguistic perspective on the (quasi-) modals of obligation and necessity in Australian English, *English World-Wide* 41(3). 267–294.

1 English modals: An outline of their forms, meanings and uses

Ilse Depraetere and Bert Cappelle

The present chapter presents some preliminaries to the study of modal verbs in English. Our survey starts with some information about their formal features, but our main aim is to reflect on some major topics in the field, such as taxonomies of modal meaning and the question of whether modals are polysemous or monosemous. We thereby frame the debate as to what is semantic and pragmatic about the meaning of modal verbs. Furthermore, we give an overview of the methods used in this volume to get a firmer grip on the meaning potentials as well as the data sets that we have compiled and exploited.

1 Modals and their formal behaviors

1.1 A varied list of verbs

The formal profile of the range of verbs that express modal meaning is diverse.[1] On the one hand, there are verbs like *have to* and *need to*, which have all the formal features of lexical verbs in that they standardly use *do*-support in NICE contexts (negation, inversion, 'code', emphasis):

(1) a. You **don't** have to hurry.
 b. **Do** we need to discuss it?
 c. Mary never has to study but John **does**.
 d. The system **DOES** need to change.

On the other hand, the so-called 'central' or 'core' modal auxiliaries (*may, might, can, could, must, shall, should, will, would*) are like the primary auxiliaries *be* and *have*, and do not require *do*-support:

---

[1] Note that we will not be concerned with inflectional mood. In others words, the subjunctive (*The government decreed that no more soldiers be sent abroad*), or so-called modal indicative forms (*If only it stopped raining!*; *I wish I had spoken to him before*), which, much like modals, do not present situations as mere facts, will not enter into the discussion. (See Section 1.2 for a comment on whether we treat non-factuality as a criterion for modality – in essence, we do not, as it would include more formal and functional categories than we could include in this book, and some of them, such as negation, are not treated as modal by any large consensus consensus.)

(2) a. It **shouldn't** matter. (cp. *It doesn't should matter.)
   b. **Can** you believe this? (cp. *Do you can believe this?)
   c. Mary could never relax but John **could**. (cp. Mary could never relax but John did: *did* is grammatical but would not be interpreted as standing for *could (sometimes/often) relax*.)
   d. This **MUST** be true! (cp. *This DOES must be true!)

The formal features that single out this second set as central or core modal auxiliaries is that (unlike the primary auxiliaries *be* and *have*, as well as *do*), they do not have non-finite forms (*to must*, *musting*) and they do not take -s in the indicative third person singular (*she musts*). Moreover, they are followed by a bare infinitive and, except in some varieties of English, they cannot be stacked (*She must can come with us*). Quirk, Greenbaum, Leech and Svartvik (1985: 137) also mention "abnormal time reference" (e.g. *You could tell her now*, in which past inflection does not communicate past time) as a further typical feature of a central modal auxiliary.

The verbs that express modal meaning do not form a closed class; all of the following expressions are mentioned in discussions on the topic:
- *dare, need, ought to, used to*
- *had better, would rather/sooner, be to, have got to*
- *be about to, be able to, be bound to, be going to, be willing to, be supposed to, etc.*
- *have to, need to, dare to*
- *want to*
- *haveta, hafta, got to, gotta, oughta, wanna*

Various terms have been used to single out categories of verbs whose formal behavior differs to varying degrees from that of the central modal verbs. Quirk et al. (1985) speak of 'marginal modals' (e.g., in the list above, *dare*, etc.), 'modal idioms' (*had better*, etc.) and 'semi-auxiliaries' (*be about to*, etc. – this category includes *have to* in their classification). Other labels are 'peripheral modal' (Depraetere and Reed 2021), 'emergent modal' (Leech 2013), 'semi-modal' (Biber et al. 2021 [1999]), 'quasi-modal' (Westney 1995, Collins 2009) and, with reference to the forms with *better, best, rather, (just) as well*, etc., 'comparative modals' (Van der Auwera and De Wit 2010). Specifically, *dare, need* and *ought to* have been called peripheral modal verbs because the former two are only used in non-assertive contexts (e.g. *Need it be stressed that*...?; cp. **It need be stressed that*...) and because the latter involves a *to*-infinitive. Semi-modals encompass modal expressions with *be*, which have all the formal features of the primary auxiliaries but only some of the features typical of the core modal auxiliaries. This label has also been used to refer to the lexical verbs *have to* and *need to*. *Want to* is included in the list above as it has acquired a modal necessity meaning with much the same meaning as *should* or *need to*, witness uses such as *You want to be careful*, used as a warning or to give advice. This 'emerging modal', as Krug (2000) calls it, is often contracted to *wanna*, just like we find contractions for many other modal expressions: *haveta, hafta, got to, gotta* and *oughta*. These and other reduced forms (e.g. *'ll, won't, can't*) do not necessarily have the same grammatical properties as the corresponding unreduced forms (Krug 2000, Lorenz 2020, Daugs 2021).

As is clear from the above overview, 'modal verb' can potentially include a large and varied set of syntactic types. The various labels mentioned above can be considered distinct categories, possibly with more or less prototypical members. The use of only a limited number of defining formal criteria makes for a taxonomy with a few basic, discrete classes such as 'central auxiliary' and 'semi-auxiliary'. However, back in 1980, Bolinger already argued for a gradient of auxiliariness, with further formal criteria resulting in finer-grained distinctions (see, e.g., Heine 1993, Krug 2000 for critical discussion). Clearly, the larger the range of features gets, the more likely it becomes that a gradient will emerge without clear-cut categorical distinctions, especially if the features have non-binary values and can be applied to a specific verb to a certain degree only, as in Bolinger's (1980) study.

The chapters following this one are to a great extent empirical studies: as explained in the introduction, we use various methods to get a clearer view on the knowledge that speakers of English draw on when they choose a modal verb. Given the large range of verbs that can – on formal grounds – be viewed as modals verbs, we have necessarily had to make a selection. In doing so, we took into account semantic considerations, that is, we chose verbs that can be thought of as the most prototypical expressions of modal meaning. As mentioned in the introductory chapter, we move beyond non-factuality as a defining feature and consider modal meaning to be crucially concerned with the expression of possibility and necessity. Accordingly, in most empirical studies presented in this book (Chapters 3 and 4, as well as Chapter 8), we have chosen to focus on the possibility verbs *can, could, may, might, be able to* and the necessity verbs *must, have to, need (to), should, ought to*. Our choice is in line with the approach in Van der Auwera and Plungian (1998), who similarly exclude volition meanings. Our selection thus includes six of the central modals, which exhibit the NICE properties (i.e., they don't need *do*-support), two so-called peripheral modals (*ought to* and the infrequently attested auxiliary *need*) and three so-called quasi-modals or semi-modals (*need to, have to, be able to*).

Will, shall and *would* enter in a less straightforward way into the possibility-necessity paradigm. However, because of the morpho-syntactic alignment with central modals such as *may* and *must*, *will* will make a justifiable appearance as a modal auxiliary in later chapters: along with *shall* and *would*, it will also be included in the set of modals used in Chapter 7, which will moreover take into account some of the modal idioms and semi-auxiliaries mentioned above (*had better, (have) got to, be allowed to* and *be supposed to*). *Will* and *shall* are likewise included in the chapter on individual variation (Chapter 6), and *shall* also features in Chapter 8. Given the attention that *will* has received in the literature, we will address in some more detail, in Section 1.2, the perennial question as to the status of *will* (as well as *shall* and *would*) as a modal auxiliary or a tense auxiliary.

1.2 *Will*, *shall* and *would*: modal auxiliaries?

Will, *shall* and *would* formally behave like the (other) core modals in NICE contexts and like *must*, *should*, *may*, *might*, *can* and *could* they don't have non-finite forms and they do not take *-s* in the indicative third person singular. However, from a semantic point of view, these verbs, and *will* in particular, have been argued to be tense auxiliaries, as their standard use is not to express 'possibility' or 'necessity', in the way *may* and *must* respectively do but to locate a situation in time (cf., e.g. Kissine 2008, Salkie 2010). We will present the kinds of arguments that have been used by the 'temporal' camp, before we present Wada's (2019) recent 'modal' approach, where *will* is linked with 'high probability', hence with non-factuality. The key question is whether non-factuality ('modal' meaning) falls out from future time (temporal meaning) rather than the other way round.

Salkie (2010) considers the following uses of *will*: (i) to refer to a future time (*It will rain in the morning, but the sun will shine later*), (ii) to build the future perfect tense (*I will have finished by tomorrow afternoon*), (iii) to express intention (*We'll do the job as soon as we can*), (iv) to express volition (*Louisa, will you please be quiet!*), (v) to express a characteristic property or activity (*Oil will float on water; He'll sit in his room all day staring at the TV*), (vi) in questions, to make a polite request or to invite someone (*Will you help me look for my purse?; Will you come to supper on Friday?*), (vii) to express a persistent habit (*Peter will fight with Paul, whatever I do*), (viii) to express a strong belief in the truth of something; to express deduction, inference, probability (*The match will be finished by now; Jean will have reached home by now*), (ix) in a conditional consequence (apodosis) (*If it rains again we'll have to cancel the match*), (x) in a conditional protasis (*If the price will come down in a few months, it's better not to buy just yet*). He considers that, apart from (viii), the uses are not clearly modal. Here's how he makes his case:

> Intention (iii) and volition (iv) are not expressed by other modals in English. Characteristic properties (v) and persistent habits (vii) are likewise not usually taken as coming under the heading of modality, though there is a parallel with *can* (*Oil can float on water / He can sit in his room all day staring at the TV*): we are in the domain of genericity here, not modality. There is a similar parallel with *can/could* in polite requests (vi): *Can/could you help me look for my purse*? It is worth pointing out that apart from the epistemic use of *will*, none of the other uses has parallels with the core modals *may* and *must* [see Salkie 2009 for reasons why these are the more prototypical modals compared to *can*, for instance]. Thus apart from the epistemic use [. . .] there is little here to convince us that *will* is fundamentally modal. (Salkie 2010: 191)

Salkie (2010) then discusses quantitative studies (Wekker 1976, Larreya 1984, Mindt 1995, 2000), which have shown that the temporal uses are by far the most frequent. However, he also mentions Coates's (1983) classification of 200 examples taken from the Survey of English Usage, which shows that non-temporal uses of *will* are not that rare; and he quotes Palmer (1990), who, taking a qualitative approach, likewise argues that there are very few examples of futurity in the Survey examples that "can be regarded as simply predicting a future event" (1990: 137–138). Further morpho-syntactic (Salkie 2010: 188–190) and typological (Salkie 2010: 198–199) arguments, amongst others, lead Salkie to conclude that *will* is temporal rather than modal.

Let us now turn to the 'modal' view. The location of a situation in the future necessarily implies reference to what-is-not-yet-factual and involves an element of prediction. For instance, *Tomorrow will be dry and sunny*, in a weather forecast, locates a situation in the future and likewise signals high confidence in that situation's actualization; *will* prototypically signals "high probability", as Wada (2001, 2019) puts it, and therefore communicates a specific epistemic stance. It is therefore not entirely surprising that *will* and its past-time counterpart *would* have been argued to be modal verbs. Wada's (2019) view is in agreement with that of Coates (1983), who associates *will* with 'epistemic prediction' (ranging from strong predictability to weak prediction) (cf. Wada 2019: 129, fn. 11 for further discussion and references).[2] Wada (2019: 151–154) further maintains that the purely factual, simple-future use of *will*, as in *He will be two tomorrow* (Huddleston and Pullum et al. 2002: 190), in which no subjective stance is involved (i.e., no prediction is made), could be seen as merely a special case of *will*, where the focus is on the future reference of the infinitival situation while the modal import of the auxiliary itself (i.e., that of high probability) has been bleached.

---

[2] However, it remains a matter of debate whether the kind of epistemic modality involved in the core meaning of *will* can be equated with epistemic *necessity*.

Wada (2019: 160–163) also argues that the root use of *will* in orders (as well as of *shall* and *would*, presumably) can be explained as extensions from the predictive-future use: *will* (arguably) communicates root necessity in *You will do as you are told*.[3] Examples like this illustrate conventional pragmatic enrichment, whereby (epistemic) prediction is strengthened to (root) necessity. Finally, some authors subsume volitional meaning (i.e., intention, willingness and insistence) under the general heading of modality (cf. Leech 2004: 87–88); given now that *will* (including its 'past' form *would*) as a tense auxiliary developed out of its use as a volition-expressing lexical verb, meaning 'desire', 'want' or 'intend' (e.g., Aijmer 1985, Bybee and Pagliuca 1987) and that its volitional origin is still present in some cases (e.g. *Will you have a biscuit?*; *The doctor will see you now*), this has been another reason why *will* has been argued to be a modal auxiliary.

While we appreciate all the evidence that is called upon in favor of a 'modal' analysis of *will*, it remains a fact that predictability, the key argument, is in line with a 'less-than-factual situation' view of modality, rather than being captured in terms of 'possible or necessary situations', which is the definition that has informed our selection of verbs in the empirical studies presented in the chapters that follow.

2 How can modals be organized in terms of the meanings they express? Towards a semantic taxonomy of modal verbs

At least as challenging a task as deciding which forms can be considered modal or not is to capture and label the range of meanings communicated by these elusive entities. In this section, we attempt to provide a relatively theory-neutral taxonomy of modal verb meanings, drawing on distinctions made in the available literature. In Section 3 we will then look at the role played by pragmatics.

The distinction between epistemic meaning and root meaning mentioned in this book's introduction is a relatively uncontroversial one (see again examples (1a) and (1c) given there, which are epistemic, and (1b) and (1d), which are root). Sentences with modal verbs that express epistemic meaning indicate how likely the speaker thinks it is that a situation is, or is not, the case. In some definitions,

---

3 *Shall* likewise has an established root necessity use, used in biblical-sounding orders and prohibitions (e.g. *Go back to the shadow. You shall not pass!*, as exclaimed by Gandalf in *The Lord of the Rings*) and in legal contexts (cf. Caliendo 2004, Williams 2005, 2009).

the notion of truth is in the foreground: "Epistemics are clausal-scope indicators of a speaker's commitment to the truth of a proposition" (Bybee and Fleischman 1995: 6). By contrast, sentences with modals that express root (or non-epistemic) meaning are concerned with the actualization of situations, that is, with the idea that it is possible or necessary for someone to do something or for something to happen or be the case.

In Table 1, we present a first broad taxonomy of modal meanings, falling into epistemic vs. non-epistemic (root) modality, a distinction that is orthogonal with that between possibility and necessity meanings.

Table 1: A broad taxonomy of modal meanings, with two crosscutting distinctions.

	Possibility	Necessity
Epistemic	[...] he fears she **may** be suicidal.[4]	This feeling ... there's no mistaking it ... it **must** be love!!
Root (non-epistemic)	You **may** kiss the bride now.	This **must** stop now.

Epistemic modality is, all in all, a fairly unproblematic area of modality and has no subdivisions other than possibility and necessity – although each of these allows for different degrees of likelihood or other subtle differences expressed by different modals. The domain of root modality (cf. the bottom row in Table 1) constitutes a greater taxonomic challenge, as we will see in Section 2.2. First, though, we briefly address, in Section 2.1, the question of whether there are any further semantic categories on a par with epistemic and root modality.

2.1 Only epistemic and root modality?

Sweetser (1990) proposes a third category of 'speech-act modality', putatively exemplified by *may* in a sentence like *He may be a university professor, but he sure is dumb*. In this posited third broad kind of modality, "the speaker (or people in general) is forced to, or (not) barred from, saying what the sentence says" (Sweetser 1990: 73). In other words, the modal meaning of possibility appears to apply here to the conversational action itself of uttering the very sentence

---

[4] Unless stated otherwise, the examples in this section and the next are taken from the COCA corpus. Any boldface has been added – ID, BC. See Section 4 for an overview of the data used for the empirical studies in this book.

('Certainly, one can very well say that ... (but ...)'). Papafragou (2000b) offers a critical discussion of Sweetser's proposal, arguing that the concessive use of *may* in this example is a special subcase of ordinary epistemic possibility (see e.g. Collins (2009: 93) for a similar view). It is necessary to tease apart the modal verb semantics from the pragmatics of the speech act of the utterance (the concessive meaning). In our view, *may* does not express epistemic possibility in such contexts: the speaker doesn't really reflect on the likelihood of the situation. Instead, she grants that the proposition can be made, so concessive *may* expresses what we will call (wide-scope) root possibility (see Section 2.4): the speaker considers the situation to be possible, but less pertinent than another one (see Leclercq 2022 for a corpus study on concessive *may*).

It is also a matter of debate whether evidential meaning (see, e.g., Aikhenveld 2018) is a subcategory of epistemic meaning, rather than a category on a par with root and epistemic modality. Evidential modality is concerned with markers that indicate whether the speaker has access to evidence (and if so, what evidence) that testifies to the truth of a proposition.

(3) **They say** he's somewhere in Texas.

As modal verbs in English do not express evidential meaning in any very obvious way, unlike for instance *sollen* in German (e.g. *Er soll krank sein* 'He is said to be ill'), we will not be addressing this concept any further.

In Section 2.2.4, we will introduce and discuss in detail the concept of 'dynamic' modality, which is a category on a par with deontic modality and epistemic modality in Huddleston and Pullum et al.'s (2002) approach, for instance. For Palmer (2001), on the other hand, dynamic and deontic modality together constitute 'event modality', which is a semantic category at the same level as epistemic modality. In other words, 'dynamic' does not feature at the same taxonomic level across authors.

Further examples of non-binary proposals will be mentioned in Section 2.3.

2.2 What are the semantic subcategories of root modality?

In this section we will address semantic distinctions that feature prominently in taxonomies of root meaning, namely ability, permission, 'deontic' modality and 'dynamic' modality. Starting from the relatively transparent categories of ability and permission (2.2.1) we will highlight the issues raised by 'deontic' modality (2.2.2 ('deontic' necessity), 2.2.3 ('deontic' possibility)) and 'dynamic' modality (2.2.4). By way of a conclusion, a selective overview will be given of existing taxonomies in Section 2.3, which visualizes conceptual and terminological agreement and disagreement across authors. The critical discussion in the present section will then pave the way for the presentation of the taxonomy that we consider to be more explicit than alternative ones (Section 2.4) and that will play an important role in this book (Chapters 2 to 4, Chapter 8).

2.2.1 Root possibility: Ability and permission

In the realm of root possibility, ability and permission are relatively transparent concepts that standardly feature in categorizations of modal meaning as expressed by modal verbs. Here is an example of each:

(4) We use the term base word for free morphemes, one-morpheme words that *can* stand on their own. (ability *can*)

(5) To reward you for your assistance, you *may* keep 20.03% of these funds as a bounty. (permission *may*)

While ability is usually defined as possibility the source of which resides in the referent of the grammatical subject – the modality is therefore said to be 'subject-internal' – there appear to have been far fewer attempts to make explicit the concept of permission, not least because this is indeed a quite intuitive notion. We could informally define it as 'allowing or authorizing someone to do something' or 'being allowed or authorized to do something' – permission can be something one gives or receives. Related to the definitional criterion of permission is whether this concept is necessarily 'deontic' in nature – is the giving of permission always a subjective and performative act or not?

A further observation is that the root possibility uses that are left when ability and permission are set aside have given rise to a diverse set of labels: 'circumstantial', 'neutral', 'dynamic', (again) 'root', etc.; this is clearly an area of meaning that is harder to capture in unambiguous terms. At this stage in the discussion, for reasons of transparency, we will use the maximally neutral label root$_{[-ABILITY, -PERMISSION]}$ to refer to this type of meaning and we will explain, in Section 2.4, how this area of meaning can be captured in a more explicit way, thus moving away from a negative (not ability, not permission) characterization:

(6) A fundamental source for understanding the Knights' attitude toward nobility **may** be found in another unpublished manuscript of the late seicento by Fra Giovanni Maria Caravita. (root$_{[-ABILITY, -PERMISSION]}$ *may*)

(7) For an overview, you **can't** beat the Vista Trail at the north end of the state's holdings, five miles north of Jenner on Highway 1. (root$_{[-ABILITY, -PERMISSION]}$ *can*)

(8) Her doctor told her to go ahead and plan for a normal future, a wide-open space where anything **might** happen. Though not anything was going to happen. (root$_{[-ABILITY, -PERMISSION]}$ *might*)

(9) We have heard from Michael Ward. You **could** still see the anger. He was seething as he took the podium for a few minutes. He, too, feels justice was served. (root$_{[-ABILITY, -PERMISSION]}$ *could*)

The two points requiring further attention that we have mentioned so far, namely, the definition of permission and its link with deontic meaning, and the definition of the category of root possibility meaning that is left when ability and permission are set aside, will be taken up in Sections 2.2.3. and 2.2.4. respectively. Before we address them, we will look at semantic subcategories of root necessity (Section 2.2.2). This will involve a discussion of deontic necessity, which will inform, in Section 2.2.3, our reflections on deontic possibility.

2.2.2 Root necessity: On 'deontic necessity'

On the root necessity side, there are no relatively clear-cut subcategories similar to those like ability and permission in the realm of root possibility. Root necessity more readily appears as a single organic block, with different uses rather than distinct meanings. 'Deontic necessity' (or 'obligation') potentially presents itself as a separate class, but there is no unanimous view on the contribution that this concept can make. Coates (1983), for instance, already argued that the modal logic term 'deontic', used by von Wright (1951) to analyze the logical relations between obligation, permission or prohibition, is inappropriate to discuss the semantics of root necessity. As she sees it, cutting up root necessity meaning (or root possibility meaning, for that matter) obscures the essential unity of root necessity utterances, which share a common, basic meaning, that is, 'it is necessary *for*', a paraphrase which differentiates this type of meaning from that used to capture the epistemic meaning, namely, 'it is necessary (i.e., necessarily the case) *that*'.

A number of basic features clearly stand out in descriptions of deontic modality. First, several authors highlight 'subjectivity' or speaker-orientedness: deontic modality is "usually subjective in that the speaker is the one who obliges, permits, or forbids" (Palmer 1990: 9). However, deontic modality is not exclusively subjective, as is clear from Huddleston and Pullum et al.'s (2002) approach: "the deontic source ... can also be objective, most obviously in reports of rules and regulations" (Huddleston and Pullum et al. 2002: 183). Van der Auwera and Plungian (1998: 81) bring in social or ethical norms as further non-subjective examples of deontic modality.

Second, the term 'performative', which broadly resonates with Searle's concept of directive, appears in various accounts.[5] Coates, for instance, gives the following example to illustrate the "psychologically" stereotypical use of "performative *must*":

(10) You **must** play this ten times over, Miss Jarrova would say, pointing with relentless fingers to a jumble of crotchets and quavers. (Coates 1983: 34)

In a similar way, Palmer suggests that modals expressing deontic meaning can be "thought of as 'performative', as indications of speech acts. That is to say, (...) deontic modals signal 'directives' ('where we get them [i.e., our hearers] to do things')" (Palmer 1990: 10).[6] That the pragmatic notion of (indirect) performativity is relevant to deontic modality is also clear from the fact that deontic meaning can be reformulated with a performative verb, *You must be back by twelve* corresponding to *I order/demand you to be back by twelve*.[7] However, not all root necessity can be captured under the heading of 'performativity', witness examples like *Clay pots [...] must have some protection from severe weather* (Coates 1983: 35).

These few observations already make it clear that the link between 'deontic meaning' and 'subjectivity' and 'performativity' is not a straightforward one, and as a result, it is hard to disentangle and compare the approaches to deontic meaning. For critical discussion, see, e.g., Nuyts, Byloo and Diepeveen (2010) and Depraetere (2015a).

Even when setting aside the functional definition of deontic modality, we can observe that the taxonomic position of deontic necessity (or deontic possibility, see Section 2.2.3) differs across authors (see Table 2 in Section 2.3): whereas for Van der Auwera and Plungian (1998), deontic and non-deontic necessity together

---

[5] See Verstraete (2001) for an insightful discussion of 'modal performativity' vs. 'interactive performativity' and their relevance to subjective and objective modality.
[6] Palmer (1990) also considers epistemic modality to be performative, in the sense that epistemic modals signal assertives ("where we tell our hearers (truly or falsely) how things are" (Palmer 1990: 10)).
[7] Applied to permission (deontic possibility, see Section 2.2.3), *You can register over there* corresponds to *I authorize you to register over there* and *You can't have a biscuit* is similar in meaning to *I forbid you to have a biscuit*.

make up the category of (root) participant-external necessity, which needs to be distinguished from (root) participant-internal necessity, for Palmer (1990) and Huddleston and Pullum et al. (2002), deontic necessity is a subcategory of modal meaning on a par with epistemic modality and what they call dynamic modality (on which more in Section 2.2.4). In the taxonomic approach we take, we refrain from equating root necessity with deonticity. We will show in Section 2.4 below how incorporating the features 'scope' and 'source' suffices to differentiate the different kinds of root necessity.

2.2.3 Permission: On 'deontic possibility'

At this stage it is interesting to briefly return to the concept of permission, which, as stated in Section 2.2.1, is standardly included in modal taxonomies; it is sometimes treated as synonymous with 'deontic possibility' (e.g. Palmer 1990). However, as in the case of modal necessity, its position in the taxonomic hierarchy is not always the same, and, secondly, there is no unanimous view on its defining features. To illustrate the former observation, in Van der Auwera and Plungian's (1998) approach to the field of possibility, a distinction is made between deontic possibility (permission) and non-deontic possibility, while, for Palmer (1990) and Huddleston and Pullum et al. (2002), deontic possibility is located at the same taxonomic level as epistemic possibility and dynamic possibility (see the similar observation about deontic necessity in Section 2.2.2 and see Table 2 below in Section 2.3). To illustrate the second issue, depending on the way in which 'deontic' is made explicit, deontic permission can be further described as 'subjective permission' (e.g. (11)) and/or as a 'performative use' of possibility (e.g. (12)); and if subjectivity and/or performativity is treated as criterial to deonticity, then cases of non-deontic permission (e.g. (13)) also need to be accounted for, which again brings up the question of the position of deontic possibility within the taxonomy overall.

(11) All [the committee members] permitted the President to declare his own inability, and four provided that he **could** declare the end of his inability whether he had made the initial determination or not. ('deontic' possibility viewed as subjective permission; the committee members determine what the president is allowed to do)

(12) "He's okay. He's here," a nurse encourages me. I don't move. "You **can** hold him while we sew up your tear. It's just a small one." ('deontic' possibility viewed as performative (speech act) permission; 'I hereby allow you to . . .')

(13) So, young babies **can** be given tea with milk, mixed in a 1:1 ratio. (web-attested) ('non-deontic' possibility viewed as non-subjective, non-performative 'permission'; 'It is permitted to . . .', 'It is acceptable to . . .')[8]

Many questions and reservations can be formulated. Suppose we identified 'deontic possibility' with 'permission' and if we further assume, for the sake of the argument, that *can* in an example such as (13) expresses some sort of permission, wouldn't such examples force us to conclude, again, that not all of deontic modality is subjective? What is the remaining conceptual space covered by possibility that is neither ability-expressing nor deontic (the latter defined as subjective and performative)? And is it possible or useful to distinguish subjective from performative uses?[9] Taking into account these complications, in the same way that we will not be using 'deontic' as a taxonomic distinction for necessity, we will not be doing so in the realm of possibility either.

2.2.4 'Dynamic' possibility and necessity

Dynamic modality is a category that commonly features in taxonomies that distinguish three semantic types of modal meaning: epistemic, deontic and dynamic, the latter two categories together therefore making up root (or non-epistemic) modality. While generally speaking, it might seem useful to differentiate a category of root meaning that is more 'subjective' ('deontic') from one that is more 'objective' ('dynamic'), given the fact that deontic modality has been argued not to be exclusively subjective (see 2.2.2 and 2.2.3), the delineation of the contours of dynamic possibility and dynamic necessity is challenging.

The definition of 'dynamic modality' offered by Huddleston and Pullum et al. (2002), for instance, does not necessarily elucidate the meaning distinctions at stake in the realm of root modality. For them, reference to "properties and dispositions of persons, etc. referred to in the clause, especially by the subject NP" (Huddleston and Pullum et al. 2002: 178) is criterial for this category. Dynamic

---

8 We put *permission* between quotation marks here because, based on the taxonomic distinctions that we propose in Section 2.4, this is not an example of permission (which is narrow-scope modality, as we argue there), but it expresses 'situation permissibility' (which is wide-scope modality).
9 Subjective uses that are not clearly performative (as in (11)) can be paraphrased as performative uses by turning the reported speech into direct speech (e.g. "and four committee members provided this: "We hereby authorize the President to declare the end of his inability . . . "").

modality is often used as a cover term for ability and volition.[10] Apart from ability, Huddleston and Pullum et al. (2002) also consider the following cases further examples of 'dynamic possibility': "[w]hat is reasonable or acceptable" (e.g., *The most we can expect is a slight cut in the sales-tax*, "[w]hat is "circumstantially possible" (e.g., *It can easily be shown that the argument is fallacious*", and "[w]hat is sometimes the case" (e.g., *Poinsettias can be red or yellow*) (Huddleston and Pullum et al. 2002: 184–185). In the realm of modal necessity, Huddleston and Pullum et al. (2002) categorize an example like the following under the heading of 'dynamic necessity'; (14) is clearly in line with their definition of prototypical dynamic modality:

(14) Ed's a guy who **must** always be poking his nose into other people's business (dynamic necessity). (Huddleston and Pullum et al. 2002: 185)

But in the realm of necessity as well, examples of what is circumstantially needed (e.g. *Now that she has lost her job she must live extremely frugally*) are considered as further illustrations of dynamic necessity.

In other words, with the exception of the clear subcategories of ability and volition, dynamic possibility and dynamic necessity constitute quite diverse conceptual areas, the boundaries with deontic modality not always being clear-cut (see, for example, Huddleston and Pullum et al. (2002: 179, 185) for observations to this effect). In the literature, the concept of dynamic modality has also been adopted and/or critically discussed by Verstraete (2001), Nuyts (2005), Gisborne (2007), Collins (2009), Van Linden and Verstraete (2011) and Portner (2018), among others.

2.3 Other distinctions in the literature

The observations made so far offer by no means an exhaustive summary of the rich literature on the topic. For instance, Narrog (2012) identifies nine different subclasses of modal meaning (epistemic, deontic, teleological, preferential, boulomaic, participant-internal, circumstantial, existential and evidential), and these are characterized in terms of two dimensions: that of 'volitivity' and that of 'speech-act orientation'. In his monograph on mood, Portner (2018) differentiates

---

10 We will not take into account, in Chapters 3, 4 and 5, the category of volition, for the reason already stated in Section 1.2 (namely, that this meaning does not relate directly to the notion of possibility or necessity).

the following three main types of modal meaning: epistemic modality, priority modality (including deontic, buletic and teleological modality), and dynamic modality (including volitional modality, with subtypes ability, opportunity and dispositional modality, as well as intrinsic modality and quantificational modality, the latter with subtypes existential and universal). The overview based on Depraetere and Reed (2021: 217) below (Table 2) shows which uses have been included in some of the previous taxonomies of modal meaning. Note that the categorical labels used converge to varying degrees only and that they do not necessarily capture (all) the same uses.

Before we present the taxonomy of modal meanings that we will adopt in Chapters 2, 3 and 4, we would still like to mention that the epistemic-deontic-dynamic model will be used (see e.g. Huddleston and Pullum et al. 2002) in Chapter 8. The aim of this later chapter is to assess to what extent the most up-to-date word representation techniques can predict the meaning of a modal verb. As this analysis builds on earlier attempts of the kind in computational sciences (such as Ruppenhofer and Rehbein 2012 and Zhou, Frank, Friedrich and Palmer 2015), it is necessary to work with the same model in order to compare the predictions made.

Irrespective of the taxonomic approach taken, actual descriptive and empirical work based on a taxonomy tends to yield a lot of observations to the effect that the borderlines between categories are fuzzy. The proliferation of subcategories in some taxonomies also shows that it is difficult to establish discriminating features. On the basis of the discussion so far, one might wonder if fuzziness is inherent in the phenomenon under study and if intersective gradience (Aarts 2007) is therefore the most suitable approach. It is our view that the boundaries between subcategories of root modality can be made more explicit than they often are.[11] In Section 2.4 we will now outline the root taxonomic distinctions that are based on Depraetere and Reed (2011) and Depraetere (2014) and that we will work with in Chapters 2, 3 and 4.

2.4 The taxonomy privileged in this book

Depraetere and Reed's (2011) aim was to pin down a number of defining criteria to distinguish root possibility meanings, to describe them as rigorously as possible, and to apply them consistently, in order to arrive at maximally transpar-

---

[11] If there is gradience at all, it is of what Aarts (2007) has called the subsective (rather than the intersective) type.

Table 2: Modal categories and their (partial) correspondence to taxonomies proposed in some of the previous literature (n.a. = not applicable, because the category at the top is not included in the taxonomy at hand; part-int = participant-internal).

epistemic modality	root, non-deontic necessity	root, non-deontic possibility excluding ability and volition	ability	obligation (deontic necessity)	permission (deontic possibility)	willingness or volition	
epistemic	root						Coates (1983), Declerck (1991)
epistemic	extrinsic		intrinsic				Quirk et al. (1985)
epistemic	n.a.	n.a.	agent-oriented				Bybee and Fleischman (1995)
propositional (evidential | epistemic)	n.a.	n.a.	dynamic	event modality		dynamic	Palmer (2001)
epistemic	dynamic			deontic		dynamic	Huddleston and Pullum et al. (2002), Nuyts (2005)
epistemic	part-int	participant-external non-deontic	non-epistemic part-int	participant-external deontic	participant-external deontic	n.a.	van der Auwera and Plungian (1998)

ent and coherent definitions that clearly bring out the similarities and dissimilarities between the different root possibility classes. This enabled the authors to describe, in a positive way, the area of root possibility that is 'not ability, not permission'. In this section, we will first describe the semantic distinctions that can in this way be made within root possibility, and we will then use the same defining features to differentiate subcategories of root necessity meaning.

Three defining criteria, *viz.* scope, source and potential barrier, are used in this taxonomy and they result in five classes of root possibility meaning (ability, opportunity, permission, general situation possibility and situation permissibility) and three classes of root necessity meaning (narrow scope internal necessity, narrow scope external necessity, general situation necessity).

The scope of a possibility modal is wide or narrow depending on whether the possibility concerns an entire proposition, as in (15) or (16), or whether 'what is possible' relates to the VP, or more precisely, whether something is possible for the subject referent to do ('to Y is possible for X (to do)'), as in (17) or (18). (See Depraetere and Reed (2011: 3–9) for some further observations about scope.)

(15) The EMF meter I have is a combination meter and thermometer, since ghosts **can** cause a sudden temperature drop in a room or a building. (wide-scope possibility: the situation of ghosts causing a sudden temperature drop is possible)

(16) How **could** these trees be there if there was an enormous flood just 4,000 years ago? (wide-scope possibility: how is the situation of these trees being there possible?)

(17) I could curse him all I wanted, but I had to survive until that ripe old age before I **could** claim the millions. (narrow-scope possibility: claim the millions is something that it would be possible for me to do)

(18) A 17-year-old girl with learning difficulties and schizophrenia refuses her depo injection. Without it you know she will become psychotic in a few days. **Can** you and her mother force her to have the injection?) (narrow-scope possibility: is force her to have the injection something that it is possible for you and her mother to do?)

Observe that both wide scope possibility and narrow scope possibility could be paraphrased as 'it is possible for X to Y '. However, what makes the possibility narrow is that the possibility to do something is predicated of the subject referent (i.e. the subject referent is said to have the possibility to do something), so that the subject stays outside the scope of what is presented as possible (namely an action, typically) ('to Y is possible for X (to do)'). With wide-scope possibility, what is presented as possible is the entire (non-modalized) proposition ('for X to Y is possible').

'Source' refers to the origin of the modality, that is, what it is that makes it possible for someone to do something (in the case of narrow-scope modality), or what it is that makes a situation possible (in the case of wide-scope modality). The source may be subject-internal, as in (19), in which case the possibility originates in innate capacities or acquired skills of the subject referent. Subject-external sources may be of different types: what lies at the origin of the possibility may be a discourse participant, as in (20), or rules and regulations, as in (21) and (22), among other possibilities.

(19) "**Can** you recall for me the last day that you felt completely well?" The doctor pauses. "There's no hurry. Take all the time you need." (subject-internal source; narrow-scope possibility)

(20) At noon, the foreman told me I **could** go home. (subject-external source: the discourse participant referred to as *the foreman* is the source; narrow-scope possibility)

(21) Under canon law someone who tortures an accused party **may** be held guilty of a capital offence if the victim dies as a consequence. (subject-external source: rules and regulations; wide-scope possibility)

(22) Adherence to the Code will be a fundamental part of professional revalidation, which comes into force at the end of this year, without which nurses will not **be able to** renew their registration. (subject-external source: rules and regulations; narrow-scope possibility)

When the source of the modality can potentially get into the way of actualization, or, put differently, when it potentially functions as a barrier to actualization, it carries the feature '+ potential barrier'. See Depraetere and Reed (2011: 13–16) for detailed discussion of this feature.

(23) But thanks to your insight, we**'re** now **able to** connect the dots. (– potential barrier; narrow-scope possibility)

(24) State law says an individual may not knowingly use multiple entities he controls to exceed the limits. But it also says no candidate **may** accept contributions that exceed allowable amounts. (+ potential barrier; wide-scope possibility)

(25) Some activists worry that the pools **could** be damaged in an earthquake. Some of the spent fuel assemblies must cool there three to five years, when they can be moved into dry cask storage. (– potential barrier; wide-scope possibility)

Table 3 shows how the different criteria define five different categories, each of which is illustrated in the list of examples that follows the table.

Table 3: Taxonomy of non-epistemic possibility.

	ability	opportunity	permission	general situation possibility	situation permissibility
scope	narrow	narrow	narrow	wide	wide
source	internal	external	external	external	external
potential barrier	– potential barrier	– potential barrier	+ potential barrier	– potential barrier	+ potential barrier

(26) "People who experienced the tsunami learned that they **could** not defeat nature," says Akihiko Sugawara, chairman of the Kesennuma chamber of commerce and industry and founder of the Kesennuma city sea wall study group. (*ability*: narrow scope, subject-internal source, – potential barrier)

(27) We asked them to keep a diary for a few days so they **could** gain some insight into their own sugar intake. (*opportunity*: narrow scope, subject-external source, – potential barrier)

(28) "He's okay. He's here," a nurse encourages me. I don't move. "You **can** hold him while we sew up your tear." (= example (12)) (*permission*: narrow scope, subject-external source, + potential barrier)

(29) Sarah had argued that the Palomar was perfect because its Palladium Room fit a hundred and thirty people perfectly, and its podium was wheelchair accessible. Her doctor told her to go ahead and plan for a normal future, a wide-open space where anything **might** happen. (*general situation possibility*: wide scope, subject-external source, – potential barrier)

(30) No part of this material **may** be duplicated or redisseminated without permission. (*situation permissibility*: wide scope, subject-external source, + potential barrier)

In the first three categories, the modality has narrow scope in that it predicates a property of the subject referent (e.g. *They could not defeat nature* ≈ 'Defeating nature is something that it is not possible for them to do'); in the case of general situation possibility (29) and situation permissibility (30), it is the entire situation that is in the scope of the possibility (e.g. 'The situation of anything happening is possible'). If the scope is narrow and the source lies within the subject referent, the meaning is that of ability (e.g. (26)); if the scope is narrow and the source is subject-external, the meaning is that of opportunity (e.g. (27)) or permission (e.g. (28)). When the source of the modality potentially functions as a barrier to actualization, the result is permission (28) or permissibility (30) meaning.

In an attempt to move away from the conceptually fuzzy notion of deontic necessity, and to arrive at greater consistency in conceptual distinctions across the realms of modal necessity and possibility, Depraetere (2014: 172) applies the same set of criteria to root necessity.[12] As with possibility, the scope can be narrow (when necessity to do something is predicated of the subject referent) or wide (when the entire situation expressed by the non-modalized proposition is claimed to be necessary). The source can also be internal or external. (The concept of source in the domain of necessity will be analyzed in more detail in Chapter 4.) This results in the identification of three categories of root necessity meaning: (a) narrow-scope internal necessity, (b) narrow-scope external necessity, (c) (wide-scope) general situation necessity.

The following examples illustrate the taxonomic distinctions:

(31) I **have to** know what Parenting readers think: I am sickened by the trend of "push" presents! (*narrow-scope internal necessity*: narrow scope, subject-internal source)

---

[12] 'Potential barrier' does not apply to necessity meaning, though. If the speaker makes it clear that it is necessary for a situation to actualize or for someone to do something, then it follows that the source of the modality cannot at the same time have source status *and* potentially act as a barrier to actualization.

(32) Because even if Donald Trump is elected president, he will **have to** deal with this Congress that is the establishment that so many of his supporters hate right now. (*narrow-scope external necessity*: narrow scope, subject-external source)

(33) In essence, to generalize an empirical index in various applications, the statistical computing **must** be flexible to represent specific conditions of a test setting. (*general situation necessity*: wide scope ('the situation of computing being flexible is necessary'), subject-external source)

It is our view that our approach to defining possibility and necessity meanings can handle some of the taxonomic challenges and shortcomings mentioned in Section 2.2. In Table 4 we provide an overview of the modal meanings we have so far discussed.

Table 4: A complete taxonomy of modal meaning categories as privileged in this book; see again Tables 3 and 4 for features distinguishing the different root modal meanings. There is no significance to the horizontal and vertical order of presentation of the categories.

	Possibility	Necessity
Epistemic	[...] he fears she **may** be suicidal.	This feeling... there's no mistaking it ... it **must** be love!!
Root (non-epistemic)	– Ability Hidden talent: I **can** juggle three basketballs. – Opportunity [...] we have oxygen in our atmosphere so we **can** breathe. – Permission Um, **can** I please speak to your daughter? – General situation possibility The symptoms **can** take up to three days to manifest. – Situation permissibility Red wine **can** be used instead of grape juice in the recipe [...].	– Narrow-scope internal necessity I just **need to** be alone for a second. – Narrow-scope external necessity Doctor, I think you **need to** take a look at this. – General situation necessity More research **needs to** be done in this area.

Having presented the taxonomic distinctions that we will use (in Chapters 2, 3 and 4), we will now address another key issue: that of the monosemy versus polysemy of modal verbs.

3 Are modals polysemous or monosemous?

3.1 Preliminaries to the discussion

While the above discussion has resulted in more rigorous and explicit descriptors for the different meanings of modal verbs, the next question is to determine whether these meanings are semantically distinct. Thus, do these different meanings constitute independent, semantic classes of their own or, rather, do all modals have just one meaning, the instantiations of which are contextual realizations of the basic semantic core? Answering that question boils down to arguing in favor of the polysemy (e.g., Lyons 1977, Traugott 1989, Bybee and Fleischman 1995, Palmer 2001, Huddleston and Pullum et al. 2002, Close and Aarts 2010, Depraetere 2010, 2014, Viebahn and Vetter 2016) or monosemy (e.g., Ehrman 1966, Tregidgo 1982, Haegeman 1983, Klinge 1993, Groefsema 1995, Papafragou 2000a) of modal verbs, respectively. Needless to say, this also involves taking a specific stance on what constitutes semantics and what constitutes pragmatics. We will clarify our view below, and this topic will be addressed in detail in the next chapter. In the present section, we will prepare the ground by presenting some major arguments that lead us to claim that modals are polysemous.

The view on the polysemy/monosemy of modal verbs considerably depends on the categories of modal meaning that are at stake: there seems to be a relative consensus that the root vs. epistemic distinction is semantic, but there is less agreement at the taxonomic level of root possibility meanings and root necessity meanings. Leech and Coates (1980), for instance, argue that epistemic and non-epistemic readings are semantically distinct, but they also observe that "*can* is essentially a monosemous modal: there are no clear divisions between permission, possibility and ability" (Leech and Coates 1980: 84). See Timotijević (2009: 227) for a similar view. This would mean that all the uses of *can* in Table 4 express just a single meaning, say 'possibility', and that the precise category labels provided there are simply interpretations that arise in context. The same would then be true for the different meanings of *need to* in that table.

A further observation is that approaches that argue in favor of semantic distinctions like deontic vs. dynamic or dynamic vs. epistemic (see Section 2.2.4 on 'dynamic' modality) all underline the existence of examples that are hard to classify (see, e.g., Palmer 1990: 20–22). A certain degree of auto-criticism or caution with respect to a principled commitment to polysemy transpires from observations of the kind we find in Collins's (2009) book, for instance:

> In the present study we assume a polysemy position, while at the same time acknowledging that the dividing line between deontic and dynamic modality will in general be less

determinate than that between epistemic modality and either of these root categories. Furthermore the three primary meanings have subsumed uses which are not always clearly distinguishable. (Collins 2009: 23)

A third preliminary observation is that the distinction between polysemy (a linguistic form having 'distinct meanings') and monosemy (a linguistic form being 'vague') is one that is notoriously hard to make.[13] It will not be possible, within the confines of this chapter, to do justice to the sophisticated literature in the field. In a nutshell, a lexical item is polysemous when it has at least two related but semantically distinct meanings (two senses). The verb *run*, for instance, has distinct but conceptually related meanings, such as 'move fast', 'function, work' (said of machines, engines, computers and the like) and 'keep being performed or shown on TV or in theatres' (said of movies, plays or TV shows). There is often an etymological link between the different meanings and one may be a metaphorical extension of another or may result from metonymical transfer.[14] A lexical item that is vague (monosemous) has a fundamental meaning but it is underspecified with respect to facets of meaning that the linguistic context allows us to flesh out. Thus, *swim* essentially means 'move through water using certain arm and leg movements' and it doesn't matter whether this action amounts to what is more specifically known as breaststroke, backstroke, crawl, etc. Likewise, *aunt* means 'sister of a parent', without 'sister of one's mother' being felt to be a sense of *aunt* that is different from 'sister of one's father'. For some further examples, see, e.g., Cruse (2011: 97–127), Depraetere and Salkie (2017: 20–23). As the meanings expressed by modal verbs (take *can* or *need to*) are related (in that they all express possibility or necessity), it follows that the key question here is whether the different meanings are different uses of a single meaning arising in context (the monosemy or vagueness position) rather than different senses or 'polysemes' to be stored in our mental dictionary (the polysemy position).

At this point, we need to make yet another terminological observation: in the modality literature, the question of the theoretical status of the meaning distinctions is referred to as the monosemy/polysemy debate. However, when pro-

---

13 The philosophical literature uses 'vague' for expressions which have unclear borderlines and give rise to the 'Sorites paradox'. A standard example is *bald*. Someone with one hair is bald, someone with half a head of hair is not bald. But at what point does 'bald' become 'not-bald'? There is no clear answer. We are focusing here on the discussion in lexical semantics, where vagueness is conceptualised in terms of *semantic underspecification*.

14 Polysemy is therefore to be distinguished from homonymy. A lexical item is homonymous when it has at least two semantically distinct meanings (two senses) that are not, or no longer felt to be, related, as in the case of *bank* 'shore' and *bank* 'financial institution' or of *board* 'long, thin, flat piece of timber' and *board* 'group of people making the decisions in a company'.

viding evidence in favor of 'polysemy', a common argument is that modals are 'ambiguous'. In lexical semantics, ambiguity is either associated with homonymy (cf. footnote 14) or it is used as a more general term to refer to semantic multiplicity, covering both homonymy and polysemy. So there is potential terminological confusion: the terms *ambiguity* and *ambiguous* are used even though it is clearly polysemy that is at stake (cf. Traugott 2003: 661 for a similar terminological point). Given that 'ambiguity' is the term that is traditionally used in discussion about the polysemy/monosemy of modals, we will continue to use it, but we will put it in inverted commas.

3.2 Submitting modals to ambiguity tests

In a seminal paper published in 1975, Zwicky and Sadock (see also Lakoff 1970) introduced a number of tests to diagnose ambiguity. The focus of their paper was on structural ambiguity, but they also discussed lexical ambiguity. They argued that various types of anaphoric constructions make it possible to decide if specific clauses are structurally ambiguous rather than vague, or, contain expressions that are lexically ambiguous rather than vague. The test runs as follows. If, in a series of clauses that can have multiple interpretations, the first clause is ambiguous, then it necessarily means that the second clause gets the same interpretation as the first clause. If, on the other hand, there is vagueness, the speaker can choose one of both interpretations in the first clause and opt for the alternative one in the second clause. The following examples can be used to illustrate the test:

(34) a. They saw her duck and so did he. (Zwicky and Sadock 1975: 24)
 b. Anne is an aunt of mine and so is Sally.

The complement(s) of *saw* in *They saw her duck* can be understood in two ways: (a) *her duck* is a Direct Object consisting of a possessive determiner followed by a noun head or (b) *her* is a personal pronoun and *duck* is a verb. If the hearer opts for interpretation (a), then *so did he* is necessarily understood as: *he also saw [her$_{pos\ det}$ duck$_N$]*. If, on the other hand, the hearer opts for interpretation (b) in the first clause, then *so did he* is necessarily understood as: *he also saw [her$_{pers\ pr.}$] [duck$_V$]*. In other words, crossed readings are ruled out (*[clause 1 interpretation (a) + clause 2 interpretation (b)] or *[clause 1 interpretation (b) + clause 2 interpretation (a)]). The conclusion that follows is that *I saw her duck* is structurally ambiguous. Alternatively, in (34b), crossed readings are not ruled out. While both Sally and Anne could be sisters of the speaker's mother or while both could be sisters of the speaker's father, a reading in which Anne is a sister of the speaker's mother and Sally a sister of the speaker's father, or vice versa, is also possible. The conclusion is that *aunt* is vague (monosemous). Summing up, if the interpretation in the second clause is necessarily the same as in the first clause, there is ambiguity (polysemy) at stake. If crossed readings are possible, there is vagueness (monosemy).[15] In lexical semantics, Zwicky and Sadock's tests have been used to identify polysemy as well as homonymy, in other words, irrespective of whether the different meanings are related or not (e.g. Geeraerts 1993, Ravin and Leacock 2002, Riemer 2010). It is therefore possible to use them to diagnose the status of the meaning distinctions in the field of modals.[16] To our knowledge, Carretero (2005) is the first discussion of modal meaning in which such a linguistic test – she speaks of "the test of substitution with SO/TOO" – is exploited, specifically to determine if *will* is polysemous.

The following examples (from Depraetere 2014: 164) can be used to test whether the taxonomic distinctions argued for in Section 2 are semantic in nature, as we believe they are, and not just pragmatic modulations of a single meaning. Let us begin with the quite uncontroversial distinction between epistemic and root modality:

(35) Sarah **may** help. ((a) epistemic possibility: 'Maybe Sarah will help'; (b) root possibility, permission: 'Sarah is allowed to help')

(36) The children **must** be hiding. ((a) epistemic necessity: 'I logically conclude that they're hiding since I can't see them anywhere'; (b) root, general situation necessity: 'The children must be hiding when grandma arrives; otherwise, it'll spoil the surprise')

Applying the identity-of-sense test clearly reveals that epistemic and non-epistemic meanings are distinct:

(37) Sarah **may** help. So **may** Sue.

(38) The children **must** be hiding. So **must** the guests.

---

15 There is also a definitional test. This hinges on the idea, going back to Aristotle, that the number of meanings of a word is determined by the number of definitions it is compatible with. A further test, the so-called logical test, stipulates that there is ambiguity or polysemy if "[f]or a given state of affairs, the sentence can be both truly affirmed and truly denied" (Gillon 1990: 407). For some critical discussion of these tests, see Gillon (1990), Geeraerts (1993) and Dunbar (2001).
16 As we pointed out in Section 3.1, in the case of modal verbs, it is polysemy that is at stake, rather than homonymy.

The sequence of clauses in (37) does not allow an interpretation whereby Sarah will perhaps help and Sue is allowed to do so, or vice versa, where Sarah is allowed to help and Sue will perhaps do so. If the first clause is given an epistemic interpretation, so must the second, and if the first is given a root interpretation, so again must the second. In (38), we see a similar restriction played out: either both clauses receive an epistemic reading or they both receive a root reading, but crossing these readings is not possible.[17] The following examples exhibit 'ambiguity' with respect to various root meanings:

(39) Jennifer **can** swim. ((a) ability; (b) opportunity; (c) permission)

(40) Jennifer **must** have that dress. ((a) narrow-scope internal necessity: 'Jennifer insists . . .'; (b) narrow-scope external necessity: 'I insist . . .')

(41) Bicarbonate **can** be added to a pool. ((a) general situation possibility: 'adding bicarbonate is technically possible, for instance, by dissolving the powder in water'; (b) permissibility: 'adding bicarbonate is permissible: swimmers won't have health problems if you do so')

The identity-of-sense test produces the same results as in the case of epistemic vs. non-epistemic meaning; crossed readings are ruled out: irrespective of the option chosen, the meaning decided on for the first clause is necessarily the one that applies to the second clause. In other words, the different non-epistemic meanings as well are indicative of the polysemy of modals:

(42) Jennifer **can** swim. So **can** Robin.

(43) Jennifer **must** have that dress. So **must** Robin.

(44) Bicarbonate **can** be added to a pool. So **can** sodium sesquicarbonate.

---

17 There are other criteria that are used to justify the semantic difference between epistemic and root meanings. First, they have different paraphrases in which the non-modalized proposition (p) is integrated (e.g. epistemic possibility: 'it is possible that p'; root possibility: 'it is possible for p'). Second, scope of negation may differentiate them. Thus, in the case of the ambiguous sentence *Sarah may not help*, we see that epistemic modality stays outside the scope of negation ('It is possible that Sarah will not help'), while root modality is precisely what gets negated ('Sarah is not allowed to help'). This latter criterion, however, does not apply across the board to all modals. For instance, epistemic *cannot* and epistemic *may not* have different scope properties (see e.g. Depraetere and Langford 2020: 270–271).

Thus, just to use (42) as an example, we cannot take this combination of clauses to mean that Jennifer is able to swim and that Robin is allowed to.

Assessing the discreteness of two senses, however, should not be conceived of as a binary decision to make. As is argued by Tuggy (1993), there is a cline from homonymy (or ambiguity in a narrow sense), to polysemy, to vagueness. This means that there are middle cases between the relatively clear cases of polysemy cited above such as *run* (fast human locomotion and proper mechanic functioning) – Tuggy (1993) gives the example of *paint* ('apply paint to a surface artistically' and 'apply paint to a surface for utilitarian purposes') – and the clear cases of monosemy given, such as *aunt*. In the next section, we will deal in more detail with cases that are difficult to classify.

3.3 'Ambiguity', merger and gradience

While we believe the results of the identity-of-sense test discussed in Section 3.2 constitute solid evidence in favor of polysemy, it is important to consider one of the main arguments of monosemists, namely that there is a great degree of indeterminacy. Starting again from the discussion on the topic in one of the first empirical studies of English modals (Coates 1983, see also Leech and Coates 1980), three types of 'indeterminacy' have been argued to exist: 'ambiguity', merger and gradience. We will briefly discuss these notions in this section.

'*Ambiguity*' has already been illustrated in many of the examples above: two or more readings are theoretically available and the hearer has to decide in context which one is intended by the hearer. For instance, *Jennifer can swim* is, out of any context, three-way 'ambiguous', but in a specific usage situation, it is likely to be taken in just one of the ways the sentence in isolation can be understood. Palmer (1990), however, objects to treating 'ambiguity' as a form of indeterminacy:

> Ambiguity is not indeterminacy and should be clearly distinguished from it. There would be ambiguity if, although it is not possible to decide in a particular context between two possible meanings of a form, it can still reasonably be stated that it must have one or other of the two, as with uncontextualized *He is fair*, where fair could mean either 'just' or 'fair-haired'; indeterminacy implies that no firm decision could, even in principle, be made. (Palmer 1990: 22)

Even though Leech and Coates (1980) explicitly list 'ambiguity' as a type of 'indeterminacy', they seem to be on one line with Palmer, as they write that '[a]mbiguities are rare in actual texts, because contextual clues generally make clear which meaning is appropriate' (Leech and Coates 1980: 81).

Merger (Coates 1983: 17) refers to contexts in which the root and epistemic meanings are mutually compatible. As in the case of 'ambiguity', there are clearly two separate meanings involved, but according to Coates, the distinction between epistemic and root necessity is 'contextually neutralized'. We have already encountered an authentic example in the introduction to this book (example (2) there). Here are two examples Coates provides:

(45) Speaker A: Newcastle Brown is a jolly good beer.
Speaker B: Is it?
Speaker A: Well it **ought to** be at that price.
(Coates, 1983: 17)

(46) It is important to note that where high concentrations are theoretically possible in the plant evaporator, the time required to build them **may** be considerable.
(Coates 1983: 145)

In (45), speaker A either means that given its price, Newcastle Brown is necessarily good beer (epistemic), or, alternatively, "the speaker is referring to the maker's obligation to provide good beer" (Coates 1983: 17) (root, general situation necessity). The sentence in (46) either expresses what we have called general situation possibility (the situation of the time required being considerable is possible), or it is interpreted in terms of epistemic likelihood: it is possible that the time required will be considerable. What is typical of merger is that the two meanings can co-exist and that the 'ambiguity' does not need to be resolved. Merger is not to be understood as an actual blend of the two meanings. It occurs in contexts in which it just so happens that either of the two (still distinct) meanings make full sense. Still, the speaker, if pressed for an answer, would be able to say which meaning she had (most clearly) in mind.[18]

Gradience, finally, applies to uses for which it is not possible, not even if we asked the speaker for her intentions, to determine which meaning is conveyed:

---

18 On the basis of the empirical analyses that we have carried out, it appears that examples with *may*, *might* and *could* can be ambiguous between wide-scope root possibility and epistemic meaning (as in (46)). Interestingly, given that epistemic meaning develops out of root meaning, and that the development is one in terms of narrow-scope root modality via wide-scope root modality to wide-scope epistemic modality (cf., e.g., Nordlinger and Traugott 1997), merger (the fact that a wide-scope root interpretation and a wide-scope epistemic interpretation seem to co-exist) may well support this path of historical change, with indeterminate examples illustrating "bridging contexts" (Enfield 2003: 28).

"an indeterminate example is said to exhibit gradience when it fits neither category a nor category b but has elements of both" (Coates 1983: 11). Gradience leaves space for examples that do not clearly belong to one category or another. For Coates, both root meaning and epistemic meaning (which, it should be noted, are mutually distinct for her) are (internally) 'fuzzy', but root meaning is even more considerably so. She treats each identifiable meaning as a 'fuzzy set', that is, "a class in which the transition from membership to non-membership is gradual rather than abrupt" (Coates 1983: 13).

In our view, indeterminacy, be it of the 'merger' or the 'gradience' type, let alone of the 'ambiguity' type (which perhaps should not even be called indeterminacy, as we have seen), does not necessarily mean that it is impossible to label the meaning expressed by a modal in context. The problem of perceived indeterminacy partly resides in the fact that taxonomic distinctions may not have been defined in a very explicit way. Consider the following two examples that supposedly illustrate that class membership is graded, under Coates's approach of modal meanings in terms of fuzzy sets:

(47) But assuming that the distinction is maintained one **may** ask which is to be analytically prior.
(Coates 1983: 143)
(supposedly peripheral example of root possibility *may*: is it still permission?)

(48) Clay pots **must** have some protection from severe weather.
(Coates 1983: 35)
(supposedly peripheral member of root necessity *must*: does it still express 'subjective', strong obligation, as in (10) above?)

In fact, these examples can easily be categorized in terms of the 5-class taxonomy of root possibility and the 3-class taxonomy of root necessity. As we see it, (47) communicates 'situation permissibility' meaning (and not permission) and (48) 'wide-scope external necessity' (cf. Section 2.4). Having said this, we do allow for the possibility that a given utterance is a clearer, more prototypical member of a semantic category than another utterance. Consider (49):

(49) Everybody freeze! There's been an employee theft in the store. Nobody **can** leave. I repeat, no one.

It cannot be denied that *can* here expresses permission (rather than any other modal meaning discussed). Still, because the subject is *nobody*, it is not the best kind of example to illustrate this category. Indeed, we typically think of permission as an action being granted to, or requested for, an identifiable Subject referent, while in this case, *nobody* has, by definition, no referent and the action referred to (*leave*) is not allowed but prohibited.

Remember that we claim that cases felt to be indeterminate can still be given precise labels and that with some effort – looking at the wider context or prompting the speaker to clarify what she intended – we can in principle settle on one of the meanings seemingly flowing together. This strongly contrasts with the position taken by Groefsema (1995), who defends a monosemy position and argues that disambiguation is not always possible – and in some cases is not even desirable.[19] For the supposed impossibility to disambiguate, consider this example:

(50) One thing you want to avoid, if you possibly **can**, is a present from my mother.
(Palmer 1979: 73, cited in Groefsema 1995: 55)

According to Palmer (1979: 73) – and this view is echoed by Groefsema (1995) – we may not be able to tell whether *can* in (50) refers to someone's ability to avoid receiving a present from the speaker's mother or with another sort of root possibility meaning. With respect to this example, however, our view is that this sentence communicates opportunity meaning ('... if circumstances make it possible for you to avoid a present'). The reason is that avoiding getting a present is not a skill that people can reasonably boast to have trained for (unlike, say, avoiding being shot in a shooter video game), while being given the opportunity (not) to end up in a situation *is* something that someone can hope for.

Summing up, the existence of examples of 'merger'/'gradience' does not necessarily imply that modals are monosemous. The meanings involved are distinct and can be made explicit. What this means in terms of the inference process that takes place is a different question, which will be addressed in the next chapter.

---

19 Groefsema uses 'disambiguation' here to refer to examples the readings of which are indeterminate between different root interpretations, which in Coates's approach point to gradience, not 'ambiguity' (which holds between root and epistemic modality meanings). So while the claim that disambiguation is not always desirable at first sight seems to resonate with Coates's (1983) definition of merger, it is important to bear in mind that Groefsema (1995) considers that modals have only one abstract meaning. In her view, unlike in Coates's work, there is no semantic distinction between epistemic and root meaning.

3.4 Pragmatics in the foreground

Apart from examples of the kind discussed in the previous section, monosemists have also made their case on the basis of examples in which illocutionary force rather than the basic 'modal meaning' seems to be in the foreground, and have therefore argued that such examples do not fit in any class either. Consider this sentence:

(51) You **must** come to dinner sometime.
(Groefsema, 1995: 57)
(message communicated: 'We would like you to come to dinner sometime')

Note that the same observation leads Facchinetti (2002: 237) and Collins (2009) to posit a different taxonomic class, which they call, after Palmer (1990), 'dynamic implication' and of which the following are some illustrations:[20]

(52) In your letter to me you say that "it is not the ownership of the NRMA that is under review." **Could** you explain that to me please? (ICE-AUS W1B-026 86)
(Collins 2009: 116)
(request)
(53) Well I **can** write on your behalf. (ICE-AUS S1A-004 116)
(Collins 2009: 104)
(offer)

In our view, the fact that a specific illocutionary force is foregrounded adds an interesting layer to the facets of meanings communicated by modals; however, contexts like these do not imply that the semantic core of the modal is wiped out (see, e.g., the discussion in Cappelle and Depraetere 2016) – or, for that matter, do not constitute separate taxonomic classes. They certainly do not provide convincing evidence in favor of monosemy.

The observations in Section 2 about taxonomy and those in Sections 3.1–3.3 about polysemy and monosemy bring up an important theoretical question: Can contextual information be considered part of the meaning of a lexical item? If so, how can this be accounted for? The issue of how modals-in-context are interpreted will be taken up in Chapter 2 in a theoretically sophisticated way, integrat-

---

20 Collins (2009) considers dynamic implication to be a subclass of dynamic modality. For Facchinetti (2002), dynamic implication is likewise a taxonomic category on a par with ability and dynamic possibility, the three of which make up dynamic modality, which itself is one of the three main categorical distinctions, together with epistemic modality and deontic modality.

ing concepts from Construction Grammar and Relevance Theory. Here, we offer some preliminary theoretical insights about this issue.

So far, we have seen that modal verbs are polysemous. The intuition is that they appear in ever-varied contexts, which hearers use to figure out what could have been the intended meaning, based on pragmatic reasoning. Yet, the crux of a full understanding of modal meaning lies in the realization that we need to acknowledge more than just the actual modal verbs as carriers of modal meanings. A hearer can often arrive at the intended meaning because modals tend to appear in recurrent phrases with conventional interpretations. For example, *Why should I . . .?* is typically used to mean something like 'I don't want to . . .', 'I see no need to . . .', 'I won't allow myself to . . .': it's an expression of defiance, more than a real, sincere question asking about the reason necessitating an action (cf. also Cappelle, Depraetere and Lesuisse 2019: 230–231). This does not mean that *should* here no longer expresses root necessity. However, this meaning is not what is at stake and is not even that relevant. The ulterior meaning of *Why should I . . .?* is conventionalized, that is, routinized or 'short-circuited', in Morgan's (1977) terms: it can be arrived at without the hearer having to work it out by means of step-by-step reasoning. The short-circuited meaning is often 'pragmatic', that is, having to do with speech acts such as requests, wishes, disbelief, etc. While not inferred (but conventionally associated with this construction), it is considered to be pragmatic because it does not contribute to the truth-conditional content of the clause. This is what we call conventional pragmatic meaning. The semantics of the modal may also arise in a similar 'short-circuited' way. In the case of *Can I please . . .?*, for instance, not only does the hearer know right away (in large part because of *please*) that a request is being made but also that the speaker is asking for *permission*, one of the semantic modal categories, and is not asking about her actual ability to do something. In other words, in *Can I please . . .?*, the 'short-circuiting' or conventional meaning concerns two levels of meaning: conventional pragmatic meaning (a request) *and* conventional semantic (permission) meaning (see our discussion of *saturation* below).

As part of their linguistic competence, language users have stored a multitude of modal verbs embedded in bits of context which come with conventionalized pragmatic interpretations. We list just a few of such contexts (in boldface) for *can't* in (54):

(54) a. **This can't be** happening.
　　 b. **I just can't** get enough of it!
　　 c. **Why can't you just** be nice?
　　 d. **You can't always** win.
　　 e. **Uh**, Sir? **You can't** operate a boat under the influence of alcohol.

In (54a), the boldfaced part often indicates that the speaker expresses stunned disbelief at a contextually salient situation. In (54b), the boldfaced part frequently signals strong emotions, in this case enthusiasm. The boldfaced part in (54c) often occurs in utterances in which the speaker expresses disapproval and exasperation. In (54d), the boldfaced sequence typically expresses resignation, accepting that it cannot be any other way. In (54e), the interjection *Uh* (often followed by a vocative or something like *hey* or *excuse me*) and *you can't* VP jointly indicate that the speaker tries to point out to the hearer that a particular action, which the hearer would like to carry out, is forbidden. As shown in Cappelle and Depraetere (2016: 25–27) and Cappelle (2017: 140), this short-circuited interpretation is so well-established that when the hearer fails to interpret it this way, willfully or out of ignorance, the effect will sound rude or comical – as when, in an episode of *The Simpsons*, the main protagonist Homer replies with "That sounds like a wager to me!".

A few of the many recurrent patterns in which we find *should* are listed in (55) (see also Cappelle, Depraetere and Lesuisse 2019):

(55) a. **Why should** I care?
 b. **You should try** this.
 c. **I don't think we should** go out anymore.
 d. Yeah, **you should never** buy technology when it's new.

We have already discussed the pattern in (55a), which the speaker uses to indicate that she sees no reason why the Subject referent (often the speaker herself) would do what's expressed by the verb phrase and hence that the Subject referent won't (allow themselves to) do this. In (55b), by contrast, the speaker recommends (doing) what is expressed by the complement of *try*, a verb that is stored along with *you should* as one of the many entrenched sequences. In (55c), the boldfaced part is used to express that perhaps it's not a good idea to do what the VP expresses. In (55d), the boldfaced part signals that the speaker is strongly convinced that you should always avoid doing what is expressed in the verb phrase.

We previously suggested that the illocutionary force is a layer added to the semantic meaning (i.e., to any of the categories in Table 4) when modals appear in utterance-level units. While this may be so, it is worth pointing out that there may be patterns in which the modal verb conveys different semantic categories but where the pragmatic specification is quite similar (and even identical, when considered with a sufficient degree of abstraction). Consider these two examples, discussed in Cappelle, Depraetere and Lesuisse (2019: 231):

(56) a. 'I've had enough of you!' she cried vehemently, not waiting for his response. '**Why should** I care what you feel when all the time you behave like a monster?' she asked rhetorically.
b. She thought, looking dubious. 'It doesn't sound likely. **Why should** there be a conspiracy? (...)'

In (56a), as in (55a) above, *should* expresses root necessity, being concerned with the need to care. In (56b), *should* expresses epistemic necessity, since a possible semantic paraphrase of this utterance is 'Why would it be necessarily the case *that* there is a conspiracy?' Despite these major semantic differences, *Why should...?* could be claimed to have the same pragmatic function, namely that of objecting to the non-modalized proposition (either to what its actual contents convey or to the 'justifiedness' of positing it as a valid one). This supports the concept of short-circuited interpretations, in this case from form to pragmatics. To the extent that the illocutionary force of objecting is felt to be what really matters in a *Why should...?* utterance, the semantics could be left underspecified as to whether it is of the epistemic or non-epistemic kind. In other words, the pragmatics of an expression encompassing a modal verb may be more in the foreground than the semantics of the modal verb. At the same time, the *effect* of objecting is clearly different when the utterance involves epistemic or non-epistemic modality. In (56a), the speaker expresses something like 'I see no reason why I should...'; hence: 'I won't (allow myself to)...'. The utterance counts as a defiant objection to the need to do something. In (56b), the illocutionary force can be formulated as 'Let's not assume/conclude too easily that...'. Having said this, while the semantic distinctions (root vs. epistemic) of the respective patterns shape and inform the nature of the objection (and are responsible for the way in which the objection is interpreted), they are at the same time subservient to the overall message that is communicated. Moreover, the way the semantic values (root vs. epistemic) interact with the general pragmatic meaning of objecting is not likely to be computed anew each time a *Why should...?* utterance is used but probably forms part of a speaker's array of stored conventions about language, in line with a usage-based perspective (Langacker 1987; see Diessel 2017 for a general overview). Figure 1 attempts to provide an informal representation of how several of the involved linguistic units that we believe are entrenched in competent speakers' cognition are connected.[21]

---

21 While Figure 1 is in itself already a (simplified) network representation of constructional nodes, the node-internal constructional information in the constructions shown here may be further represented as links between 'leaner' nodes, for example between a node specifying just

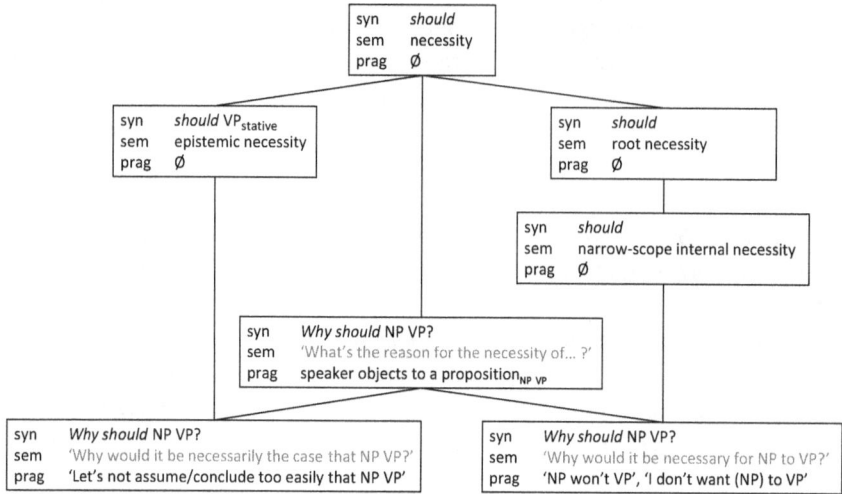

Figure 1: Simplified network representation of some entrenched linguistic units (the nodes enclosed in rectangles), containing formal ('syn'), semantic ('sem') and, if available, pragmatic ('prag') information.

Should as a modal verb, at the top, expresses necessity and has, in and of itself, no particular pragmatic properties. At a lower level of generality, we can identify epistemic *should*, which formally (virtually) requires an environment where the VP is stative (cf. Wärnsby 2006), and root *should*, both of which of course still express necessity. Root necessity *should* has, among other subtypes (not included in Figure 1), a narrow-scope internal necessity sense. So far, the pragmatic specification of these units remains empty. It is only when *should* occurs in the sequence *Why should* NP VP? that we can specify a conventional pragmatic value of this entire unit. The semantics of this sequence is backgrounded (indicated in Figure 1 by a lighter text color). By the way, it is backgrounded only in this entrenched sequence with this particular pragmatic value. Indeed, nothing prevents *Why should* NP VP? to be used semantically compositionally and pragmatically neutrally, as when a teacher asks their students, "Why should this method be chosen here?" and thereby intends to convey no criticism at all about the adoption of the method referred to. Finally, depending on whether *should* is used epistemically or non-epistemically in this stored sequence, we get a different semantic specification (still backgrounded) and also a more specific pragmatic value.

---

the form of *should* and another node specifying its meaning. See Chapter 9 for a proposal along those lines.

When pragmatics is included in a unit, it is not of the 'inferential' kind involving, for instance, the use of Gricean maxims to make sense of an utterance in a given discourse situation. Nevertheless, when a hearer decides whether a given sequence is to be understood as an entrenched one with 'pre-installed' or conventional pragmatics or, rather, as a purely compositional combination, this decision is itself one that relies on inferential pragmatics. In the example just given of a teacher using the sequence *Why should* NP VP? to make them come up with justifications for the (non-ironically presented) usefulness of a method to solve a problem, the hearer will have to conclude on the basis of quite complicated situational and contextual clues that the utterance was assembled fully compositionally and should likewise be interpreted fully compositionally. In line with the observations just made, Chapter 2 will therefore argue for an approach to pragmatics which gives due space to conventional pragmatics as well as to inferred pragmatic content (see, e.g. Cappelle 2017, Depraetere 2015b, Leclercq and Depraetere 2022, Leclercq 2020). To illustrate the different ways in which *pragmatic(s)* has been approached and is involved in utterance interpretation, we can use the construction *Can you* VP?, instantiated as *Can you open the window?* In Table 6 we present various conceptions of *pragmatic(s)*, applied to how this utterance is understood in a particular usage situation. These conceptions are non-identical, as we will show in the comments that follow.

Table 6 shows that *pragmatic(s)* is sometimes used as a label to capture 'reference to the context', be it the linguistic context (e.g. *can* in *She can play the flute* is more likely to be interpreted as expressing ability than in *She can enter the concert hall at 8 pm*) or the extra-linguistic context (e.g. *can* is more likely

Table 6: Different ways in which the term *pragmatic* is often used, applied to the utterance *Can you open the window?*

[Situation: it's not particularly hot in the classroom, which does however feel a little stuffy; the teacher then addresses John.] *Can you open the window?*		
Pertaining to \ Based on	linguistic context: ***pragmatic*** in the sense of 'co-text-dependent'	extra-linguistic context: ***pragmatic*** in the sense of 'situation-based'
meaning resulting from saturation (truth-conditional semantics)	*can* = 'have the *ability* to', not e.g. 'have *permission* to'	*you* = 'John'
Pragmatic meaning in the sense of (conventional or non-conventional) non-truth-conditional meaning (e.g. speech acts)	The utterance is (conventionally understood as) a *request*, backgrounding the basic ability meaning[22]	The utterance is (indirectly understood as) covert *criticism* by the speaker that there's an unpleasant smell in the room

to express ability in the context described than in that of a visitor addressing a patient in hospital and inquiring into the house rules: teachers, who have relative power over pupils, generally do not need to inquire about whether the latter are *allowed* to do something but they can, and often do, wonder whether pupils are *capable* of doing something.

Alternatively, and more in line with how 'prag(matics)' is represented in Figure 1, *pragmatic* can also be used to refer to non-truth conditional, for instance, 'implicated' aspects of meaning, some of which can become part of the meaning conventionally expressed by constructions, some others of which remain purely inferred and non-conventional and would not necessarily arise in a different setting. Table 6 shows how these subtypes of pragmatic meaning can be differentiated. The speech act conventionally associated with *Can you open the window?* is a request; this is conventional (or 'short-circuited') pragmatic meaning. We indeed consider this to be *pragmatic* meaning: even though it is not situationally inferred, it is not part of the truth-conditional content of the utterance (more on which shortly). Additional non-conventional pragmatic meaning may be inferred: given an appropriate situational context, the hearer may gather that *Can you open the window?* is a critical comment by the speaker. Neither is this 'extra' meaning part of the truth-conditional content of the utterance.

Pragmatic aspects of meaning in the second sense (i.e., non-truth-conditional meaning) are to be contrasted with *saturated* aspects of meaning. *Saturation* (Recanati 1989) refers to information that is often inferred in context and that, unlike implicated meaning, contributes to the truth-conditional content of the proposition. Saturation is linguistically mandated and obligatory in the sense that it is necessary in order to arrive at a propositional form to which a truth value can be assigned. For instance, the assignment of a specific referent to *you* will impact on the truth-conditional content of *You can come in*. As we see it – but this is a matter of debate – disambiguation is also a case of saturation: the truth value of *Susan can speak French* may well be different depending on whether permission or ability meaning is communicated.[23] It is important to make the following observation: the position of the disambiguation of *can* (*can* = 'have the *ability* to', not e.g. 'have *permission* to') as an illustration of the impact of the linguistic co-text in Table 6 might be interpreted to mean that this saturation process is

---

22 While the ability meaning is typically backgrounded, it can be re-foregrounded in certain contexts, as when the speaker actually wants to check whether the addressee has the physical skills to open the window. Indeed, the window in question might be known to be hard to open, and the speaker might want to present opening it as a challenge. This shows that the request reading, though conventionalized in the *Can you* VP? pattern, is still a cancellable implicature.
23 Saturation will be addressed in more detail in Chapter 2.

determined by the linguistic co-text only. This is not our view, however: saturation depends on the immediate linguistic co-text as well as on the wider discourse context and on extra-linguistic background. For instance, *She can speak French* will communicate permission rather than ability when embedded in a context like *No one will take offence here; she can speak French* rather than in the following context: *Isn't it amazing, this little girl is perfectly bilingual; she can speak French as well!* And even in the absence of such clear linguistic clues, the hearer will have to figure out which interpretation was meant.

Note that the meaning that is inferred through saturation impacts on the truth-conditional content of the sentence. So here, two approaches are in principle possible: one might want to argue that, because the meaning of *can* is *inferred*, we should consider it to be pragmatic. But – and this is the view we take – as the inferred meaning contributes to the truth-conditional content (*can* expressing ability vs. *can* expressing permission), it can also be – and in fact should be – considered to be semantic in nature. Note again that ambiguity tests can be used to show that the utterance can be true in one sense but false in the other.

Furthermore, as we know, *can* conventionally expresses possibility, which is information that does not appear in Table 6 but that is similar to what is represented in Figure 1, where *should* is shown to encode necessity in the highest, most general node of the network. This is the level of conventional, truth-conditional semantics where no pragmatics comes into play. Additionally, as argued with respect to *Can I please . . .?*, where the modal features in a particular stored sequence (i.e. a modal verb construction), there can be 'short-circuiting' at the semantic level, and the meaning of 'permission' will get conventionally saturated in this expression.

Summing up, with respect to our example, *Can you open the window?*, the conventional semantic (truth-conditional) meaning of this utterance includes the fact that *can* communicates possibility meaning; an inferred semantic (i.e., truth-conditional) aspect of meaning consists in *can* being disambiguated as communicating ability meaning; a conventional pragmatic (non-truth-conditional) aspect of meaning is that the utterance (given the form *Can you . . .?*) communicates a request; an inferred pragmatic (i.e., non-truth-conditional) aspect of meaning could be that there is an unpleasant smell in the room being criticized.

It is against the background of these distinctions between inferred/conventional and truth-conditional/non-truth-conditional meaning that the semantics-pragmatics interface will be explored in more detail in Chapter 2.

4 Theoretical models, methods and datasets used in this book

The title of this chapter promised an *outline* of the uses of modal verbs, as well as of their forms and meanings. It should be clear from the few examples discussed here that we cannot give a complete overview of the myriad different ways in which modal verbs are used. We nonetheless hope to have given a general sketch of a cognitively plausible model that recognizes that modal verbs are not just to be described as 'atoms', as they also occur in cognitively entrenched chunks associated with particular communicative functions. While above we have proposed a network with quite detailed nodes, at the end of this book, in Chapter 9, Martin Hilpert and Susanne Flach will present a different kind of network model, in which the links between nodes are more important and the nodes themselves are leaner. In line with the title of this volume, and as explained in the introduction of this book (Section 2 there), we analyze modals from different perspectives: in the next chapter, it will be argued by Benoît Leclercq that combined insights from Relevance Theory and Construction Grammar can offer a solid theoretical basis for the analysis of modal meaning, making explicit the respective roles of knowledge and inference during the interpretation. The focus will be on conceptual and procedural meaning and their relative contributions to the profile of a modal in context, and the model presented will build on the concept of lexically regulated saturation.

As for the methods adopted in this book, we also adopt a broad array of approaches. The present and the next chapter largely use (what we believe to be sound) introspective linguistics, but some of the claims advanced are also based on empirical research into recurrent patterns and qualitative data analysis that probes into the meaning of modal verbs. 'Traditional' corpus linguistics, coupled with statistical analyses, will be used in Chapters 3 and 4, co-authored (in varying combinations) by Bert Cappelle, Ludovic De Cuypere, Ilse Depraetere, Cyril Grandin and Benoît Leclercq, where findings on the choice of semantically roughly equivalent modals (five possibility modals, or five necessity modals) are based on manual annotation of various linguistic predictors. The extent to which the most discriminating predictors identified in this type of research also play a role in language users' preference for one of two competing modals is then investigated by means of a psycholinguistic experiment in Chapter 5, co-authored by Susanne Flach, Bert Cappelle and Martin Hilpert. In the experimental task, subjects had to rate the acceptability of two modals (*must* and *have to*) presented in a range of stimuli pairs that were designed to exhibit different values of the predictors tested. Apart from a manual-labor-intensive corpus-linguistic approach and the associated psycholinguistic validation experiment, we also present methods belonging to the growing field of AI (artificial intelligence). We use machine learning not just to try to predict the meaning of modal verb in any given context – (Chapter 8, co-authored by Mathieu Dehouck and Pascal Denis) but also to categorize language productions according to six levels (A1, A2, B1, B2, C1 and C2 in the Common European Framework of Reference for Languages) (Chapter 7, co-authored by Natalia Grabar, Thierry Hamon and Benoît Leclercq). For the latter, different sets of linguistic and textual properties will be considered, including the occurrence of modal verbs in texts. These methods build complex probabilistic models of a large dataset to make accurate predictions about unseen cases. Statistical comparison of collective versus individual language usage will lead to an assessment of the degree to which different speakers have incorporated in their language use highly personal routines around the use of a modal verb (Chapter 6, co-authored by Clemens Hufeld and Hans-Jörg Schmid).

The empirical dataset that is used in Chapters 3, 4, 5 and 8 is a sample of (roughly) 5,000 tokens of modal verbs, randomly selected from COCA (Davies 2008–), consisting of circa 500 contextualized instances of 10 modal verbs (*can, could, may, might, be able to, must, should, ought to, need (to) and have to*). This dataset has been annotated in terms of 36 features that are syntactic, semantic, pragmatic and lexical in nature. This 'REM' dataset (with *REM*, as noted before, short for *Re-thinking English Modal constructions*) is available from the publisher's website (https://www.degruyter.com/document/isbn/9783110734157/html). The corpus annotation guide has also been made available as an online companion to the volume. This is not the only dataset used in this book. Chapter 6 uses data from the British National Corpus 2014. Chapter 7 relies on the EFCamDat corpus (https://corpus.mml.cam.ac.uk/efcamdat2) (Geertzen, Alexopoulou and Korhonen 2013; Huang et al. 2018), which contains linguistic productions by adult learners of English from different L1 backgrounds. The exploited set of this corpus contains 83 million words written by some 175,000 learners. These productions are categorized according to the six CECRL levels from A1 (beginners) to C2 (fluent). Chapter 8 builds on several datasets: MPQA, EPOS and the REM dataset. The MPQA (Multi-Perspective Question Answering) is a 11,114-sentence corpus that was collected and annotated by Wiebe et al. (2005) (https://mpqa.cs.pitt.edu/corpora/mpqa_corpus/). Ruppenhofer and Rehbein (2012) extracted the sentences containing modal verbs and annotated their senses, and this resulted in a dataset (http://ruppenhofer.de/pages/Data%20sets.html) with 1,248 annotated modals. The EPOS corpus (Zhou et al. 2015) is a 2,453-sentence corpus (https://heidata.uni-heidelberg.de/dataset.xhtml?persistentId=doi:10.11588/data/JEESIQ) of annotated English modals based on sense projection from German-English parallel sentences from the OPUS corpus (Tiedemann 2012).

5 Conclusion

In this chapter, we have laid some of the conceptual groundwork for the study of English modals. We first established which verbs, based on their formal properties, can be considered modal verbs. We devoted some attention to the question of whether *will*, *would* and *shall* are tense or modal auxiliaries. Our position is that they are primarily tense forms but that they have modal uses, which is the reason why they are considered in only some of the chapters to follow. Most of the present chapter was concerned with semantic distinctions (epistemic, root, deontic, etc.) that play a role in modal taxonomies proposed in the literature. We have argued here for a taxonomy that distinguishes between epistemic and root meanings and between possibility and necessity, and that further recognizes different root meanings based on the binary features scope, source and (for possibility) potential barrier. We further argued that these different meanings are distinct semantic categories that need to be 'disambiguated' via saturation, thus taking a polysemy position to modal meaning and reassessing perceived cases of semantic indeterminacy. We also considered the role of pragmatics, emphasizing the existence of conventionalized aspects of non-truth-conditional meaning that have become part of what speakers know about constructions. Our chapter ended with a specification of the theoretical approaches taken in this book (namely a broadly constructionist model combined, in the next chapter, with Relevance Theory), as well as of the methods and the datasets that are used.

References

Aarts, Bas. 2007. *Syntactic Gradience: The Nature of Grammatical Indeterminacy*. Oxford: Oxford University Press.

Aijmer, Karin. 1985. The semantic development of *will*. In Jack Fisiak (ed.), *Historical Semantics. Historical Word-Formation*, 11–21. Berlin: Mouton de Gruyter.

Aikhenvald, Alexandra Yurievna. 2018. Evidentiality: The framework. In Alexandra Yurievna Aikhenvald (ed.), *The Oxford Handbook of Evidentiality*, 1–46. Oxford: Oxford University Press.

Biber, Douglas, Stig Johansson, Geoffrey Leech, Susan Conrad & Edward Finegan. 2021 [1999]. *Grammar of Spoken and Written English*, 2nd edn. Amsterdam: John Benjamins.

Bolinger, Dwight. 1980. WANNA and the gradience of auxiliaries. In Gunther Brettschneider & Christian Lehmann (eds.), *Wege zur Universalienforschung: Sprachwissenschaftliche Beitrage zum 60. Geburtstage von Hansjakob Seiler*, 292–299. Tübingen: Gunter Narr.

Bybee, Joan L. & William Pagliuca. 1987. The development of future meaning. In Anna Giacalone Ramat, Onofrio Carruba & Giuliano Bernini (eds.), *Papers from the 7th International Conference on Historical Linguistics*, 109–122. Amsterdam: John Benjamins.

Bybee, Joan L., & Suzanne Fleischman. 1995. Modality in grammar and discourse: An introductory essay. In Joan L. Bybee & Suzanne Fleischman (eds.), *Modality in Grammar and Discourse*, 1–14. Amsterdam: John Benjamins.

Caliendo, Giuditta. 2004. Modality and Communicative Interaction in EU Law. In Christopher N. Candlin & Maurizio Gotti (eds.), *Intercultural Discourse in Domain-specific English*. 241–259. Bern: Peter Lang.

Cappelle, Bert. 2017. What's pragmatics doing outside constructions? In Ilse Depraetere & Raphael Salkie (eds.), *Semantics and Pragmatics: Drawing a Line*, 115–151. Cham: Springer.

Cappelle, Bert & Ilse Depraetere. 2016. Short-circuited interpretations of modal verb constructions: Some evidence from *The Simpsons*. *Constructions and Frames* 8 (1). 7–39.

Cappelle, Bert, Ilse Depraetere & Mégane Lesuisse. 2019. The necessity modals *have to, must, need to* and *should*: Using n-grams to help identify common and distinct semantic and pragmatic aspects. *Constructions and Frames* 11(2). 220–243.

Carretero, Marta. 2005. Explorations of the use of English *will/be going to* contrasted with the Spanish future indicative *ir a*. In Roberta Facchinetti & Frank Palmer (eds.), *English Modality in Perspective*, 205–230. Frankfurt-am-Main: Peter Lang.

Close, Joanne & Bas Aarts. 2010. Current change in the modal system of English. A case study of *must, have to* and *have got to*. In Ursula Jenker, Judith Huber & Robert Malhammer (eds.), *English Historical Linguistics 2008: Selected Papers from the Fifteenth International Conference on English Historical Linguistics (ICEHL 15), Munich, 24-30 August 2008. Volume I: The History of English Verbal and Nominal Constructions*, 165–182. Amsterdam: John Benjamins Publishing Company.

Coates, Jennifer. 1983. *The Semantics of the Modal Auxiliaries*. London and Canberra: Croom Helm.

Collins, Peter. 2009. *Modals and Quasi-modals in English*. Amsterdam and New York: Rodopi.

Cruse, Alan. 2011 [2000]. *Meaning in Language. An Introduction to Semantics and Pragmatics*. 3rd edn. Oxford: Oxford University Press.

Daugs, Robert. 2021. Contractions, constructions and constructional change: Investigating the constructionhood of English modal contractions from a diachronic perspective. In Martin Hilpert, Bert Cappelle & Ilse Depraetere (eds.), *Modality and Diachronic Construction Grammar*, 12–52. Amsterdam: John Benjamins.

Davies, Mark. 2008–. The Corpus of Contemporary American English (COCA): 560 million words, 1990-present. Available online at https://www.english-corpora.org/coca/

Declerck, Renaat. 1991. *A Comprehensive Descriptive Grammar of English*. Tokyo: Kaitakusha.

Depraetere, Ilse. 2010. Some observations on the meaning of modals. In Bert Cappelle & Naoaki Wada (eds.), *Distinctions in English Grammar, Offered to Renaat Declerck*, 72–91. Tokyo: Kaitakusha.

Depraetere, Ilse. 2014. Modals and lexically-regulated saturation. *Journal of Pragmatics* 7. 160–177.

Depraetere, Ilse. 2015a. Categorization principles of modal meaning categories: A critical assessment. *Anglophonia* [online], URL: http://anglophonia.revues.org/453; DOI : 10.4000/anglophonia.

Depraetere, Ilse. 2015b. Modality. In Nick Riemer (ed.), *The Routledge Handbook of Semantics*, 370–386. London and New York: Routledge.

Depraetere, Ilse & Chad Langford. 2020 [2011]. *Advanced English Grammar: A Linguistic Approach*. 2nd edition. London: Bloomsbury.

Depraetere, Ilse & Susan Reed. 2011. Towards a more explicit taxonomy of root possibility. *English Language and Linguistics* 15(1). 1–29.

Depraetere, Ilse & Susan Reed. 2021 [2006]. Mood and modality in English. In Bas Aarts, April McMahon & Lars Hinrichs (eds.), *The Handbook of English Linguistics*. 2nd edn. 207–227. Oxford/Malden, MA: Wiley-Blackwell.

Depraetere, Ilse & Raphael Salkie. 2017. Pragmatic enrichment and saturation, completion and expansion: a view from linguistics. In Ilse Depraetere and Raphael Salkie (eds.), *Semantics and Pragmatics: Drawing a line*, 11–38. Cham: Springer.

Diessel, Holger. 2017. Usage-based linguistics. In Mark Aronoff (ed.), *Oxford Research Encyclopedia of Linguistics*. New York: Oxford University Press.

Dunbar, George L. 2001. Towards a cognitive analysis of polysemy, ambiguity and vagueness, *Cognitive Linguistics* 12. 1–14.

Ehrman, Madeline. 1966. *The Meanings of the Modals in Present-day American English*. The Hague: Mouton and Co.

Enfield, Nicolas James. 2003. *Linguistic Epidemiology: Semantics and Grammar of Language Contact in Mainland Southeast Asia*. London: Routledge.

Facchinetti, Roberta. 2002. *Can* and *could* in contemporary British English: a study of the ICE-GB corpus. In Pam Peters, Peter Collins & Adam Smith (eds.), *New Frontiers of Corpus Research. Papers from the Twenty-first International Conference on English Language Research on Computerized Corpora Sydney 2000*, 229–46. Amsterdam and New York: Rodopi.

Geeraerts, Dirk. 1993. Vagueness's puzzles, polysemy's vagaries. *Cognitive Linguistics* 4. 223–272.

Geertzen Jeroen, Dora Alexopoulou & Anna Korhonen. 2013. Automatic linguistic annotation of large scale L2 databases: The EF-Cambridge open language database (EFCAMDAT). *31st Second Language Research Forum (SLRF)*.

Gibbs, Dorothy A. 1990. Second language acquisition of the English modal auxiliaries *can, could, may*, and *might. Applied Linguistics* 11(3). 297–314.

Gillon, Brendan S. 1990. Ambiguity, generality and indeterminacy: tests and definitions. *Synthese* 85. 391–416.

Gisborne, Nikolas. 2007. Dynamic modality. *SKASE Journal of Theoretical Linguistics* 4(2). 44–61. Available online: http://www.skase.sk/Volumes/JTL09/pdf_doc/4.pdf. Accessed 28 September 2021.

Groefsema, Marjolein. 1995. *Can, may, must* and *should*: A relevance-theoretic account. *Journal of Linguistics* 31. 53–79.

Haegeman, Liliane. 1983. The semantics of *will* in present-day British English: a unified account. Brussels: Verhandeling Letteren, jrg. 45, nr. 103.

Heine, Bernd. 1993. *Auxiliaries: Cognitive Forces and Grammaticalization*. Oxford and New York: Oxford University Press.

Huddleston, Rodney & Geoffrey K. Pullum et al. 2002. *The Cambridge Grammar of the English Language*. Cambridge: Cambridge University Press.

Huang, Yan, Akira Murakami, Theodora Alexopoulou & Anna Korhonen. 2018. Dependency parsing of learner English. *International Journal of Corpus Linguistics* 23(1). 28–54.

Kissine, Mikhael. 2008. Why *will* is not a modal. *Natural Language Semantics* 16. 129–155.

Klinge, Alex. 1993. The English modal auxiliaries: From lexical semantics to utterance interpretation. *Journal of Linguistics* 29. 315–357.

Krug, Manfred G. 2000. *Emerging English Modals*. Berlin: Mouton de Gruyter.

Lakoff, George. 1970. A note on vagueness and ambiguity. *Linguistic Inquiry* 1. 357–359.
Langacker, Ronald W. 1987. *Foundations of Cognitive Grammar. Vol.1: Theoretical Prerequisites.* Stanford, CA: Stanford University Press.
Larreya, Paul. 1984. *Le Possible et le Nécessaire: Modalité et Auxiliaires Modaux en Anglais Britannique.* Paris: Nathan.
Leclercq, Benoît. 2020. Semantics and pragmatic in Construction Grammar, *Belgian Journal of Linguistics* 25: 225–234.
Leclercq, Benoît. 2022. The post-modal grammaticalization of concessive *may* and *might*. Presentation at *La postmodalité et les cycles de vie des expressions modales*. University of Caen Normandie, Caen, France. 2–3 June.
Leclercq, Benoît & Ilse Depraetere. 2022. Making meaning with *be able to*: modality and actualization. *English Language and Linguistics*, 26(1). 27–48.
Lee, Young Mi & Mun Koo Kang. 2012. A study on *will* as modal or non-modal. *English Language and Literature Teaching* 18(3). 175–190.
Leech, Geoffrey N. 2004 [1971]. *Meaning and the English Verb*. 3rd edn. New York: Longman.
Leech, Geoffrey N. 2013. Where have all the modals gone? An essay on the declining frequency of core modal auxiliaries in recent standard English. In Juana I. Marín-Arrese, Jorge Marta Carretero, Jorge Arús Hita & Johan van der Auwera (eds.), *Modality: Core, Periphery, and Evidentiality*, 95–116. Berlin: Mouton de Gruyter.
Leech, Geoffrey N. & Jennifer Coates 1980. Semantic indeterminacy and the modals. In Sidney Greenbaum, Geoffrey N. Leech & Jan Svartvik (eds.), *Studies in English linguistics: For Randolph Quirk*, 79–90. London: Longman.
Lorenz, David. 2020. Converging variations and the emergence of horizontal links: To-contraction in American English. In Lotte Sommerer & Elena Smirnova (eds.), *Nodes and Networks in Diachronic Construction Grammar*, 243–274. Amsterdam: John Benjamins.
Lyons, John. 1977. *Semantics*. Cambridge: Cambridge University Press.
Mindt, Dieter. 1995. *An Empirical Grammar of the English Verb: Modal Verbs*. Berlin: Cornelsen.
Mindt, Dieter. 2000. *An Empirical Grammar of the English Verb System*. Berlin: Cornelsen.
Morgan, Jerry L. 1977. Two types of convention in indirect speech acts. Technical report No. 52. University of Illinois at Urbana-Champaign. https://www.ideals.illinois.edu/bitstream/handle/2142/17765/ctrstreadtechrepv01977i00052_opt.pdf?seque
Narrog, Heiko. 2012. *Modality, Subjectivity, and Semantic Change: A Cross-Linguistic Perspective*. Oxford: Oxford University Press.
Nordlinger, Rachel & Elizabeth C. Traugott. 1997. Scope and the development of epistemic modality: Evidence from *ought to*. *English Language and Linguistics* 1. 295–317.
Nuyts, Jan. 2005. The modal confusion: On terminology and the concepts behind it. In Alex Klinge & Hendrik Hegel Müller (eds.), *Modality: Studies in Form and Function*, 5–38. London: Equinox.
Nuyts, Jan, Pieter Byloo & Janneke Diepeveen. 2010. On deontic modality, directivity and mood: the case of Dutch *moeten* en *mogen*. *Journal of Pragmatics* 41.1. 16–34.
Palmer, Frank R. 1979. *Modality and the English Modals*. London: Longman.
Palmer, Frank. R. 1990 [1979]. *Modality and the English Modals*. 2nd edn. London: Longman.
Palmer, Frank. R. 2001 [1986]. *Mood and Modality*. 2nd edn. Cambridge: Cambridge University Press.
Papafragou, Anna. 2000a. *Modality: Issues in the Semantics-Pragmatics Interface*. Amsterdam: Elsevier.

Papafragou, Anna. 2000b. On speech-act modality. *Journal of Pragmatics* 32. 519–538.
Portner, Paul. 2009. *Modality*. Oxford: Oxford University Press.
Portner, Paul. 2018. *Mood*. Oxford: Oxford University Press.
Quirk, Randolph, Sidney Greenbaum, Geoffrey Leech & Jan Svartvik. 1985. *A Comprehensive Grammar of the English Language*. London: Longman.
Ravin, Yael & Claudia Leacock. 2002. Polysemy: an overview. In Yael Ravin & Claudia Leacock (eds.), *Polysemy: Theoretical and Computational Approaches*, 1–29. Oxford: Oxford University Press.
Recanati, François. 1989. The pragmatics of what is said. Mind and Language 4. 294–328.
Riemer, Nick. 2010. *Introducing Semantics*. Cambridge: Cambridge University Press.
Ruppenhofer, Josef & Ines Rehbein. 2012. Yes we can!? Annotating English modal verbs. In *Proceedings of the Eighth International Conference on Language Resources and Evaluation (LREC'12)*, 1538–1545. Istanbul, Turkey, May 2012. European Language Resources Association (ELRA).
Salkie, Raphael. 2010. *Will*: Tense or modal or both? *English Language and Linguistics* 14 (2). 187–215.
Sweetser, Eve. 1990. *From Etymology to Pragmatics*. Cambridge: Cambridge University Press.
Tiedemann, Jörg. 2012. Parallel data, tools and interfaces in OPUS, *Proceedings of the Eighth International Conference on Language Resources and Evaluation* (LREC'12). 2214–8. Istanbul, Turkey: European Language Resources Association (ELRA). http://www.lrec-conf.org/proceedings/lrec2012/pdf/463_Paper.pdf.
Timotijevič, Jelena. 2009. *The semantic domain of possibility in English and German*. Brighton: University of Brighton dissertation.
Traugott, Elizabeth C. 2003. Approaching modality from the perspective of relevance theory. *Language Sciences* 25. 657–669.
Traugott, Elizabeth C. 1989. On the rise of epistemic meanings in English: An example of subjectification in semantic change. *Language* 65(1). 31–55.
Tregidgo, Paul. 1982. MUST and MAY: Demand and permission. *Lingua* 56. 75–92.
Tuggy, David. 1993. Ambiguity, polysemy and vagueness. *Cognitive Linguistics* 4. 273–91.
Van der Auwera, Johan & Astrid De Wit. 2010. The English comparative modals – A pilot study. In Bert Cappelle & Naoaki Wada (eds.), *Distinctions in English Grammar, Offered to Renaat Declerck*, 127–147. Tokyo: Kaitakusha.
Van der Auwera, Johan & Vladimir A. Plungian. 1998. Modality's semantic map. *Linguistic Typology* 2. 79–124.
Van Linden, An & Jean-Christophe Verstraete. 2011. Revisiting deontic modality and related categories. A conceptual map based on the study of English modal adjectives. *Journal of Pragmatics* 43. 150–163.
Verstraete, Jean-Christophe. 2001. Subjective and objective modality: Interpersonal and ideational functions in the English modal auxiliary system. *Journal of Pragmatics* 33(10). 1505–1528.
Viebahn, Emanuel & Barbara Vetter. 2016. How many meanings for *may*? The case for modal polysemy. *Philosophers' Imprint* 16(10). 1–26.
Wärnsby, Anna. 2006. *(De)coding Modality: The Case of Must, May, Måste and Kan*. (Lund Studies in English 113). Lund: Department of English, Centre for Language and Literature, Lund University.
Wada, Naoaki. 2001. *Interpreting English Tenses: A Compositional Approach*. Tokyo: Kaitakusha.

Wada, Naoaki. 2019. *The Grammar of Future Expressions in English*. Tokyo: Kaitakusha.
Westney, Paul. 1995. *Modals and Periphrastics in English*. Tübingen: Niemeyer.
Wekker, Herman. 1976. *The Expression of Future Time in Contemporary British English*. Amsterdam: North-Holland.
Wiebe, Janyce, Theresa Wilson & Claire Cardie. 2005. Annotating expressions of opinions and emotions in language. *Language Resources and Evaluation* 39. 165–210.
Williams, Christopher. 2005. *Tradition and Change in Legal English: Verbal Constructions in Prescriptive Texts*. Bern: Peter Lang.
Williams, Christopher. 2009. Legal English and the 'modal revolution'. In Raphael Salkie, Pierre Busuttil & Johan van der Auwera (eds.), *Modality in English: Theory and Description*, 199–210. Berlin and New York: Mouton de Gruyter.
Wright, Georg Hendrik Von. 1951. *An Essay in Modal Logic*. Amsterdam: North Holland Pub Co.
Zhou, Mengfei, Anette Frank, Annemarie Friedrich & Alexis Palmer. 2015. Semantically Enriched Models for Modal Sense Classification. In *Proceedings of the EMNLP Workshop LSDSem: Linking Models of Lexical, Sentential and Discourse-level Semantics*, Lisbon, Portugal. 44–53.
Zwicky, Arnold M. & Jerrold M. Sadock. 1975. Ambiguity tests and how to fail them. In John P. Kimball (ed.), *Syntax and Semantics*. 1–36. New York: Academic press.

2 Modality revisited: Combining insights from Construction Grammar and Relevance Theory

Benoît Leclercq

1 Introduction

Modality has been and remains a very active field of research (cf. Nuyts and van der Auwera 2016; Abraham 2020; Hohaus and Schulze 2020), and some of the most fundamental questions are still being debated: how to define modality (Cornillie and Pietrandrea 2012: 2110), how modality interacts with other semantic categories (Squartini 2016), whether modals are monosemous or polysemous (Depraetere 2014: 162), how to distinguish between different modal meanings (Depraetere and Reed 2021), how to differentiate the semantics of modals from other pragmatic effects (Depraetere 2019), and what meanings (semantic and pragmatic) exactly are expressed by a given modal expression (e.g. Leclercq and Depraetere's (2022) analysis of *be able to*). Linguists clearly struggle to come to grips with the meanings of modals and this struggle starkly contrasts with the impressive ease with which we acquire, use and process sentences with modals. This chapter offers a theoretical discussion of how speakers manage to make meaning with modals.

This discussion takes meaning conventions as a starting point. The previous chapter established that several meaning distinctions are usually made: a first distinction concerns the difference between *epistemic* and *root* modality; finer-grained distinctions are then often made within the category of root modality (cf. Depraetere and Reed (2021) for an extensive overview of taxonomies of modal meaning). That such distinctions exist has been widely acknowledged in the literature. The main challenge is to decide whether these distinct meanings are contextually derived interpretations of a single meaning (hence adopting a monosemy approach) or if they are conventionally associated with the modal verb used (thereby adopting a polysemy approach). Some have argued that modals have a unitary meaning from which different interpretations (both root and epistemic) are derived in context (e.g. Joos 1964; Ehrman 1966; Kratzer 1977; Walton 1988; Klinge 1993; Groefsema 1995; Papafragou 1998, 2000; Boogaart 2009). Others defend the view that modal verbs are polysemous, i.e. that they encode the different senses identified (e.g. Lyons 1977; Bybee and Fleischman 1995; Palmer 2001; Huddleston and Pullum et al. 2002; Collins 2009; Depraetere 2010, 2014). Alternatively, Coates (1983) and Sweetser (1990) propose an intermediate stage where modals are polysemous between a root and an epistemic reading only, the different root interpretations being derived in context.

https://doi.org/10.1515/9783110734157-003

In this book, we believe that modals are polysemous (see Chapter 1), and we adopt the taxonomy of modal meanings developed in Depraetere and Reed (2011) and Depraetere (2014). Whether or not modals are monosemous or polysemous is therefore not at issue here. Rather, the main challenge that this chapter aims to resolve is how this knowledge is then put to use in conversation. No matter which taxonomy is used, the interpretation of a modal verb (or any linguistic sign, for that matter) does not merely consist in selecting one of its encoded senses. That is, context-dependence also applies in the case of polysemy.[1] The idea that words provide 'meaning potentials' and/or that the interpretation of an utterance involves a process of 'meaning construction' is now accepted wisdom in linguistic theory (cf. Halliday 1973; Bezuidenhout 2002; Allwood 2003; Fauconnier and Turner 2003; Croft and Cruse 2004; Recanati 2004; Evans and Green 2006; Noren and Linell 2007; Verschueren 2018; *inter alia*). So the main challenge here is how exactly to reconcile polysemy and context-dependence for modal verbs. Depraetere (2010, 2014) makes a very interesting proposal in that regard, which she spells out in terms of a process of *lexically-regulated saturation*. This view will be fully presented in Section 5. It will be shown that some crucial elements are missing from Depraetere's analysis, however, and that it does not yet fully capture the complexity of what is involved in understanding a modal utterance. Importantly, what is needed is a more comprehensive view on how linguistic and extra-linguistic factors contribute to this process of lexically-regulated saturation (i.e. to the interpretation process of a modal verb). That is, it is not enough to posit the context-dependence of modal meaning, it must also be stated what it involves exactly.

As was already shown in Chapter 1, a multitude of theoretical approaches and conceptual tools have been put forward to pin down and explain the use of modal verbs. The view in this book is that, rather than relying on one particular approach, greater precision can be achieved through theoretical and methodological triangulation. In Chapters 3 to 5, the results of different empirical and experimental studies are presented and compared. This chapter is focused on theoretical models. The aim is to show that, just like various empirical methods can complement one another in identifying the impact of specific features on the choice of a modal, comparing different theoretical approaches makes it possible to finetune the conceptual tools needed for the description of modality in English. I will especially focus on (Cognitive) Construction Grammar (henceforth CxG; Goldberg 1995, 2006; Hilpert 2019) and Relevance Theory (henceforth RT; Sperber

---

1 Here, the term 'context' is used as a cover term for both the linguistic and extra-linguistic environment.

and Wilson 1995; Clark 2013). Both these approaches grew out of a concern for cognitively accurate descriptions of linguistic knowledge and language use. Their goals are ultimately different, however. While Construction Grammar mainly focuses on linguistic representations, Relevance Theory is much more interested in the pragmatic side of communication. For that reason, I strongly believe that a combination of these two approaches, which I view as complementary, can be fruitfully applied to the topic at hand and help us gain insights into the domain of modality.

In Section 2, I will briefly introduce each theory and discuss some of the analyses of modality that have been conducted within each framework. In Section 3, attention is given to the structural side of modality. I argue that some of the challenges faced in understanding the way modals are used depends in the first place on one's underlying conception of the formal properties that these constructions have, and I claim that a view in terms of a complex network of (semi-schematic) modal constructions is most promising. The next question that falls out of these observations is that of the nature of modal meaning. I will pick up an issue already addressed in Chapter 1, namely the definition of modality. I will also reflect on the distinct semantic and pragmatic features that modal constructions can have. It will be argued that modals are hybrid and have both conceptual and procedural functions. I will show in Section 5 what is the exact contribution that all this knowledge makes in actual language use. It will be shown that positing complex networks of modal constructions is not sufficient and that a great deal of work is performed online in accordance with the principle of relevance.

2 The modal enigma in RT and CxG

RT and CxG have both attempted to account for the uses and meanings of modal verbs. There has been very little interaction between both theories, even though they both present themselves as theories of cognition. My aim is to show that combined insights result in a richer understanding. In a first step, I will present each theory in turn and explain how the meaning of modal verbs is analysed in each framework.

2.1 Modality in RT

Relevance Theory is essentially a theory of information processing that aims to unravel the cognitive underpinnings that enable us to make sense of our world.

More specifically, with respect to the domain of verbal communication, RT aims to pin down the underlying factors involved in establishing the content of an utterance (Sperber and Wilson 1995). The theory was developed around the notion of *relevance*, a technical term that refers to the value of an input to an individual and that is defined in terms of a processing cost-benefit balance: the more cognitive effects obtained in processing the input, the more relevance; the more effort spent in processing the input, the less relevance (Sperber and Wilson 1995: 125). A key principle in RT is that we humans have certain expectations of relevance. In particular, any ostensive use of language carries with it a presumption of optimal relevance, whereby a speaker's utterance should provide enough cognitive effects to be worth the hearer's processing effort (idem: 260). And this principle is argued to play a major guiding role in the co-construction of meaning. It constrains speakers into making linguistic choices that will guarantee this level of relevance, and it gives hearers a general direction of where the intended interpretation is to be found. This guiding role is essential as it is assumed in RT that the words we use can never fully determine the speaker's intended meaning and, therefore, that verbal communication remains by and large an inferential affair (Carston 2002: 19). The principle of relevance is thus viewed as one of the main cognitive forces behind inferential processes. For instance, it is used to explain how *implicatures* are derived (Sperber and Wilson 1995: 193f.). But more importantly here, it is also used to explain how the explicit content of an utterance is contextually fleshed out. Sperber and Wilson (1995: 182) coined the term *explicature* to capture the hybrid nature (partly encoded, partly inferred) of 'what is said' (see also Carston 1999, 2004, 2009, 2010). A much discussed process involved in the derivation of explicatures is the systematic creation of *ad hoc* concepts, i.e. context-specific lexical meanings (cf. Carston 2012). Consider the sentences in (1) and (2), for instance.

(1) This has certainly not been the pregnancy I imagined. I've never been one of those women who **loves** being pregnant. I've lost my appetite, my craving is wine and, just like the first time round, I spent the first trimester sick as a dog. (Coronavirus corpus)[2]

(2) He says he had planned on dating a lot of different women before he met me. He says that he probably **loves** me and definitely adores me and that he is almost ready to just be with me. (COCA)

---

[2] Most of the examples used in this chapter were extracted from corpora available on Mark Davies' interface (cf. Davies 2008–, 2019–): the *Coronavirus* and COCA (*Corpus of Contemporary American English*) corpora.

In (1), the verb *love* is used by the speaker to indicate that the view she takes on being pregnant is not one of great pleasure. In (2), it refers to the romantic feeling of affection (probably) experienced by the subject referent. From the perspective of RT, the interpretation of *love* in (1) and (2) primarily consists in an inferential operation, with the principle of relevance as the main driving force, which results in the creation of specific *ad hoc* concepts. Accordingly, while the (repeated) creation of *ad hoc* concept has been argued to be at the root of polysemy (cf. Carston 2016a, 2021), the observation that *ad hoc* concepts are systematically derived has at the same time fostered the assumption that a monosemous view of meaning is more convincing:

> I am uneasy with the assumption that a monosemous analysis is always to be preferred to a polysemous one, though the 'if at all possible, go pragmatic' strategy that it entails is one that I generally follow myself, as it makes for much more elegant analyses and because, for the time being, we lack any other strong guiding principle. (Carston 2002: 219)

This is not the strategy adopted in this book. However, it is exactly the view defended by authors who have worked on English modals from a relevance theoretic perspective (cf. Walton 1988; Haegeman 1989; Groefsema 1992, 1995; Klinge 1993; Berbeira Gardón 1996, 1998, 2006; Nicolle 1996, 1997a, 1998a; Papafragou 2000; Kisielewska-Krysiuk 2008).[3] All of them confront polysemous analyses of modal auxiliaries by (implicitly) referring to the *polysemy fallacy* (Sandra 1998: 368) and a modified Occam's Razor argument, i.e. they argue that modal auxiliaries should not be given distinct senses beyond measure, especially given the "modal's apparent semantic anarchy" (Walton 1988: 43). According to them, the only way to describe modality in English is through the combination of a monosemous analysis of modal verbs together with a solid pragmatic account, which Relevance Theory provides.

These analyses are for the most part consistent with the main relevance theoretic tenets and are, as such, theoretically valid. It is unclear however whether they truly manage to reflect the speaker's cognitive reality, a goal that RT is supposedly committed to. I will discuss some of the limits of these approaches in the following paragraphs (though see Salkie (2002, 2014: 340), Traugott (2003), Depraetere (2014: 168), and Leclercq (2019a: 184f.) for more in-depth critical discussions), and I will explain how other key RT concepts can be fruitfully applied to the domain of modality in the rest of this chapter.

---

3 Likewise, see e.g. De Saussure (2014, 2017) for a monosemous analysis of French modal verbs.

The main observation that can be made is that these analyses often provide anecdotal evidence against polysemous approaches to modals. Groefsema (1995), for instance, argues that the interpretation of *must* in (3) in terms of volition ('We would like you to come to dinner') does not tally with any of the root meanings (of necessity or obligation) usually associated with the modal verb. Likewise, she discusses examples like that in (4), in which the verb *can* is allegedly ambiguous between a 'mere possibility' and an 'ability' meaning.

(3) You *must* come to dinner sometime. (Groefsema 1995: 57)

(4) One thing you want to avoid, if you possibly *can*, is a present from my mother. (Palmer 1990: 85)

What these examples are supposed to show is that polysemy (i.e. different encoded senses) cannot account for all possible interpretations of a modal verb. Not only is it difficult to identify all possible senses of a modal verb, but more importantly, some contexts make disambiguation impossible or undesirable (Groefsema 1995: 57). This view of polysemy is problematic however, as it seems to be based on the assumption that disambiguating a polysemous expression necessarily requires selecting one of the senses encoded by that expression. This is too restrictive though, for polysemy does not preclude context sensitivity (cf. Introduction; see also Carston 2021 for a recent discussion). Nevertheless, it appears that relevance theorists would rather explain "the different interpretations of the modals in a unified way" (Groefsema 1995: 57). In other words, the monosemous analyses they defend are also due to considerations of (theoretical) elegance: why rely on more theoretical constructs than necessary? While I agree that theoretical elegance matters, I doubt whether it should be upheld at the expense of descriptive accuracy. This also seems to be the position adopted by Berthelin (2017) who, in her relevance-theoretic analysis of Uummarmiutun modals, argues that a "polysemy account is better equipped than a unitary account for capturing linguistic realities" (p. 266). See discussion in Section 4.

Beyond the general concern just presented, there are other issues with the monosemous approach to English modals largely adopted in RT. The main challenge is to identify, for each modal expression, what exactly constitutes their distinctive unitary meaning. This is no easy task, which explains why no consensus can be found (see in particular the critical discussions in Nicolle 1996; Berbeira Gardón 1998; Papafragou 2000 and Kisielewska-Krysiuk 2008). Nevertheless, various researchers have provided descriptions that are by and large cut from the same cloth. Consider for instance the different descriptions of the meaning of *can*:

(5) *Potential* (the potential exists that p) (Walton 1988: 50)

(6) POTENTIAL (The SITUATION REPRESENTATION turns out to be a true description of a WORLD SITUATION and the SITUATION REPRESENTATION turns out not to be a true description of a WORLD SITUATION.) (Klinge 1993: 334)

(7) *p* is compatible with the set of all propositions which have a bearing on *p* (Groefsema 1995: 62)

(8) *p* is compatible with the set of all propositions which have a bearing on *p*, and the world type is potential. (Berbeira Gardón 1998: 15)

(9) p is compatible with $D_{factual}$ (Papafragou 2000: 43)

These proposals deserve more space than I can give them here. It is worth noting however that all of them are largely inspired by the approach adopted in Kratzer (1977, 1981, 1991) in terms of possible world semantics. In spite of the limits of the possible-worlds model (cf. Papafragou (2000: 33) and Gosselin (2010: 44–49) for discussion), this approach enables the various authors to capture one of the central features of modal meaning, namely the distinction between possibility and necessity. In (5) to (9), for instance, the terms *potential* and *compatible* are used to focus on the notion of possibility associated with the modal *can*. Although the concepts of possibility and necessity are central to the semantic category of modality, they alone do not exhaust the complexity of modal meaning. Part of this complexity stems from the relation that the speaker establishes between the notion of possibility/necessity and the embedded proposition, as is nicely reflected in the semantic descriptions. It is surprising to note however that, while RT offers precise conceptual tools to account for this type of relation (especially the notion of *procedural* semantics and *higher-level explicatures*, introduced by Blakemore 1992 and Wilson and Sperber 1993), the authors above rely on many diverse conceptual tools, not necessarily relevance-theoretic, to make their case (such as *constraints, operators, restrictors, situation representation, procedures*, etc.), and as a result the theoretical apparatuses are at times heavy and hard to grasp. This heterogeneity affects the clarity of their analysis and adds unnecessary complexity (cf. discussions in Salkie 2002, 2014; Traugott 2003; Depraetere 2014; and Leclercq 2019a). In Section 4, it will be shown how the analysis of modal meaning can benefit from a more systematic application of the fine conceptual tools developed in RT.

2.2 Modality in CxG

Construction Grammar, in the variant addressed here, is a cognitively-oriented theory of language that primarily focuses on what constitutes linguistic knowledge (Goldberg 1995, 2006). The theory was developed around the notion of *constructions*, a technical term which can be unsettling when you are not familiar with the theory. In CxG, the term *construction* does not only refer to complex combinations or grammatical structures such as is usually the case elsewhere in linguistics. Rather, all objects of linguistic knowledge are argued to be constructions: lexemes, idioms as well as larger phrasal and syntactic patterns (Goldberg 2003: 219). In CxG, what defines a construction is not its internal complexity but its symbolic nature: constructions are conventional pairings of a specific form and a particular semantic or discourse function (Goldberg 1995: 4, 2006: 5). CxG thus rejects the modular dichotomy between words on the one hand (i.e. the 'lexicon') and abstract syntactic rules on the other (i.e. 'grammar'). Instead, Goldberg (2003: 223, 2006: 18) argues that it is "constructions all the way down." At the same time, not just any linguistic pattern will count as a construction. Traditionally, it is assumed that a pattern must either show a degree of (formal or functional) idiosyncrasy and/or occur with sufficient frequency in order to obtain construction status (Goldberg 2006: 5). From this perspective, units like *roof*, ADJ-*ish* (e.g. *yellowish*), *private property*, *break the ice*, the X *is the new* Y construction (e.g. *Strong is the new skinny*, COCA), or the CAUSED-MOTION construction [SUBJ V OBJ OBL] (e.g. *My constituents will vote me out of office*, COCA) all qualify as constructions (cf. discussion in Leclercq 2019a). Constructions thus take various shapes. As Figure 1 illustrates, they vary in size (from fully atomic, e.g. *roof*, to more complex, e.g. *as soon as possible*) and in schematicity (from fully lexically specific, e.g. *break the ice*, to fully schematic, e.g. the CAUSED-MOTION construction [SUBJ V OBJ OBL]) (cf. Croft and Cruse 2004: 255).

Such gradience is argued to follow naturally from the usage-based nature of language, whereby constructions directly emerge from language use and are ac-

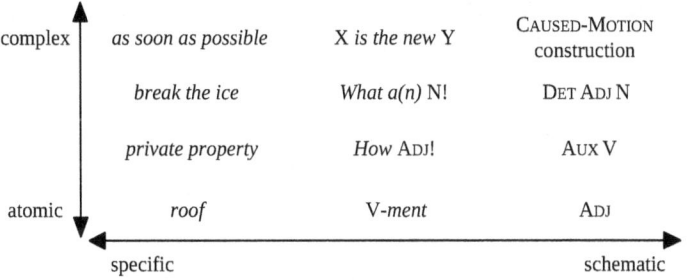

Figure 1: Constructions, complexity and schematicity.

quired via general processes of categorization (and generalization) over specific instances (Goldberg 2006: 44; Diessel 2013: 347). What is important for our discussion (cf. Section 3) is that it is thus possible for the same sign to be stored redundantly across different constructions (cf. Hilpert 2019: 68). The lexeme *word*, for instance, is also found in constructions like *in other words*, *have the final word* or *put words into* someone's *mouth*, each of which is associated with its own semantic and pragmatic properties. As a result, a person's linguistic knowledge is viewed as a vast network of interrelated constructions called the *construct-i-con* (Goldberg 2003: 219).

A fundamental assumption in CxG is that all constructions, including the more schematic (or 'syntactic') ones, are associated with a specific function that directly contributes to the interpretation of the utterance in which they occur. In the examples in (10), for instance, it is assumed that, beyond the valency of each individual verb, the schematic form [SUBJ V OBJ OBL] is itself associated with the meaning 'X *causes* Y *to move* Z', which together form the CAUSED-MOTION construction (Goldberg 1995: 152). Knowledge of this construction is argued to explain how the verb *sneeze* in (11) receives a 'caused motion' interpretation even though it does not originally encode this meaning. This interpretation is coerced onto the lexeme, which inherits the semantic and pragmatic properties attached to the position it occupies in the schematic CAUSED-MOTION construction (cf. Michaelis 2004: 25; Leclercq 2019b).

(10) a. Aaron puts his hands over his ears. (COCA)
 b. You were very nice. You threw me out of your office. (COCA)
 c. The U.S. Navy moved some of its ships to the western side of Japan. (COCA)

(11) Frank *sneezed* the tissue off the table. (Goldberg 1995: 152)
 (*sneeze* in verbal position of [SUBJ V OBJ OBL])

In the domain of modality, this kind of approach has in particular inspired Wärnsby (2002) Boogaart (2009). Though not a construction grammarian herself, Wärnsby (2002) tries to see if the constructionist approach can be used to answer the following question:

> When speakers are confronted with modal expressions in their native language, especially those that contain a modal verb, they are immediately able to interpret these expressions as being either epistemic or non-epistemic. What then is it that enables the speakers to interpret these modal expressions accurately? (p. 1)

In keeping with the view presented previously, Wärnsby explores the possibility that modal sentences inherit their modal meaning not only from the use of a modal verb (e.g. *may*, *must*, *can*, etc.), but also from the use of larger, more schematic modal constructions in which modal verbs occur. That is, just like the verb *sneeze* in (11) inherits part of its interpretation from the schematic CAUSED-MOTION construction in which it is used, modal verbs such as *could* in (12) might likewise inherit their meaning (epistemic, in this case) from a larger schematic modal construction.

(12) Oliver *could* call you today. (*could* in modal position of [?])

In particular, Wärnsby looks into the possibility that there are (at least) two distinct schematic modal constructions in which modal auxiliaries occur: a 'root' modal construction and an 'epistemic' modal construction,[4] each individually contributing to the recognition of either interpretation.[5] While formulating their arguments differently, similar hypotheses can be found in Boogaart (2009) who contends that the relative ease with which the value of a modal verb is determined is to be explained in terms of schematic modal constructions that directly contribute to the interpretation process. In this case, the challenge is to identify the distinct formal and functional properties of the schematic modal constructions (taking into account all the possible forms that a modal sentence can take). Using corpus data, Wärsnby (2002, 2016) convincingly shows that it is nearly impossible to identify these properties, however. Given the multitude of patterns in which modal verbs can be found, the form of e.g. the 'epistemic' modal construction would have to result from an extreme kind of abstraction (e.g. SUBJ MOD$_e$ VP; where subscript *e* stands for epistemic). But what use would such an abstraction have? First, it is not clear how much it can actually help the hearer arrive at the intended interpretation. (After all, how exactly would such an abstraction really differ from that of a schematic 'root' modal construction?) But more importantly, postulating such an abstract construction raises the question of the extent to which it really is part of the speaker's knowledge, or only an idealisation of the analyst. Wärnsby (2002, 2016) thus casts strong doubt on the existence of fully schematic modal constructions (see also Leclercq (2019a) for further arguments against this hypothesis). Wärnsby actually goes further as to suggest that CxG might altogether fail to provide an adequate approach to the analysis of modal expressions. As I see it, this conclusion is too rash (see also Trousdale (2016) for a convincing response). Indeed, between

---

[4] On the distinction between root and epistemic modality, see Section 4.
[5] To put it differently, the question is whether or not the root/epistemic interpretation of modal verbs in English is actually 'coerced' from schematic constructions in which modals occur.

words and schematic patterns, as mentioned in the description above, there are many other levels at which linguistic knowledge can be represented. And contra Wärnsby, there have been rather fruitful applications of CxG in the domain of modality.

These specific applications will be discussed in Section 3, which addresses the morphosyntax of modality. It will be shown exactly how the conceptual tools developed with CxG can be applied to modals and help us gain insights into the contribution of constructional knowledge to the interpretation of a modal sentence. Before that, there is two final observations I wish to make. First, note that in CxG it is typically assumed that conventional polysemy is the norm (cf. Goldberg 1995: 31, 2019: 20). And the domain of modality is in that regard no exception. To my knowledge, only Boogaart (2009) adopts a monosemous approach to modals in CxG. Second, it is interesting to note that the CxG analyses discussed above, in terms of schematic modal constructions, especially try to account for the root/epistemic distinction and that a clear difference is therefore made between, on the one hand, the central concepts of 'possibility' and 'necessity' and, on the other, the way these concepts apply to the propositions they are attached to (i.e. the root/epistemic values). That is, like relevance theorists, constructionists are aware of the complex nature of modal meaning, which cannot be reduced to the concepts of possibility or necessity (see Section 4).

3 A network of modal constructions

Modals are *constructions* in the technical sense of the term since they combine specific formal and functional properties. Accounting for the formal pole of modal verbs is often perceived as unproblematic. There is a variety of verbs that can be used to express modality (e.g. *could, must, have to, be able to*), and their formal idiosyncrasies have been adequately addressed in the descriptive literature (cf. Quirk et al. 1985: 121; Palmer 2001: 100; Huddleston and Pullum et al. 2002: 108; Collins 2009: 12; Biber et al. 2021: 482; *inter alia*).[6] In this section, in keeping with the view developed in CxG, the aim is to show that the domain of modality is not limited to the knowledge of specific modal verbs (or modal adjectives, adverbs or nouns) and their individual morphosyntactic features but in fact consists of a complex network of modal constructions. This is an important step towards identifying the underlying factors that determine the meaning of a modal sentence,

---

6 See Chapter 1, Section 1 for a critical discussion.

for it will be shown that a variety of modal constructions directly contribute to the interpretation process.

The essential insight argued for in this section is that attention thus needs to be given to the level beyond that of modal verbs alone. In the literature on modality, there is a general tendency to look at modal auxiliaries as atomic constructions (and to assume that just like speakers of English know the noun *table*, they also know the auxiliary verb *could*). This is exactly the view adopted by the authors mentioned in Section 2, and I believe it is the reason why their analyses fail to capture the complexity of modal meaning. From the perspective of Construction Grammar, as Hilpert (2006, 2008, 2013, 2016) convincingly argues, modal verb constructions (in English) do not constitute atomic, fully specified constructions (i.e. *can, must, might*, etc) but instead are partly schematic: *can* V-INF, *must* V-INF, *might* V-INF, etc (see also the discussion in Daugs 2020). Indeed, a distinctive formal property of modal auxiliary constructions (and auxiliary verbs in general) is that they systematically select a verb in the infinitive. Consider the following examples (from Hilpert 2016: 68):

(13) a. We *will arrive* in a few minutes on platform number five.
      b. You *can borrow* my umbrella.
      c. *Should* I *leave* the door open?
      d. *Would* you *mind* if I opened the window?

Hilpert agrees that one particular way to look at this selection constraint is to assume that modal verbs have this specific behaviour because they are typically used in a more general AUXILIARY PLUS INFINITIVE construction (Hilpert 2019: 21). Therefore, the property of systematically selecting a verb in the infinitive need not be attributed to the specific modal auxiliaries themselves but to a more general construction which actually accounts for the behaviour of all auxiliaries in English.[7] According to Hilpert, there are reasons to believe, however, that this formal property is part and parcel of the different modal auxiliary constructions and constitute knowledge that speakers have about these constructions. Indeed, Hilpert provides solid evidence that speakers of English do not use just any verb after a modal auxiliary, but that different auxiliaries are typically used with different types of verbs. Hilpert (2016) points out that these particular "collocational preferences are not predictable from any other knowledge of language that speakers

---

[7] Hilpert (2016: 68, 2019: 21) acknowledges that, at first glance, some constructionhood criteria typically used in CxG (notably, the identification of semantic and/or formal idiosyncrasies) support this view.

of English can be assumed to have" (p. 70) and therefore that this "must be seen as an integral part of speakers' linguistic knowledge" (Hilpert 2016: 70).[8] As will be shown more fully in Chapter 9, this type of knowledge enables individuals to create associative (semasiological and onomasiological) links between different constructions (see also Bergs 2010; Goldberg and van der Auwera 2012; Traugott 2016), hence the idea of a modal network. What matters for the present discussion is that modal verb constructions are therefore partially schematic, a feature that will be shown to be crucial when discussing their semantic contribution to the interpretation process in section 4.

As mentioned above, it is important to understand however that there is more to the modal constructicography than mere knowledge of constructions such as *can* V-INF, *must* V-INF, and *might* V-INF. First, in keeping with the view defended by Hilpert, Daugs (2020: 27) argues that contracted and negated modal schemas (e.g. SUBJ*'ll* V-INF, SUBJ*'d* V-INF, *won't* V-INF, *can't* V-INF) are also likely to be stored as separate constructions, since these patterns show distinct collocational (and functional) preferences compared to their canonical alternatives (see, for instance, Bybee's (2010: 151) comparative analysis of *can* and *can't*) which cannot be predicted. In addition, it has been shown that modals can also be found (i.e. redundantly represented, cf. page 68) in larger patterns whose meaning is non-predictable. De Haan (2012), who focuses on *must*, argues that the pattern in (14), for instance, which almost systematically involves an epistemic interpretation, must be "stored as such as part of the grammar" (de Haan 2012: 723). Similarly, he argues that the pattern in (15) must also receive independent construction status since it (almost) systematically involves a deontic interpretation, a functional preference that cannot be predicted from any of the constituting elements of that construction.

(14) SUBJ *must be* V-ing
People are reading newspapers less than they used to and I guess that means *they must be reading* magazines and, you know, other written stuff less too.

(15) *I must* V
Here I am at my own home, locked out, so *I must stand* in the road!!

Likewise, Cappelle, Depraetere and Lesuisse (2019) and Leclercq (2022), who apply the corpus methodology developed in Cappelle and Depraetere (2016a,

---

8 In his analysis of English, Hilpert has particularly focused on the collocational preference of *will*, *shall* and *may* (cf. Hilpert 2008, 2016).

2016b), identify large sets of '(semi)-idiomatic' constructions that contain the verbs *have to, must, need to, should, can, could* and *be able to*. Consider, for instance, the examples in (16) to (18).

(16) SUBJ *must surely* VP
She *must surely* be the most beautiful in the world. (Cappelle, Depraetere and Lesuisse 2019: 231)

(17) *I don't think we should* VP
It was kind of Anne to think of it and not condemn us, but – well, we've managed so far being discreet about it, and *I don't think we should* change things now. (Cappelle, Depraetere and Lesuisse 2019: 232)

(18) *I can't tell you how* . . .
Sweet loyal Jack. *I can't tell you how* good it is to see you. (Leclercq 2022: 239)

In (16), *must* receives a strong epistemic interpretation. In (17), the verb *should* gets a root interpretation and the construction (which provides a hedging context that weakens the value of *should*) serves as an invitation not to perform the action denoted by the VP (i.e. *let's not* VP). The construction in (18), which primarily indicates one's inability to be specific about various types of (metaphorical) quantities, is used by the speaker to put particular emphasis on her feelings (positive, in this case) with regard to the particular situation described.[9]

In other words, the construct-i-con is composed of many additional '(semi)-idiomatic' modal constructions that have their own semantico-pragmatic profiles.[10] This is an important observation, for this means that, although these constructions naturally add up to the complexity of modality, they also provide new insights about the type of knowledge that goes into understanding modal sentences. Exactly how these constructions contribute to the interpretation process will be discussed in Section 5. For the time being, there is one last type of modal construction that I wish to look at. Leclercq (2022: 243) shows that *can* is most probably (redundantly) stored in the construction '*I don't think we can* VP':

(19) And so, on the basis of this, some claim that Lincoln was a homosexual. Well, I don't think he can be called a homosexual. But at the same time, *I don't think we can* call Lincoln a heterosexual either. (COCA)

---

9 See also Chapter 1, Section 3.4 for a similar discussion of the construction '*Why should* . . . ?'.
10 See Leclercq (2020) for a discussion of the use of the terms *semantics* and *pragmatics* in CxG.

Putting aside the verb *can*, this construction is formally and functionally similar to the pattern with *should* discussed in (17). In both cases, the modal verb receives a root interpretation and the construction is used as an invitation not to perform the action denoted by the VP. Further investigation reveals that the verbs *have to* (20), *need to* (21) and *ought to* (22) are also highly frequent in this pattern.

(20) Well, I agree with you. *I don't think we have to* give up any liberties. But we've got to work smarter and not just harder. (COCA)

(21) And let me be clear on this. *I don't think we need to* have our boots on the ground. The Kurds are a very viable military force. (COCA)

(22) *I don't think we ought to* attack the Social Security system. It is the last line of defense that Americans have when they lose their pensions. (COCA)

For that reason, in Leclercq (2022: 246) I argue that, in addition to knowing (at least) the two idiomatic patterns with *should* and *can*, speakers of English most probably also store a more general construction '*I don't think we* MOD VP'. It is this construction that licenses the use of the modals *have to*, *need to* and *ought to* in examples (20) to (22). It is also this construction, I believe, that licenses the unusual use of *may* in (23) and that projects its function onto the modal sentence.

(23) *I don't think we may* consider Trump as a "coronabuster", on the contrary, but at least the cartoon is well rendered.[11]

While the discussion has so far focused on constructions that contain specific modal verbs (e.g. **might** V-INF, *I* **must** V, *I* **can't** *tell you how* . . ., etc.), this type of example shows that the interpretation of a modal sentence can also be determined by constructions in which the modal slot is left open. For instance, speakers of English probably also store the construction in (24), which typically trigger an epistemic interpretation of the modal verb (cf. Coates 1983: 20; see also Wärnsby 2002 for a critical discussion).

---

11 From: https://twitter.com/LatuffCartoons/status/1265597766186786816. Last accessed: May 20th, 2021.

(24) SUBJ MOD *be* COMPL
   a. They could be anywhere. (COCA)
   b. Colorado residents might be growing weary of tax increases. (COCA)
   c. You must be the neighbor. (COCA)

Constructions of this type, i.e. with an open modal slot, thus also affect the interpretation by imposing a certain meaning that is inherited by (or coerced onto) the modal verb used.

Overall, this section has shown, contra Wärnsby (2002, 2016), that Construction Grammar can be fruitfully applied to the domain of modality. Modals, like the rest of our linguistic knowledge, can be analysed in terms of complex networks of interconnected constructions that each contribute, in their own way, to the understanding of an utterance. How exactly the different types of constructions affect the interpretation process will be discussed in Section 5. Before doing so, it is important to look into more detail at the functional pole of modal constructions.

4 Modals as conceptual-procedural hybrids

Even a quick investigation of the literature shows that defining modality is not a straightforward task (cf. Kiefer 1987: 67; Krug 2000: 39; Palmer 2001: 1; Narrog 2005: 165; Portner 2009: 1; Salkie 2009: 79; Declerck 2011: 21; Cornillie and Pietrandrea 2012: 2110). A number of different criteria have been used to define the notion of modality, giving rise to a plethora of analyses (see Nuyts 2005, 2016; Depraetere and Reed 2021; and references cited therein), and it still remains unclear what exactly the term *modality* captures. According to van der Auwera and Plungian (1998: 80), there is "no one correct way" to define modality. Nevertheless, it is important for the purpose of this discussion to try and characterize this notion as exactly as possible as it will enable me to explain how modal meaning comes about in context. Two different views particularly stand out in the literature. On the one hand, some have defined modality as a cover term for all the expressions that convey the (logical) notions of 'possibility' and 'necessity' (e.g. Kratzer 1981: 39; van der Auwera and Plungian 1998: 80; von Fintel 2006: 1; Leech 2006: 64). On the other hand, modality has been described as marking non-factuality (or irreality), and often in terms of the speaker's assessment of the truth or actualization of the proposition (e.g. Palmer 1990: 2; Papafragou 2000: 3; Huddleston and Pullum et al. 2002: 173; Collins 2009: 11; Declerck 2011: 27). Of course, advocates of the latter approach also acknowledge the particular status of possibility and necessity inside the category of modality but do not use them as defining criteria.

The second approach seems more convincing. First of all, it is essential to note that the concepts of possibility or necessity do not exhaust what is commonly considered to be modal. Other notions have often been discussed under the same category (e.g. volition, hypotheticality, etc.). Importantly, it seems intuitively logical that a definition of modality should capture what is common to all modal expressions, yet the concepts of possibility and necessity each apply to different subsets of modal expressions. As Collins (2009: 11) points out, what all the different modal expressions identified in the literature really "have in common is that they all involve some kind of non-factuality." This aspect of modal meaning is particularly salient when comparing modal sentences to their non-modal counterparts, as in (25) to (27). These sentences share the same proposition, identified in (28). In the (non-modal) sentence in (25), the proposition is represented as factual, i.e. as actualizing. In the modal sentences in (26) and (27), the proposition is not represented as factual, but is rather being commented upon by the speaker. In the sentence in (26), it is the truth of the proposition that is being assessed (epistemic modality), while in the sentence in (27) it is its actualization potential (root modality).

(25) Tom is eating cookies.

(26) Tom *might* be eating cookies.

(27) Tom *should*n't be eating cookies.

(28) Tom / be eating cookies.

I endorse the view that this specific attitude (or judgement) of the speaker towards the proposition expressed (cf. Huddleston and Pullum et al. 2002: 173; Depraetere and Reed 2021: 207) indeed defines modal meaning. Of course, the notions of possibility and necessity are central to modal expressions and also constitute distinctive features of modal sentences. But these two notions, I want to argue, only contribute to a modal sentence by qualifying the type of attitude that a speaker adopts. This analysis thus leads me to put forward the hypothesis that modals in English are conceptual-procedural hybrids.

The functional distinction between *concepts* and *procedures* was introduced in Relevance Theory via the work of Blakemore (1987, 1990, 2002). A key assumption in RT, as mentioned in Section 2.1, is that communication is primarily an inferential affair and that language is merely used as a tool (albeit an efficient one) to guide the hearer towards optimal relevance (cf. Sperber and Wilson 1995: 172). It follows logically from this view that language might not only give us access to specific mental representations but also provide us with the tools to compute these mental representations. And this is exactly what the distinction between *concepts* and *procedures* is meant to capture. In addition to making specific mental representations available (i.e. concepts), language is also used to provide information about how to compute these mental representations and directly constrain the inferential process involved during the search for optimal relevance (i.e. procedures). Blakemore (1992: 151) explicitly describes procedural expressions as items that "encode instructions for processing propositional representations." Specifically, procedures can constrain the recovery of three different types of information: *implicatures*, *explicatures* or *higher-level explicatures*. Typical constraints on the recovery of implicatures (i.e. implicit propositions) are discourse markers such as *so*, *but* and *therefore*. In Grice's (1989: 25) famous example '*He is an Englishman; he is, therefore, brave*', the discourse marker *therefore* is used to constrain the derivation of the implicated premise *Englishmen are brave*. Constraints on the recovery of explicatures (i.e. explicit propositions, cf. Section 2.1) include pronouns and demonstratives, which provide instructions for the identification of specific referents (cf. Wilson and Sperber 1993; Scott 2011, 2013, 2016). The term *higher-level explicature* is a technical notion that refers to an intermediate level of communication where the explicature is embedded under specific meta-representations, including speech acts and speaker attitudes (Wilson and Sperber 1993: 4). For instance, recovering the thought expressed in (29) requires the hearer to embed the explicit proposition under (at least) one higher-level representation such as the ones in (30).

(29)   Andy thinks it's raining. (Clark 2013: 208)

(30)   a.   *Ken says that* Andy thinks it's raining
      b.   *Ken wonders whether* Andy thinks it's raining.

While higher-level explicatures are typically inferred (like implicatures), use of procedural items can also constrain their recovery. For instance, Clark (1991) argues that sentence types, such as imperatives or exclamatives, are precisely meant to recover the speaker's attitude towards the embedded proposition. Having presented the conceptual/procedural distinction, it is now important to explain in what sense modals are conceptual-procedural hybrids.

Had modality been solely described in terms of possibility and necessity, it could be easily argued that modals are strictly conceptual (e.g. de Saussure, 2014). Indeed, possibility and necessity are easily mentally recalled (which is often used as a defining criterion of conceptual meaning, see Carston, 2016b: 159). Moreover, these two notions are expressed in various ways (e.g. possibility, necessity, permission, ability, obligation, etc.) and are largely subject to contextual variation (another distinctive criterion of conceptual meaning, idem: 160). However, this is not how modality was defined above. Instead, it was defined in terms of a speaker's attitude towards the proposition. That is, when modality is used, the proposition is not represented as factual, as actualizing, but the speaker indicates to the hearer that she is assessing (the truth/actualization of) the proposition, i.e. she indicates to the hearer how to understand and manipulate the proposition. And such a definition of modality comes very close to a procedural analysis of meaning, rather than a conceptual one. Indeed, as was just explained, procedural meaning is typically defined as "information about how to manipulate [conceptual representations]" (Wilson and Sperber 1993: 97). In this case, the procedural information encoded by modal constructions in English can thus be described as providing a constraint on the recovery of higher-level explicatures. For instance, the modal *might* in (31) directly contributes to recovering the higher-level explicature in (32).

(31) Rhys might apply for a scholarship.

(32) *Jane thinks it is possible that* Rhys will apply for a scholarship.

Note that in the (relevance-theoretic) literature, different perspectives have been adopted. Some have argued – notably given the particular salience of possibility and necessity in modal expressions – that modals must be conceptual in nature (e.g. de Saussure, 2014). But most relevance-theoretic approaches adopt a different view. As it happens, the choice for a conceptual/procedural analysis often depends on which type of modal meaning is at stake (root or epistemic). The assumption is that root meanings are essentially conceptual whereas epistemic modality is procedural (see for instance Papafragou (2000: 70; in Traugott 2003: 663); Traugott and Dasher 2002: 11). Unfortunately, it is not clear what exactly motivates this distinction, and especially the conceptual treatment of root modality. In RT, epistemic modality is often described as an indication of the speaker's (subjective) propositional attitude (e.g. Papafragou 2000: 82; Wilson 2012). Wilson (2012: 38) says, for instance, that epistemic modality enables the speaker to express "[her] degree of confidence about the truth of [her] assertion." And this view allows an analysis in procedural terms since expressions that "point to or index the speaker's attitude" (Traugott 2003: 661) generally receive a procedural analysis in RT (see above). By contrast, the reason why root modality is preferably discussed in conceptual terms follows from the (implicit) assumption that, unlike epistemic modality, it does not indicate a particular attitude. Yet it is clear from the literature that root modality is no less attitudinal, and therefore no less procedural, than epistemic modality.[12] Root modality also gives the hearer the tools to process the status of the situation that is represented by the proposition. A differentiated approach to root and epistemic meaning is possible only if one considers one category as not constituting modal meaning at all (e.g. Nuyts 2005). However, this is not the view adopted here (nor in the majority of research on modal meaning). Given the definition of modality adopted previously, root and epistemic modality should receive the same, procedural, analysis. In RT, only Klinge (1993) and Nicolle (1997b) have explicitly adopted this view.

Now, as mentioned before, this view does not ignore the fact that the notions of possibility and necessity are equally central to the meaning of modals in English. These two notions are undeniably linked to modality and part of the content of modal verb constructions; they therefore need to be included in the analysis. This is particularly true since 'possibility' and 'necessity' are not procedural but conceptual notions. Modality therefore cannot be described either in conceptual terms or in procedural terms. Rather, modality is the complex combination of both types of meanings: procedural (the speaker's attitude, i.e. the distinction between root and epistemic meaning) and conceptual (possibility and necessity).[13] The challenge involved in defining and analysing modal meaning thus follows from the complexity of having both types of meaning associated with the same expression. This difficulty is enhanced by the fact that the conceptual material that contributes to the understanding of modal expressions is particularly salient. Nevertheless, a clear distinction should be made between the procedure that constrains the recovery of the speaker's attitude (and which contributes to the higher-level explicature) and the concepts of possibility and necessity, which serve to (further) qualify the nature of this attitude.

This hypothesis is in line with Nicolle's work (1997b, 1998b, 2007, 2011, 2015) on the nature of procedural meaning and aspects of proceduralization. Nicolle particularly highlights the relation between grammaticalization and the development of procedural meaning. As it happens, modal auxiliary verbs in English have long been used as case studies of grammaticalization. Plank (1984: 308) refers to modals as the "paradigm case of grammaticalization." From this per-

---

12 Although sometimes only epistemic modality is described in terms of the speaker's attitude to the proposition, the entire category of modality can be discussed in those terms (e.g. Palmer 1990: 10; Simpson 1993: 43; Bybee Perkins and Pagliuka 1994: 176; Huddleston and Pullum et al. 2002: 173; Nuyts 2005: 23; Radden and Dirven 2007: 233; Besnard 2017: 252). That is, the notion of 'attitude' is not a distinctive property of epistemic modality. (It is interesting to note that Palmer (2001: 7–8) actually refers to the speaker's 'attitude' only in relation to root modality.)
13 Cf. Traugott and Dasher (2002: 11) for a similar treatment of epistemic modality.

spective, analysing modals in procedural terms is not surprising since "grammaticalization begins with the addition of procedural information" (Nicolle, 2011: 408). At the same time, it is equally not surprising to argue that modal verbs in English give access both to conceptual and procedural types of information since the process of *proceduralization* does not systematically lead to the complete deletion of the conceptual material. Instead, conceptual elements can still exist alongside the new procedural meaning, which Nicolle (1998b: 24) refers to as "conceptual retention".[14] This therefore reinforces the view that modal constructions in English can be described both in conceptual and procedural terms (cf. Leclercq 2019a for further discussion on the relation between grammatical constructions and procedural encoding).

A precise definition of modality having been outlined, I can now explain in what way exactly the different conceptual and procedural features of modal verbs are put to use in specific contexts.

5 Modals in use

Discussing the form and function of modal constructions is important as it directly informs us about the type of knowledge that goes into the interpretation of a modal sentence. It has been shown that speakers of English possess a vast network of semantically complex constructions. The remaining issue is to pin down exactly how this knowledge is actually made use of. Specifically, one major challenge is to try and reconcile assumptions about rich conceptual knowledge (i.e. polysemy) with the observation that the process of meaning construction is primarily a pragmatic affair (i.e. context-dependent) and not a matter of word recognition and sense selection. In the domain of modality, this question has been directly addressed by Depraetere (2010, 2014), who introduces the notion of *lexically-regulated saturation* to account for the process at work.[15]

Depraetere (2014: 170) contrasts *lexically-regulated* saturation with *open-ended* saturation. The term *saturation* was originally introduced by Recanati (1989: 304) to refer to a type of pragmatic process that is required by linguistic items that are considered to include variables. In particular, saturation is often discussed in relation to pronouns for instance, for which a specific referent needs to be selected, or

---

14 It is worth noting that Traugott and Dasher (2002: 148) argue that "the acquisition of modal meaning involves the acquisition of procedural in addition to content meaning."
15 See Leclercq (2019a), who extends the notion of *lexically-regulated saturation* outside the field of modality.

gradable adjectives (e.g. *tall*, *strong*, etc.) which can only be understood in relation to a specific reference (e.g. *tall [for a building]*, *strong [for a child]*, etc.). Depraetere (2014) refers to this type of saturation as *open-ended*, since these items can be saturated with any kind of information that is not pre-determined by the items themselves. That is, it is relatively unconstrained. However, in the case of the English modals, Depraetere (2014) uses the term *lexically-regulated* saturation. She argues the notions of 'possibility' and 'necessity' are context-independent, and form the core meaning of modal auxiliaries. In contrast, the three criteria used in her taxonomy (i.e. 'source', 'scope' and 'potential barrier', cf. Chapter 1, Section 2.4) to distinguish between the various root senses are argued to be context-dependent; they have to be contextually provided in order to arrive at one of the alternative meanings. In that way, the interpretation of modal verbs in English necessarily involves a saturation process, from the core notions of 'necessity' and 'possibility' to one of the more specific senses. This saturation is lexically-regulated, however, since modals cannot be saturated with any kind of information, but rather require specific information to be provided (with respect to defining criteria that constrain the number of possible interpretations). Depraetere (2014) thus develops a layered structure of modal meaning in order to capture both the polysemy of modals and their context-dependence. Table 1, for instance, captures the layered polysemy of *may*, and Table 2 captures that of *must*.

Table 1: Modal meaning grid for *may* (in Depraetere 2014).

Context-independent semantics	POSSIBILITY			
Context-dependent semantics (obligatory layer)	EPISTEMIC		ROOT	
Context-dependent semantics (obligatory layer)	NO FURTHER DISTINCTION	Permission	GSP	Permissibility
Pragmatic meaning (optional)	– Effect of illocutionary force – Effect of context of speech (pragmatic strengthening) etc.			

Depraetere (2010, 2014) thereby proposes a more dynamic approach to the meaning of modal auxiliaries in English and in this way reconciles monosemous and polysemous approaches. I largely endorse this view myself, but there are two limits to this approach that need to be addressed.

First of all, it is not clear how one is to distinguish, in the first layer of 'context-dependent semantics', between root and epistemic interpretations. The three

Table 2: Modal meaning grid for *must* (in Depraetere 2014).

Context-independent semantics	NECESSITY			
Context-dependent semantics (obligatory layer)	EPISTEMIC		ROOT	
Context-dependent semantics (obligatory layer)	NO FURTHER DISTINCTION	Narrow-scope internal necessity	Narrow-scope external necessity	GSN
Pragmatic meaning (optional)	– Effect of illocutionary force – Effect of context of speech (pragmatic weakening) – Effect of strength of the modality etc.			

distinguishing criteria used by Depraetere and Reed (2011) only relate to the categories identified within root modality, and cannot be used to distinguish between epistemic and root modality. How is a hearer therefore expected to contextually distinguish between root and epistemic interpretations in the first place? That is, it needs to be specified how the notions of possibility and necessity can be saturated into one or the other type of modality, before being saturated into further subtypes. In keeping with the view developed in Section 4, I want to argue that this is because Depraetere solely focuses on the conceptual notions of 'possibility' and 'necessity' whereas modal meaning also involves a procedural component. That is, modals primarily provide the hearer with an indication of the type of attitude that the speaker is most certainly holding, either assessing the actualization potential of the residue (root interpretations) or its truth (epistemic interpretation). It is this procedure that helps the hearer to recover what Depraetere (2010, 2014) refers to as the first 'context-dependent semantics' layer of modal meaning. That is, the procedure guides the hearer towards one of the alternative attitudes that form the basis of the modal meaning intended by the speaker. Once the hearer has recovered a particular attitude, he will build on the conceptual notions of 'possibility' or 'necessity' that each modal construction also gives access to so as to (further) qualify the nature of this attitude (which Depraetere (2010, 2014) refers to as the second 'context-dependent semantics' layer of meaning). Hearers here reconstruct the content of the modal expression via the process of *lexically-regulated saturation*.

Second, although Depraetere puts forward a more dynamic account of how modals are interpreted in context, it remains unclear how much variation actually occurs between the various uses of the same modal construction in different utterances. From one perspective, it seems that only the three criteria discussed in the taxonomy need to be contextually established in order to derive one of the alternative (root) meanings. Although described as a process of saturation, this resembles a 'selection' view of disambiguation more than a 'meaning construction' view, where assigning the value for each of the three variables suffices to select one of the alternative senses. That is, it is not clear how co(n)textual information can affect the interpretation of a modal verb (other than fixing pre-determined values) and as a result whether the inferential process involved has any impact on the 'semantic layers' of modal meaning. Yet, as mentioned in the introduction, the interpretation process remains primarily an inferential process rather than a selective one, even in the case of polysemy; it is therefore unlikely that the process of saturation only consists in specifying for these values. In line with the view defended in Relevance Theory, I want to argue that – beyond determining the value of the three criteria – a large part of the interpretation is due to intention recognition and considerations of relevance. From this perspective, lexically-regulated saturation is primarily an *inferential* process guided by the search for relevance that builds upon one's knowledge (which, in the case of modal constructions, consists of conceptual-procedural information). The primarily inferential nature of the interpretation process allows one to explain why examples like (3) and (4), repeated here in (33) and (34), are possible in the first place, for instance. The volition reading of *must* in (33) (not typical of the modal verb) and the indeterminate reading of *can* in (34) (between 'ability' and 'mere possibility') are derived simply because these interpretations meet the hearer's expectations of relevance. (A 'selection' view of disambiguation fails to explain how these interpretations are possible.) I thus view lexically-regulated saturation not as a meaning-selection process but as a linguistically-informed inferential process guided by the search for relevance.

(33)　You *must* come to dinner sometime. (Groefsema 1995: 57)

(34)　One thing you want to avoid, if you possibly *can*, is a present from my mother. (Palmer 1990: 85)

The aim of course is not to minimize the role of one's knowledge during the interpretation process. The following chapters provide plenty of evidence to the effect that many formal and functional factors directly help us choose and understand specific modal constructions. The aim is only to steer clear of the undesirable conclusion that understanding modal constructions merely boils down to identifying these features, thereby adopting a pre-determined, almost mechanistic, approach to verbal communication (inherent in the *Conduit Metaphor*) that both RT and CxG supposedly reject (Wilson 2009: 57). The view defended here is that the search for relevance constitutes one of the main factors during the construction and interpretation of a modal utterance.

At the same time, as was explained in Section 3, there is a vast network of (modal) constructions that support this process of lexically-regulated saturation, which will naturally give different results depending on which construction is used. There are in particular two ways in which this process can be affected (See Leclercq 2019a for further details). First, lexically-regulated saturation can be *guided* whenever a modal verb appears in an other modal construction (which can give rise to coercion effects). This is the case, for instance, in examples (35) and (36).

(35) It's so incredible what your mother did. She *must* be a saint. (COCA)

(36) And, you know, when you hear so many criticisms, people callously getting, you know, getting on the case of video game makers, of gangster rappers, well, here's a guy who wasn't portraying violence, who was actually committing it. And *I don't think we need to* be glorifying that. (COCA)

In example (35), the epistemic interpretation of *must* is in part due to its being used in the 'SUBJ MOD *be* COMPL' construction with which this meaning is associated; in example (36), the root interpretation combined with an invitation not to perform the action denoted by the VP is inherited from the '*I don't think we* MOD VP' construction in which *need to* is used (cf Section 3). That is, in those examples, the interpretation of the modal verbs is not only driven by their own semantic potential and by the search for relevance but is also constrained by the function of the larger constructions in which they occur.

Second, lexically-regulated saturation can also be *suspended*, such as when a modal idiom is used. This is the case, for instance, in the following examples:

(37) As a scientific man himself, Mr. Harris *must surely* see the value in that. (COCA)

(38) *I can't tell you how* proud we are to host tonight's event with President Obama. (COCA)

Here, much like in the case of homonymy, the interpretation process requires the hearer to identify which of the modal verb (i.e. *must* or *can*) or the modal idiom (i.e. 'SUBJ *must surely* VP' or '*I can't tell you how* . . .') is used by the speaker. This identification process is largely guided by considerations of relevance (cf. discussion in Leclercq 2019a), and early stages of the comprehension process systematically involve *lexically-regulated saturation* (i.e. reconstruction of the modal meaning). However, this process may simply be suspended (i.e. in the sense of interrupted) in case processing the meaning of the idiom seems more relevant to the hearer.

In either case, the interpretation process remains primarily guided by the search for relevance. This is important for this then enables us to explain how speakers that do not possess exactly the same network of modal constructions (whether partially schematic or more idiom-like) can still understand each other. It is to be expected for instance that speakers of different varieties of English will store different sets of constructions. Even at the level of individual speakers do we find some variation (see Chapter 8). In this case, communication succeeds because of individual considerations for relevance. This is why both models are needed to provide an accurate description of how speakers make meaning with modals.

6 Conclusion

Modality is often taken as a case study when looking at the semantics-pragmatics interface, and answers to the various questions raised at the beginning of this chapter vary greatly depending on the theoretical approach in which they are couched. The aim of this chapter was to provide a cross-theoretical understanding of the type of knowledge required in using and understanding modal expressions in English and of the underlying pragmatic skills employed in doing so.

Particular attention was given to the views developed in Relevance Theory and Construction Grammar. First, I presented each theory and illustrated how English modals have been analysed in either model. It was shown in Section 3 that a necessary starting point, as suggested in CxG, is to consider that speakers' knowledge consists of a vast network of modal constructions that each contribute in their own way to the understanding of a modal sentence. It was then shown in Section 4 that understanding modal sentences proves to be particularly complex since modal constructions combine two types of meaning. On the one hand, they provide information about the speaker's attitude (root or epistemic) with regard to the proposition. On the other, modals also provide more specific information that further qualify the different types of attitudes, typically in terms of possibility or necessity. The former kind of meaning was analysed in procedural terms while the latter was discussed in conceptual terms. What this discussion shows is that the complexity of understanding how the meaning of modal constructions emerges in context also follows from the fact that hearers need to combine these two aspects during the interpretation process. In accordance with the procedural information, hearers need to recover the type of attitude held by the speaker (root or epistemic), which is enriched into a more specific interpretation on the basis of the conceptual material provided by the modal verb (i.e. possibility or necessity).

Eventually, I tried to reconcile the polysemy view of modal meaning with more context-dependent approaches (such as in RT) and I argued that understanding modal constructions is not reduced to a process of sense selection but rather consists in a process of meaning construction. In accordance with the account developed in Depraetere (2010, 2014), I argued that interpreting modal constructions typically involves an inferential process of lexically-regulated saturation, whereby the meaning of modal verbs is systematically reconstructed in context in accordance both with the principle of relevance and the various senses made accessible by modal verbs. This process may be guided or suspended, depending on which other modal constructions are used, but the central claim remains that the search for relevance constitutes a key factor to (modal) utterance comprehension.

References

Abraham, Werner. 2020. *Modality in Syntax, Semantics, and Pragmatics*. Cambridge: Cambridge University Press.

Allwood, Jens. 2003. Meaning potential and context. Some consequences for the analysis of variation in meaning. In Hubert Cuyckens, René Dirven & John Taylor (eds.), *Cognitive Approaches to Lexical Semantics*, 29–65. Berlin: Mouton de Gruyter.

Berbeira Gardón, José Luis. 1996. *Los Verbos Modales Ingleses: Estudio Semántico-Pragmático*. Cádiz: Cádiz University, Servicio de Publicaciones.

Berbeira Gardón, José Luis. 1998. Relevance and modality. *Revista Alicantina de Estudios Ingleses* 11. 3–22.

Berbeira Gardón, José Luis. 2006. On the semantics and pragmatics of *will*. In Marta Carretero, Laura Hidalgo Downing, Julia Lavid, Elena Martínez Caro, Joanne Neff, Soledad Perez de Ayala & Esther Sánchez-Pardo (eds.), *A Pleasure of Life in Words: A Festschrift for Angela Downing* (vol. 1), 445–465. Madrid: Universidad Complutense de Madrid.

Bergs, Alexander. 2010. Expression of futurity in contemporary English: A Construction Grammar perspective. *English Language and Linguistics* 14(2). 217–238.

Berthelin, Signe Rix. 2017. *The Semantics and Pragmatics of Uummarmiutun Modals*. PhD thesis, Norwegian University of Science and Technology.

Besnard, Anne-Laure. 2017. *Be likely to* and *be expected to*, epistemic modality or evidentiality? Markers of (non)commitment in newspaper discourse. In Juana Isabel Marín Arrese, Gerda Haßler & Marta Carretero (eds.), *Evidentiality Revisited: Cognitive Grammar, Functional and Discourse-Pragmatic Perspectives*, 249–269. Amsterdam: John Benjamins.

Bezuidenhout, Anne. 2002. Truth-conditional pragmatics. *Philosophical Perspectives* 16. 105–134.

Biber, Douglas, Stig Johansson, Geoffrey Leech, Susan Conrad & Edward Finegan. 2021. [1999]. *Grammar of spoken and written English*. 2nd edn. Amsterdam: John Benjamins.

Blakemore, Diane. 1987. *Semantic Constraints on Relevance*. Oxford: Blackwell.

Blakemore, Diane. 1990. Constraints on interpretation. *Proceedings of the 16th Annual Meeting of the Berkeley Linguistics Society*. 363–370.

Blakemore, Diane. 1992. *Understanding Utterances*. Oxford: Blackwell.

Blakemore, Diane. 2002. *Relevance and Linguistic Meaning: The Semantics and Pragmatics of Discourse Markers*. Cambridge: Cambridge University Press.

Boogaart, Ronny. 2009. Semantics and pragmatics in Construction Grammar: The case of modal verbs. In Alexander Bergs & Gabriele Diewald (eds.), *Contexts and Constructions*, 213–241. Amsterdam: John Benjamins.

Bybee, Joan. 2010. *Language, usage and cognition*. Cambridge: Cambridge University Press.

Bybee, Joan & Suzanne Fleischman. 1995. *Modality in Grammar and Discourse*. Amsterdam: John Benjamins.

Bybee, Joan, Revere Perkins & William Pagliuca. 1994. *The evolution of grammar: Tense, aspect and modality in the languages of the world*. Chicago: University of Chicago Press.

Cappelle, Bert & Ilse Depraetere. 2016a. Short-circuited interpretations of modal verb constructions: Some evidence from *The Simpsons*. *Constructions and Frames* 8(1). 7–39.

Cappelle, Bert & Ilse Depraetere. 2016b. Response to Hilpert. In *Constructions and Frames* 8(1). 86–96.

Cappelle, Bert, Ilse Depraetere & Mégane Lesuisse. 2019. The necessity modals *have to*, *must*, *need to* and *should*: Using n-grams to help identify common and distinct semantic and pragmatic aspects. *Constructions and Frames* 11(2). 220–243.

Carston, Robyn. 1999. The semantics/pragmatics distinction: A view from Relevance Theory. In Ken Turner (ed.), *The Semantics/Pragmatics Interface from Different Points of View*, 85–125. Oxford: Elsevier.

Carston, Robyn. 2002. *Thoughts and Utterances: The Pragmatics of Explicit Communication*. Oxford: Blackwell.

Carston, Robyn. 2004. Explicature and semantics. In Steven Davis & Brendan Gillon (eds.), *Semantics: A Reader*, 817–845. Oxford: Oxford University Press.

Carston, Robyn. 2009. The explicit/implicit distinction in pragmatics and the limits of explicit communication. *International Review of Pragmatics* 1. 35–62.

Carston, Robyn. 2010. Explicit communication and 'free' pragmatic enrichment. In Belén Soria & Esther Romero (eds.), *Explicit communication: Robyn Carston's Pragmatics*, 217–285. Basingstoke: Palgrave Macmillan.

Carston, Robyn. 2012. Word meaning and concept expressed. *The Linguistic Review* 29. 607–623.

Carston, Robyn. 2016a. Linguistic conventions and the role of pragmatics. *Mind and Language* 31(5). 612–624.

Carston, Robyn. 2016b. The heterogeneity of procedural meaning. *Lingua* 175. 154–166.

Carston, Robyn. 2021. Polysemy: Pragmatics and sense conventions. *Mind & Language* 36(1). 108–133.

Clark, Billy. 1991. *Relevance Theory and the Semantics of Non-declaratives*. PhD thesis. University College London.

Clark, Billy. 2013. *Relevance Theory*. Cambridge: Cambridge University Press.

Coates, Jennifer. 1983. *The Semantics of the Modal Auxiliaries*. London and Canberra: Croom Helm.

Collins, Peter. 2009. *Modals and Quasi-modals in English*. Amsterdam and New York: Rodopi.
Cornillie, Bert & Paola Pietrandrea. 2012. Modality at work. Cognitive, interactional and textual functions of modal markers. *Journal of Pragmatics* 44(15). 2109–2115.
Croft, William & Alan Cruse. (2004). *Cognitive Linguistics*. Cambridge: Cambridge University Press.
Daugs, Robert. 2020. Revisiting global and intra-categorial frequency shifts in the English modals: A usage-based, constructionist view on the heterogeneity of modal development. In Pascal Hohaus & Rainer Schulze (eds.), *Re-assessing Modalising Expressions: Categories, co-text, and context*, 17–46. Amsterdam: John Benjamins.
Davies, Mark. 2008–. *The Corpus of Contemporary American English (COCA)*. Available online at https://www.english-corpora.org/coca/.
Davies, Mark. 2019–. *The Coronavirus Corpus*. Available online at https://www.english-corpora.org/corona/.
Declerck, Renaat. 2011. The definition of modality. In Adeline Patard & Frank Brisard (eds.), *Cognitive Approaches to Tense, Aspect and Epistemic Modality*, 21–44. Amsterdam and Philadelphia: John Benjamins.
de Haan, Ferdinand. 2012. The relevance of constructions for the interpretation of modal meaning: the case of *must*. *English Studies* 93(6). 700–728.
Depraetere, Ilse. 2010. Some observations on the meaning of modals. In Bert Cappelle & Naoaki Wada (eds.), *Distinctions in English grammar, offered to Renaat Declerck*, 72–91. Tokyo: Kaitakusha.
Depraetere, Ilse. 2014. Modals and lexically-regulated saturation. *Journal of Pragmatics* 7. 160–177.
Depraetere, Ilse. 2019. Meaning in context and contextual meaning: A perspective on the semantics-pragmatics interface applied to modal verbs. *Anglophonia. French Journal of English Linguistics* 28. https://doi.org/10.4000/anglophonia.2453
Depraetere, Ilse & Susan Reed. 2011. Towards a more explicit taxonomy of root possibility. *English Language and Linguistics* 15(1). 1–29.
Depraetere, Ilse & Susan Reed. 2021. [2006] Mood and modality in English. In Bas Aarts, April McMahon & Lars Hinrichs (eds.), *The Handbook of English Linguistics*, 207–227. 2nd edn. Oxford: Blackwell.
de Saussure, Louis. 2014. Verbes modaux et enrichissement pragmatique. *Langages* 193. 113–126.
de Saussure, Louis. 2017. Why French modal verbs are not polysemous, and other considerations on conceptual and procedural meanings. In Joanna Blochowiak, Cristina Grisot, Stephanie Durrleman & Christopher Laenzlinger (eds.), *Formal Models in the Study of Language*, 281–296. Berlin: Springer.
Diessel, Holger. 2013. Construction Grammar and first language acquisition. In Thomas Hoffmann & Graeme Trousdale (eds.), *The Oxford Handbook of Construction Grammar*, 347–363. Oxford: Oxford University Press.
Ehrman, Madeline. 1966. *The Meanings of the Modals in Present-Day American English*. The Hague: Mouton de Gruyter.
Evans, Vyvyan & Melanie Green. 2006. *Cognitive Linguistics: An Introduction*. Edinburgh: Edinburgh University Press.
Fauconnier, Gilles & Mark Turner. 2003. Polysemy and conceptual blending. In Brigitte Nerlich, Zazie Todd, Vimala Herman & David Clarke (eds.), *Polysemy: Flexible Patterns of Meaning in Mind and Language*, 79–94. Berlin: Mouton de Gruyter.

Goldberg, Adele. 1995. *Constructions: A Construction Grammar Approach to Argument Structure*. Chicago: University of Chicago Press.
Goldberg, Adele. 2003. Constructions: A new theoretical approach to language. *Trends in Cognitive Science* 7(5). 219–224.
Goldberg, Adele. 2006. *Constructions at Work: The Nature of Generalization in Language*. Oxford: Oxford University Press.
Goldberg, Adele. 2019. *Explain me this: Creativity, Competition and the Partial Productivity of Constructions*. Princeton, NJ: Princeton University Press.
Goldberg, Adele & Johan van der Auwera. 2012. This is to count as a construction. *Folia Linguistica* 46(1). 109–132.
Gosselin, Laurent. 2010. *Les Modalités en Français: La Validation des Représentations*. Amsterdam/New York: Rodopi.
Grice, Paul. 1989. *Study in the way of words*. Cambridge: Harvard University Press.
Groefsema, Marjolein. 1992. 'Can you pass the salt?': A short-circuited implicature? *Lingua* 87. 103–135.
Groefsema, Marjolein. 1995. *Can, may, must* and *should*: A relevance-theoretic account. *Journal of Linguistics* 31. 53–79.
Haegeman, Liliane. 1989. *Be going to* and *will*: A pragmatic account. *Journal of Linguistics* 25. 291–317.
Halliday, Michael. 1973. *Explorations in the Functions of Language*. London: Edward Arnold.
Hilpert, Martin. 2006. Distinctive collexemes and diachrony. *Corpus Linguistics and Linguistic Theory* 2(2). 243–256.
Hilpert, Martin. 2008. *Germanic Future Constructions: A Usage-based Approach to Grammaticalization*. Amsterdam and Philadelphia: John Benjamins.
Hilpert, Martin. 2013. *Constructional Change in English: Developments in Allomorphy, Word Formation, and Syntax*. Cambridge: Cambridge University Press.
Hilpert, Martin. 2016. Change in modal meanings: Another look at the shifting collocates of *may*. *Constructions and Frames* 8(1). 66–85.
Hilpert, Martin. 2019. [2014]. *Construction Grammar and its Application to English*. 2nd edn. Edinburgh: Edinburgh University Press.
Hohaus, Pascal & Rainer Schulze (eds.). 2020. *Re-assessing Modalising Expressions: Categories, Co-text and Context*. Amsterdam: John Benjamins.
Huddleston, Rodney & Geoffrey Keith Pullum et al. 2002. *The Cambridge Grammar of the English Language*. Cambridge: Cambridge University Press.
Joos, Martin. 1964. *The English Verb: Form and Meanings*. Madison: University of Wisconsin Press.
Kiefer, Ferenc. 1987. On defining modality. *Folia Linguistica* 21. 67–94.
Kisielewska-Krysiuk, Marta. 2008. The epistemic/non-epistemic distinction as exemplified by *must*: A relevance-theoretic perspective. In Ewa Mioduszewska & Agnieszka Piskorska (eds.), *Relevance Round Table I*, 43–65. Warsaw: Warsaw University Press.
Klinge, Alex. 1993. The English modal auxiliaries: From lexical semantics to utterance interpretation. *Journal of Linguistics* 29. 315–357.
Kratzer, Angelika. 1977. What 'must' and 'can' must and can mean. *Linguistics and Philosophy* 1. 337–355.
Kratzer, Angelika. 1981. The notional category of modality. In Hans-Jürgen Eikmeyer & Hannes Rieser (eds.), *Words, Worlds, and Contexts*, 38–74. Berlin: Mouton de Gruyter.

Kratzer, Angelika. 1991. Modality. In Arnim von Stechow & Dieter Wunderlich (eds.), *Semantics: An International Handbook of Contemporary Research*, 639–650. Berlin: Mouton de Gruyter.

Krug, Manfred. 2000. *Emerging English Modals*. Berlin: Mouton de Gruyter.

Leclercq, Benoît. 2019a. *On the Semantics-Pragmatics interface: A Theoretical Bridge between Construction Grammar and Relevance Theory*. PhD thesis, University of Lille.

Leclercq, Benoît. 2019b. Coercion: A case of saturation. *Constructions and Frames* 11(2). 270–289.

Leclercq, Benoît. 2020. Semantics and pragmatics in Construction Grammar. *Belgian Journal of Linguistics* 34. 228–238.

Leclercq, Benoît. (2022). From modals to modal constructions: An n-gram analysis of *can*, *could* and *be able to*. *Constructions and Frames*. 14(2). 226–261.

Leclercq, Benoît & Ilse Depraetere. 2022. Making meaning with *be able to*: modality and actualisation. *English Language and Linguistics*. 26. 27–48.

Leech, Geoffrey. 2006. *A Glossary of English Grammar*. New York, NY: Columbia University Press.

Lyons, John. 1977. *Semantics*. Cambridge: Cambridge University Press.

Michaelis, Laura Adrienne. 2004. Type-shifting in Construction Grammar: A unified model of aspectual coercion. *Cognitive linguistics* 15. 1–67.

Narrog, Heiko. 2005. On defining modality again. *Language Sciences* 27(2). 165–192.

Nicolle, Steve. 1996. *Conceptual and Procedural Encoding in Relevance Theory: A Study with Reference to English and Kiswahili*. PhD thesis, University of York.

Nicolle, Steve. 1997a. A relevance-theoretic account of *be going to*. *Journal of Linguistics* 33. 355–377.

Nicolle, Steve. 1997b. Conceptual and procedural encoding: Criteria for the identification of linguistically encoded procedural information. In Marjolein Groefsema (ed.), *Proceedings of the University of Hertfordshire Relevance Theory Workshop*, 47–56. Chelmsford: Peter Thomas and Associates.

Nicolle, Steve. 1998a. *Be going to* and *will*: a monosemous account. *English Language and Linguistics* 2. 223–243.

Nicolle, Steve. 1998b. A relevance theory perspective on grammaticalization. *Cognitive Linguistics* 9. 1–35.

Nicolle, Steve. 2007. The grammaticalization of tense markers: A pragmatic reanalysis. In Louis de Saussure, Jacques Moeschler & Genoveva Puskas (eds.), *Tense, Mood and Aspect: Theoretical and Descriptive Issues*, 47–65. Amsterdam and New York: Rodopi.

Nicolle, Steve. 2011. Pragmatic aspects of grammaticalization. In Heiko Narrog & Bernd Heine (eds.), *The Oxford Handbook of Grammaticalization*, 401–412. Oxford: Oxford University Press.

Nicolle, Steve. 2015. Diachronic change in procedural semantic content. *Cahiers de Linguistique Française* 32. 133–148.

Norén, Kerstin & Per Linell. 2007. Meaning potentials and the interaction between lexis and contexts: An empirical substantiation. *Pragmatics* 17. 387–416.

Nuyts, Jan. 2005. The modal confusion: On terminology and the concepts behind it. In Alex Klinge & Henrik Høeg Müller (eds.), *Modality: Studies in Form and Function*, 5–38. London: Equinox.

Nuyts, Jan. 2016. Analyses of the modal meanings. In Jan Nuyts & Johan van der Auwera (eds.), *The Oxford handbook of modality and mood*, 31–49. Oxford: Oxford University Press.
Nuyts, Jan & Johan van der Auwera (eds.). 2016. *The Oxford Handbook of Modality and Mood*. Oxford: Oxford University Press.
Palmer, Frank Robert. 1990. [1979]. *Modality and the English Modals*. 2nd edn. London: Longman.
Palmer, Frank Robert. 2001. [1986]. *Mood and Modality*. 2nd edn. Cambridge: Cambridge University Press.
Papafragou, Anna. 1998. Modality and semantic indeterminacy. In Villy Rouchota & Andreas Jucker (eds.), *Current Issues in Relevance Theory*, 237–270. Amsterdam: John Benjamins.
Papafragou, Anna. 2000. *Modality: Issues in the Semantics-Pragmatics Interface*. Amsterdam: Elsevier.
Plank, Frans. 1984. The modals story retold. *Studies in Language* 8. 305–366.
Portner, Paul. 2009. *Modality*. Oxford: Oxford University Press.
Quirk, Randolph, Sidney Greenbaum, Geoffrey Leech & Jan Svartvik. 1985. *A Comprehensive Grammar of the English Language*. London: Longman.
Radden, Gunter & René Dirven. 2007. *Cognitive English Grammar*. Amsterdam: John Benjamins.
Recanati, François. 1989. The pragmatics of what is said. *Mind and Language* 4. 294–328.
Recanati, François. 2004. *Literal meaning*. Cambridge University Press, Cambridge.
Salkie, Raphael. 2002. Review of Papafragou 2000. *Journal of Linguistics* 38. 716–718.
Salkie, Raphael. 2009. Degrees of modality. In Raphael Salkie, Pierre Busuttil & Johan van der Auwera (eds.), *Modality in English: Theory and Description*, 79–103. Berlin: Mouton de Gruyter.
Salkie, Raphael. 2014. Enablement and possibility. In Werner Abraham and Elizabeth Leiss (eds.), *Modes of Modality: Modality, Typology and Universal Grammar*, 319–352. Amsterdam: John Benjamins.
Sandra, Dominiek. 1998. What linguists can and can't tell you about the human mind: A reply to Croft. *Cognitive Linguistics* 9. 361–378.
Scott, Kate. 2011. Beyond reference: Concepts, procedures and referring expressions. In Victoria Escandell-Vidal, Manuel Leonetti & Aoife Ahern (eds.), *Procedural Meaning: Problems and Perspectives*, 183–203. Bingley: Emerald Group Publishing.
Scott, Kate. 2013. This and that: A procedural analysis. *Lingua* 131. 49–65.
Scott, Kate. 2016. Pronouns and procedures: Reference and beyond. *Lingua* 175–176. 69–82.
Simpson, Paul. 1993. *Language, Ideology and Point of View*. London: Routledge.
Sperber, Dan & Deirdre Wilson. 1995. [1986]. *Relevance: Communication and cognition*. 2nd edn. Oxford: Blackwell.
Squartini, Mario. 2016. Interactions between modality and other semantic categories. In Jan Nuyts & Johan van der Auwera (eds.), *The Oxford Handbook of Modality and Mood*, 50–67. Oxford: Oxford University Press.
Sweetser, Eve. 1990. Modality. In Eve Sweetser (ed.), *From Etymology to Pragmatics: Metaphorical and Cultural Aspects of Semantics*, 49–75. Cambridge: Cambridge University Press.
Traugott, Elizabeth Closs. 2003. Approaching modality from the perspective of relevance theory. *Language Sciences* 25. 657–669.
Traugott, Elizabeth Closs. 2016. Do semantic modal maps have a role in a constructionalization approach to modals? *Constructions and Frames* 8(1). 98–125.
Traugott, Elizabeth Closs & Richard Dasher. 2002. *Regularity in Semantic Change*. Cambridge: Cambridge University Press.
Trousdale, Graeme. 2016. Response to Wärnsby. *Constructions and Frames* 8(1). 54–65.

van der Auwera, Johan & Vladimir Alexander Plungian. 1998. Modality's semantic map. *Linguistic Typology* 2. 79–124.
Von Fintel, Kay. 2006. Modality and Language. In Donald Borchert (ed.), *Encyclopedia of Philosophy*, 20–27. Detroit: MacMillan Reference USA.
Verschueren, Jef. 2018. Adaptability and meaning potential. In Rajend Mesthrie & David Bradley (eds.), *The Dynamics of Language: Plenary and Focus Papers from the 20th International Congress of Linguists*, 99–109. Cape Town: UCT Press.
Walton, Alan Leslie. 1988. *The Pragmatics of English Modal Verbs*. PhD thesis, University of London.
Wärnsby, Anna. 2002. Modal constructions? *The Department of English in Lund: Working Papers in Linguistics*, 2.
Wärnsby, Anna. 2016. On the adequacy of a constructionist approach to modality. *Constructions and Frames* 8. 40–53.
Wilson, Deirdre. 2009. Parallels and differences in the treatment of metaphor in Relevance theory and Cognitive Linguistics. *Studies in Pragmatics* 11. 42–60.
Wilson, Deirdre. 2012. Modality and the conceptual-procedural distinction. In Ewa Wałaszewska & Agnieszka Piskorska (eds.), *Relevance Theory: More than Understanding*, 24–43. New Castle upon Tyne: Cambridge Scholars Publishing.
Wilson, Deirdre & Dan Sperber. 1993. Linguistic form and relevance. *UCL Working Papers in Linguistics* 2. 95–112.

3 Possibility modals: Which conditions make them possible?

Bert Cappelle, Ludovic De Cuypere, Ilse Depraetere, Cyril Grandin and Benoît Leclercq

1 Introduction

English has several modals that can express possibility: the periphrastic expression *be able to* (a 'quasi-modal' or 'semi-modal'), the modal auxiliaries *can* and *could*, and the modal auxiliaries *may* and *might*. On what basis do language users make a choice between them? There are arguably multiple factors involved. Some obvious ones are (morpho-)syntactic in nature. For instance, the members making up this set of options are not equally likely candidates to be hosts of a contracted negator: *can't, couldn't, isn't/aren't/weren't able to* are much more likely than *mayn't*, which is hardly ever used (Huddleston and Pullum et al. 2002: 1611), or *mightn't*, which is less rare but still very uncommon (Palmer 1987: 17–18; Huddleston, Pullum and Reynolds 2021: 52). Looking at the left co-text, *be able to* is the only modal option to be encountered after the infinitive marker *to* and, at least in standard English, it is the only option to be used after an auxiliary: we can say, *I think he'll be able to come tomorrow,* but not *I think {*he'll can / *he'll could / *he'll may / *he'll might} come tomorrow* (Palmer 1986: 33–34, 1987: 15, Huddleston and Pullum et al. 2002: 105).

The latter syntactic factor can also be treated as a semantic one, as temporal *will* (or *'ll*) explicitly refers to the future. We can therefore hypothesize that future-time reference sets *be able to* apart from the four 'core' modals. Time of reference may be relevant among those four core modals, too, given that *could* and *might* are historically past-tense forms related to *can* and *may*, respectively. Thus, speaking about the past, we can say, *When I was a child, I could* (but not **can*) *watch TV as much as I wanted*, or *I thought I might* (but not **may*) *throw up if I had another bite* (Huddleston and Pullum et al. 2002: 196–197). However, it is well known that *could* and *might* are far from always used with past-time reference (e.g. *Warning: this could/might get loud*; cf. Huddleston and Pullum et al. 2002: 200), so temporal location may only play a limited role in what guides language users in their choice. Another factor, one that is more clearly semantic, is whether the modality is 'epistemic' or 'root'. To express epistemic meaning, *be able to* cannot be selected and *can* is constrained to non-affirmative contexts, while *could* and definitely *may* and *might* are likely choices (e.g. *You {*are able to / *can / can't / could / may / might} be right*; Coates 1983: 131ff; Huddleston

https://doi.org/10.1515/9783110734157-004

and Pullum et al. 2002: 182, 200; but see Coates 1995 and Collins 2009: 98, for instance, for putative examples of epistemic *can* in affirmative contexts). Within the root meanings, different semantic categories may again preferentially trigger different modals, for instance ability favoring *be able to* (e.g. *She was able to make me blush*; see Leclercq and Depraetere 2022: 36) and general situation possibility *can* or *could* (e.g. *What {can / could} be done to combat climate change?*).

Pragmatic aspects of the utterance could also be assumed to exert an influence on modal verb selection. For instance, a request for action can be expressed with *Can you . . .?* or *Could you . . .?*, while *Are you able to . . .?* is not very likely, let alone *May you . . .?* However, when the speaker requests to do something herself, that is, when asking the addressee for permission, then it *is* possible to use *May I . . .?* (Depraetere and Langford 2020: 275). We also observe that specific lexical contexts, such as the following verb, trigger the use of specific modals, as in *You may want to try this*. Note, furthermore, that while in this example the speaker is making use of a possibility modal, there is pragmatic enrichment: the utterance is conventionally understood as expressing necessity. An important realization, therefore, is that factors cannot be treated on their own. There can be a complex interplay between them, for example, in the case just mentioned, between speech act and person of the subject. We have mentioned another case before, namely when we pointed out that *can* cannot be selected to express epistemic modality in affirmative contexts. Or consider again the ability example we gave above, which was shortened from *She was able to make me blush more than men could*, a sentence taken from the REM dataset (on which, see below and Chapter 1, Section 4). In this sentence, *could* expresses ability, just like *was able to*, but appears without a verbal complement – it is used in a context known as 'code', which provides the 'C' in the acronym NICE (cf. Chapter 1, Section 1.1) – and this special syntactic context might have played a role here. In view of such interactions, it is essential not just to look at the individual effects of each potential factor separately but to evaluate the simultaneous (i.e., multivariate) effect of all motivating factors taken together. Only then can we hope to unravel the relative impact effects of the various factors and their possible interactive effects. For an overview of all the factors that we investigated – a total of 36 – and how they were conceptualized, operationalized and annotated, we refer to the annotation guide of the REM project, which can be found on the companion website of this book (https://www.degruyter.com/document/isbn/9783110734157/html). These factors were applied to the REM dataset, which includes 2,500 tokens, extracted from COCA: circa 500 tokens of each of the five modal forms that express possibility.[1]

---

[1] The REM dataset contains approximately another 2,500 tokens of necessity modals, which this chapter is not concerned with; see Chapter 4 for a comparison of the necessity modals (five of

2 Statistical data analysis

Data preparation and data analysis were performed with R (R Core Team 2021) in Rstudio (Rstudio Team 2021). Data preparation mainly consisted of rebinning certain highly unbalanced variables (so we merged categories with low numbers together), which we used as a preemptive measure to avoid fitting issues in the multivariate analysis. Upon examination of the data, we identified several variables with highly skewed numbers of observations per level; using the nearZeroVar() function from the caret package (Kuhn 2021), we excluded variables that were too skewed. All details of the data preparation and data analysis are reported in an open R markdown document shared on the companion website (for the URL, see the end of the previous section).

With regard to the data analysis reported below, we initially performed a bivariate analysis as a preliminary investigation of the associations between the five modal auxiliaries (i.e., outcome variable 1) and the various predictor variables extracted from the corpus. We then examined the multivariate effect of the predictors by means of the classification tree approach. Classification trees are fitted by recursively splitting the data based on associations between the outcome variables and a combination of predictor variables. Multiple algorithms exist to fit a classification tree to a dataset. We fitted Conditional Inference Trees (CIT), using the ctree() function (Hothorn, Hornik and Zeileis 2006), as well as Conditional Random Forests (CRF), using cforest() (Hothorn et al. 2006, Strobl et al. 2007, 2008). The latter were used to measure the predictive accuracy of the CITs as well as to identify the variable importance. Single classification trees may overfit the data. Overfitting means that a tree may have good classification accuracy for the data under analysis but performs poorly for unseen data. Classical learning algorithms (such as Classification and Regression Trees (CART), which recursively splits the data based on chi squared testing) may also display a bias towards predictors with multiple levels, which allows for multiple splits. The CIT algorithm counters both the overfitting and bias issues, but a random forest is even better suited because multiple trees are fitted based on subsets of the data and the predictors.

---

them: *must, have to, need to, should, ought to*) with respect to SOURCE of modality, a crucial variable for that set. Cyril Grandin's contribution to the present chapter and to Chapter 4 has been that of annotating the large dataset for the ten modal forms. He compiled the dataset and annotated the extracted examples for 33 out of the 36 predictors. Benoît Leclercq annotated three of them, namely CONTEXTUAL EFFECTS (STRENGTHENING AND WEAKENING), SPEECH ACT, and DIRECTNESS/ INDIRECTNESS.

After fitting a general model on all data with the five modal verbs as the outcome variable (outcome 1), we performed additional subset analyses by zooming in on three further outcome variables:
- outcome 2: *be able to, can, could* vs. *may* and *might*
- outcome 3: *be able to* vs. *can* vs. *could*
- outcome 4: *may* vs. *might*

With respect to model building, we fitted various models and retained the one with the best classification accuracy based on out-of-the-box cross-validation of the CRF. The same tree-growing options were used for both the CITs and the CRFs. For more details, see the R notebook on the companion webpage.

3 Results

3.1 Bivariate analysis

The final corpus sample consists of N = 2496 sentences, with a near-equal number of observations for each modal verb. (Four observations were omitted because the general meaning of the sentence could not straightforwardly be interpreted.) Table 1 summarizes the bivariate relation between the modal verbs and 31 predictor variables. The numbers in the left column correspond to those in the annotation guide, to which we refer for more information on the different variables.[2] Each individual association was tested by means of a chi squared test of independence. Cramér's *V* is additionally given as an effect size estimator.

---

[2] GENRE has been added here as a variable; this factor does not feature in the annotation guide, as it is one of the metadata that did not have to be annotated manually. Three variables with a large number of levels are excluded from the table: LEMMA FORM OF THE VERB (predictor 17; 760 types), SUBCLAUSE INTRODUCTION (MAIN ITEM) (predictor 24; 219 different items), LEMMA FORM OF THE ADVERB (predictor 36; 256 adverbs or adverbial phrases). We excluded the variable POSSIBILITY VS. NECESSITY (predictor 5), as the dataset for the analysis reported in this chapter contains tokens with possibility modals only. Two more variables were not included here (predictors 2 and 3) as they pertained to annotations that just apply to *be able to* and not to the other possibility modals, namely whether or not there is *do*-support and what the form is of *be able to* (present, past, present perfect, past perfect, future, past future, past future perfect, infinitive, *-ing* form).

Table 1: Descriptive statistics of the bivariate relation between the five modal auxiliaries and the predictor variables under analysis.

#	Predictor	*Be able to* n = 500	*Can* n = 500	*Could* n = 499	*May* n = 500	*Might* n = 497
	Extra-linguistic variable					
0	**GENRE**					< 0.001 (0.17)*
	academic	97 (17%)**	109 (20%)	58 (10%)	205 (37%)	89 (16%)
	fiction	59 (12%)	62 (13%)	182 (38%)	48 (10%)	132 (27%)
	magazine	95 (19%)	108 (22%)	87 (18%)	87 (18%)	113 (23%)
	news	100 (22%)	110 (24%)	88 (19%)	80 (18%)	76 (17%)
	spoken	149 (29%)	111 (22%)	84 (16%)	80 (16%)	87 (17%)
	LEVEL 1: Modal verb					
1	**NEXT CONSTITUENT**					< 0.001 (0.12)
	adverb	13 (7%)	49 (26%)	39 (21%)	47 (25%)	42 (22%)
	none (code)	2 (6%)	12 (36%)	12 (36%)	2 (6%)	5 (15%)
	subject	0 (0%)	34 (51%)	18 (27%)	9 (13%)	6 (9%)
	verb	482 (22%)	395 (18%)	429 (20%)	433 (20%)	432 (20%)
4	**MEANING**					< 0.001 (0.82)
	epistemic	0 (0%)	8 (1%)	121 (12%)	453 (45%)	435 (43%)
	root	500 (34%)	492 (33%)	378 (26%)	47 (3%)	62 (4%)
6	**SCOPE**					< 0.001 (0.63)
	narrow	420 (47%)	225 (25%)	206 (23%)	19 (2%)	19 (2%)
	wide	80 (5%)	275 (17%)	293 (18%)	481 (30%)	478 (30%)
7	**SOURCE**					< 0.001 (0.80)
	non-'subjective'	500 (35%)	466 (32%)	370 (26%)	37 (3%)	61 (4%)
	'subjective' (discourse-internal)	0 (0%)	34 (3%)	129 (12%)	463 (44%)	436 (41%)
8	**CATEGORY**					< 0.001 (0.45)
	ability	182 (50%)	85 (23%)	97 (27%)	1 (0%)	0 (0%)
	epistemic	0 (0%)	8 (1%)	121 (12%)	453 (45%)	435 (43%)
	gen. sit. poss.	72 (13%)	257 (46%)	169 (30%)	20 (4%)	40 (7%)
	opportunity	226 (49%)	111 (24%)	100 (22%)	8 (2%)	19 (4%)
	permission	20 (22%)	39 (42%)	12 (13%)	18 (20%)	3 (3%)
9	**ACTUALIZATION**					< 0.001 (0.37)
	no	295 (39%)	219 (29%)	199 (27%)	19 (3%)	17 (2%)
	yes	125 (91%)	4 (3%)	7 (5%)	0 (0%)	2 (1%)

Table 1 (continued)

#	Predictor	Be able to n = 500	Can n = 500	Could n = 499	May n = 500	Might n = 497	
10	**TEMPORAL LOCATION**						< 0.001 (0.40)
	future	90 (94%)	0 (0%)	3 (3%)	1 (1%)	2 (2%)	
	past	164 (39%)	0 (0%)	238 (57%)	0 (0%)	16 (4%)	
	past in subclause	14 (12%)	1 (1%)	44 (38%)	7 (6%)	51 (44%)	
	present	232 (12%)	499 (27%)	214 (11%)	492 (26%)	428 (23%)	
11	**TEMPORAL RELATION**						< 0.001 (0.19)
	anterior	0 (0%)	1 (1%)	12 (9%)	63 (47%)	57 (43%)	
	posterior	1 (3%)	0 (0%)	10 (29%)	15 (43%)	9 (26%)	
	simultaneous	499 (21%)	499 (21%)	478 (21%)	422 (18%)	431 (19%)	
	LEVEL 2: Verbal complement						
12	**INFINITIVAL FORM**						< 0.001 (0.23)
	perfect inf.	0 (0%)	1 (1%)	40 (24%)	64 (38%)	62 (37%)	
	present inf.	496 (22%)	482 (21%)	444 (19%)	433 (19%)	426 (19%)	
13	**MEANING OF PERF. INF.**						_ ***
	actualized	0 (0%)	0 (0%)	2 (67%)	1 (33%)	0 (0%)	
	anterior	0 (0%)	1 (1%)	5 (4%)	63 (53%)	50 (42%)	
	counterfactual	0 (0%)	0 (0%)	16 (84%)	0 (0%)	3 (16%)	
	past	0 (0%)	0 (0%)	17 (63%)	0 (0%)	10 (37%)	
14	**GRAMMATICAL ASPECT**						< 0.001 (0.13)
	progressive	0 (0%)	2 (5%)	3 (7%)	15 (37%)	21 (51%)	
	non-progressive	496 (21%)	481 (20%)	481 (20%)	482 (20%)	467 (19%)	
15	**VOICE**						< 0.001 (0.14)
	active	496 (21%)	427 (19%)	454 (20%)	463 (20%)	458 (20%)	
	passive	3 (2%)	56 (37%)	30 (20%)	34 (22%)	29 (19%)	
16	**SITUATION TYPE**						< 0.001 (0.32)
	dynamic	422 (28%)	337 (23%)	291 (20%)	209 (14%)	228 (15%)	
	static	74 (8%)	146 (15%)	193 (20%)	288 (30%)	260 (27%)	
	LEVEL 3: Subject						
18	**SUBJECT EXTRAPOSITION**						< 0.001 (0.12)
	yes	0 (0%)	3 (9%)	2 (6%)	19 (59%)	8 (25%)	
	no	500 (20%)	497 (20%)	497 (20%)	481 (20%)	489 (20%)	

Table 1 (continued)

#	Predictor	*Be able to* n = 500	*Can* n = 500	*Could* n = 499	*May* n = 500	*Might* n = 497	
19	PERSON						< 0.001 (0.20)
	1st	106 (28%)	105 (28%)	105 (28%)	24 (6%)	35 (9%)	
	2nd	48 (19%)	97 (39%)	35 (14%)	35 (14%)	34 (14%)	
	3rd	325 (18%)	296 (16%)	358 (19%)	438 (24%)	424 (23%)	
20	ANIMACY						< 0.001 (0.39)
	yes	464 (28%)	354 (22%)	350 (21%)	218 (13%)	253 (15%)	
	no	14 (2%)	144 (17%)	147 (18%)	279 (34%)	240 (29%)	
21	AGENTIVITY						< 0.001 (0.47)
	yes	397 (38%)	240 (23%)	211 (20%)	75 (7%)	115 (11%)	
	no	82 (6%)	257 (18%)	285 (20%)	422 (30%)	377 (26%)	
22	GENERICITY						< 0.001 (0.16)
	yes	109 (24%)	138 (31%)	54 (12%)	89 (20%)	62 (14%)	
	no	390 (19%)	362 (18%)	445 (22%)	411 (20%)	435 (21%)	
LEVEL 4: Clause							
23	CLAUSE TYPE						< 0.001 (0.15)
	main clause	233 (17%)	303 (22%)	261 (19%)	332 (24%)	245 (18%)	
	subclause	267 (24%)	196 (17%)	238 (21%)	168 (15%)	252 (22%)	
25	SENTENCE TYPE						< 0.001 (0.16)
	declarative	204 (16%)	267 (21%)	235 (19%)	325 (26%)	238 (19%)	
	non-declarative	12 (14%)	35 (41%)	25 (29%)	7 (8%)	6 (7%)	
26	POLARITY						< 0.001 (0.18)
	negative	56 (26%)	31 (14%)	44 (20%)	50 (23%)	34 (16%)	
	contracted *not*	33 (20%)	76 (45%)	59 (35%)	0 (0%)	0 (0%)	
	positive	411 (19%)	393 (19%)	397 (19%)	450 (21%)	463 (22%)	
27	SCOPE OF NEGATION						< 0.001 (0.95)
	over modality	59 (24%)	96 (39%)	85 (35%)	2 (1%)	2 (1%)	
	over proposition	0 (0%)	1 (1%)	0 (0%)	41 (60%)	26 (38%)	
28	HABITUALITY						= 0.15
	yes	3 (27%)	2 (18%)	5 (45%)	1 (9%)	0 (0%)	
	no	497 (20%)	498 (20%)	494 (20%)	499 (20%)	497 (20%)	
29	COUNTERFACTUALITY						< 0.001 (0.13)
	yes	6 (16%)	0 (0%)	21 (57%)	0 (0%)	10 (27%)	
	no	494 (20%)	500 (20%)	479 (19%)	500 (20%)	487 (20%)	

Table 1 (continued)

#	Predictor	Be able to n = 500	Can n = 500	Could n = 499	May n = 500	Might n = 497	
30	**HYPOTHETICAL MEANING**						< 0.001 (0.14)
	yes	8 (14%)	23 (39%)	25 (42%)	1 (2%)	2 (3%)	
	no	492 (20%)	477 (20%)	747 (19%)	499 (20%)	495 (20%)	
31	**CONTEXTUAL EFFECT**						< 0.001 (0.09)
	strengthening	0 (0%)	5 (12%)	3 (7%)	19 (48%)	13 (32%)	
	weakening	0 (0%)	2 (100%)	0 (0%)	0 (0%)	0 (0%)	
	none	500 (20%)	493 (20%)	496 (20%)	481 (20%)	484 (20%)	
32	**SPEECH ACT**						< 0.001 (0.15)
	assertive	444 (20%)	415 (18%)	456 (20%)	475 (21%)	467 (21%)	
	non-assertive	56 (23%)	85 (36%)	43 (18%)	25 (10%)	30 (13%)	
33	**DIRECTNESS**						= 0.03
	direct	475 (20%)	457 (19%)	476 (20%)	476 (20%)	470 (20%)	
	indirect	25 (18%)	43 (30%)	23 (16%)	24 (17%)	27 (19%)	
34	**ADVERB STRENGTH**						= 0.01
	strong	0 (0%)	0 (0%)	3 (21%)	5 (36%)	6 (43%)	
	weak	5 (26%)	3 (16%)	7 (37%)	1 (5%)	3 (16%)	
35	**ADVERB POSITION**						< 0.001 (0.16)
	initial	22 (24%)	15 (16%)	18 (20%)	33 (36%)	4 (4%)	
	initial-medial	17 (44%)	4 (10%)	7 (18%)	8 (21%)	3 (8%)	
	medial	56 (22%)	53 (21%)	42 (16%)	57 (22%)	50 (19%)	
	pre-end	1 (3%)	12 (32%)	9 (24%)	13 (34%)	3 (8%)	
	end	28 (24%)	40 (35%)	17 (15%)	21 (18%)	9 (8%)	

*P-value based on a chi-squared test for independence (effect size as estimated by Cramér's V).
**Number of observations and conditional proportions (probability of the outcome level, conditional on the predictor level). For example, 17% = probability of *be able to*, given that the genre is academic.
***No statistical analysis is performed due to data sparsity (too many empty cells).

Table 1 suggests that the choice of modal auxiliary is possibly associated (at least on a bivariate level) with most predictor variables (26 out of 29 chi squared tests are significant at the 5% significance level).[3] With such a large number of

---

3 Whenever we use the words "choice" or "decision" in our description of the statistical models we do not intend to imply that these are also cognitive choices or decisions made by the speakers. We use the statistical models as a means to explore multivariate associations between the

observations, small deviations may easily turn out to be significant. Looking at the effect sizes (estimated based on Cramér's *V*), we see eight variables that yield a particularly strong effect. Six of these variables are features of the modal verb, i.e., MEANING (predictor 4), SCOPE (predictor 6), SOURCE (predictor 7), CATEGORY (predictor 8), ACTUALIZATION (predictor 9), and TEMPORAL LOCATION (predictor 10). One predictor is related to the Subject, i.e., AGENTIVITY (predictor 21), and one, namely SCOPE OF NEGATION (predictor 27), to the clause (or to the modal verb, if the scope is over the modality). Note that SCOPE OF NEGATION is only relevant to a small subset of the data (N = 312), which implies that its effect in the full data sample is very limited.

Table 1 further indicates that six predictors have extremely low variability in relation to the outcome variable. Using the nearZeroVar() function from the caret package (Kuhn 2021), the following variables were identified as having near zero variability and were accordingly excluded from further analysis: GRAMMATICAL ASPECT (predictor 14), SUBJECT EXTRAPOSITION (predictor 18), HABITUALITY (predictor 28), COUNTERFACTUALITY (predictor 29), HYPOTHETICAL MEANING (predictor 30), and CONTEXTUAL EFFECT (predictor 31).

3.2 Multivariate analysis

The results we reported above show for each individual variable how strongly it is associated, if at all, with the use of a possibility modal. As was explained in the introduction, we need to take into account the simultaneous effect of the predictor variables on the outcome variable, which requires a multivariate analysis.

Note that the definition of the variable CATEGORY is largely based on a combination of SCOPE and SOURCE (see Table 4 in the annotation guide; see also Chapter 1, Section 2.4), which implies that these variables exhibit near-complete collinearity, as can be seen in Table 2. We prefer to use CATEGORY rather than SCOPE and SOURCE in the analyses below, because CATEGORY offers the most finegrained measurement of the semantic feature of interest, and using one variable rather than two gives the most parsimonious model.

---

outcome variable modal verb and a set of predictor variables. We do not regard these multivariate models as cognitive or generative models.

Table 2: The distribution of category in function of scope and source.

CATEGORY	SCOPE	SOURCE	
		non-'subjective'	'subjective' (discourse-internal)
ability	narrow	365	0
	wide	0	0
epistemic	narrow	0	0
	wide	0	1017
gen. sit. poss.	narrow	0	0
	wide	548	10
opportunity	narrow	461	3
	wide	0	0
permission*	narrow	32	28
	wide	28	4

*Permission and permissibility were taken together to avoid data sparsity.

Note also that CATEGORY and MEANING are completely collinear, in that all levels of the former predictor variable, except 'epistemic', correspond to the level 'root' of the latter predictor variable. This follows naturally from the definition of these levels. As the predictor variable CATEGORY makes more fine-grained distinctions than the very general predictor variable MEANING, we did not include the latter variable in the analyses either.

Another general observation about the data that we need to mention here is that several variables had a very large number of missing values. Those were mostly secondary variables that provided annotations for a specific level of a more general variable. For instance, as we pointed out at the end of Section 3.1, SCOPE OF NEGATION is only relevant when the POLARITY is negative. Variables with more than a thousand missing values were not included in the models reported below. These variables are: FORM OF BE ABLE TO (predictor 2; cf. also fn. 2), ACTUALIZATION (predictor 9), SUBCLAUSE INTRODUCTION (MAIN ITEM) (predictor 24; cf. also fn. 2), SENTENCE TYPE (predictor 25), SCOPE OF NEGATION (predictor 27), COUNTERFACTUALITY (predictor 29), ADVERB STRENGTH (predictor 34), ADVERB POSITION (predictor 35), and LEMMA FORM OF THE ADVERB (predictor 36; cf. also fn. 2). Finally, variables with more than ten levels were not included either, namely (SPECIFIC) SOURCE OF THE TEXT (i.e. one of the metadata entered into the dataset), LEMMA FORM OF THE VERB (predictor 17), and again LEMMA FORM OF THE ADVERB (predictor 36, which had already been excluded for the previously-mentioned reason). The subsections below always start by mentioning which variables were tested in the models.

3.2.1 Outcome 1: *be able to* vs. *can* vs. *could* vs. *may* vs. *might*

We fitted a CIT and CRF based on the following predictor variables:

> Outcome ~ GENRE + NEXT CONSTITUENT + CATEGORY + TEMPORAL LOCATION + TEMPORAL RELATION + INFINITIVAL FORM + VOICE + SITUATION TYPE + PERSON + ANIMACY + AGENTIVITY + GENERICITY + CLAUSE TYPE + POLARITY + SPEECH ACT + DIRECTNESS

Based on the CIT, visualized in Figure 1, we found evidence that the distribution of the five modal verbs is associated with four predictors: (i) CATEGORY, (ii) TEMPORAL LOCATION, (iii) POLARITY, and (iv) NEXT CONSTITUENT.

The CIT visualization is readily interpretable as a decision tree. The splits from the top down can be interpreted as a series of subsequent decisions leading to a preferred choice of modal verb. The Y-axis gives the predicted probability for the final decision based on the steps taken. For instance, node 4 at the bottom left shows a clear preference for the verb *be able to*. Let's look at the specific combination of predictor variables that lead to this particular outcome. Starting from the top (node 1) and going to the left reads: if CATEGORY is equal to either 'ability', 'general situation possibility', 'opportunity' or 'permission', we arrive at node 2. Again going to the left: if TEMPORAL LOCATION is equal to 'future', 'past', or 'past in a subclause', we arrive at node 3. Going once more to the left: if TEMPORAL LOCATION is equal to 'future', then the modal *be able to* is the most likely choice of modal;[4] the other modal verbs have an extremely low probability, which confirms a hypothesis we raised in the introduction. With TEMPORAL LOCATION equal to 'past' or 'past in subclause', *could* is the most likely option, in line with its 'past' morphology, closely followed by *be able to*, by virtue of *be* allowing past-tense inflection.

Ideally, every combination of the predictor variables in the decision tree leads to a 'pure' node, which means that there is a clear preference for one of the five outcomes. This is clearly not the case in this tree, and so there is still a considerable amount of variation unaccounted for by the statistical model. There are nevertheless several associative tendencies that can be distilled from the classification tree. For instance, *can* appears to be associated with a combination of root possibility CATEGORY and present TEMPORAL LOCATION, and this probability is slightly higher with the variable CATEGORY equal to 'general situation possibility' or 'permission'. The modals *may* and *might* are mostly associated with CATEGORY equal to 'epistemic' (i.e., the right branch of the tree). There is a (small) additional effect of POLARITY,

---

[4] This may appear to be a trivial finding, as only *be able to* can combine with *will*, as we noted in the introduction. Future-time reference, however, is treated here as a semantic factor, as it need not involve the auxiliary *will*. It can (very) occasionally be found with the core modals (e.g. *Future research may focus on . . .*, although even in this example, there could be discussion as to whether the modality itself is located in the future).

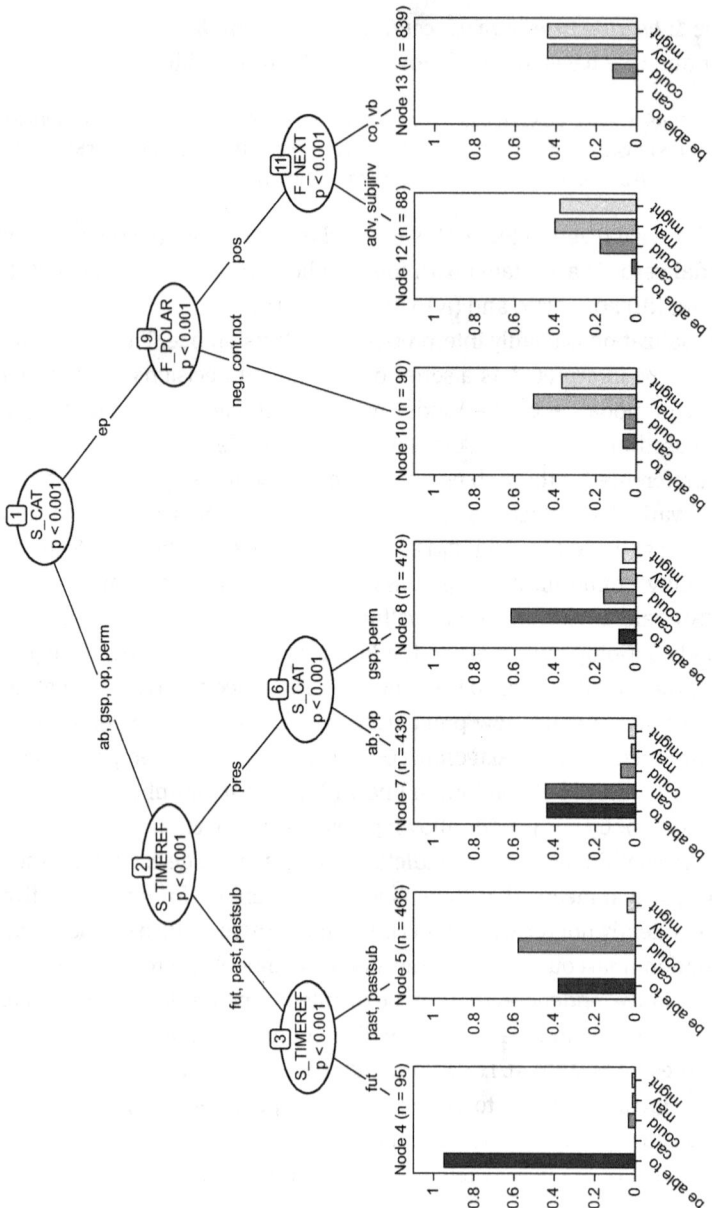

Figure 1: Conditional Inference Tree for the outcome with five modal auxiliary verbs. The y-axis represents the predicted probability for each outcome based on the CIT, i.e., based on the combinations between the various predictor variables in the model.[5]

---

5 For the full versions of the abbreviations used in this and further figures, see Appendix 1.

in that negative polarity has a small positive effect on *may* (note that the predicted probability of *may* is around 50% in node 10, while around 40% in nodes 12 and 13). Other combinations and decisions can be readily read from the visualized tree in Figure 1. The CIT thus allows one to create a list of decision 'rules' in which each modal auxiliary is associated with a specific combination of predictor levels.

One of the advantages of a classification tree analysis, apart from the fairly straightforward interpretation, is that the top node of the tree can also be regarded as the most important predictor variable. Because the algorithm recursively splits the data based on the predictor that has the strongest association with the outcome, the first node is the predictor with the strongest association of all variables tested in the model. In this case, the semantic variable CATEGORY appears to have the strongest association with the outcome variable. The two lower nodes can then be taken as the second most important predictors.

To verify the reliability of the effects of the predictors, we additionally built a Conditional Random Forest (CRF) model, which allows one to verify the variable importance in multiple subsamples of the data. Figure 2 shows the relative

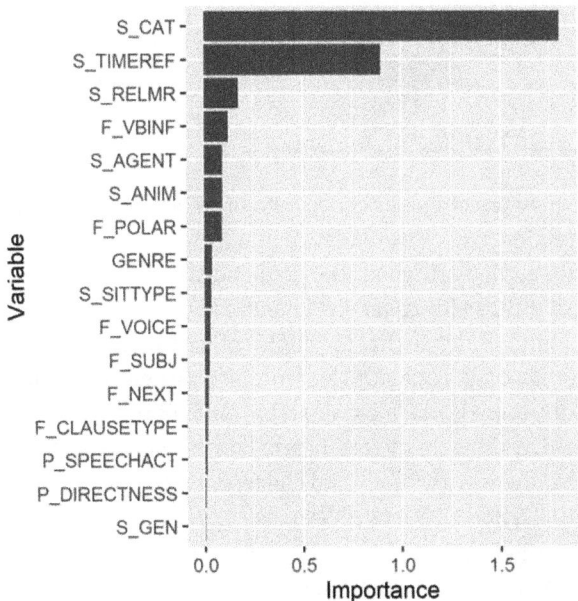

Figure 2: Variable importance for the Conditional Random Forest fitted to outcome 1. Variable importance is measured as the mean decrease in accuracy, with accuracy being defined as the fraction of sample observations correctly classified by the model out of the total number of sample observations. Thus, dropping S_CAT from the model results in the largest average loss in accuracy in comparison to all the other variables.

importance of the predictors based on the Conditional Random Forest. This and all other variable importance plots were made with ggplot2 (Wickham et al. 2016).

The CRF confirms that CATEGORY and TEMPORAL LOCATION yield the strongest effect. The effects of POLARITY and NEXT CONSTITUENT are not retained by the CRF. Looking at nodes 10, 12, and 13 in Figure 1, we can see that the effect of the latter two is indeed small.

To evaluate the predictive quality of the CIT model we compare the outcome predicted by the model and the observed outcomes in the data. We specifically look at the prediction accuracy of the CRF. Table 3 presents the classification table for observed and predicted outcomes. The prediction is done on different subsamples of the data in order to get an honest classification rate.

Table 3: Classification table based on the Random forest model based on out-of-bag cross-classification.

	Predicted					
Observed	be able to	can	could	may	might	% Correct
be able to	246	197	57	0	0	49%
can	22	470	0	5	3	94%
could	96	102	181	87	33	36%
may	3	43	1	368	85	74%
might	5	44	15	249	184	37%

Overall, the CRF model has a correct classification rate of 58%, which is better than random guessing (a random choice would result in a 20% correct classification on average), but still not particularly good. The predictions for *can* (94%) and *may* (74%) are very good, but those for *could* (36%) and *might* (37%) are rather poor. So, even though we found evidence that the choice of modal verbs is associated with CATEGORY and TEMPORAL LOCATION, and to a lesser extent with POLARITY and NEXT CONSTITUENT, there is still a considerable amount of variation in the data that is not explained by these predictors. Figure 1 further suggests, rather unsurprisingly perhaps, that there are actually two clusters of modal auxiliaries: *may* and *might* (cf. nodes 10, 12, and 13) vs. *be able to*, *can* and *could* (cf. nodes 4, 5, 7, and 8). This distinction is mostly associated with CATEGORY.

We additionally performed a behavioral profile analysis (Gries 2010), which involves clustering the modal verbs based on the available predictor variables, and this analysis additionally confirms that the modal verbs can be clustered into two groups. This is clearly indicated by the dendrogram in Figure 3: the first group consists of *may* and *might*, the second group of *be able to*, *can* and *could*.

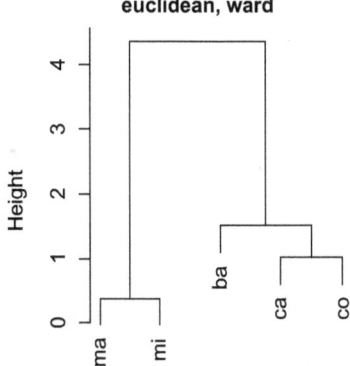

Figure 3: Dendrogram visualizing the result of a behavioral profile analysis clustering the modal verbs based on predictor variables (ma = *may*, mi = *might*, ba = *be able to*, ca = *can*, co = *could*). The clustering algorithm uses the Euclidean distance metric and Ward's amalgamation strategy; other strategies give similar results.

We examine this binary outcome in the next section.

3.2.2 Outcome 2: *be able to*, *can* and *could* vs. *may* and *might*

The following formula was used to fit our CIT and CRF:

> Outcome ~ GENRE + NEXT CONSTITUENT + CATEGORY + TEMPORAL LOCATION + TEMPORAL RELATION + INFINITIVAL FORM + VOICE + SITUATION TYPE + PERSON + ANIMACY + AGENTIVITY + GENERICITY + CLAUSE TYPE + POLARITY + SPEECH ACT + DIRECTNESS

Based on a CIT, visualized in Figure 4, we found evidence for the effect of two variables: (i) CATEGORY and (ii) POLARITY.

The effect of CATEGORY is consistent with what we observed for the analysis of all the modal verbs (cf. Section 3.2), as the predictor is associated with the main split between the two clusters of modal verbs. CATEGORY appears to have an additional effect in that *may* and *might* have the lowest predicted probability with the categories ability and opportunity. The CIT further suggests an effect of POLARITY within the subset of CATEGORY equal to 'epistemic': negative polarity appears to have a positive effect on the use of *may* and *might*; however, when the negator is contracted, the relative likelihood of *can*, *could* and *be able to* increases again, confirming what was suggested in the introduction.

The variable importance plot in Figure 5 provides further evidence for the effects of CATEGORY and POLARITY.

108 — 3 Possibility modals: Which conditions make them possible?

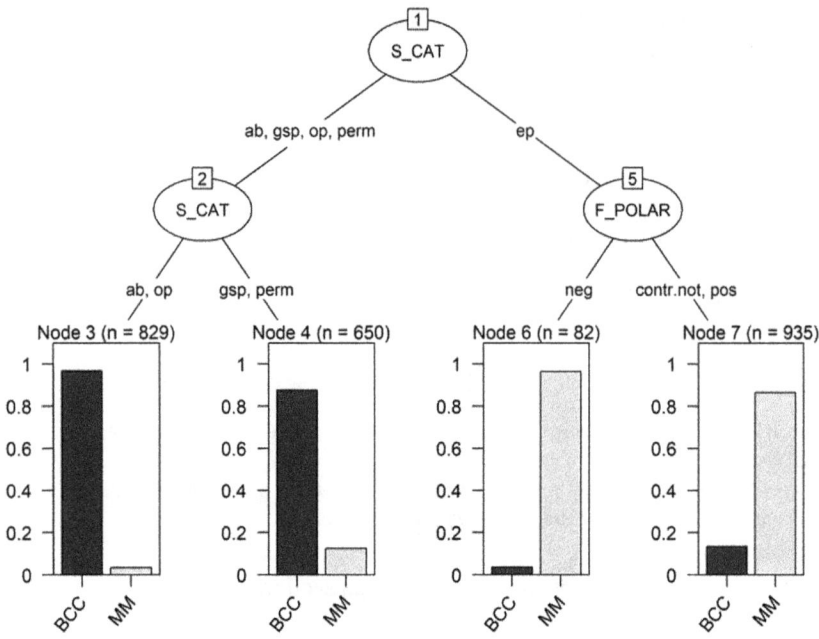

Figure 4: CIT for the binary outcome *be able to*, *can* and *could* (BCC) vs. *may* and *might* (MM).

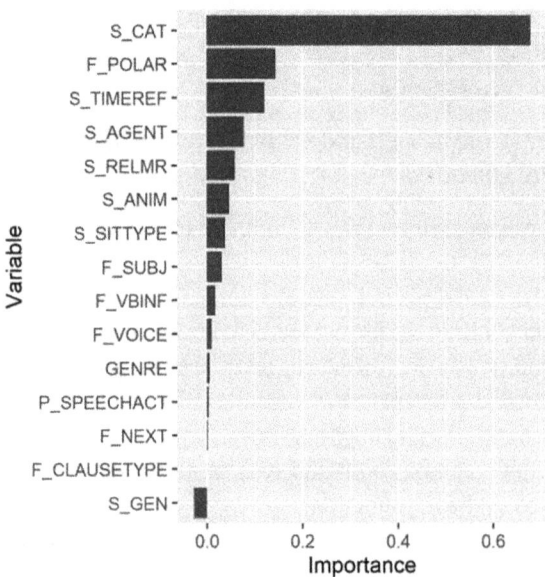

Figure 5: Variable importance plot for the Conditional Random Forest for the binary outcome between *be able to*, *can* and *could* vs. *may* and *might*.

As shown in Table 4, the predictive quality of the CFR is outstanding, with an overall correct classification of 90%.

Table 4: Classification table for the Conditional Random Forest for the binary outcome between *be able to*, *can* and *could* vs. *may* and *might*.

	Predicted		
Observed	*be able to/can/could*	*may/might*	% Correct
be able to/can/could	1370	127	91%
may/might	110	887	89%

3.2.3 Outcome 3: *be able to* vs. *can* vs. *could*

For this particular dataset, we added ACTUALIZATION and SENTENCE TYPE to the model formula, because these variables no longer had more than 1000 missing values:

Outcome ~ GENRE + NEXT CONSTITUENT + CATEGORY + TEMPORAL LOCATION + TEMPORAL RELATION + INFINITIVAL FORM + VOICE + SITUATION TYPE + PERSON + ANIMACY + AGENTIVITY + GENERICITY + CLAUSE TYPE + POLARITY + SPEECH ACT + DIRECTNESS + ACTUALIZATION + SENTENCE TYPE

A CIT, visualized in Figure 6, returned three variables as significant: (i) TEMPORAL LOCATION, (ii) ACTUALIZATION, and (iii) CATEGORY.

Based on the CIT, we can formulate the following general tendencies. First, *be able to* is again associated with future TEMPORAL LOCATION (node 3). Second, *could* is preferred with TEMPORAL LOCATION equalling 'past' or 'past in subclause' and when there is no ACTUALIZATION (node 5); however, when there *is* ACTUALIZATION, then *be able to* is preferred (node 6). This ties in with what is described in grammar books (e.g. Depraetere and Langford 2020: 281), namely that for the expression of past possibility *could* is reserved for so-called 'general' or 'unlimited' ability or opportunity (e.g. *In those days, you could always get ice cream cones for 1 cent* (web-attested)), while *be able to* is used for ability or opportunity that was actually made use of on a specific moment (e.g. *Today I was able to taste wasabi ice cream* (web-attested)). Third, *could* is also associated with a present TEMPORAL LOCATION, particularly when CATEGORY equals 'epistemic' (node 11): as we noted in the introduction, in spite of its diachronically past morphology, *could* is far from always semantically past. Fourth, both *be able to* and *can* are equally preferred with present TEMPORAL LOCATION and when CATEGORY equals 'ability' or 'opportunity' (node 9). *Can*, though, is preferred when CATEGORY equals 'general situation possibility' or 'permission' (node 10).

TEMPORAL LOCATION and CATEGORY yield the strongest effects, as confirmed by the variable importance plot in Figure 7. However, the status of ACTUALIZATION

110 — 3 Possibility modals: Which conditions make them possible?

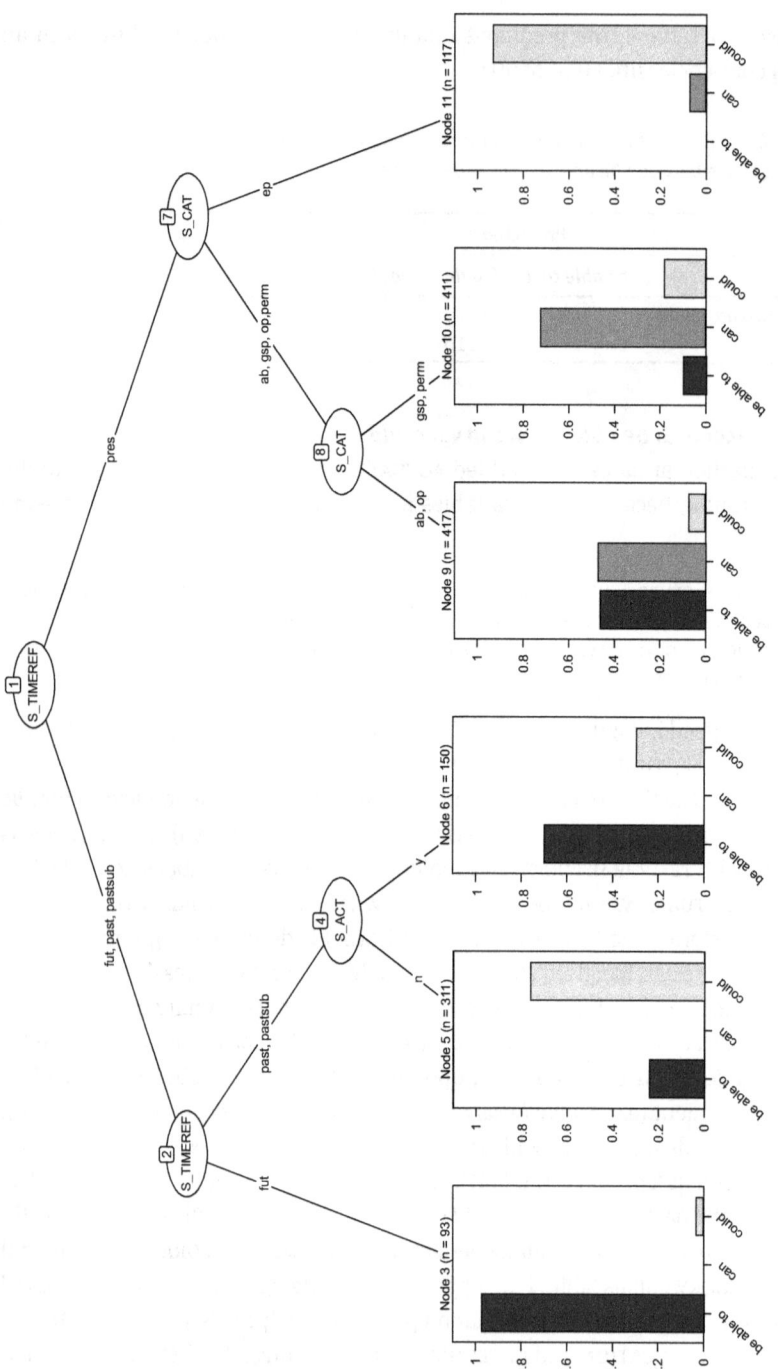

Figure 6: CIT for the triadic outcome *be able to* vs. *can* vs. *could*.

as the next most predictive variable is not confirmed. The CRF suggests that the variable INFINITIVAL FORM is more important, which is perhaps related to the fact that *could* also occurs with perfect infinitival forms, which is not, or hardly, the case for *be able to* and *can* (cf. Table 1).

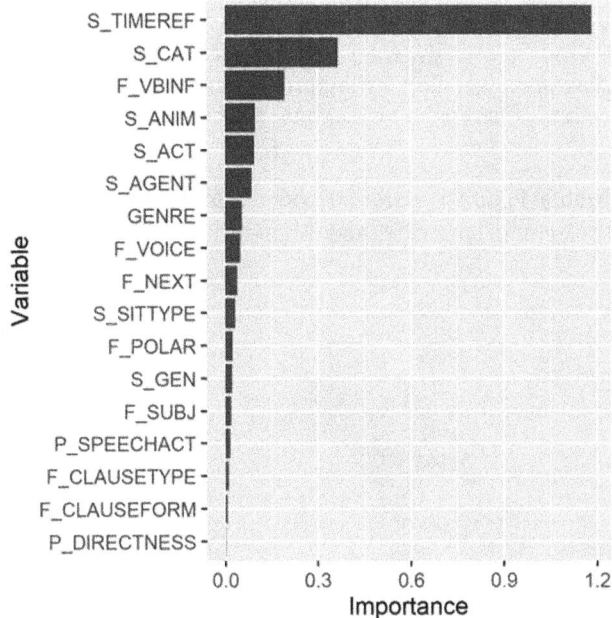

Figure 7: Variable Importance plot for the Conditional Random Forest fitted for the triadic outcome *be able to* vs. *can* vs. *could*.

The predictive quality of the model is very good, with an overall correct classification of 70% (where chance prediction would be 33.3%; cf. Table 5). *Can* is particularly well identified by the model.

Table 5: Classification table for the CRF for the triadic outcome between *be able to* vs. *can* vs. *could*.

	Predicted			
Observed	be able to	can	could	% Correct
be able to	299	148	53	60%
can	64	428	8	86%
could	87	93	319	64%

3.2.4 Outcome 4: *may* vs. *might*

For this outcome, we added MEANING OF PERFECT INFINITIVE, SCOPE OF NEGATION, ADVERB STRENGTH, and ADVERB POSITION, because these variables have fewer than 1000 missing values in this particular dataset. This amounts to the following list of predictor variables tested:

> Outcome ~ GENRE + NEXT CONSTITUENT + CATEGORY + TEMPORAL LOCATION + TEMPORAL RELATION + INFINITIVAL FORM + VOICE + SITUATION TYPE + PERSON + ANIMACY + AGENTIVITY + GENERICITY + CLAUSE TYPE + POLARITY + SPEECH ACT + DIRECTNESS + MEANING OF PERFECT INFINITIVE + SENTENCE TYPE + SCOPE OF NEGATION + ADVERB STRENGTH + ADVERB POSITION

Based on the CIT, visualized in Figure 8, we found evidence for the effect of three variables: (i) GENRE, (ii) TEMPORAL LOCATION, and (iii) CATEGORY.

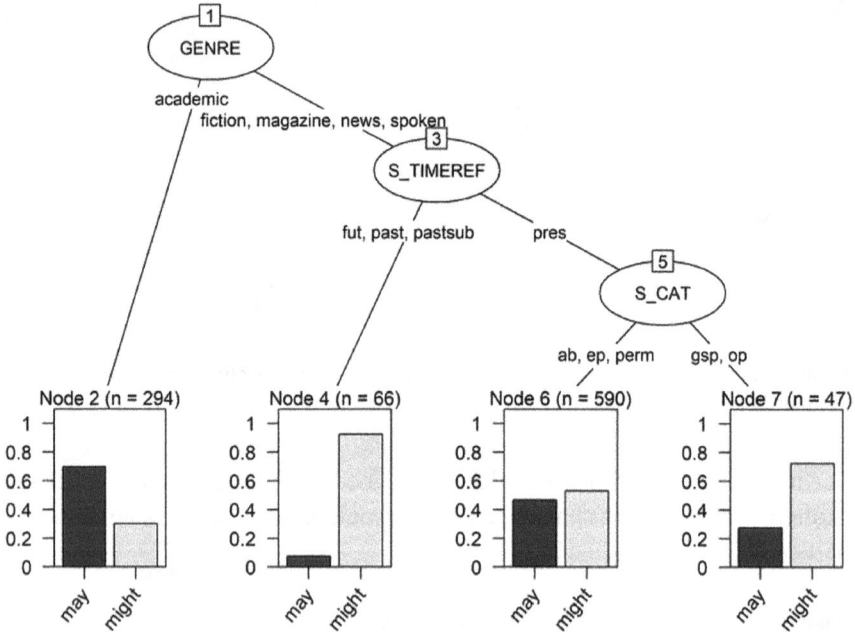

Figure 8: CIT for the binary outcome *may* vs. *might*.

The use of *may* is more probable in academic texts (node 2), while *might* is more probable in fiction, magazines, news and spoken texts. *Might* is particularly preferred with non-present TEMPORAL LOCATIONS (node 4). Most of these concern past contexts. This observation is in line with its originally past-tense morphology, which we mentioned in Section 1. With a present TEMPORAL LOCATION, *might* is preferred when CATEGORY equals 'general situation possibility' or 'opportunity', and *may* and *might* are almost equally frequent with the other values for CATEGORY, although we can see from Table 1 that it is epistemic modality (rather than ability or permission, which we also find in that cluster) that produces this result. (There are only few instances in the dataset in which *may* or *might* locates the modality in the future, as can also be seen in Table 1.)

The variable importance of TEMPORAL LOCATION and GENRE is confirmed by a CRF, but not that of CATEGORY, as shown in Figure 9. The effect of clause type is not observed in the CIT above, but Table 1 suggests that *may* is more likely in main clauses, while *might* is preferred in subclauses.

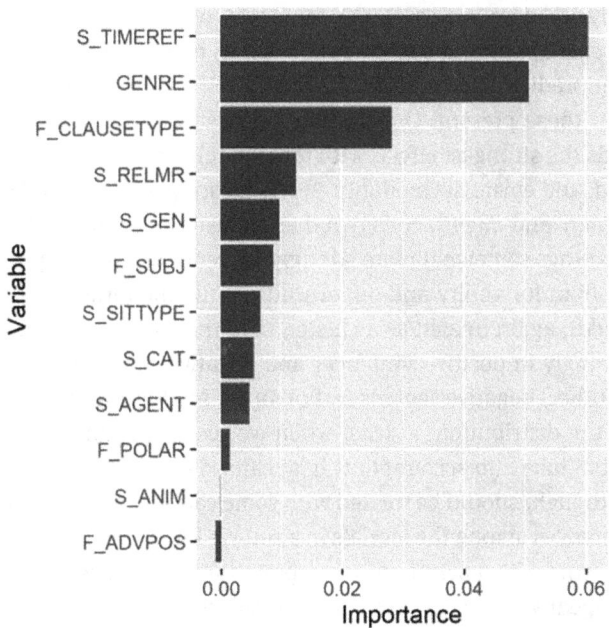

Figure 9: variable importance plot for the Conditional Random Forest for the binary outcome *may* vs. *might*.

The CFR has an overall correct prediction accuracy of 61%. Table 6 shows considerable misclassification for both verbs.

Table 6: Classification table based on the CRF for the binary outcome *may* vs. *might*.

	Predicted		
Observed	may	might	% Correct
may	303	197	61%
might	193	304	61%

4 Conclusion

Our multifactorial analysis based on ca. 2,500 sentences with the possibility modals *be able to*, *can*, *could*, *may* and *might* has allowed us to identify the most important variables that predict these modals' choice as well as the nested conditions ('if (if . . .)') that these present. Our findings suggest that the semantic variable CATEGORY yields the strongest effect, with root modality clearly favoring *be able to*, *can* and *could*, and epistemic modality clearly favoring *may* and *might*. The latter two modals (*may* and *might*), considered as a cluster of choices, hold their ground in root meanings somewhat more strongly for general situation possibility and permission than for ability and opportunity, while the former three (*be able to*, *can* and *could*), again treated as a cluster, hold their ground in epistemic contexts more strongly in positive sentences and negative sentences with contracted *not* than in (other) negative sentences. POLARITY, in other words, also contributes strongly to the distribution, at least when we see this predictor not as a simple binary one but take into account how it is realized (morpho)syntactically. Such clusterings, though, should be treated with some caution, as they may obscure individual differences among the modals in a set. We know, for instance, that *might* hardly ever occurs with a permission interpretation and that *be able to* and *can* almost never appear with an epistemic interpretation.

When we consider the cluster of the modals *be able to*, *can* and *could* separately, we find that the TEMPORAL LOCATION of the modality is the most important factor in their distribution. *Be able to* comes out as the clear winner when the modality is located in the future. When the TEMPORAL LOCATION is past, ACTUALIZATION appears to be a further distinguishing factor, namely between *be able to* (focus on a concrete instance in which the possibility actualized) and *could* (no such focus). When we look at variable importance, though, ACTUALIZATION is not such a strong predictor. With the modality located in the present, we find that the semantic CATEGORY again exerts its influence: with epistemic meaning, *could* is favored; with ability and opportunity, *be able to* and *can* are roughly equally frequent, while with general situation possibility and permission, *can* is more frequent than *be able to*.

Focussing on the pair *may* and *might* separately, we see that GENRE has the strongest predictive force, as in academic discourse, *may* is clearly more frequent than in the other main genres in COCA (fiction, magazines, news, spoken). The contrast between past and present TEMPORAL LOCATION – there are virtually no cases with future time reference with *may* and *might* – next plays the most important role in making a split between the two modals. With modality situated in the past, we almost exclusively find *might*. With modality situated in the present, it is again the kind of semantic CATEGORY that would appear to be strongly predictive: with epistemic modality, *may* and *might* seem to be fairly equal in distribution; with general situation possibility and opportunity, we seem to especially find *might*. In fact, though, this semantic variable (CATEGORY) could be shown to play a rather weaker role for this pair of modals than CLAUSE TYPE, i.e., whether or not the modal appears in a main clause (in which case *may* is favored) or in a subclause (where *might* is more likely).

We would like to argue that these findings are not just descriptively useful. In language pedagogy, for example, they could inform the development of materials that pay attention to those variables that are most relevant for the distribution of the possibility modals. Theory and practice in the language learning class could focus on the semantic CATEGORY expressed by the modal (epistemic modality versus root modality, and among root modality, the different more specific kinds), on POLARITY (and whether or not *not* is contracted), on the TEMPORAL LOCATION of the modality, and perhaps on a small number of further factors that are strongly discriminating. Variables that seem to make no or hardly any contribution in our 2496-sentence dataset, such as the GRAMMATICAL ASPECT of the complement or the PERSON of the subject, can safely be left out of the picture.

Appendix 1

Abbreviations in this paper can be read as follows:

ab	ability
adv	adverb
ba	*be able to*
BCC	*be able to*, *can* and *could*
ca	*can*
co	*could* or (as a level of F_NEXT) code
contr.not	contracted *not*
F_ADVPOS	ADVERB POSITION

F_CLAUSEFORM	SENTENCE TYPE
F_CLAUSETYPE	CLAUSE TYPE
F_NEXT	NEXT CONSTITUENT
F_POLAR	POLARITY
F_SUBJ	PERSON
F_VBINF	INFINITIVAL FORM
F_VOICE	VOICE
fut	future tense
gsp	general situation possibility
ma	*may*
mi	*might*
MM	*may* and *might*
n	number of occurrences
neg	negative (not involving a contracted negator)
op	opportunity
P_DIRECTNESS	DIRECTNESS
P_SPEECHACT	SPEECH ACT
past	past tense
pastsub	past in a subclause
perm	permission
pos	positive
pres	present tense
S_ACT	ACTUALIZATION
S_ADVSTR	ADVERB STRENGTH
S_AGENT	AGENTIVITY
S_ANIM	ANIMACY
S_CAT	CATEGORY
S_GEN	GENERICITY
S_HAVE	MEANING OF PERFECT INFINITIVE
S_NEGSCOPE	SCOPE OF NEGATION
S_RELMR	TEMPORAL RELATION (between modal and residue)
S_SITTYPE	SITUATION TYPE
S_TIMEREF	TEMPORAL LOCATION
subjinv	INVERTED SUBJECT
vb	verb
y/n	yes/no

The *F_* at the beginning of some predictors stands for 'formal', the *S_* for 'semantic', and the *P_* for 'pragmatic'.

References

Coates, Jennifer. 1983. *The Semantics of Modal Auxiliaries*. London: Croom Helm.
Coates, Jennifer. 1995, Root and epistemic possibility in English. In: Bas Aarts & Charles F. Meyer (eds.), *The Verb in Contemporary English: Theory and Description*, 145–156. Cambridge: Cambridge University Press.
Collins, Peter. 2009. *Modals and Quasi-modals in English*. Amsterdam and New York: Rodopi.
Depraetere, Ilse & Chad Langford. 2020 [2012]. *Advanced English Grammar: A Linguistic Approach*. 2nd edition. London: Bloomsbury Academic.
Gries, Stefan Th. 2010. BehavioralProfiles 1.01. A program for R 2.7.1 and higher.
Hothorn, Torsten, Peter Buehlmann, Sandrine Dudoit, Annette Molinaro & Mark Van Der Laan. 2006. Survival Ensembles. *Biostatistics* 7(3). 355–373.
Hothorn, Torsten, Kurt Hornik & Achim Zeileis. 2006. Unbiased Recursive Partitioning: A Conditional Inference Framework. *Journal of Computational and Graphical Statistics* 15(3). 651–674.
Huddleston, Rodney & Geoffrey K. Pullum et al. 2002. *The Cambridge Grammar of the English Language*. Cambridge: Cambridge University Press.
Huddleston, Rodney, Geoffrey K. Pullum & Burt Reynolds. 2021. *A Student's Introduction to English Grammar*. Cambridge: Cambridge University Press.
Kuhn, Max. 2021. Caret: Classification and Regression Training. R package version 6.0-90. https://CRAN.R-project.org/package=caret
Leclercq, Benoît & Ilse Depraetere. 2022. Making meaning with *be able to*: modality and actualization. *English Language and Linguistics* 26(1). 27–48.
Palmer, Frank. 1986. *Mood and Modality*. Cambridge: Cambridge University Press.
Palmer, Frank. 1987 [1974]. *The English Verb*. 2nd edition. London: Longman.
R Core Team. 2021. R: A language and environment for statistical computing. R Foundation for Statistical Computing, Vienna, Austria. URL https://www.R-project.org/.
RStudio Team. 2021. RStudio: Integrated Development Environment for R. RStudio, PBC, Boston, MA URL http://www.rstudio.com/.
Strobl, Carolin, Anne-Laure Boulesteix, Thomas Kneib, Thomas Augustin & Achim Zeileis. 2008. Conditional variable importance for random forests. *BMC Bioinformatics* 9(307).
Strobl, Carolin, Anne-Laure Boulesteix, Achim Zeileis & Torsten Hothorn. 2007. Bias in random forest variable importance measures: Illustrations, sources and a solution. *BMC Bioinformatics* 8(25).
Wickham, Hadley, Danielle Navarro & Thomas Lin Pederson. 2016. *ggplot2: Elegant Graphics for Data Analysis*. New York: Springer.

4 Necessity modals and the role of source as a predictive factor

Benoît Leclercq, Bert Cappelle, Ilse Depraetere and Cyril Grandin

1 Background and aims

One of the aims of this book is to find out what drives the speaker's choice of modal verb, and to gauge the impact of the lexico-grammatical context as well as various syntactic, semantic and pragmatic features (see, e.g., Chapter 3 for a discussion of the possibility verbs). In this chapter, we turn to necessity modals, more specifically, *must, have to, need to, ought to*, and *should*, when they express root meaning.

One of the striking features in taxonomic discussions is that, compared to possibility modals, far less clearly delineated meaning distinctions stand out in the realm of necessity (Depraetere 2015, Depraetere and Reed 2021). Admittedly, the main distinction between epistemic and root (non-epistemic) modality is found in both conceptual domains and is as clear for the necessity modals as it is for the possibility modals. For instance, *She must be in her room* has two very different readings (as a conclusion or as a claim about an obligation), which are as distinct as the two readings of *She could have gone home* ('It is possible that she went home' or 'She had the possibility to go home'). However, while root possibility can be broken down into fairly clearly distinct subcategories (e.g. 'ability' and 'permission'), the borderlines between subcategories of root necessity meaning appear to be far more blurry. These subcategories are also harder to characterize. For instance, although the concepts of deontic and dynamic necessity are commonly used, it is not clear where to put 'non-performative' necessity (e.g. *These plants must have plenty of water if they are to survive*, an example provided in Huddleston and Pullum et al. (2002: 185) as one that falls in between these categories) (see Chapter 1, Section 2.2.2 on deontic necessity and Chapter 1, Section 2.2.4 on dynamic modality).

Furthermore, epistemic and root necessity appear to be different with respect to which modals are suitable to encode these categories. Indeed, necessity modals differ in how readily they express (certain shades of) epistemic modality (compare, e.g., *He {must really / *should really / *really needs to / ??really has to / ??really ought to} love you to give you such a nice complement!*).[1] By contrast,

---

[1] In Chapter 1, we have not made any taxonomic distinctions within epistemic necessity, but as was noted there, there may nonetheless be differences in the degree of likelihood of the situation, and various more subtle differences, among the individual modals.

it is possible to find non-epistemic contexts in which all of them can occur (e.g. *You {must / should / need to / have to / ought to} be careful*). This would seem to suggest that root necessity is a semantic category that allows a range of different encoding options, which can be seen as largely synonymous (and then we are not even considering alternative forms such as *want to* and *had better*). Pinning down the factors that drive the choice of a root necessity verb therefore seems to involve a bigger challenge than explaining the choice of a root possibility verb.

One predictor that has been advanced as relevant is that the necessity modals exhibit differences in STRENGTH (see, for instance, Sweetser 1990: 540, Bybee, Perkins and Pagliuca 1994: 186, Myhill 1995: 162, Hoye 1997: 110, Palmer 2001: 73, Smith 2003: 242, Tagliamonte and Smith 2006: 345, Collins 2009: 61). For instance, *must* is probably stronger than all the other necessity verbs. Judgments are more delicate, though, when we attempt to position *all* necessity verbs on a scale of strength. Importantly, there have as yet been few attempts to operationalize this concept for corpus analysis (see, e.g., Verhulst, Depraetere and Heyvaert 2013, Schützler and Herzky 2021 for discussion). For these reasons, the REM dataset was not annotated for strength.

In this chapter, we will zoom in on 'SOURCE of the necessity', which we define as the driving force behind the necessary state of affairs. For instance, in sentences (1) and (2), it is the speaker who wants the addressee (not) to bring about a state of affairs. Alternatively, in (3), it is the widespread concerns about the deficit that make it necessary for the subject referent to be careful about how they frame it:

(1) "Pishima, I am coming back as soon as I finish school," I declared one night. "No! You *mustn't* come back. You mustn't. I want you to go away. You mustn't waste your life."[2]

(2) Good heavens! You're coming to Portland? Clearly you *must* contact me when you arrive so that we can do some sort of bizarre joint blog post.

(3) Everyone is concerned about the deficit, and that's why we *have to* be careful how we frame this.

Our choice to focus on 'source' is inspired by discussions that stress the importance of this factor as driving the choice of necessity modals (see Section 2 for discussion). The aim is therefore to pin down the extent to which SOURCE can predict

---

[2] All the examples in this chapter have been extracted from COCA.

the choice of a root necessity verb. By singling out this particular predictor, we will inevitably ignore any influence that other predictors might simultaneously exert.

In Section 2, we will present the classification of modal sources used in the project and we will embed the discussion within previous research. In Section 3, we will present and interpret the results of the data analysis based on the REM dataset. We used Pearson residuals and *configural frequency analysis* (CFA) to establish which verbs are typically attracted to, or repelled by, which sources, in order to shed light on an overarching question addressed in this book. Section 4 will formulate our conclusion.

2 Five sources of modality

The intuitive idea that if a situation is necessary, there must be an extra-linguistic element that is at the origin of this necessity is one that features quite often in the literature, especially in discussions of so-called deontic modality. For instance, Lyons (1977) argues that "deontic necessity typically proceeds, or derives, from some source or cause" (Lyons 1977: 824). Likewise, Heine (1995), referring to Jespersen, writes that agent-oriented (root) uses of German modals involve "some force (F) that is characterized by "an element of will" (Jespersen 1924: 320–321), i.e. that has an interest in an event either occurring or not occurring" (Heine 1995: 29); "F may be either a human authority, e.g. the speaker, or a non-human (e.g., religious, institutional, or moral) power" (Heine 1995: 30). Diewald (2001) distinguishes between an internal source, which is located within the subject (and which accounts for volitional meaning), and an external source, which is not (and which accounts for deontic meanings).

In Kratzer's formal approach, the concept of a modal source is inherent in the notion of 'conversational backgrounds' (cf. Kratzer 1977, 1981, 1991). For instance, phrases like *given the regulations* and *in view of what the law provides* capture a deontic modal base; *in view of my goals* and *in view of the circumstances* capture a *teleological* and a *circumstantial* modal base, respectively. *Bouletic* conversational backgrounds have to do with preferences and wishes. While there are restrictions on the kinds of conversational backgrounds that can be used to interpret modals, they mainly serve to determine taxonomic distinctions (bouletic, teleological, epistemic, etc.). In a somewhat similar way, Huddleston and Pullum et al. (2002) put forward 'force' as a defining feature of deontic vs. dynamic modality when they write: "The person, authority, convention, or whatever from whom the obligation, etc. is understood to emanate we refer to as **deontic source**" (Huddleston and Pullum et al. 2002: 178; original emphasis); dynamic necessity is typically associated with "someone's properties/disposition" (Huddleston and Pullum et al. 2002: 185), and circumstantial necessity is more peripheral to this category.

In Chapter 1, we explain how to operationalize the factor of 'source', treated as a binary 'external' vs 'internal' feature, for the purposes of building a taxonomy of modal meanings (see Section 2.4 in that chapter). Here, in the present chapter, source is not discussed through the lens of taxonomic distinctions, but rather as a non-binary context-based factor that drives the choice of one modal verb of necessity rather than another. That is, we do not differentiate semantic (taxonomic) classes of modals on the basis of each of the five types of source. Yet, that does not mean that the finer-grained distinctions we will propose shortly cannot constitute a variable (co-)determining the choice of modals (in the same way as the other 35 predictors that were annotated in the REM dataset do not result in taxonomic distinctions – rather, they characterize the contexts of use).

SOURCE thus features among the 36 variables in terms of which the REM dataset was annotated.[3] As mentioned in the introduction, we define 'source' as the underlying driving force (or factor) that makes a certain state of affairs necessary. The following five-way distinction has been used; it is inspired by the discussions in Depraetere and Verhulst (2008), Depraetere and Reed (2011) and Depraetere (2014, 2022):

(i)   subject-internal source
(ii) discourse-internal source
(iii) conditional source
(iv) rules and regulations
(v)   circumstantial source

Subject-internal source is in the foreground in discussion of root possibility: the modal class of 'ability' is standardly defined as a possibility that resides in the referent of the grammatical subject. On the necessity side, 'subject-internal' modality is typically associated with *need to*, and we will address the ways in which this feature has been described before in Section 2.1. Discourse-internal source resonates with what has been called 'subjective' modality; for reasons that will be explained below, we prefer to use the term 'discourse-internal source': it is either the speaker – in declarative sentences – or the hearer (addressee) – in interrogative sentences. The final three types of source are so-called 'objective' sources: the

---

[3] As observed in Chapter 3 (fn. 1), Cyril Grandin's contribution to this chapter has likewise been that of compiling the dataset and annotating the examples for 33 out of the 36 predictors, including SOURCE.

hypothesis here is that the finer-grained distinctions can help explain the contexts of use of root necessity modals. In each of the following subsections, we will illustrate our classification, explain how the distinctions have been operationalized for corpus analysis, and position them with respect to previous research.

2.1 Subject-internal source

Ability meanings are standardly described as involving skills internal to the subject referent (e.g. Depraetere and Langford 2020: 279). Van der Auwera and Plungian (1998), for instance, use the label 'participant-internal possibility' to capture the meaning expressed by *can* in examples like *Boris can get by with sleeping five hours a night*, the necessity counterpart of which is 'participant-internal necessity', as in *Boris needs to sleep ten hours every night for him to function properly*. They define this meaning as "necessity internal to a participant engaged in the state of affairs" (1998: 80).

We speak of a 'subject-internal' source if the source of the necessity lies within the referent of the grammatical subject. The following examples are cases in point:

(4) "I *have to* have something to read, I *have to* have my iPod, I *have to* have my snacks. This is like a nine-hour flight with connections. I'd go crazy."

(5) We've finally reached the stage where he takes his time-out himself. If he sees he's getting upset, he says, "I *need to* be alone."

It is important to add that the subject referent is clearly the agent: in (4) the subject referent is determined to take something to read, an iPod and some snacks with her; in (5), the subject referent makes it clear what he wants, what he finds necessary for him to do. In other words, agentivity is taken as the defining criterion for 'subject-internal' source in sentences with an animate subject referent. In this case, the modal can be paraphrased by *want to*. Agentivity is taken here in the sense of what Cruse (1973) calls 'volitive' meaning, which "is present when an act of will is stated or implied" (Cruse 1973: 18).[4]

---

[4] Cruse uses *agentive* as a broader category: the feature *agentive* "is present in any sentence referring to an action performed by an object which is regarded as using its own energy in carrying out the action" (Cruse 1973: 21). Van Valin and Wilkins (1996) introduce the term 'effector', "roughly, the dynamic participant doing something in an event" (Van Valin and Wilkins 1996: 291), which they argue is a concept that is more basic than that of agent, agentivity arising as a result of an agent implicature. For instance, though *Larry killed the deer* will normally be under-

2.2 Discourse-internal source (speaker- or hearer-based)

We use the term 'discourse-internal' source to refer to cases in which it is the speaker who imposes an obligation or who simply voices an opinion and makes it clear that in her view, it is necessary for someone to do something or for a situation to actualize. The label 'subjective' is commonly used to capture this meaning. The term 'discourse-internal' is preferred to the notion of 'subjectivity', though, as the latter often carries different conceptual loads depending on the empirical and theoretical background in which it is couched (see, e.g., De Smet and Verstraete 2006, Tagliamonte and Smith 2006, Nuyts 2012, Nokkonen 2017: 49; see Verstraete 2001, Narrog 2012, Ziegeler 2019 for interesting overviews and discussion).[5] The view taken here is that the source of the root necessity is discourse-internal so long as the speaker's (or hearer's) personal opinion exhaustively makes up the source of modality, a view that can be operationalized in a fairly straightforward way in a corpus study. The following are some cases in point:

(6) "Come away from the window, Jewell," her mother said in a low voice. "You *must* not appear as though you're aware of any of this."

(7) I think one of the questions that *ought to* be on the table here today is Ken Starr and what is going on with that investigation.

(8) Even though there is no pain involved with hair loss, people *should* know that it is very hard to live with.

Coates (1983: 33) has characterized the clearly performative/directive uses of *must* in (6) as a 'psychological', though not a quantitative, stereotype: it is the first kind of example that comes to mind but it is not the most frequent use. In this example, the speaker, who is in a position of authority, makes it clear to her

---

stood in terms of Larry, the effector, intentionally performing the action, this is merely a default pragmatic inference (since Larry is a human being and since the actions of humans are often willful). If there is information to the contrary, as in *Larry accidentally killed the deer*, the effector will not be construed as an agent (cf. Van Valin and Wilkins 1996: 309–310).

5 Whenever we use inverted commas around 'subjective/-ity' and 'objective/-ity', this is to make it clear to the reader that we are adopting these generic concepts in the way these have been generally intended in the empirical literature on modal verbs since Coates (1983), that is, as referring to cases where the speaker/hearer is, or is not, crucially involved as the sole driving force.

daughter that she needs to behave in a specific way. Likewise, in (7), the host wants their co-hosts to talk about Ken Starr's investigation. Not all examples with a 'discourse-internal' source are performative/directive, however. Example (8), for instance, is not a direct order or request, whereby the speaker is in an authoritative position and is telling the addressee what to do. It is clear though that here again, it is the speaker who feels it is necessary for certain questions to be addressed, and that she feels it is important that people be informed about the hardship caused by hair loss.

In declarative sentences such as in (6)-(8), it is the speaker who is the source, but in interrogatives, it is the hearer, as is clear from the paraphrases added between brackets to each of the following examples (see, e.g., Huddleston and Pullum et al. 2002: 183):

(9) "So, my little storm cloud," my mother says from the front seat. "Are you comfortable back there?"
I grunt instead of speaking.
"You're not hungry, you don't care what music we listen to, you haven't said one word." "She'll eat if we stop at Cracker Barrel," Travis says. "She likes the buffet."
"What do you say, Beck? *Should* I get off the highway?" (*Do you think it is necessary for me to get off the highway?*)

(10) GEORGE-WILL-1-ABC# (Off-camera) [. . .] Never mind the possibility as Secretary Clinton has said that this could wind up an enormous Somalia. We just hope things are going to be better.
JAKE-TAPPER-1-ABC (Off-camera) You're a former admiral. *Should* we have intervened?
JOE-SESTAK-1FORME I was not supportive of our intervention. When I was at the National Security Council, as director of policy for President Clinton, the one thing I really learned there is you got to make sure that your military force actually matches the political objective. (*Do you think it was necessary for us to intervene?*)

In either case, 'discourse-internal' source reflects a type of modality that is crucially grounded in the speaker's or hearer's personal view on what is necessary or what should necessarily (not) happen. In that regard, it is the only truly 'subjective' source in the five-class classification adopted here, and we believe it plays a major role in the choice of modal verb. For instance, it is often argued that *must* is more 'subjective' than *have to* or that *should* is more 'subjective' than *ought to* (cf. Cappelle and De Sutter 2010, Depraetere and Verhulst 2008 and Verhulst and

Heyvaert 2015 for references and critical discussion), claims that will be put to the test in our corpus analysis.

2.3 Circumstantial sources

In the examples below, it is circumstances, be it the (narrow or broader) context of speaking, or more generally, 'the nature of things' that make it necessary for a situation to actualize or for someone to do something. It has been argued that sentences that express circumstantial necessity do not have a source but express "an inevitability inherent in the situation as a whole" (Nuyts 2005: 8) (cf. also Larreya and Rivière 2019: 103, Verstraete 2001: 1508). In our view, any root necessity is linked up with a source: if there is reference to a necessity it must originate somewhere. In (11), it is the low number of 'religious consumers' that forces churches to be competitive; in (12), it is (increasing) student enrollment that determines the need to build a new campus; in (13), it is teacher placement that requires certain factors to be addressed. Examples (14) and (15) illustrate circumstantial sources that have to do with 'the nature of things', either the mortal condition of human beings (14) or the biological attributes of hermit crabs (15).

(11) Since there are only so many of us religious consumers to go around, churches *have to* compete with one another to acquire and keep as many consumers as possible.

(12) "A district with a static student enrollment does not *need to* construct three to four new campuses per year," Cy-Fair spokeswoman Kelli Durham said.

(13) When placing a pre-service teacher (PST), certain factors *need to* be addressed.

(14) But just because all men *must* die, that doesn't mean we can't have some fun.

(15) Every hermit crab, land or sea, *must* bear the burden of carrying its home on its back whenever it travels.

Circumstantial necessity features quite prominently in research on modal sources, and different labels are used, such as 'external necessity' (Quirk et al. 1985: 226, Palmer 1990), 'circumstantial necessity' (Declerck 1991: 383, Huddleston and Pullum et al. 2002: 185), 'neutral necessity' (Palmer 1990), 'objective necessity'

(Coates 1983: 36) and 'general objective necessity' (Goossens 2000: 161). As stated before, when we introduced the five kinds of sources, 'circumstantial' as it is used here singles out one kind of 'objective' source and it is to two other kinds, 'conditional sources' and 'rules and regulations', that we now turn.

2.4 Conditional source

In examples that we have classified as 'conditional', the actualization of a situation is said to be necessary in order for another one to materialize (cf., e.g., Furmaniak (2020: 292) for a similar view). Put differently, a situation is necessary (or it is necessary for someone to do something) if a specific purpose is to be achieved (i.e. 'X is necessary in order to Y' or 'if Y is to actualize, X is necessary'). It is important to point out the temporal sequence that is typical of examples of this kind: situation X needs to actualize at time t in order for another situation to actualize at time $t+1$. The purpose can be made explicit in various ways: it may take the form of an adverbial subclause of purpose, as in (16) and (17) or an *if*-clause, as in (18):

(16) To reach the cabin you *must* walk at least 15 hours.

(17) We *need to* pass legislation that contains both carrots and sticks to encourage the use of recycled materials.

(18) "If you want to continue living in poverty without clothes and food," I told them, "then go and drink in the shebeens. But if you want better things, you *must* work hard. We [cannot] do it all for you; you must do it yourselves."

Alternatively, it may be more implicitly communicated, in which case the context plays a crucial role. In (19), for instance, the purpose takes the form of an implicit conditional clause ('if maternal death is to be avoided'); in (20), it is an implicit adverbial subclause of purpose ('in order to have reliable material'); in (21), *for this reason* refers to the risk posed by ingesting a live leech. A reason is not, actually, a purpose, the latter of which here remains implicit ('to avoid the risk posed by a leech in the throat passage').

(19) Statins should be discontinued # Venous Thromboembolism (VTE) Pulmonary embolism (PE) accounts for a third of all maternal deaths and is the leading cause of maternal death in the UK. 2 Warfarin therapy is contraindicated in pregnancy due to its teratogenicity and risk of placental

abruption and *should* be stopped prior to pregnancy. Following specialist intervention, the woman may be switched to heparin or low-dose aspirin. It is recommended that all women with a personal or family history of VTE are screened for inherited and acquired thrombophilia.

(20) KELLY-MATHESON Most of the video that we see on YouTube and that goes viral and on the media is about the crime. [...]. An important part of my job is to teach people also how to document who did it and how it was done, so that we can convict perpetrators, the people who are committing these crimes, in court.
HARI-SREENIVASAN Part of the training emphasizes basic video shooting techniques, such as holding a steady shot for at least 10 seconds, proper framing of people and objects and gathering a variety of shots that show details like I.D. badges, street signs and license plate numbers. Senior program manager Priscila Neri oversees the organization's work in Latin America.
PRISCILA-NERI, -Sen You need to do things like not deleting your original file. You *need to* do things like making sure you can prove that that [was] filmed the day you say it was filmed, and making sure you can find it later, and that it's stored in a safe place.

(21) It is true that a live leech could adhere to your throat passage, and for this reason they *should* be killed first or thoroughly chewed.

It may be useful to add that the presence of an *if*-clause or a *to*-infinitive clause is not necessarily the instantiation of a conditional source. In the following example, for instance, the source is a rule or a regulation (see Section 2.5) and the *if*-clause specifies the circumstances that make a certain situation necessary:

(22) However at my hospital it is policy that if you are not feeling well in any way you *must* wear a mask.

A further, related observation concerns examples like (23) and (24), in which speakers clearly express their own opinion ('discourse-internal' source) but which also contain a purpose clause ('conditional' source). Examples like these were annotated as having 'discourse-internal' source (cf. Section 2.2), since this feature is more central to the meaning communicated by the speaker.

(23) Like other specialists working in the field, Hayman emphasizes the ways in which bats help to maintain healthy forests by keeping insect populations

in check, pollinating plant species, and distributing fruit seeds far and wide. He and colleagues explained the case last year: "[P]athogen transfer *should* be an active area of research in order to develop evidence-based policies to minimize risks, while conserving bats and the irreplaceable ecosystem services they provide."

(24) PRESIDENT-GEORGE-W: The desire by the North Koreans to convince the world that they're in the process of developing a nuclear arsenal is nothing new. I mean, we've known that for a while. And therefore, we *must* continue to work with the neighborhood to convince Kim Jong Il that his decision is an unwise decision.

It is thus crucial to understand that, while there may well be reasons (circumstantial, or other) why the speaker views a particular situation as necessary, these reasons do not automatically constitute the source of the modality. In examples (23) and (24), for instance, what is key is that the necessity ultimately stems from the speaker's personal opinion (and therefore the source is said to be 'discourse-internal'). In both (23) and (24), the scope of the modality is wide (see Chapter 1): the situation referred to in the subclause of purpose is part of the proposition that is modalized, that is, part of the proposition that the speaker argues should necessarily be brought about (the situation of pathogen transfer being an active area of research in order to develop evidence-based policies to minimize risks is necessary, and it is the speaker who considers that this situation should be brought about). In a similar way, in (24) President Bush voices his opinion on the situation that needs to actualize, namely that of the US continuing to work with the neighborhood to convince Kim Jong Il that his decision is an unwise decision. Here again, the proposition in the subclause is part of the situation that the speaker feels should be brought about; this situation is not the source that drives the actualization of the proposition in the main clause.[6]

---

[6] That the subclause situation is included in the proposition that is in the scope of the modal is also clear from the fact that we can provide the following close paraphrase of Bush's statement:

(i) .... And therefore, we must continue to work with the neighborhood *in an effort to* convince Kim Jong Il that his decision is an unwise decision.

In other words, the subclause in (24), which functions as an adverbial Adjunct of the main clause, encodes a situation that, just like the main clause situation, needs to be actualized.

2.5 Rules and regulations

In examples that we classify under 'rules and regulations', the compelling source can be a law, as in (25), household rules, as in (26), or instructions for use, as in (27):

(25) Under RFRA (Religious Freedom Restoration Act), if a law substantially burdens someone's religious practice, the government *must* prove that the burden is necessary to advance a compelling government interest.

(26) The Post welcomes letters up to 150 words on topics of general interest. Letters *must* include full name, home address and day and evening phone numbers. Letters may be edited for length, grammar and accuracy.

(27) After eMule software has been installed in the computer, you *must* close the browser such as Internet Explorer or Firefox and re-open it. After you re-open the browser, under Online Audio download page, just click the eMule download link for any file you would like to download.

This category also encompasses weaker binding forces such as commonly accepted social patterns, or what seems to be morally right:

(28) The United States and the North Atlantic Alliance are probably stronger than ever, so helping the reformers in Russia and in the former Soviet Union is not letting our guard down, it's not doing anything that we shouldn't do. It's doing exactly what we *ought to* be doing.

(29) WALTERS Let me ask each of you very quickly, if a doctor has a patient who is terminally ill, who does want to die, who is mature, who is in sound mind, should that doctor be allowed to help the patient kill himself?
LYNN No, because that would be very bad public policy. Not because it might not be arguably correct in this particular case, but allowing it in this case is going to allow many, many more cases to come to this that ought to have been ministered to, that we *ought to* have served. And if we instead make it easy for people to be dead rather than to be helped, then we will completely discount the possibility of correction

In (28) and (29), it is clearly what is morally right, or what seems ethically sound, that constitutes the driving force and serves as motivation for a specific way of going about things.

2.6 Complications

An important question, in the context of the annotation process, is whether the categories are mutually exclusive.[7] We already touched upon this issue in our discussion of examples (23) and (24). Another case in point is example (30). In this example, the situation seems to be grounded in the context of some institutional rule. This example nevertheless was coded as an instance of 'conditional' source (cf. Section 2.4), since in spite of this general context, the speaker makes it clear that being nominated by a sponsor constitutes the particular condition that needs to be met if one is to apply for a visa.

(30) There are several types of visas in Australia. There are subcategories of subcategories but it's all pretty cut and dry and can be found with ease online. You will definitely *need to* be nominated by a sponsor (an employer) in order to apply for a visa. Contact your local consulate or embassy.

Note that while the main clause situation refers to a condition to be met, it is the subclause situation that we consider to be the 'conditional' source of the necessity: it is what drives the main clause situation. As we observed in Section 2.4, conditional examples are typically associated with a specific temporal order: the proposition in the subclause of purpose is typically posterior to the situation that necessarily needs to be brought about: situation X needs to actualize at time t in order for situation Y to actualize at time $t+1$. This is clearly also the case in the example in (30).

---

[7] This question is not just a valid one for the purposes of annotation. Does it *conceptually* make sense to treat the five kinds of sources discussed here as mutually exclusive? We certainly acknowledge that more than one source may appear to be at stake and that it may be challenging to decide which type we are dealing with. We thus allow for the conceptual possibility that sources are not fully mutually exclusive. Consider the following two (constructed) examples:

(i) If you want to get into the second year of college, you need to study harder.
(ii) You need to study harder! Especially if you want to get into the second year of college.

In (i), there is clearly a conditional source that drives the main clause situation. In (ii), however, we would annotate the same situation as being driven by a discourse-internal source (i.e., coming from the speaker), while the addressee's getting into the second year of college is now offered by the speaker as (just) an extra motivation (in addition to, say, just earning some transferable credits for another first-year programme). It may be clear that the (main-clause) situation of studying harder is also driven, to a certain degree, by a discourse-internal source (the speaker) in (i) and by a condition in (ii). This would then mean that multiple sources can in principle exert their influence at the same time and that deciding which source is the single most important one in a given example sometimes proves difficult, as is witnessed by the less-than-perfect agreement among annotators (cf. Section 3.1).

Another classificatory question is whether conditional sources and rules and regulations should not be regarded as a kind of circumstance. In other words, do 'circumstances' not encompass 'rules and regulations' and 'conditional sources'? While this is a possible approach, we have set apart the latter two categories as they have been argued in the literature to trigger the use of a specific modal, and it is hypotheses of the kind that will be tested in the empirical study described in the next section.

3 Source and necessity modals: empirical analysis

3.1 Data and methods

Our aim is to identify potential correlations between SOURCE and root necessity verbs. We are interested to find out if specific modal verbs are typically attracted to or repelled by specific sources. The REM dataset extracted from COCA, and described in Chapter 1, served as the basis for the analysis. It contains around 500 tokens of each of the necessity modals *must*, *have to*, *need to*, *ought to* and *should*. Epistemic uses were excluded from the analysis.[8] Each example was annotated in terms of one of the five categories presented in the previous section. The distribution of sources within the selected sample is shown in Table 1.

SOURCE is a semantico-pragmatic feature: the linguistic co-text as well as the extra-linguistic context needs to be taken into account to identify the source of the necessity. For that reason, the initial classification, inspired by previous descriptions, was put to an extensive qualitative data test. Four subsets of 100 examples

---

8 As a result, the totals (which are lower than 500) in Table 1 correspond to the number of root uses of each verb. Epistemic modality (see Chapter 1, Section 2.1) is inherently 'subjective' (that is, 'discourse-internal' in terms of the classification used here (see Section 2.2)), as it is by definition the speaker's judgment about the likelihood that something is the case. (Lyons has argued for a distinction between '*subjective* epistemic modality' and '*objective* epistemic modality' (Lyons 1977), but his definitions of 'subjective' and 'objective' are different from ours.) We did not include the tokens that express epistemic necessity for several reasons. First, the nature of the modality is clearly different: root modality is concerned with the actualization of a situation. Second, since *have to*, *must*, *ought to* and *should* can communicate epistemic meaning, an inherently subjective source cannot function as a predictive factor for the choice of (epistemic) necessity verbs. The removal of the epistemic data therefore enables us to pin down more clearly any attraction between 'discourse-internal source' and root uses of necessity verbs. With respect to the *have to* sample, there were 13 sentences with root (*have*) *got to/gotta* which were not taken into account in the analysis either. As for *need to*, this is a shorthand here for both the semi-modal *need to* itself and the peripheral modal need, the latter of which is instantiated in our dataset by only about twenty tokens.

Table 1: Distribution of sources in the REM dataset (root necessity).

	subject-internal	discourse-internal	circumstantial	conditional	rules & regulations	Total
must	1 (0.3%)	84 (23.5%)	128 (35.8%)	69 (19.8%)	76 (21.2%)	358
have to	6 (1.4%)	77 (18.7%)	272 (63%)	45 (10.4%)	28 (6.5%)	428
need to	4 (1.2%)	96 (19.7%)	283 (57.2%)	95 (18.9%)	16 (3.1%)	494
ought to	0	223 (48.3%)	192 (41.6%)	22 (4.8%)	25 (5.4%)	462
should	0	174 (38.1%)	202 (44.2%)	42 (9.2%)	39 (8.5%)	457
						2,199

randomly selected from the REM dataset, epistemic uses included, were coded by three different annotators. The first two sets were used to make the guidelines more explicit and to determine the exact contours of each category. The final two sets were used to calculate kappa scores and in this way to check the rate of agreement among the three annotators. Kappa scores are considered to be a more trustworthy measure than percent agreement calculation, as they take into account agreement occurring by chance. More specifically, we used Randolph's (free-marginal) kappa score (Randolph 2008), which is a statistical method that allows researchers to measure multi-rater agreement when "raters do not know a priori the quantities of cases that should be distributed into each category" (Randolph 2005: 3), as is the case in our study. The kappa scores for the final two sets ranged from 0.57 (65.83% agreement) to 0.66 (73% agreement), which means that there is moderate to substantial agreement (cf. Landis and Koch 1977: 165) and, accordingly, that the feature can be exploited for corpus analysis. Finally, the REM dataset was coded in terms of SOURCE by one annotator.

For the purposes of the statistical analysis, we removed data points where the value of source was 'subject-internal'. This is because we only found 11 examples in that category (out of 2199, cf. Table 1), distributed across *must*, *have* to and *need to*, and because some modals have zero instances of this type of source.[9]

---

[9] One of the reviewers mentions two factors that might explain the low number of 'subject-internal' examples in our data set. First, their hypothesis being that 'subject-internal' source is more typical of the spoken register, they argue that our data points might not be distributed evenly across genres (with the spoken genre being under-represented), which would explain the results. The REM data set is well-balanced between different genres and spoken is even not particularly under-represented (NEWS: 16.9%; FIC: 19.7%; MAG 18.2%; SPOK 25.1%; ACAD 20.3%). Second, the reviewer also shares their intuition that 'subject-internal' source might be typical of the forms (*have*) *got to* and *gotta*, which were excluded from the analysis (cf. footnote 8). However, after inspection, none of the 17 instances of (*have*) *got to/gotta* in our dataset have a 'subject-internal' source. Neither hypothesis can thus explain the low number of examples with a 'subject-internal' source.

3.2 Quantitative overview

Using the vcd package in R (R Core Team 2018), we found that the distribution between the choice of modal and type of source is not random: $\chi^2(12) = 300.54$, $p < 0.001$. The effect size is moderate: Cramér's V = 0.214. We then calculated Pearson residuals, visualized in Figure 1, in order to determine the contribution of each cell to the overall significance and to identify individual directions of deviation (i.e. attraction or repulsion).

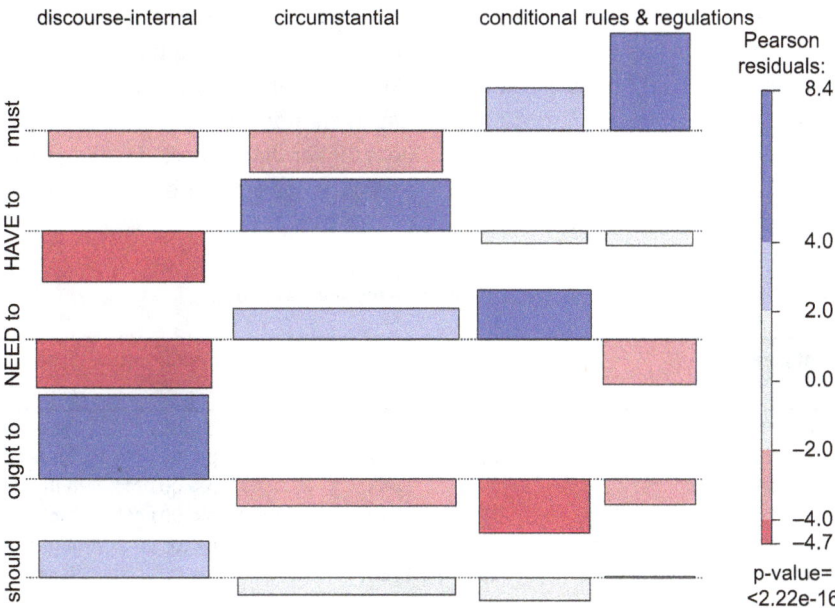

Figure 1: Residual-based association plot of five necessity modals by source.

Bars appearing above the dotted line next to a modal point to an association (i.e. attraction) between that modal and the source indicated at the top, compared to the other modals; bars below the dotted line indicate that the modal and the source are typically not associated (i.e., there is repulsion). The higher up or deeper down the bars reach, and the darker their filling is, the more strongly the observed value deviates from the expected value. (The width of a bar corresponds to the squared root of the expected value in a cell. This is related to the different numbers of tokens for each modal in the data set, as well as to the different number of tokens for each particular type of source in it.)

Figure 1 enables us to make a number of generalizations about the impact of SOURCE on the choice of modal necessity verb. We will discuss each of them in turn in Section 3.3. Before doing so, we need to complement our quantitative analysis with the following two observations.

First, it is important to bear in mind that the association plot in Figure 1 only shows the contribution of each cell to the overall significance of deviation. It does not tell us whether the deviation (from the expected value) of a given cell reaches significance or not, however. That is, it does not tell us which of the individual patterns of attraction/repulsion shown are indeed significant. The height of a bar and its hue may provide strong clues, but this needs to be statistically verified as well. We checked this in R (using the cfa package) with a two-level *configural frequency analysis* (Von Eye et al. 2013). The results of this analysis are reported in Table 2. In this table, significant patterns of deviation (p < 0.05) are called 'types' when the value is higher than expected (i.e., in cases of attraction) and 'anti-types' when the value is lower than expected (i.e., in cases of repulsion).

Table 2: Configural frequency analysis of five necessity modals by source.

Configuration	Obs.freq	Exp.freq	Chi.squared	Significance	Type vs. anti-type
Must – 'rules & regulations'	76	30.0219	70.4146	p < .001 ***	Type
Ought to – 'discourse-internal'	223	138.0932	52.2050	p < .001 ***	Type
Ought to – 'conditional'	22	57.6444	22.0407	p < .001 ***	Anti-type
Have to – 'circumstantial'	272	207.7212	19.8909	p < .001 ***	Type
Have to – 'discourse-internal'	77	126.1371	19.1415	p < .001 ***	Anti-type
Need to – 'conditional'	95	61.1380	18.7548	p < .001 ***	Type
Need to – 'discourse-internal'	96	146.4625	17.3875	p < .001 ***	Anti-type
Need to – 'rules & regulations'	16	41.2066	15.4192	p < .01 **	Anti-type
Must – 'conditional'	69	44.5434	13.4279	p < .01 **	Type
Must – 'circumstantial'	128	175.7262	12.9622	p < .01 **	Anti-type
Should – 'discourse-internal'	174	136.5987	10.2406	p < .05 *	Type
Need to – 'circumstantial'	283	241.1929	7.2466	n.s.	NA
Ought to – 'circumstantial'	192	227.4104	5.5138	n.s.	NA
Ought to – 'rules & regulations'	25	38.8519	4.9386	n.s.	NA
Must – 'discourse-internal'	84	106.7084	4.8325	n.s.	NA
Should – conditional'	42	57.0206	3.9568	n.s.	NA
Should – 'circumstantial'	202	224.9493	2.3413	n.s.	NA
Have to – 'rules & regulations'	28	35.4881	1.5800	n.s.	NA
Have to – 'conditional'	45	52.6536	1.1125	n.s.	NA
Should – 'rules & regulations'	39	38.4314	0.0084	n.s.	NA

Table 2 indicates, for instance, that there is significant attraction between *must* and 'rules and regulations', as one may have predicted from the dark blue box in Figure 1. It also shows that *need to* is not significantly attracted to circumstantial source, however, unlike what the light blue box in Figure 1 may seem to suggest. It is therefore mostly the figures in Table 2 that will inform our discussion in Section 3.3 below.

Second, note that *have to* and *need to* are lexical verbs that are quite frequently considered to be suppletive forms of *must*, *should* and *ought to* in the past (i.e., *had to*, *needed to*) and the future (i.e., *will have to*, *will need to*). These forms were included in the analysis presented here. It could of course be argued that this may have an impact on the interpretation of our results, in the sense that these forms dilute the contrasts that we are trying to establish among necessity verbs. We have reasons to believe that our analysis is fully justified, however. Even though they are the only available forms in the past and the future, the two verbs that have these forms do not merely serve as formal substitutes in those contexts. If they did, then they should have the same semantico-pragmatic profiles as the verbs that they supposedly represent. That is, the two lexical verbs should be associated with the exact same sources as the three auxiliaries which they are said to stand for (i.e., as we will see, with 'discourse-internal' for *ought to*, with 'conditional' for *must* and with 'rules and regulations' again for *must*). Yet, this is not the case. To see this let us look at the patterns which emerge from Figure 1 and Table 2. It can be observed that *have to* and *need to* have distinct patterns of attraction, compared to the other modals. The verb *have to*, for instance, shows significant attraction to a 'circumstantial' source, which none of the other modal verbs do. This suggests that *have to* has its own pragmatic profile. This claim holds when we analyze the non-present-tense and present-tense uses of the verb separately. In fact, as shown in Figure 2 below, the non-present-tense uses of the verb (row 'S.HAVE to', where 'S' stands for 'suppletive') appear to contribute to a greater extent to the verb's overall attraction to 'circumstantial' source than the present-tense uses (row 'NS. HAVE to', with 'NS' for 'non-suppletive'). It is therefore warranted to keep the (so-called) 'suppletive' uses of *have to* in our analysis. In the case of *need to*, the story is different, as it does indeed compete with *must* in the context of a 'conditional' source. However, Figure 2 reveals that the attraction of *need to* to 'conditional' source does not vary depending on the form ('suppletive' or not) that the verb takes. (This observation is supported by the results of a distinct CFA test, cf. Table 4 in the appendix.) This suggests that *need to* has a homogeneous pragmatic profile across all contexts of use, and that the generalizations made previously apply to all uses of the modal verb. In keeping with the choice to include 'suppletive' forms of *have to*, it also makes sense to keep 'suppletive' forms of *need to*.

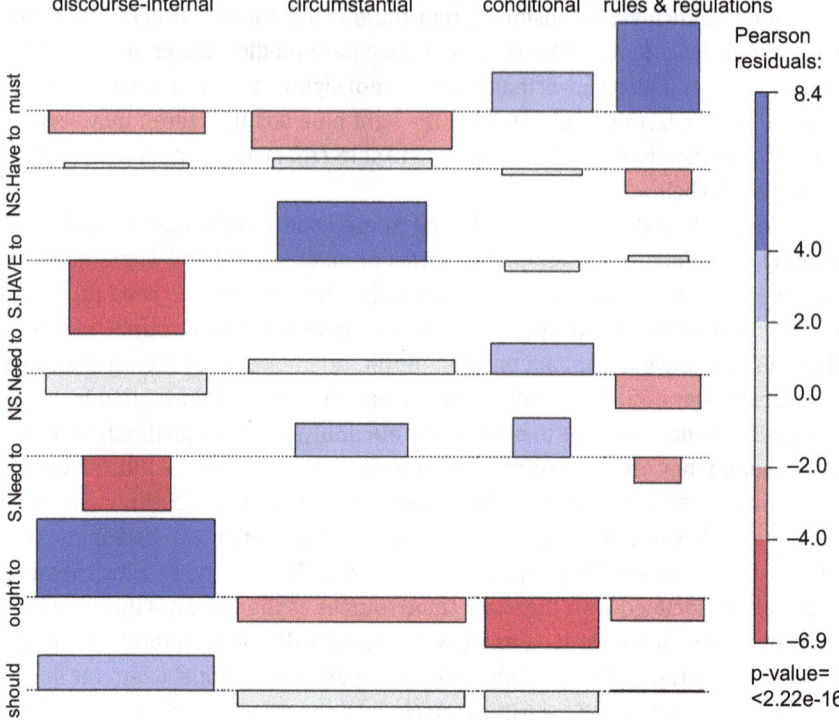

Figure 2: Residual-based association plot (with 'suppletive' vs. 'non-suppletive' forms) of five necessity modals by source.[10]

On the basis of the different observations made in this section, we will now turn to a more qualitative analysis of our data.

3.3 Analysis of the results

First, the verb *must* is especially used in the context of 'rules and regulations' (examples (31) and (32)) and it is also typically used in conditional contexts (examples (33) and (34)); it is typically not used with circumstantial sources.

---

10 Note that individual association plots with only the 'non-suppletive' and 'suppletive' uses of the verbs were also drawn. These can be found in the appendix (as Figures 3 and 4, respectively). They show more clearly the unique contribution of each type of use to the overall attraction of the quasi-modal verbs to the different sources and they corroborate our findings.

(31) In Michigan, for instance, death certificates *must* be certified not only by a doctor but also by a funeral director, and then the body must remain "under the supervision of a person licensed to practice mortuary science in this state."

(32) To be eligible, the home purchase must be an individual's principal residence. Homebuyers cannot claim the credit if the home is a vacation home or rental property. The "main home" *must* be where residents spend 50 percent or more of their time.

(33) As the craft approaches Jupiter, the sunlight reaching Rosetta's solar panels dwindles to just a fraction of its strength near Earth. To preserve power (and to weather funding cuts in Europe), Rosetta *must* go into hibernation for the final third of its trip.

(34) It is important to note that within Native American communities, there are a number of specific subgroups, each presenting unique issues that *must* be addressed if culturally appropriate and effective approaches to HIV/AIDS prevention and intervention are to be developed.

These findings are somewhat unexpected as *must* has been argued to be typically 'subjective' (cf. Coates 1983: 37, Quirk et al. 1985: 225, Tagliamonte and Smith 2006: 363, Larreya and Rivière 2019: 101).[11] Interestingly though, Palmer (1990: 36, 70), Huddleston and Pullum et al. (2002: 181), Leech (2004: 86–87) and Collins (2009: 35) have observed that *must* has 'subjective' as well as 'objective' uses. Our dataset confirms the latter view and shows that a finer-grained taxonomy of sources can shed new light on the typical contexts of use: it is not the discourse-oriented use of *must* that stands out; rather, *must* is preferably used in 'rules and regulations' contexts and conditional contexts. The latter two are 'sources' that have been less in the foreground in discussions about the semantic profile of modal verbs; our findings show that they are relevant categories.

Second, our data suggest that *have to*, compared to the other modals, is typically used with a circumstantial source (cf. examples (35) and (36)) and typically disprefers a discourse-internal source.

---

11 In their corpus-based grammar, Biber et al. (2021) also find that *must* is typically not 'subjective', which they too find intriguing given the "expectation of personal involvement" (Biber et al. 2021: 493) usually associated with the verb.

(35) His father dropped his voice, changed the tone, so Jack Peter *had to* creep closer to the register.

(36) Steinhart has received so many complaints about their treatment of the dolphins that they've *had to* post a notice trying to assure the public that the dolphins were born in captivity and that everything is somehow OK because of it.

The results confirm observations in the literature to the effect that *have to* expresses circumstantial necessity: Coates (1983: 55), Perkins (1983), Huddleston and Pullum et al. (2002: 206), for instance, have argued that *have to* is "objective" (see also Sweetser 1990: 53): "*Have* and *have got* are most commonly used for deontic necessity [. . .]. Here they characteristically differ from *must* in being objective rather than subjective" (Huddleston and Pullum et al. 2002: 206). Similar observations are also made by Quirk et al. (1985: 225–226), who also contrast *have (got) to* and *must*: "Thus *must*, unlike *have (got) to*, typically suggests that the speaker is exercising his authority. [. . .] In the obligation sense [. . .], *have (got) to* is often felt to be more impersonal than *must*, in that it tends to lack the implication that the speaker is in authority." Tredidgo (1982: 81) writes that this modal verb is not 'subjective' (he uses the term 'speaker-oriented') and Larreya and Rivière (2019: 133) qualify this verb as expressing "neutral necessity", that is, necessity that is "independent of the speaker" (our translation, "nécessité vue comme neutre (indépendante de l'énonciateur)"). Moreover, our findings point to repulsion between *have to* and discourse-internal sources, compared to the other four modals.

Third, compared to the other four necessity verbs, *need to* is especially used with a conditional source (examples (37) and (38)); it is typically not used with rules and regulations or, especially, a discourse-internal source.[12]

(37) What behaviors do choral music educators *need to* exhibit in order to create an atmosphere in the choral rehearsal that motivates students to learn?

---

[12] The fact that *need to* is typically not used with a discourse-internal source is at odds with the hypothesis about the semantic profile of *need to* (compared to *must* and *have (got) to*) in Scottish Standard English (SSE) and Southern British Standard English (SBSE) which is put forward by Schützler and Herzky (2021).

(38) But they really feel like they want to have this thing signed by the president by the State of the Union address, which is in late January. To do that, certain things have to happen at certain times. They *need to* pass it through the Senate by the end of the year. And, then, of course, there is going to be an agreement between the House and the Senate. They need to pull that off. And then the two Houses have to vote again in January.

Interestingly, we found observations in two grammars written in the 1990s (Declerck 1991: 386, Dekeyser et al. 1999) to the effect that "that *need to* in affirmative sentences [. . .] mostly emphasizes what is required for a specific purpose" (Dekeyser et al. 1999: 111). In general, though, this context of use is not in the foreground in discussions about *need to*. *Need to* has been described in the literature in terms of "internal compulsion" (Nokkonen 2006, Collins 2009: 73), "participant-internal *need to*" (Van der Auwera and Plungian 1998, Nokkonen 2010) (see also Smith 2003: 244–245), and "self-motivated obligation" (Schützler and Herzky 2021: 20). A lot depends of course on how concepts like these are interpreted (see Depraetere 2022 for discussion). However, the dataset first and foremost shows that, if it is supposed to capture a source that lies within the reference of the grammatical subject, such a source is not typical of the semantico-pragmatic profile of *need to* (or any other modal verb of necessity, for that matter).

It follows from our empirical observations that *need to* competes with *must* in the case of conditional sources. Further multifactorial analyses (e.g. of the kind implemented in Hohaus 2020, whose work is focused on modal verbs in syntactically dependent contexts) are needed to determine which other factors differentiate the contexts of use of both verbs. The formal profile of these verbs, such as the fact that *need to*, unlike *must*, is a lexical verb that can be inflected for future-time and past-time reference, could be a potential important factor. However, as observed in Section 3.2, the CFA analysis does not confirm this hypothesis.

Finally, *ought to* is typically used with a discourse-internal source (examples (39) and (40)); it is typically not used with a conditional source. *Should* is also typically used with a discourse-internal source (examples (41) and (42)), but this preference is less pronounced. In this data set, *should*, unlike *ought to*, is only weakly attracted or repelled by the other types of sources.

(39) Maybe so, but now I think we *ought to* accept this change, embrace it, be positive about it because change can be very exciting.

(40) You can't hide this. It's going to come out sooner or later. And people ought to know it and the common people *ought to* be able to make their own judgments.

(41) It's time the Vatican hierarchy remembered that they are there to serve the people, not the other way around. They *should* start by providing an English translation that is literate and understandable.

(42) This image – this is everyday life. This *should* not be on the front page of The New York Times.

These findings put into perspective the views that have been put forward in the literature. *Should* and *ought to* are both classified as 'subjective' by Huddleston and Pullum et al. (2002: 186), but some grammarians claim that *ought to* is more 'objective' than *should*. Consider this quote from Declerck (1991):

> Although *should* and *ought to* are often interchangeable, there is a slight difference of meaning between them. When using *should* the speaker expresses his own subjective view; *ought to* is more objective and is used when the speaker wants to represent something as a law, duty or regulation. For this reason *ought to* may sound more emphatic than *should*.
>
> e.g. You should / ought to congratulate her.
> > I ought to congratulate her, but I don't think I will. (*Should* would sound odd here: it would be strange to give yourself advice and then add that you were not going to follow it).
>
> (Declerck 1991: 377, fn. 21)

Similar statements can be found in Swan (1980: 550) and Larreya and Rivière (2019: 130). Collins (2009: 45) writes that *should* can be both 'subjective' and 'objective', but also adds that "[e]ven in those instances where *should* expresses the desirability of an action deriving not from the speaker, or from some moral or legal consideration, but merely from circumstantial expediency [. . .], we understand the action to be recommended by the speaker or by some external body representing the deontic source" (2009: 44).

Given that, compared to the four other necessity modals, *should* is not significantly repelled by circumstantial and conditional sources, and not repelled at all by 'rules and regulations' (cf. e.g. instructions like *All abstracts should be submitted electronically through the abstract submission system*), it is clearly more objective than *ought to*, which, in comparison, shows clear repulsion of circumstantial and conditional sources and 'rules and regulations' (see e.g. Close 1981: 120–122, Westney 1995: 172 and Cappelle and De Sutter 2010: 117–118, for discussion of 'rules and regulations' examples).

As in the case of the overlapping typical contexts of use of *must* and *need to* referred to above, we should take into account a wider range of factors to pin down additional differentiating features between the contexts of use of *should* and *ought to*. Previous studies have identified a number of factors that could play a role: Cappelle and De Sutter (2010) looked into twenty-six potential predictors and found that among the most significant ones in British English, there are many that relate to the fact that *should*, as a core modal, is syntactically different from *ought*, which takes a *to*-infinitive. Thus, *should* much more easily undergoes inversion (cp. *Should we do that?* vs. *Ought we to do that?*), is far more often followed by the contracted form of the perfect auxiliary (cp. *You should've had more sense* vs. *You ought to've had more sense*), more often occurs with an adverb, if present, right after it (cp. *You should probably ignore this* vs. *You ought probably to ignore this*), and more often uses negation with *not* or *-n't* (cp. *We shouldn't do this* vs. *We oughtn't to do this*). Other factors include the use of the modal for past-time reference, in which case *ought to* but not *should* is acceptable (e.g., *She told me I {ought to / ??should} go, so I said goodbye and left*) and, in case the modalized proposition is embedded, the semantics of the subordinating verb (e.g. *should* is less often used than *ought to* in the complement clause of a cognition verb, which again undermines the claim that it is more subjective than *ought to*). Verhulst, Depraetere and Heyvaert (2013) have argued that it is important to look at who/what the actualized situation is beneficial to. Their hypothesis is that in the case of *ought to*, it is typically someone other than the discourse-internal source who benefits from the actualization of the situation, as in the examples below:

(43) If people have any questions on individual presentations then I think we *ought to* take those questions while the group is up here. (2013: 216)

(44) If we're to take this motion seriously, the Tories are suggesting that council housing should be restricted to those most in need. Now on the face of that, that seems fairly sensible, y'know – If somebody is in need we *ought to* be doing something about it. (2013: 217)

4 Conclusion

In this chapter, we have addressed the semantico-pragmatic feature of SOURCE. This notion is present in discussions about the semantic profile of modal verbs, but it has not been systematically applied to a range of root necessity verbs on the basis of extensive corpus annotation. We have shown how 'source' can be exploited in quantitative corpus analysis. First, we have illustrated the five types of source in our classification and we have made explicit the ways in which they were operationalized as non-overlapping subcategories. Given the fact that SOURCE is a qualitative notion, there is room for interpretation. The results of the interrater reliability tests have shown that SOURCE is a concept that can be used to identify significant differences in the distribution of modal verbs.

The patterns observed can be summarized as follows. *Must* is especially frequently embedded in 'rules and regulations' contexts and it is also attracted to conditional source contexts. *Have to* usually has a circumstantial source and is not often used when there is a discourse-internal source. *Need to* is especially attracted to conditional sources and also to circumstantial ones; it is repelled by discourse-internal sources and, to a slightly lesser extent, by rules and regulations. Finally, *should* and (particularly) *ought to* are typically used with a discourse-internal source, while the latter modal is not often used with any of the other sources, especially conditional ones.

Presenting the findings from a different perspective, for each kind of source (apart from the very infrequently attested subject-internal source) there is a different modal that is associated with it most strongly (cf. Table 3):

Table 3: Four kinds of sources and the necessity modal most strongly associated with them.

Source	Most strongly associated modal	Example
Rules and regulations	must	CFLs must be properly recycled.
Conditional	need to	If you want to succeed, you need to do this.
Discourse-internal	ought to	I think we ought to call it a day here.
Circumstantial	have to	Something's come up back in Vance Township. I'm afraid I have to leave.

Should is not associated with any of these sources more strongly than any of the other modals. However, it does come close to *ought to* in also showing significant preference for a discourse-internal source (*You should be thanking me*).

We have shown that some, but not all of these conclusions, resonate with the characterization of the various verbs in previous work. Furthermore, while SOURCE is a useful concept to explain the choice of modal verb, the conclusions show that it is not the only motivating factor. In other words, while the analysis has brought to light significant patterns, a multifactorial approach of the kind presented in the previous chapter is necessary to complement the analysis.

Appendix

Table 4: Configural frequency analysis of five necessity modals by source (suppletive vs. non-suppletive forms).

Configuration	Obs.freq	Exp.freq	Chi.squared	Significance	Type vs. anti-type
Must – 'rules & regulations'	76	30.0219	70.4146	$p < .001$ ***	type
Ought to – 'discourse-internal'	223	138.0932	52.2050	$p < .001$ ***	type
S.HAVE to – 'discourse-internal'	6	58.5850	47.1995	$p < .001$ ***	anti-type
S.HAVE to – 'circumstantial'	151	96.4771	30.8129	$p < .001$ ***	type
S.NEED to – 'discourse-internal'	4	33.7761	26.2498	$p < .001$ ***	anti-type
Ought to – 'conditional'	22	57.6444	22.0407	$p < .001$ ***	anti-type
S.NEED to – 'conditional'	28	14.0992	13.7053	$p < .01$ **	type
Must – 'conditional'	69	44.5434	13.4279	$p < .01$ **	type
Must – 'circumstantial'	128	175.7262	12.9622	$p < .01$ **	anti-type
Should – 'discourse-internal'	174	136.5987	10.2406	$p < .05$ *	type
NS.NEED to – 'rules & regulations'	14	31.7038	9.8861	$p < .05$ *	anti-type
S.NEED to – 'circumstantial'	79	55.6220	9.8258	$p < .05$ *	type
NS.NEED to – 'conditional'	67	47.0388	8.4706	n.s.	n.s.
S.NEED to – 'rules & regulations'	2	9.5027	5.9237	n.s.	n.s.
Ought to – 'circumstantial'	192	227.4104	5.5138	n.s.	n.s.
NS.HAVE to – 'rules & regulations'	9	19.0055	5.2674	n.s.	n.s.
Ought to – 'rules & regulations'	25	38.8519	4.9386	n.s.	n.s.
Must – 'discourse-internal'	84	106.7084	4.8325	n.s.	n.s.
Should – 'conditional'	42	57.0206	3.9568	n.s.	n.s.
NS.NEED to – 'discourse-internal'	92	112.6865	3.7975	n.s.	n.s.
Should – 'circumstantial'	202	224.9493	2.3413	n.s.	n.s.
NS.NEED to – 'circumstantial'	204	185.5708	1.8302	n.s.	n.s.
NS.HAVE to – 'circumstantial'	121	111.2441	0.8556	n.s.	n.s.

Table 4 (continued)

Configuration	Obs.freq	Exp.freq	Chi.squared	Significance	Type vs. anti-type
S.HAVE to – 'conditional'	20	24.4552	0.8116	n.s.	n.s.
S.HAVE to – 'rules & regulations'	19	16.4826	0.3845	n.s.	n.s.
NS.HAVE to – 'conditional'	25	28.1984	0.3628	n.s.	n.s.
NS.HAVE to – 'discourse-internal'	71	67.5521	0.1760	n.s.	n.s.
Should – 'rules & regulations'	39	38.4314	0.0084	n.s.	n.s.

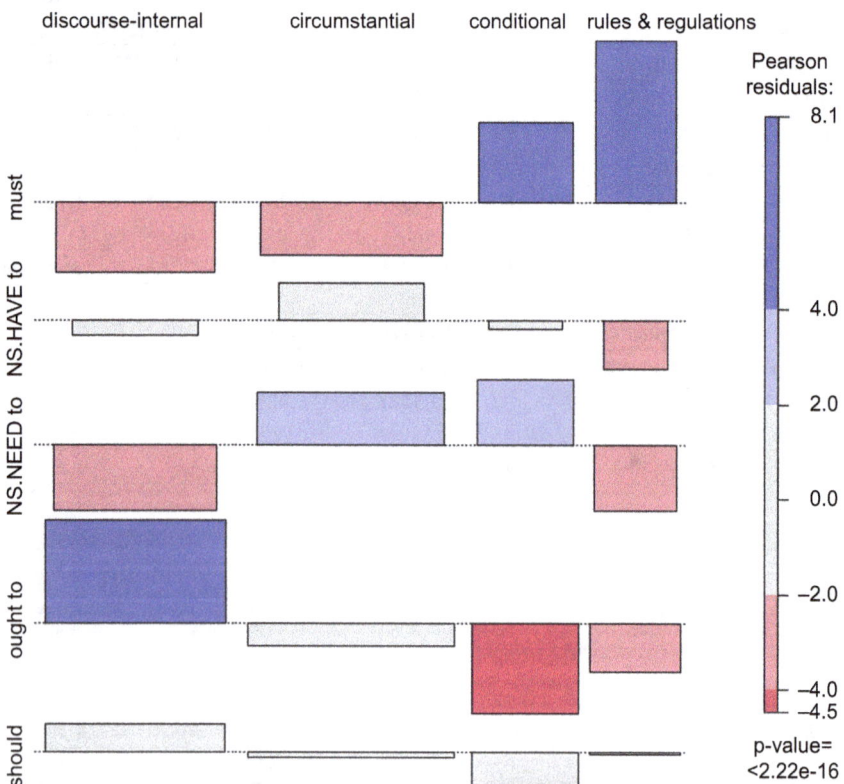

Figure 3: Residual-based association plot of five necessity modals by source ('non-suppletive' forms).

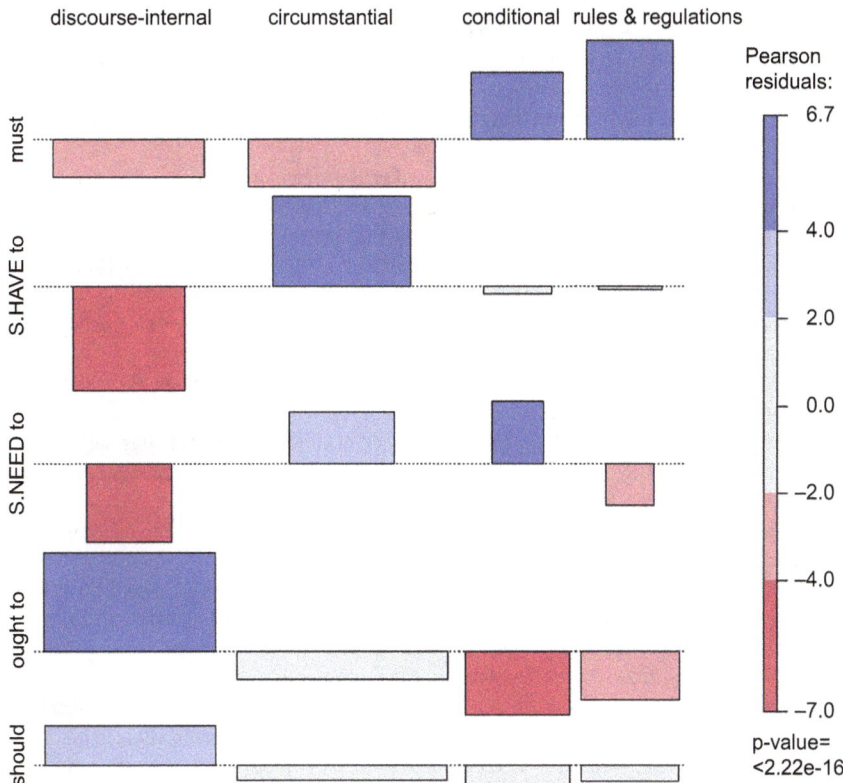

Figure 4: Residual-based association plot of five necessity modals by source ('suppletive forms').

References

Biber, Douglas, Stig Johansson, Geoffrey Leech, Susan Conrad & Edward Finegan. 2021. [1999] *Grammar of Spoken and Written English*, 2nd edn. Amsterdam: John Benjamins.
Bybee, Joan, Revere Perkins & William Pagliuca. 1994. *The Evolution of Grammar: Tense, Aspect and Modality in the Languages of the World*. Chicago: University of Chicago Press.
Cappelle, Bert & Gert De Sutter. 2010. *Should* vs. *ought to*. In Bert Cappelle & Naoaki Wada (eds.), *Distinctions in English Linguistics, Offered to Renaat Declerck*, 92–126. Tokyo: Kaitakusha.
Close, Reginald A. 1981. [1962] *English as a Foreign Language: Its Constant Grammatical Problems*. 3rd edn. London: George Allen & Unwin.
Coates, Jennifer. 1983. *The Semantics of the Modal Auxiliaries*. London/Canberra: Croom Helm.
Collins, Peter. 2009. *Modals and Quasi-modals in English*. Amsterdam/New York: Rodopi.
Cruse, Alan. 1973. Some thoughts on agentivity. *Journal of Linguistics* 9. 11–23.

Declerck, Renaat. 1991. *A Comprehensive Grammar of English*. Tokyo: Kaitakusha.
Dekeyser, Xavier, Betty Devriendt, Steven Geukens & Guy Tops. 1999. *Foundations of English Grammar*. Leuven/Amersfoort: Acco.
Depraetere, Ilse. 2014. Modals and lexically-regulated saturation. *Journal of Pragmatics* 7. 160–177.
Depraetere, Ilse. 2015. Categorization principles of modal meaning categories: a critical assessment. *Anglophonia* 19. https://doi.org/10.4000/anglophonia.476
Depraetere, Ilse. 2022. Sources of modal necessity: the case of *'need to'*. *English Language and Linguistics*. https://journals.sagepub.com/doi/10.1177/00754242221124129. [Online first version]
Depraetere, Ilse & Chad Langford. 2020. [2011] *Advanced English Grammar: A Linguistic Approach*. 2nd edn. London and New York: Continuum.
Depraetere, Ilse & Susan Reed. 2011. Towards a more explicit taxonomy of root possibility in English. *English Language and Linguistics* 15(1). 1–29.
Depraetere, Ilse & Susan Reed. 2021. [2006] Mood and modality in English, In Bas Aarts, Lars Hinrichs & April McMahon (eds.), *The Handbook of English Linguistics*, 207–227. 2nd edn. Oxford/Malden, MA: Wiley-Blackwell.
Depraetere, Ilse & Ann Verhulst. 2008. Source of modality: a reassessment. *English Language and Linguistics* 12(1). 1–25.
Diewald, Gabriele, 2001. A basic semantic template for lexical and grammaticalized uses of the German modals. In Johan van der Auwera & Patrick Dendale (eds.), *Modal Verbs in Germanic and Romance Languages*, 23–41. Amsterdam: John Benjamins.
Furmaniak, Grégory. 2020. On the (con)textual properties of *must, have to* and *shall*: An integrative account. In Pascal Hohaus & Rainer Schulze (eds.), *Re-assessing Modalising Expressions: Categories, Co-text and Context*, 281–310. Amsterdam: John Benjamins.
Goossens, Louis. 2000. Patterns of meaning extension, 'parallel chaining', subjectification, and modal shifts. In Antonio Barcelona (ed.), *Metaphor and Metonymy at the Crossroads: A Cognitive Perspective*, 149–169. Berlin: Mouton de Gruyter.
Heine, Bernd. 1995. Agent-oriented vs. epistemic modality: Some observations on German modals. In Joan Bybee & Suzanne Fleischman (eds.), *Modality in Grammar and Discourse*, 17–53. Amsterdam: John Benjamins.
Hohaus, Pascal. 2020. S*ubordinating Modalities. A Quantitative Analysis of Syntactically Dependent Modal Verb Constructions*. Berlin: J.B. Metzler.
Hoye, Leo. 1997. *Adverbs and Modality in English*. London/New York: Longman.
Huddleston, Rodney & Geoffrey K. Pullum et al. 2002. *The Cambridge Grammar of the English Language*. Cambridge: Cambridge University Press.
Jespersen, Otto. 1924. *The Philosophy of Grammar*. London: Allen and Unwin.
Kratzer, Angelika. 1977. What 'must' and 'can' must and can mean. *Linguistics and Philosophy* 1. 337–355.
Kratzer, Angelika. 1981. The notional category of modality. In Hans-Jürgen Eikmeyer & Hannes Rieser (eds.), *Words, Worlds, and Contexts*, 38–74. Berlin: Mouton de Gruyter.
Kratzer, Angelika. 1991. Modality. In Arnim von Stechow & Dieter Wunderlich (eds.), *Semantics: An International Handbook of Contemporary Research*, 639–650. Berlin: Mouton de Gruyter.
Landis, Richard & Gary Koch. 1977. The measurement of observer agreement for categorical data. *Biometrics* 33. 159–174.

Larreya, Paul & Claude Rivière. 2019. [1996] *Grammaire Explicative De L'anglais*. 5th edn. France: Pearson Education.
Leech, Geoffrey N. 2004 [1971]. *Meaning and the English Verb*. 3rd edn. New York: Longman.
Lyons, John. 1977. *Semantics*. Cambridge: Cambridge University Press.
Myhill, John. 1995. Change and continuity in the function of the American modals. *Linguistics* 33. 157–211.
Narrog, Heiko. 2012. *Modality, Subjectivity, and Semantic Change. A Cross-linguistic Perspective*. Oxford: Oxford University Press.
Nokkonen, Soili. 2006. The semantic variation of NEED TO in four recent British English corpora. *International Journal of Corpus Linguistics* 11. 29–71.
Nokkonen, Soili. 2010. How many taxis there needs to be? The sociolinguistic variation of need to in spoken British English. Corpora 5(1): 45–74.
Nokkonen, Soili. 2017. Modals of obligation in dialogic registers of British English. In Juan Rafael Zamorano-Mansilla, Carmen Maíz, Elena Domínguez & Victoria Martín De la Rosa (eds.), *Thinking Modally: English and Contrastive Studies on Modality*, 47–76. Newcastle upon Tyne: Cambridge Scholars Publishing.
Nuyts, Jan. 2005. The modal confusion: On terminology and the concepts behind it. In Alex Klinge & Henrik Høeg Müller (eds.), *Modality: Studies in Form and Function*, 5–38. London: Equinox.
Nuyts, Jan. 2012. Notions of (inter)subjectivity. *English Text Construction* 5(1). 53–76.
Palmer, Frank. 1990 [1979]. *Modality and the English Modals*. 2nd edn. London: Longman.
Palmer, Frank. 2001 [1986]. *Mood and Modality*. 2nd ed. Cambridge: Cambridge University Press.
Quirk, Randolph, Sidney Greenbaum, Geoffrey Leech & Jan Svartvik. 1985. *A Comprehensive Grammar of the English Language*. London: Longman.
R Core Team. 2018. R version 3.5.0. R: A language and environment for statistical computing. R Foundation for Statistical Computing Platform, Vienna, Austria. https://www.R-project.org/.
Randolph, Justus. 2005. Free-marginal multirater kappa: an alternative to Fleiss' fixed-marginal multirater kappa. Paper presented at: *Joensuu University Learning and Instruction Symposium 2005*, Joensuu, Finland, October 14–15.
Randolph, Justus. 2008. Online Kappa Calculator [Computer software]. Retrieved from http://justus.randolph.name/kappa.
Schützler, Ole & Jenny Herzky. 2021. Modal verbs of strong obligation in Scottish Standard English. *English Language and Linguistics*. 1–27.
Smet, Hendrik de & Jean-Christophe Verstraete. 2006. Coming to terms with subjectivity. *Cognitive Linguistics* 17(3). 365–392.
Smith, Nicholas. 2003. Changes in the modals and semi-modals of strong obligation and epistemic necessity in recent British English. In Roberta Facchinetti, Manfred Krug & Frank Palmer (eds.), *Modality in Contemporary English*, 241–266. Berlin: Mouton de Gruyter.
Swan, Michael. 1980. *Practical English Usage*. Oxford: Oxford University Press.
Sweetser, Eve. 1990. *From Etymology to Pragmatics: Metaphorical and Cultural Aspects of Semantic Structure*. Cambridge: Cambridge University Press.
Tagliamonte, Sali & Jennifer Smith. 2006. Layering, competition and a twist of fate: The deontic modality system in English dialects. *Diachronica* 23(2). 341–380.

Tregidgo, Philip. 1982. MUST and MAY: Demand and permission. *Lingua* 56. 75–92.

Van Valin, Robert & David Wilkins. 1996. The case for 'effector': Case roles, agents, and agency revisited. In Masayoshi Shibatani & Sandra Thompson (eds.), *Grammatical Constructions: Their Form and Meaning*, 289–322. Oxford: Clarendon.

van der Auwera, Johan & Vladimir A. Plungian. 1998. Modality's semantic map. *Linguistic Typology* 2. 79–124.

Verhulst, An, Ilse Depraetere & Liesbet Heyvaert. 2013. Source and strength of modality: An empirical study of root *should, ought to* and *be supposed to* in present-day British English. *Journal of Pragmatics* 55. 210–222.

Verhulst, An & Liesbet Heyvaert. 2015. Root modal uses of *should, ought to* and *be supposed to* in present-day English: From patterns and profiles to proficiency guidelines. *English Studies* 96(5). 562–595.

Verstraete, Jean-Christophe. 2001. Subjective and objective modality: Interpersonal and ideational functions in the English modal auxiliary system. *Journal of Pragmatics* 33(10). 1505–1528.

von Eye, Alexander, Eun-Young Mun, Patrick Mair & Stefan von Weber. 2013. Configural frequency analysis. In Todd D. Little (ed.), *The Oxford Handbook of Quantitative Methods: Statistical Analysis*, 74–105. New York: Oxford University Press.

Westney, Paul. 1995. *Modals and Periphrastics in English: An Investigation into the Semantic Correspondence between Certain English Modal Verbs and their Periphrastic Equivalents*. Tübingen: Niemeyer.

Ziegeler, Debra. 2019. Mood and modality. In Bas Aarts, Jill Bowie & Gergana Popova (eds.). *The Oxford Handbook of English Grammar*, 418–438. Oxford: Oxford University Press.

5 You *must*/*have to* choose: Experimenting with choices between near-synonymous modals

Susanne Flach, Bert Cappelle and Martin Hilpert

1 Introduction

English modal auxiliaries are notoriously polyfunctional: most have more than one function – most broadly those of root and epistemic meanings – and the same proposition can be encoded by more than one expression with virtually no change in meaning. In this chapter, we take a closer look at factors that underlie speakers' choices between two near-synonymous modal expressions: how do speakers choose between the root uses of *have to* and *must* as in *You must / have to see this for yourself*?

We approach this question from both a corpus-based and an experimental perspective: do factors that distinguish between both expressions in corpus data also predict preferences in a rating task? Specifically, we address the following: (i) Which of the factors that are frequently discussed in the literature distinguish between the root uses of *have to* and *must* in a regression model of corpus data? (ii) Which of these factors also predict speaker choices in a judgement experiment? And, (iii), where do corpus and experimental data show similar patterns and where do they differ? The last point addresses common questions about the degree to which corpus data allow for insights into the mental representation of linguistic expressions. Most broadly, corpus data provide a window into usage patterns, which generate new hypotheses that can be followed up upon using experimental tasks which aim to tap into more specific questions. However, the set of research questions and the methodological goal of combining corpus and experimental perspectives present specific challenges in the current context, primarily because we are investigating a choice between near-synonymous alternatives, and because factors that influence the choice of a modal expression are of a semantic-pragmatic rather than a phonological, morphological or syntactic nature.

The chapter is organized as follows. We discuss the alternation of *have to* and *must*, the nature of the data set, and the resulting challenges in Section 2. Sections 3 and 4 are dedicated to the corpus analysis and the experiment, respectively. The discussion in Section 5 compares the results of both analyses and discusses our main insight: while some factors that distinguish between the two expressions in corpus data also predict preference ratings in the experiment, most notably the source of modality, this does not hold for other (presumably more latent) factors.

Section 6 concludes with a discussion of the theoretical implications for models of modal auxiliaries in the context of recent dynamic network models.

2 Background

We begin this section by reviewing the alternation of the two root necessity modals *have to* and *must* and where they overlap with regard to the propositions they can express (Section 2.1). We proceed to a discussion of central distinguishing factors that have previously been discussed in the literature (Section 2.2). We conclude the section with remarks on the design and the challenges of the study (Section 2.3).

2.1 Alternating necessity

Among modal expressions, root uses of *have to* and *must* are considered to express "strong obligation", compared to the "medium-strength modality" necessity modals *should, ought to* or *be supposed to* (Depraetere and Verhulst 2008: 14–15, Huddleston and Pullum et al. 2002: 175–177, Verhulst et al. 2013: 211; see also Coates 1983). Between the two, it has been argued that *must* conveys a stronger necessity than *have to* (see the discussion in Chapter 4). However, in most cases, if we come across sentences as in example (1), it is difficult if not impossible to determine which alternative the speaker or writer chose:

(1) If the Tea Party wants to be respected and wants to be part of the mainstream in this country, they { ***have to*** | ***must*** } act in a responsible way. [COCA, NEWS]

With the exception of some formal conditions we discuss below, *have to* and *must* are interchangeable: there are no unambiguous cues as to which modal expression occurs in the original. We may have intuitions, for instance regarding collocational preferences, as dynamic contexts (indicated by the verb *act*) tend to be associated more with *have to* than with *must* (cf. Section 3). On the other hand, we may hypothesize that *must* is more likely in this situation because of the more formal news context (see also Section 3; Chapter 9). Except for formal cases discussed next that exclude alternation, *have to* and *must* in their root meaning are interchangeable without a loss in meaning, and a choice for one or the other is ultimately probabilistic.

To illustrate which contexts and data points we excluded, let us discuss the non-alternating contexts. There are formal, semantic or situational circumstances that either rule out one expression or at least make one option highly unlikely. These include past tense contexts (2a), expressions preceded by a(nother) core modal (2b), inversion, negation and/or *do*-support (2c), idiomatic chunks including binomials (2d) and quasi-fixed expressions (2e):

(2) a. New variables { ***had to*** | ****musted*** } be added. [COCA, MAG]
 b. Then I won't { ***have to*** | ****must*** } ask her – I'll get it out of you. [COCA, FIC]
 c. ... for he { ***must*** | ?***has to*** } never know how ill he was ... [COCA, ACAD]
 d. Brazil can and { ***must*** | ?***has to*** } find a way to balance stability with expansion. [COCA, ACAD]
 e. Do what you { ***must*** | #***have to*** } to get in here. [COCA, FIC]

The contexts in (2a,b) rule out *must* for formal reasons. Example (2c) illustrates that some sentences would have to be rephrased syntactically in order to be conventional with *have to*, likely with a substantial change in meaning (*for he doesn't have to know* ...). Examples (2d,e) illustrate that collocational preferences often make the other option highly unlikely (cf. Cappelle et al. 2019, Hilpert 2016, Flach 2020b). Since non-alternating contexts are not part of our study of near-synonymous expressions, we excluded them from the REM data for the corpus analysis (for a more detailed description of the REM data, see Chapter 1 and Section 3.2 below).

2.2 Factor selection

What determines the choice between *have to* and *must* has been the topic of extensive debate. The source of the modality (here: necessity) is of crucial importance for the profile of root necessity modals (Depraetere and Verhulst 2008). As discussed in depth in Chapter 4, there is a perceived "cause" of the necessary state of affairs in root necessity modals (Lyons 1977: 824). In the REM data set, the factor SOURCE refers to the origin of the necessity, i.e., "'who' or 'what' makes actualization possible or necessary" (Lesuisse et al. 2022: 15). As laid out in Chapter 4, the REM data set distinguishes five levels of SOURCE. In this chapter, for the most part, we collapse SOURCE to two levels, i.e., "rules and regulations" (henceforth 'rule') and "non-rule", illustrated in examples (3) and (4), respectively:

(3) a. I mean, "American Idol" is great, but you ***have to*** be 26 and that's as old as you can be. [COCA, SPOK]
 b. Shallow described a game where, at each round, players ***must*** either double their bet or drop out. [COCA, FIC]

(4) a. And, said the senator: We have to commit ourselves to freedom. But freedom also **has to** be sustainable freedom. [COCA, MAG]
b. This nanorobot **must** be small enough to travel through the blood stream or the smallest capillaries in the human body. [COCA, ACAD]

The non-rule contexts, such as those in in (4), include examples classified as "subject-internal", "discourse-internal", "circumstantial", and "conditional" (see discussion of their details in Chapter 4). Grouping these together is conceptually warranted because the resulting binary distinction best captures the contrast with regard to the deontic source in the context of *have to* and *must*. It is also supported by the corpus analysis in Section 3 below, which shows that *must*, but not *have to*, is associated with "rules and regulations" (see Chapter 4 for similar results). In addition, there are methodological benefits of binary variables, which we will address in more detail in the next subsection. We confine the remainder of this subsection to three related factors that enter into our analyses, namely, PERSON, AGENTIVITY, and GENERICITY.

The category PERSON of the grammatical subject has been discussed extensively in the literature (e.g., Collins 2009, Coates 1983, Cappelle and De Sutter 2010, Nokkonen 2006, Schützler and Herzky 2022, Tagliamonte and Smith 2006, Westney 1995). For example, Collins (2009: 37) reports that more than two thirds of *must* uses occur with a third-person subject, which also correlates with a rule source; Schützler and Herzky (2021) report a similar skew of *must* towards third-person subjects in British English dialects. Coates (1983: 37) remarks that second-person subjects generally occur in utterances with stronger force than first-person subjects, which in turn tend to occur with stronger force than third-person subjects. These earlier results are not directly applicable to the present study, especially in their details, owing to differences in the application of concepts, their operationalization in the annotation and the analysis of the data. However, they do indicate that PERSON is a crucial factor in the paradigmatic choice between *have to* and *must*.

PERSON is related to AGENTIVITY: first- or second-person subjects will usually be animate and hence they are more likely agentive, while third person subjects will also include inanimate and non-agentive referents. Since *have to* and *must* are preferentially used with different persons, the distribution of *have to* and *must* across PERSON and AGENTIVITY will differ; hence we included both factors as predictors of the choice. SOURCE is not unrelated to AGENTIVITY, as the source of the necessity is sometimes tied to the agentivity of the referent of the grammatical subject, namely in the case of subject-internal necessity (cf. Chapter 4; see also Cruse 1973: 18). While Cruse (1973) uses a broader definition of AGENTIVITY than that adopted for the REM data (Lesuisse et al. 2022), both refer to the fact that the referent of the grammatical subject has control over the actualization of the proposition. Consider the agentive context in (5) vs. the non-agentive context in (6):

(5) a. Players ***must*** complete a monthly community service project on a Saturday. [COCA, NEWS]
 b. Almost all residents and nonresidents ***must*** obtain a fishing license before fishing in the public waters of Texas. [COCA, NEWS]

(6) a. Letters ***must*** include full name, home address and day and evening phone numbers. [COCA, NEWS]
 b. ... for he ***must*** never know how ill he was ... [COCA, ACAD]

Agentive contexts as in (5) almost necessarily have an animate subject (robots, self-driving cars, etc. being possible exceptions, but the REM data set does not contain such examples). Non-agentive contexts as in (6) can have either inanimate (6a) or animate subjects (6b); with inanimate referents, the modal complement nearly always consists of an adjectival copula (e.g., *must be* ADJ), a passive (e.g., *the medication must be administered*), or a verb low in agentivity (e.g., *believe, contain, know*).

Finally, PERSON and AGENTIVITY are related to GENERICITY. In a similar vein that there is a connection between PERSON and AGENTIVITY (i.e., first- or second-person subjects are more likely agentive than third-person subjects), there is also a potentially influential distributional pattern between PERSON and GENERICITY. Consider the examples in (7) and (8), illustrating non-generic and generic subjects, respectively:

(7) a. If the Tea Party wants to be respected and wants to be part of the mainstream in this country, they ***have to*** act in a responsible way. [COCA, SPOK]
 b. To enhance provider communication with HIV-positive patients of reproductive age about their reproductive desires and intentions, these gaps ***must*** be addressed. [COCA, ACAD]

(8) a. If teachers want to provide better support for their families, they ***have to*** become principals or leave education entirely. [COCA, ACAD]
 b. To move toward greater health care empowerment the provider ***must*** acknowledge, foster, and respect the patient's autonomy and value to the collaborative [COCA, ACAD]

GENERICITY distinguishes whether a subject is "kind-referring" (generic) or not (non-generic). While this factor does not feature prominently in the debate so far (but see comments on similar concepts such as "habitual reference" or "impersonal *you*" in Nokkonen 2006, Tagliamonte and Smith 2006, Palmer 1990, or Westney 1995), the fact that *have to* emerged historically primarily in generic contexts (Ziegeler 2014) supports the assumption that genericity may have retained some relevance for contemporary use. As the distribution across GENERICITY in the REM data is conspicuous, we include it as a factor; *have to* occurs, in fact, relatively *less* often with generic subjects than *must*. However, it has to be borne in mind that the REM project uses a different operationalization than Ziegeler's work. In the REM data, GENERICITY is coded with regard to the subject referent (Lesuisse et al. 2022), while in Ziegeler (2014: 221) it refers to the situation.

In sum, we included four factors which, apart from AGENTIVITY, have received considerable previous discussion in analyses of modal verb choice. Amongst those, *must* appears to be favored in situations of rule-based contexts, and/or with third-person, non-agentive, and/or generic subjects. As with all monofactorial analyses, it is difficult to determine which factors remain influential when controlled for the other factors in a multifactorial analysis, and how skews in the data affect this influence (e.g., as non-agentive subjects are heavily skewed towards passives and psych verb complementation). In addition, there are several methodological challenges, which we discuss in the next section. We need to remember that, perhaps with the exception of PERSON, all factors are semantic, not formal. We will return to this issue in Section 5.

2.3 Methodological approaches and challenges

One aim of our study is to combine an observational and an experimental perspective by using stimuli that are modelled on factors that account for speaker choices in production, i.e., factors found significant in corpus data. One challenge is that conflicting requirements and limitations of both methodologies have to be reconciled. Usage data is messy and distributionally highly skewed. While such skews are generally considered meaningful for modelling linguistic knowledge (e.g., Ellis et al. 2014), they also present the analyst with some difficulties. For example, skewed distributions in which most observations are concentrated around one or two frequent variants clash with the necessity of tightly controlled and fully balanced experimental stimuli. This is especially problematic if one also wants to keep comparable but lexically varied stimuli of the same factor combinations as natural as possible. Not only do stimuli need to be balanced across all factors; deriving stimuli from usage data always involves a significant trade-off between "the maximum number of potentially interesting usage factors" (corpus data), and "the minimum number of factors" (experiments).

As a simple example, it is very difficult to find, "in the wild", felicitous sentences that are non-agentive and in the active voice, since non-agentive subjects near-exclusively occur in stative copula or passives (see the discussion on AGENTIVITY above). Trying to solve this issue by balancing voice creates new problems, as agentive subjects do not co-occur with passives. However, since passive complements are heavily skewed towards *must*,[1] a stronger preference of participants for *must* in passive stimuli may solely be due to the usage skew of the passive complement towards *must*. This property would make it difficult to assess the effect of all other factors. In this case, it is easier to exclude voice as a factor altogether, because the added complexity probably outweighs its insights. Similar limitations apply to other factors in the REM dataset, many of which are not available for a majority of data points (because they don't apply to the contexts in question). The factors we chose to include – SOURCE, AGENTIVITY, PERSON, and GENERICITY – are the factors that are least affected by this problem, especially since we conflate SOURCE to a binary variable.

A related challenge is that different factor combinations will require different lexical material to sound natural. Previous corpus-linguistic research on modal complementation has shown that modal expressions have distinct co-occurrence profiles with the surrounding lexical material (Hilpert and Flach 2021), particularly with infinitival complements (Hilpert 2016) and adverbs (Flach 2021a). Statistically speaking, the distinguishing preferences are especially pronounced in analyses that contrast alternating expressions (e.g., in Distinctive Collexeme Analysis), which suggests that, given a choice, participants may tip their preference towards one option solely based on which modal expression the verb complement is more strongly attracted to. Since it is impossible to design stimuli that are systematically controlled for co-occurrence preferences, i.e., where attraction can be held constant, we control the statistical association between a modal expression and the infinitive by including a control variable ASSOCIATION that captures a verb's attraction or repulsion. Since a similar problem exists for adverbs following a modal expression, we refrain from using post-modal adverbial modification in our stimuli.

A final challenge concerns the choice of task for the experiment. Experimental paradigms are broadly classified as on-line and off-line. On-line tasks are designed to monitor automatic sentence processing, while responses in off-line

---

[1] In the REM data set where *have to* and *must* alternate (see next section), root uses of *have to* have a passive complement in 9 out of 248 cases (4%) and *must* in 62 out of 329 cases (19%).

tasks access higher-order cognitive processes after more immediate processing has been completed (Kaiser 2013). Typical off-line tasks are acceptability/grammaticality judgements; on-line tasks include self-paced reading or eye-tracking. Because on-line tasks can measure processing effects below the level of consciousness, they tend to be better suited to tap into covert mental phenomena, whereas off-line tasks allow a more pronounced focus on interpretation effects that are inaccessible to on-line methods.

We opted for an off-line task for two reasons. First, it suits the research question about a *choice* (here: preference) between two near-synonymous expressions, which is similar to an analysis of choice in production (here: in corpora). Second, on-line methods such as self-paced reading capitalize on the assumption that participants slow down or make more errors at or after a critical region. This property makes self-paced reading tasks well-suited for the study of phenomena involving formal violations with a relatively clearly identifiable critical region. However, the choice between *have to* and *must* in our experiment is not related to the presence or absence of formal elements, but is driven predominantly by semantic-pragmatic factors. As most of these factors are highly abstract, it is difficult to determine a critical region and thus formulate predictions about where participants (should) slow down. In addition, the value of semantic variables such as GENERICITY or AGENTIVITY in a given stimulus becomes apparent only after the full sentence has been processed (or at least not until the verbal complement has been read) by the participant. It would be extremely difficult to design natural-sounding sentences that have clearly identifiable or universal critical regions. Off-line methods do not have this problem, because the required experimental reaction occurs after the participants had access to the full context.

3 Corpus analysis

3.1 Data source

The corpus analysis is based on the REM data set (version 20/09/12). The full set contains 4,936 annotated data points for six core modals (*may, could, can, must, might,* and *should*), as well as four semi-modals (*be able to, ought to, need to,* and *have to*) that were randomly sampled from the *Corpus of Contemporary American English* (COCA; Davies 2008). All observations were annotated for 36 variables, including semantic factors such as epistemic vs. root meaning, scope, source of modality, or animacy, syntactic factors such as voice, clause type, negation, or *do*-support, and pragmatic factors such as speech act type or specific context effects (Lesuisse et al. 2022). The REM set contains 499 data points for *must* and

460 for *have to*, for a total of 959 tokens. The data set and analysis scripts for both analyses are available at https://osf.io/nc9ue/.

3.2 Data processing

The 959 tokens for *have to* and *must* had to be processed and filtered in three steps. First, we only used data points with a root meaning (removing 156 tokens). This is motivated by the fact that the focus of the analysis is on the choice between *have to* and *must* rather than on epistemic vs. root meaning; that is, an epistemic *must* cannot alternate with a root *have to* (and vice versa).

Second, we removed data points with only a few tokens for a given variable level, or where the value for a variable level is missing (marked as NA in the data set). This led to the exclusion of tokens where SOURCE is subject-internal (7 tokens) or NA (12 tokens). We also removed data points without a main verb (11 tokens, mostly elliptic uses). This step was necessary in order to assign a value of modal–verb$_{inf}$ attraction to each data point (the control variable ASSOCIATION). We further removed all tokens with NA values for AGENTIVITY and/or GENERICITY (6 tokens).

The third step was to remove observations where there is no alternation between *have to* and *must* (see Section 2.1 above), either for morphosyntactic reasons or because the use of an alternative would involve a significant change in meaning and/or syntactic structure. Such contexts include (i) preterite, participial or gerundial *have to* (*we had to, they'd had to, her irritability at having to*), (ii) negation (*won't have to, don't have to, mustn't, must never*), (iii) *do*-support (*we did have to talk to him*), (iv) *have to* as the complement of another modal (*you may have to consider*), and (v) quasi-idiomatic coordination (*this can and must happen*). We retained cases where *have to* follows *would/'d* or *will/'ll*, based on the assumption that these expressions have future reference that can be expressed by *must* without a significant change in meaning (*You'll have to ask her* vs. *You must ask her*; see, however, Depraetere 2012 for subtle temporal differences) or where *would* primarily acts as a politeness marker (*You'd have to ask her* vs. *You must ask her*). This step removed 181 non-alternating tokens. In total, the cleaning procedure left a data set of 586 observations, 329 (56.1%) for *must* and 257 (43.9%) for *have to*.

3.3 Data annotation

We used the annotations of the REM data with some adjustments. The order of the variable levels discussed below are in the hypothesized direction of an effect, and the first-mentioned level(s) indicate(s) a predicted preference for *have to*.

The variables AGENTIVITY (levels: agentive, non-agentive) and GENERICITY (levels: non-generic, generic) are taken from the REM factors S_AGENT and S_GEN, respectively. We extracted PERSON (levels: 1st, 2nd, 3rd) from the factor F_SUBJ (levels: 1s, 2s, 3s, 1p, 2p, 3p). (We excluded NUMBER, primarily as there are too few data points for 2nd.PL, which is insufficient for a robust regression analysis.)

Based on the S_SOURCE factor in the REM data, we created the variables SOURCEMULT (circ, cond, disint, rule) and SOURCE (non-rule, rule). The binary variable SOURCE conflates the SOURCEMULT levels circ(umstantial), cond(itional), and dis(course-)int(ernal), as discussed in Section 2.1. A binary variable makes it easier to compare the corpus with the experimental results, and binary variables are preferable in an experimental setting to avoid complexity (see Section 4.1). As we shall see in Section 3.4, the conflation is also supported by the results of the corpus data analysis.

In addition, we included the variable GENRE in the REM data set (levels: spok, fic, mag, news, acad) to minimally control for genre effects. While there is no expectation of a substantial change in the direction of effects, we use GENRE as a proxy to formality, since the context of a modal expression contains many "soft" factors that can plausibly activate certain parts of the constructional network (cf. Section 5, Chapter 9).

Finally, we added ASSOCIATION, which captures the strength of the lexical association or dissociation between a modal and an infinitive. As discussed in Section 2.3, modals have distinct collocational profiles (e.g., Hilpert 2016), which can also affect experimental behavior (Flach 2020). Thus, we added a binary variable ASSOCIATION (levels: *have to*, *must*), which indicates, for each observation, whether the infinitive follows the modal more often than expected. We used the REM variable VB to extract the verb information, but since the REM data lists the base form of the verb participle in cases of passives (rather than *be*, e.g., it lists *recognise* for *must be* recognised), we changed the value for VERB to *be* for passive examples. The association of infinitives with either *must* or *have to* was determined by a Distinctive Collexeme Analysis (Gries and Stefanowitsch 2004; Flach 2021b) over all *must* + V_{inf} and *have to* + V_{inf} strings in the late 2015 offline version of COCA. If a lexical verb occurs more often than expected with *must* than with *have to*, the value for ASSOCIATION was coded as *must* (and vice versa), irrespective of whether the association is statistically (highly) significant (88.6% of data points have statistically significantly associated collexemes at $G^2 > 3.84$, $p < 0.05$). We opted for the binary ASSOCIATION variable at the expense of the numerical LogLikelihood (G^2), because the binary variable facilitates the comparison with the other variables, and it also facilitates comparison of corpus and experiment data (cf. below).[2]

3.4 Analysis

We submitted the data to a binary logistic regression with MODAL as the outcome variable, and SOURCE, PERSON, AGENTIVITY, GENERICITY, ASSOCIATION, and GENRE as the predictor variables (using treatment coding, i.e., contrasting each level of a variable to a specified reference level as baseline). Given the make-up of COCA and the REM data, there is not enough information to control for idiosyncrasies of corpus files in a fixed-effects model. However, the REM set contains fewer than 500 randomly selected observations per expression, which is only a fraction of their corpus total (e.g., 0.2% of *must* and <0.1% for *have to*), which makes it unlikely that a substantial number of observations in the set come from the same file and/or speaker/writer (the REM data has no information on corpus files).

Table 1 provides the regression results. The model is overall statistically significant (LR $\chi^2(12)$ = 219.27, $p < 0.001$), discriminates well (C = 0.83; D_{xy} = 0.66) and the classification accuracy is significantly higher than the baseline (74.6% vs. 56.1%; $\chi^2(1)$ = 134.77, $p < 0.001$, Cramér's V = 0.47). There is no issue with collinearity, as all variance inflation factors (VIFs) < 1.6. The 95% confidence intervals (CIs) were confirmed by a bootstrapping procedure (2,000 repetitions) which we ran to ascertain the stability of the model, given the considerable skew across some variables and variable levels. Where the CI includes 0, that level is not significantly different from the reference level.

The results in Table 1 are interpreted as follows. The values in the estimate column are the coefficients for the respective variable levels. They indicate the direction of an effect of that level: a positive coefficient means – all other variables being at their reference level – that this variable level increases the odds for *must*. An intuitive, illustrative example is the coefficient of ASSOCIATION: this is positive for the level *must*, which means that an infinitive that is statistically associated with *must* also increases the odds for a *must* choice (and, conversely, that a weaker *must*-infinitive association decreases the odds for *must*).

---

[2] There is at least one additional reason why binary ASSOCIATION is preferable in the current context, due to the heavy skew of verb association with *must*: compared to *have to*, *must* has far fewer strongly associated types. That is, a handful of top-attracted items (*be*, *have*) are strongly associated due to their high co-occurrence (G^2 values between 500–20,0000), dwarfing the majority of strongly associated, but less frequent verbs types (G^2 values between 3.86–50). Such extreme skews mask (true) association effects of less frequent verbs (e.g., *acknowledge*, *adhere*).

Table 1: Output of binary logistic regression model (corpus data).

Coefficients:	Estimate	Std.Err.	95% CI		z-value	Pr(>|z|)	Sig.
(Intercept)	−2.332	0.321	−2.962	−1.703	−7.26	<0.001	***
SourceMult = cond	0.420	0.319	−0.204	1.045	1.32	0.187	ns
SourceMult = disint	0.371	0.251	−0.120	0.862	1.48	0.139	ns
SourceMult = rul	1.245	0.353	0.554	1.937	3.53	<0.001	***
Person = 2nd	−0.517	0.351	−1.204	0.170	−1.47	0.140	ns
Person = 3rd	0.639	0.265	0.121	1.158	2.42	0.016	*
Agentivity = nonagt	−0.085	0.261	−0.597	0.426	−0.33	0.744	ns
Genericity = gen	0.764	0.252	0.270	1.258	3.03	0.002	**
Association = must	1.009	0.261	0.498	1.521	3.87	<0.001	***
Genre = fic	1.724	0.332	1.073	2.374	5.20	<0.001	***
Genre = mag	0.980	0.310	0.372	1.589	3.16	0.002	**
Genre = news	1.461	0.320	0.833	2.089	4.56	<0.001	***
Genre = acad	2.698	0.362	1.989	3.407	7.46	<0.001	***

Number of observations: 586, Likelihood Ratio (LR) $\chi^2(12)$ = 219.27, p < 0.001
Model: Modal ~ SourceMult + Person + Agentivity + Genericity + Association + Genre.

There are two other binary variables that allow for a straightforward interpretation. Genericity has a positive coefficient, which means that a generic subject increases the odds for *must*. The coefficient for Agentivity is negative, but as indicated by the confidence intervals, Agentivity is not a statistically significant factor (coef = −0.085, z = −0.33, p = 0.74). While we will return to this in the discussion below, it should be mentioned at this point that Agentivity is a significant factor in a model *without* Association (coef = 0.461, z = 2.17, p = 0.03). This suggests that *must* is associated more strongly with situations over which the subject referent has less control. However, the fact that Association cancels the effect of Agentivity suggests that verb association captures a fair amount of agentivity already. This is not an implausible assumption given the logic of collocational profiles and the principle of semantic similarity: if a subject has agentive control, these situations will be encoded by agentive verbs (and vice versa). If, then, a modal is more likely in situations with a certain degree of agentivity, it will also co-occur with agentive verb types. This is reflected in the Distinctive Collexeme Analysis: the top attracted collexemes of *have to* are activity verbs (*go, do, say, deal, take, ask*), while *must* is distinguished by stative verbs or verbs low in activity (*be, have, understand, know*).

The variables with more than two levels are less straightforward to interpret: the coefficients indicate whether the respective level significantly the odds for *must* over the variable's reference level. For example, if the source is conditional or discourse-internal, the odds for *must* are not significantly increased over a circumstantial source. However, *must* is significantly more likely if the source is a rule, compared to when it is circumstantial. Yet, the coefficients in Table 1 do not allow for a direct inference of whether rules are also significantly different from both conditional and discourse-internal sources. Indeed, a Bonferroni-corrected pairwise comparison between the levels of SOURCEMULT only confirms that rule is significantly different from circumstantial (z: –3.53, $p < 0.01$).[3] Put differently, the levels of SOURCEMULT that distinguish best between *have to* and *must* are circumstantial (favoring *have to*) and rule (favoring *must*).

The same logic applies to the interpretation of PERSON. While – when compared to first-person subjects – second-person subjects favor *have to* (negative coefficient), this is not significant. On the other hand, third-person subjects significantly increase the odds for *must* (positive coefficient). A Bonferroni-corrected pairwise comparison between the levels 2nd and 3rd confirms that they are different (z: –3.56, $p < 0.01$), and they are the two levels that best distinguish between *have to* and *must*.

The variable GENRE was included as a control variable and/or a coarse-grained proxy to formality. Statistically, the inclusion of GENRE reduces the absolute values of the coefficients of all other variables, but does not cancel, let alone reverse, any effect discussed above. Thus, while GENRE generally does not change the direction of an effect of another predictor, the patterns in the GENRE coefficients indicate a "formality" effect: more formal contexts increase the odds for *must*. We ordered the levels along a hypothesized informal–formal continuum from spoken as the most informal COCA register to academic as the most formal or highly conventionalized one. The pattern from the regression largely confirms this continuum, with the exception of fiction.

As a preliminary summary, we can discuss three points at this juncture. First, the results broadly mirror the results in Chapter 4: circumstantial and rule sources best distinguish between *have to* and *must*, while discourse-internal and conditional do not. Second, at face value, GENERICITY, which favours *must*, goes against what could be expected from earlier observations about at least *have to*. Remember that *have to* was noted by Ziegeler (2014) to have emerged especially in generic environments (cf. Section 2.2). However, it does not necessarily follow that a historic context of one expression makes this context a distinguishable variable in comparison with another expression. Third, AGENTIVITY is not an influential factor once ASSOCIATION is factored in.

---

[3] Determined via the emmeans() function in the R package {emmeans}.

4 Experiment

4.1 Design and materials

4.1.1 Design

Following the discussion in Section 2.3, we opted for a variant of the off-line split-100 task (Bresnan 2007, Bresnan and Ford 2010). In this paradigm, participants are asked to split 100 points between two options and distribute the points according to the strength of their (dis)preference for either option. For example, in stimuli where one option is ungrammatical, the grammatical alternative would (likely) get a value of close to 100 (and the other option one closer to 0). Should both options be roughly equal, each would get a value of 50 (and so on). The split-100 task is particularly suited in contexts where experimenters assume the choice to be less clear-cut, as in the study of near-synonymous expressions; designs using a Likert scale, where at any moment in the experiment only one option is shown, would not be able to provide choice-based information to begin with.

The split-100 task is similar to other off-line tasks such as acceptability rating, magnitude estimation or forced-choice. The primary difference to acceptability ratings is that participants see both options at the same time; the difference to forced-choice tasks is that participants can indicate the extent of a preference. An advantage of the split-100 task over magnitude estimation is that it is conceptually easy to understand. A mathematical advantage is that the responses can be transformed into a binary response relative to the neutral 50 points position. This possibility combines the potential increase in informativity of scaled ratings and the clarity of a forced-choice rating. However, in practice, there might be little substantial difference in the informativity of binary vs. numerical responses for these kinds of experiments (Weskott and Fanselow 2011). The transformation into a binary variable can be a good statistical option given that the split-100 task is prone to a bimodal distribution on numerical responses, which causes issues for regressions (cf. Section 4.4).

4.1.2 Materials

We constructed 64 sentences in a 2x2x2x2 design. That is, there were 16 conditions, which together exhaustively represent the possible combinations of values for four variables, and for which we created four lexically different versions. Following the discussion in Section 2, we crossed SOURCE (rule, non-rule), AGENTIVITY (non-agentive, agentive), GENERICITY (non-generic, generic) and PERSON (2nd, 3rd).

In a complex experimental setting with four crossed variables, it is preferable to keep the number of variable levels as low as possible: the higher the number of levels, the higher the number of required stimuli. Thus, we use the variable Source with binary levels. The corpus analysis has shown that the two levels of SourceMult that most clearly distinguish between *have to* and *must* are circumstantial and rule, while the other two levels are not clearly separable from either circumstantial or rule. Hence, we opted for a binary split, contrasting non-rule vs. rule, and most non-rule examples are modelled on the REM definition of "circumstantial".

As pointed out before, the sentences were inspired by corpus sentences in the REM data and amended for an experimental setting. Given the importance of situational context as well as the semantic-pragmatic and highly abstract character of the variables, it is necessary to provide a fair amount of context to force the reading of a particular variable level. Thus, each target clause (the modal expression) was preceded by a "carrier" (a matrix clause, a complex subject or an adverbial adjunct). For example, to force a rule reading, a carrier clause like *The court ruling means that* preceded the target sentence *you have to/must accept the settlement*. Two examples are given in (9); the full list of stimuli is provided in the supplementary material (https://osf.io/nc9ue/).

(9) a. Carrier: *If you want to reduce violence,*
   Targets: *you must change people's living conditions.*
   you have to change people's living conditions.
   Factor level combination:
   Source: non-rule
   Agentivity: agentive
   Genericity: generic
   Person: 2nd

b. Carrier: *During official meetings,*
   Targets: *all three committee members must be present.*
   all three committee members have to be present.
   Factor level combination:
   Source: rule
   Agentivity: non-agentive
   Genericity: non-generic[4]
   Person: 3rd

---

[4] Note again that genericity, in the REM data set, is treated as a property of the subject, not of the situation.

Recall that in contrast to experiments on morphosyntactic phenomena where the factors of interest are salient, formal variables, a central characteristic of the current experiment is the fact that all factors are semantic-pragmatic and highly abstract. This presents two challenges. First, it means that the intended reading for a factor level can often only be provided by a specific lexical carrier that may in turn be unavailable for another level of that factor. For example, it is straightforward to vary an item for the factor SOURCE in an example such as *If you want to go fishing there, you have to/must* ... with a continuation in either *get a permit* (rule) or *get a good bait* (non-rule). However, such manipulations are often not possible across all factors and/or factor levels, if the goal is to create naturally sounding sentences (see Section 2.3). Thus, for item variation, we constructed propositionally different sentences not just per factor level combination (4 different sentences, each assigned to a different list) but also across factor level combinations, rather than trying to change a sentence along only a small lexical dimension that would lead to unidiomatic sentences. On that note, we did not include negation or adverbial modification to avoid unintended effects of collocational preferences (see Flach 2020b on modal + adverb collocations).

Second, since AGENTIVITY, GENERICITY, and SOURCE index concepts that are difficult to express in the space of a carrier and a target clause, the stimuli were also annotated by Cyril Grandin, the main coder of the REM data, to ascertain the intended readings. Cyril, who was unaware of our decision on a binary SOURCE variable, was given all 64 stimuli sentences, randomly in either the *have to* or *must* variant, and asked to annotate for SOURCE, AGENTIVITY, and GENERICITY. The interrater reliability was substantial across all variables (SOURCE: κ = 0.69, 84%; AGENTIVITY: κ = 0.75, 88%; GENERICITY: κ = 0.69, 84%), which is remarkable considering the subtlety of the variables and the fact that only a short sentence or phrase was available for context. We took disagreement to mean that the desired reading was not sufficiently obvious, and in such cases, we changed either the carrier or the target clause to increase the likelihood of a particular reading.

In total, the 64 sentences were distributed over four lists and each participant was randomly assigned to one list. Each list contained 16 sentences, so that each participant saw each factor combination only once.

4.1.3 Fillers

In addition to the 16 target items, each participant rated sentences from three classic alternation phenomena, i.e., the dative alternation (*You can send a letter to them.* vs. *you can send them a letter*), *to-* vs. *-ing-*complementation (*We avoid {discussing / to discuss} politics*), and morphological vs. periphrastic comparative

(*It was never {easier / more easy} to create a start-up*). The primary function of the filler items was less to distract from the modal expressions, which is difficult to achieve for lexically-specific *have to* and *must* stimuli anyway, but rather to alleviate two issues of the experimental paradigm, especially since it is administered online. A near-synonymous alternation where both options are acceptable and fully grammatical provides far fewer incentives to use the extreme ends of the scale (apart from participants who only make 0–100 splits). Thus, participants can easily get bored or become uncooperative. Unless they have reason to engage closely with the items and employ different splits occasionally, they might quickly resort to providing random and meaningless responses. With regard to the latter, participant cooperation is a possible concern in anonymous online implementations to begin with, where a number of checks have to be implemented with the purpose of evaluating the quality of the responses and potentially removing the data from uncooperative participants.

Therefore, in order to safe-guard against uncooperativeness and to have a means of evaluating participant attention, we marked 22 of the 41 fillers as "control" items; these were pairs where one option is clearly ungrammatical and which should trigger very clear native speaker preferences (**She explained him the task*). The preferences for fillers were determined by collostructional attraction based on data sets of previous studies (e.g., Gries and Stefanowitsch 2004 for the dative alternation; Hilpert 2008 for the comparatives). Thus, each participant also responded to 22 "control" items which we used to determine a participant's error rate.

4.2 Implementation

4.2.1 Software and plattform

The experiment was set up in PCIbex and ran on the PCIbex farm (Zehr and Schwarz 2018). The split-100 task can be implemented in two ways, either by asking participants to type the splits for each option or by presenting a slider that participants can move as much or as little as they feel appropriate.

We opted for a slider with 100 increments of 1. The thumb (the circle to be moved along the track) was in the central position at the start of each trial, and the slider was CSS-modified to show a green thumb on a grey track, which ensured that the slider was identical across all browsers. A slider does not require participants to split and sum numbers to 100 correctly; such a requirement could tempt participants to resort to coarse-grained splits (100–0, 80–20, 50–50, etc.) for no reason other than to avoid mistakes and/or save time, which would cancel the advantage of graded preferences.

In anonymous online participant recruitment, experimenters usually do not have control over the devices that participants access the experiment with (especially small-screen mobile phones). To ensure that all participants saw carriers, targets, and sliders in a similar fashion and without awkward line breaks due to a small screen, the welcome page required pressing the spacebar to proceed, which is only possible on devices with physical keyboards.

The carrier was centered at the top, followed by the targets in a new line, situated above either ends of the slider (cf. Figure 1). Whether the target clauses appeared on the left or right was random for each trial. The order of the sentences was randomized per participant. The experiment paused every 16 sentences, at which point participants could take a break.

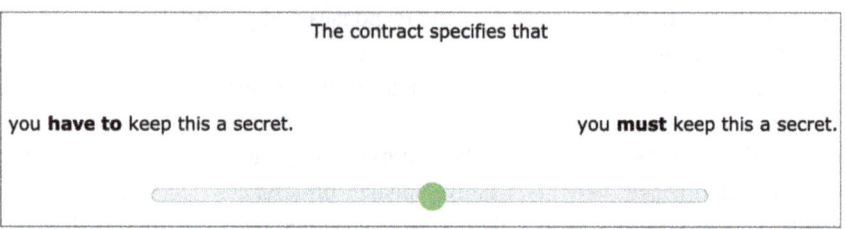

Figure 1: Split-100 implementation (visually identical across browsers).

4.2.2 Instructions

After collecting informed consent, participants were told that they took part in a study on how and when learners of English come closer to native speaker preferences in grammatical contexts where two options are available that express roughly the same meaning. Their task was to provide their native speaker intuitions about sentences with alternations that are notoriously difficult for learners (e.g., modals, dative alternation, comparative). Participants were instructed to be quick and rely on their gut-feeling, but were asked to read each sentence and both continuations carefully. The experiment was preceded by five training items that covered the full range of acceptability to familiarize participants with the behavior of the slider.

4.2.3 Participants

We recruited 100 native speakers of North American English via Prolific[5] (47 females, 1 NA; average age 31 years, $sd = 10.4$); 38 participants reported to be

---

[5] Prolific.ac (Palan & Schitter 2018).

college-level students. To get a native speaker participant pool, we made use of Prolific's pre-screening options, which ensured that the experiment was only available to monolingual participants who were born in the US or Canada, and have spent a maximum of 6 months outside their country of birth. While self-reported criteria are not a guarantee of native speaker proficiency, the combination of demographic criteria is likely sufficient for this purpose. To reduce the risk of uncooperativeness, a further requirement was that a participant had a 100% approval rate, which indexes cooperation in earlier studies.

The median completion time was 9 minutes. No participant was identified as uncooperative and all were paid £1.35. They were asked to provide voluntary feedback at the end, which about half of the participants did.

4.3 Data processing

As every participant responded to 16 target items, there were 1,600 responses.[6] Roughly 15% of participants gave (near-)exclusively binary responses for the modal stimuli, i.e., moved the slider all the way across in every trial. We removed the data for four participants who only gave either *have to* or *must* responses ("non-alternating participants"). This left 1,536 data points from 96 participants.

As the software records responses on a scale from 0 to 99, and because targets were randomly shown on the left or right, the data needed to be transformed, such that preferences for *have to* have values from −49 to 0, while preferences for *must* have values from 1 to 50. From these numerical responses we created a binary response variable CHOICE by assigning the level *have to* to all negative values (and 0) and the level *must* to all positive values. This was necessary given the response pattern by a sizable portion of participants with essentially binary choices and because the numerical responses are not normally distributed (cf. Figure 3, right panel).

---

[6] Unfortunately, the distribution of participants across the lists turned out to be very uneven (L1: 30, L2: 17, L3: 38, L4: 11). This results from the fact that PCIbex uses a counter for list assignment, which is incremented once a participant *completes* the experiment rather than when they *start* it (despite a setting to prevent this from happening). Since a number of participants recruited from a platform tend to take the experiment simultaneously (as soon as an experiment is available), this can lead to imbalances. To check if this distorted the results, the analyses were also performed on a random subset of the data with 10 participants per list, with virtually the same results, which indicates that the uneven list distribution does not affect the interpretation of the results in our context.

As with the corpus data, we added the variable ASSOCIATION. This is not only motivated by the effect of collocational preferences (see Section 3), but is even more relevant in an experiment. Recall that a preference rating given for near-synonymous choices with identical lexical material might well swing towards one option for no other reason than a more "chunk-like" association between the modal and the infinitive. Thus, we used the same binary ASSOCIATION variable as for the corpus data, based on a Distinctive Collexeme Analysis (91% of responses involved a statistically significant collexeme at $G^2 > 3.84$, $p < 0.05$).

4.4 Analysis

Let us first look at general descriptive statistics of the responses. Figure 2 shows a histogram of the responses for example control items with an ungrammatical option, where responses are skewed in the expected direction. This suggests that the paradigm works in an online context and that participants were cooperative and attentive (mean error rate for the control items: 4.4%, sd = 0.06). Figure 3 shows that the preferences for target items with *have to* and *must* are less clear, as expected. Indeed, many participants commented specifically on the difficulty of assigning preferences for *have to* and *must* in the debriefing feedback section in their post-experiment feedback.

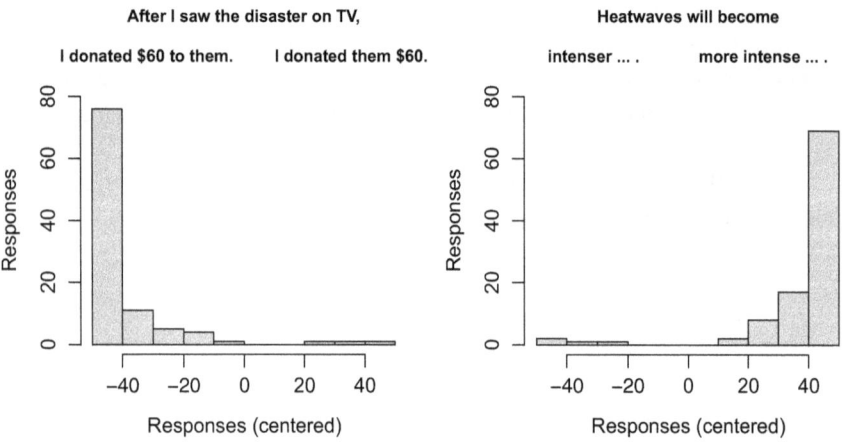

Figure 2: Distribution of preferences for the dative alternation (left) and the comparative (right).

As Figure 3 shows, the numerical responses are not normally distributed: responses tend to cluster around both extremes rather than the middle. This is not ideal for a

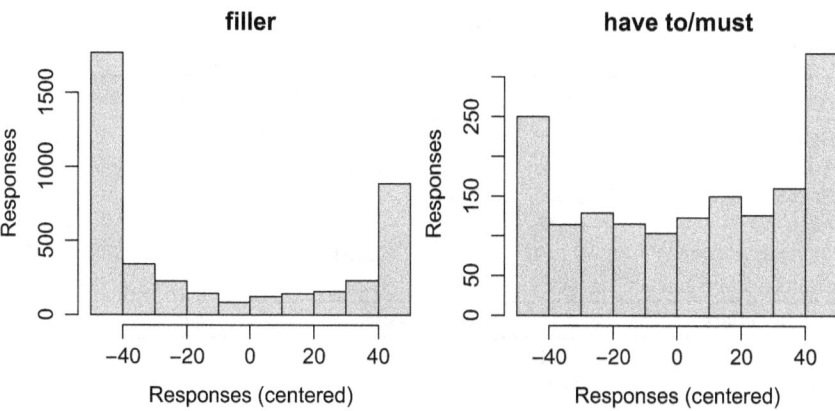

Figure 3: Distribution of preferences for filler items (left) and targets (right).

regression model. While response data need not necessarily be normally distributed, the residuals of the model have to be, and if we predict the numerical responses in a linear regression, the residuals are not normally distributed. Hence, we report a logistic regression, predicting the binary response CHOICE (for which the results and interpretation are essentially identical to the model with a numerical predictor). A binary response also makes this analysis straightforwardly comparable to the corpus analysis.

We fit a mixed-effects model with CHOICE as the outcome variable, and SOURCE, PERSON, AGENTIVITY, GENERICITY, and ASSOCIATION as the predictor variables (AGE, GENDER, and STUDENT status had no effect and were removed). PARTICIPANT and ITEM were specified as random effects. The results are given in Table 2. As before, the reference level for CHOICE is *have to*, and positive coefficients indicate increasing odds for *must*, and where the CI includes 0, the factor level does not predict CHOICE above chance.

The main results are that participants were more likely to prefer *must* when the SOURCE was a rule (as opposed to circumstantial). Expectedly, if the verb is associated with *must*, this increases the odds for *must*. Neither PERSON, nor AGENTIVITY, nor GENERICITY had an influence on participants' preferences.

As a minor insight, in a model without ASSOCIATION, PERSON is a significant factor and its coefficient is elevated (coef = 0.548, $z = 2.82$, $p < 0.01$), such that 3rd person subjects increase the odds for *must*. However, in this model, neither AGENTIVITY (coef = 0.058, $z = 0.30$, $p = 0.77$) nor GENERICITY (coef = –0.054, $z = -0.28$, $p < 0.78$) have a significant effect.

Table 2: Output of mixed-effects regression model (experiment data).

Fixed effects:	Estimate	Std.Err.	95% CI		z-value	Pr(>|z|)	Sig.
(Intercept)	−0.408	0.219	−0.837	0.021	−1.86	0.062	.
SOURCE = rule	0.761	0.186	0.397	1.126	4.09	< 0.001	***
PERSON = 3rd	0.300	0.201	−0.094	0.694	1.49	0.136	ns
AGENTIVITY = nonagt	−0.115	0.192	−0.491	0.261	−0.60	0.549	ns
GENERICITY = gen	−0.045	0.182	−0.402	0.312	0.25	0.805	ns
ASSOCIATION = must	0.628	0.215	0.206	1.051	2.92	0.004	**
Random effects:	Name		Variance		Std.Dev.		
PARTICIPANTID	Intercept		0.5726		0.7567		
ITEM	Intercept		0.2913		0.5398		

Observations: 1,536; Participants: 96; Items: 64

CHOICE ~ SOURCE + PERSON + AGENTIVITY + GENERICITY + ASSOCIATION + (1|ParticipantID) + (1|ITEM)

5 Discussion

We begin with a comparison of both the corpus and the experimental models, where their results converge and where they diverge. We then discuss the results in the light of other results throughout this book and the relevance for models of modal auxiliaries (cf. Chapter 9).

Let us begin with a summary of the results of the corpus analysis and the experiment task in a direct comparison. To make the models comparable, we refit a regression analysis with the corpus data including the binary variable SOURCE instead of SOURCEMULT (we also set the reference level of PERSON to 2nd, as in the experiment data). The results for this corpus model are identical in magnitude to the model from Section 3.4.

Figure 4 plots the model coefficients for the corpus data in blue and the experiment data in green. The dots and squares represent the coefficients (log odds ratio), and the horizontal lines show the 95% Confidence Intervals. If the CI includes 0, the indicated variable level is not distinct from the reference level. Note that for the corpus model, the coefficients for GENRE are not shown, as these were not available for the experimental data.

The variables SOURCE, ASSOCIATION, PERSON, and GENERICITY emerged as significant predictors of *must* choices in the corpus data (blue), while AGENTIVITY did not significantly improve the model. The preferences in the experiment were predicted by SOURCE and ASSOCIATION, but not by PERSON, GENERICITY, and AGENTIVITY (green). In other words, the results indicate that choices and

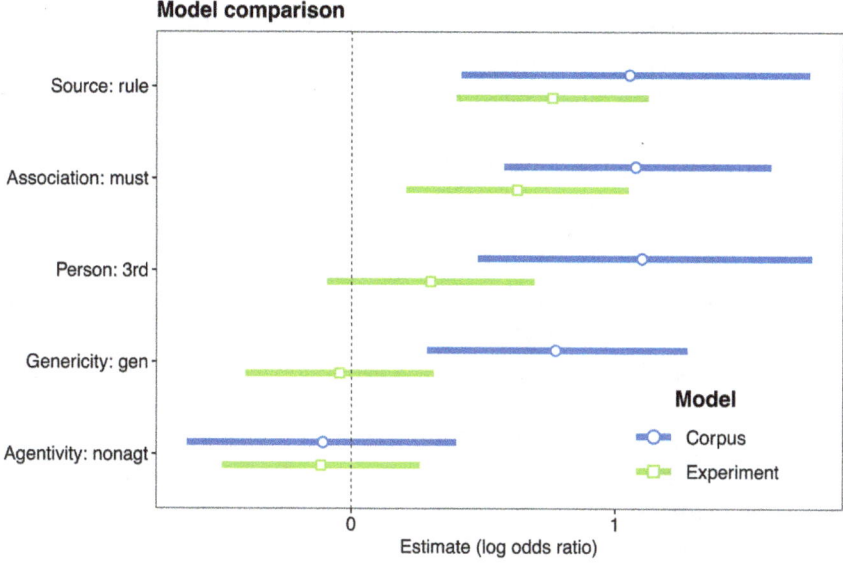

Figure 4: Comparing corpus and experiment model coefficients with 95% CI.

preferences for either *have to* and *must* are primarily explained by SOURCE (i.e., rule-based stimuli favor *must*), which is a phenomenon-specific factor, and by ASSOCIATION (i.e., whether the post-modal infinitive is more strongly associated with either *have to* or *must*), which is a general usage factor. SOURCE and ASSOCIATION were the only significant predictors in both types of data. Despite these differences, however, no factor's effect was "reversed" between the data sets, i.e., the direction of influence is stable across both data types. As a methodological insight, it is noteworthy that verb association explained a large share of the choices in both the corpus data and the experiment; it is a processing-related factor, i.e., not unique to modal auxiliaries. The large role played by this variable suggests that association measures should feature more frequently in the analysis of especially experimental data.

The main results converge with the discussion in Chapter 4 along those dimensions that are comparable: *have to* favors non-rule sources (in the experiment mainly of the circumstantial kind) and *must* favors rule sources. As we discuss below, this may well be the most salient of these abstract semantic-pragmatic factors. We need to bear in mind that SOURCE appears most distinctive when all non-rule categories are collapsed.

At face value, the results may be taken to mean that there is less "converging evidence" between corpus and experimental results. However, we should discuss three points in this context. First, the choice for participants was among two acceptable alternatives. The fact that many participants explicitly commented on the *have to* and *must* stimuli (rather than on the alternations used for the fillers) underlines their near-equivalence. Thus, one reason that some factors are predictive of corpus choices, but not of preferences, could lie in the fact that the experimental conditions varied only by semantic-pragmatic variables, especially the highly abstract categories GENERICITY or AGENTIVITY. It may well be that such "soft" factors are too weak to trigger (noticeable) behavioral differences, as opposed to "hard" form-related factors that are usually tested in experiments. This fuzziness and abstractness might explain part of the divergent use and operationalization of these factors by different authors. Yet, SOURCE, as a significant factor in both analyses, is not uncontroversial in terms of concepts and operationalization either (see Chapter 4). It is, however, the most salient. In our study, we simplified this context by presenting participants with examples with clear rule and non-rule readings. It may well be that more fine-grained distinctions for the non-rule contexts and/or equally abstract subjectivity/objectivity distinctions would likely have only very subtle or even no effects, similar to GENERICITY and AGENTIVITY.

Second, corpus analyses in the modal paradigm have repeatedly demonstrated the relevance of context. Recall that researchers frequently comment on the difficulty to annotate data; annotators are probably more likely to agree if sufficient extralinguistic context is available that provides reliable cues regarding SOURCE, GENERICITY, and AGENTIVITY. Hence, it is very difficult to implement clear and concise contextual cues in experimental stimuli, especially in the design used here, where context was only provided through a short carrier fragment. In other words, the context that is available to speakers or writers (i.e., in corpus data) is as rich (and unique) as the situation in which a conversation or a piece of writing takes place; by contrast, the context is nowhere near as rich for participants in controlled experimental settings. It is somewhat doubtful that longer carriers could provide substantially more reliable cues (although that is a testable hypothesis for increasingly richer contexts). After all, when it comes to SOURCE conceived of as a binary factor, enforcing rule-based readings could be achieved in as little as one carrier clause (e.g., *The **law** states that* ...).

Third – related to the previous point – the present study compares productive "choice" (corpus data) and receptive preference (offline experiment), and thus measures different things. In other words, a speaker's (or writer's) "selection" of a particular modal in an utterance is made with a plethora of unique contextual information available to the speaker (or writer). By contrast, a language user in the offline experiment is explicitly presented with two targets, each of which is inevitably brought to the participant's consciousness; making a forced choice between them is not quite the same as letting oneself be guided by the complex interplay of factors in an actual communicative situation. We would thus claim that although the results overlap in important ways, some differences are to be expected, since the underlying phenomena each have characteristics of their own.

This leads to a discussion of the theoretical implications, which we base on the arguments put forth in more detail Chapter 9 on modelling modals in a dynamic network of associations (e.g., Schmid 2020, Diessel 2019). In brief, a network model assumes that speaker knowledge consists primarily of knowledge about associations and links between linguistic elements rather than knowledge about feature–value pairs, which are specified in the constructions themselves. A dynamic network perspective works around the "fat node" problem. Put simply, if we assume that properties, be they semantic, formal, or probabilistic, are specified in the nodes of a network (the constructions), then nodes are heavily inflated. This inflation can be avoided if we assume that many relationships between linguistic units reside in associations, and there is ample psycholinguistic evidence to this effect (cf. Chapter 9). Three such associations are distinguished: (i) syntagmatic relationships, which concerns the sequence of units, e.g., the association between a modal and the following verb; (ii) paradigmatic associations, which concerns alternation, e.g., the choice between *have to* and *must*; and (iii) pragmatic associations, e.g., contextual information that makes the activation of some links more likely than others (e.g., a rule-based situation activates *must* more readily than *have to*). Under this view, the experimental results are plausible given the assumption that the highly salient association with rules vs. non-rules is enough to trigger a particular response, while this is not the case for less salient associations that are simply not available or active for the experimental participant.

6 Concluding remarks

In this chapter, we looked at the choice between two near-synonymous root modal expressions, *have to* and *must* from both a corpus and an experimental perspective. The main goal, i.e., to investigate to what extent predictive factors in language production also predict preference ratings, suggests that the choice between the two modals, given the variables included, is predicted primarily by the SOURCE of the root necessity (a phenomenon-specific property) and verb association (a processing-related property). More latent semantic-pragmatic factors either showed effects only in the corpus data (e.g., GENERICITY) or not at all (e.g., AGENTIVITY). The results can be accounted for in terms of dynamic network models that prioritize associative links over feature-based analyses: since the semantic-pragmatic factors are examples of pragmatic associations, they increase the odds for one over another alternative, but this "triggering" force is more easily available in language production than in language comprehension.

Experiment

Instructions

In English, speakers can often choose between two expressions that mean (roughly) the same, but if your native language is English, you will usually have a preference.

Our team studies the circumstances under which learners of English come close(r) to preferences of native English speakers, so we are interested in your intuitions.

Your task

You will see sentences with choices that are difficult for learners. Your task is to judge which is more acceptable by dragging a slider towards the better-sounding option.

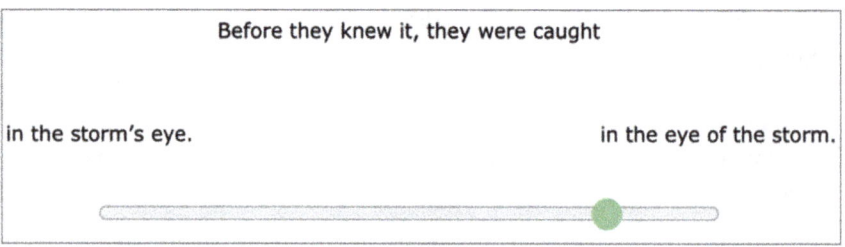

Sometimes both options are more or less equally good, so you can or should indicate the strength of your preference by how far you move the slider.

For some sentences, one option sounds clearly "off", move the slider all the way across, while for others you may want to move it only a little towards a (slightly) better option.

Important: We are interested in your gut-feeling, so you should decide quickly, but we do ask you to read both alternatives carefully.

Press SPACE to proceed to some training sentences to test the slider.

References

Bresnan, Joan. 2007. Is syntactic knowledge probabilistic? Experiments with the English dative alternation. In Sam Featherston & Wolfgang Sternefeld (eds.), *Roots: Linguistics in search of its Evidential Base*, 77–96. Berlin: Mouton de Gruyter.

Bresnan, Joan & Marilyn Ford. 2010. Predicting syntax: Processing dative constructions in American and Australian varieties of English. *Language* 86(1). 168–213.

Cappelle, Bert, Ilse Depraetere & Mégane Lesuisse. 2019. The necessity modals *have to, must, need to*, and *should*: Using n-grams to help identify common and distinct semantic and pragmatic aspects. *Constructions and Frames* 11(2). 220–243.

Cappelle, Bert & Gert De Sutter. 2010. *Should* vs. *ought to*. In Bert Cappelle & Naoaki Wada (eds.), *Distinctions in English Grammar. Offered to Renaat Declerck*, 92–126. Tokyo: Kaitakusha.

Cappelle, Bert & Gert De Sutter. 2010. *Should* vs. *ought to*: A corpus-based, multivariate analysis revealing distinct patterns of usage. In Bert Cappelle & Naoaki Wada (eds.), *Distinctions in English grammar: Offered to Renaat Declerck*, 92–126. Tokyo: Kaitakusha.

Coates, Jennifer. 1983. *The Semantics of the Modal Auxiliaries*. London: Croom Helm.

Collins, Peter. 2009. *Modals and Quasi-Modals in English*. Amsterdam: Rodopi.

Cruse, D. Alan. 1973. Some thoughts on agentivity. *Journal of Linguistics* 9. 11–23.

Davies, Mark. 2008. *The Corpus of Contemporary American English: 450 million words, 1990–present*. https://www.english-corpora.org/coca/.

Depraetere, Ilse. 2012. Time in sentences with modal verbs. In Robert I. Binnick (ed.), *The Oxford Handbook of Tense and Aspect*, 989–1019. Oxford: OUP.

Depraetere, Ilse & Susan Reed. 2011. Towards a more explicit taxonomy of root possibility. *English Language and Linguistics* 15(1). 1–29.

Depraetere, Ilse & An Verhulst. 2008. Source of modality: A reassessment. *English Language and Linguistics* 12(1). 1–25.

Diessel, Holger. 2019. *The Grammar Network: How Linguistic Structure is Shaped by Language Use*. Cambridge: Cambridge University Press.

Ellis, Nick C., Matthew Brook O'Donnell & Ute Römer. 2014. The processing of verb-argument constructions is sensitive to form, function, frequency, contingency and prototypicality. *Cognitive Linguistics* 25(1). 55–98.

Flach, Susanne. 2020a. Schemas and the frequency/acceptability mismatch: Corpus distribution predicts sentence judgements. *Cognitive Linguistics* 31(4). 609–645.

Flach, Susanne. 2021a. Beyond modal idioms and modal harmony: A corpus-based analysis of gradient idiomaticity in MOD+ADV collocations. *English Language and Linguistics*. 743–765.

Flach, Susanne. 2021b. Collostructions: An R implementation for the family of collostructional methods. Version 0.2.0. https://sfla.ch/collostructions/.

Flach, Susanne & Martin Hilpert. under review. There must be a connection between sound and meaning: Phonetic properties of *must* in spoken American English distinguish meaning differences.

Forster, Kenneth I., Christine Guerrera & Lisa Elliot. 2009. The maze task: Measuring forced incremental sentence processing time. *Behavior Research Methods* 41(1). 163–171.

Gries, Stefan Th. & Anatol Stefanowitsch. 2004. Extending collostructional analysis: A corpus-based perspective on "alternations." *International Journal of Corpus Linguistics* 9(1). 97–129.

Hilpert, Martin. 2008. The English comparative: Language structure and language use. *English Language and Linguistics* 12(3). 395–417.

Hilpert, Martin. 2016. Change in modal meanings: Another look at the shifting collocates of *may*. *Constructions and Frames* 8(1). 66–85.

Hilpert, Martin & Susanne Flach. 2021. Disentangling modal meanings with distributional semantics. *Digital Scholarship in the Humanities*. 36(2). 307–321.

Huddleston, Rodney D. & Geoffrey K. Pullum et al. 2002. *The Cambridge grammar of the English language*. Cambridge: Cambridge University Press.

Kaiser, Elsi. 2013. Experimental paradigms in psycholinguistics. In Robert Podesva & Devyani Sharma (eds.), *Research Methods in Linguistics*, 135–168. Cambridge: Cambridge University Press.

Lesuisse, Mégane, Benoît Leclercq, Bert Cappelle, Ilse Depraetere & Cyril Grandin. 2022. *Annotation Guide REM project – Rethinking English Modal Constructions: From Feature-Based Paradigms to Usage-Based Probabilistic Representations*. Université de Lille.

Lyons, John. 1977. *Semantics*. Cambridge: Cambridge University Press.

Nokkonen, Soili. 2006. The semantic variation of need to in four recent British English corpora. *International Journal of Corpus Linguistics* 11(1). 29–71.

Palan, Stefan & Christian Schitter. 2018. Prolific.ac: A subject pool for online experiments. *Journal of Behavioral and Experimental Finance* 17. 22–27.

Palmer, Frank R. 1990. [1979]. *Modality and the English Modals*. 2nd edn. London: Longman.

Perkins, Michael R. 1983. *Modal Expressions in English*. Norwood: Ablex.

Schmid, Hans-Jörg. 2020. *The Dynamics of the Linguistic System: Usage, Conventionalization, and Entrenchment*. Oxford: Oxford University Press.

Schützler, Ole & Jenny Herzky. 2022. Modal verbs of strong obligation in Scottish Standard English. *English Language and Linguistics* 26(1). 133–159.

Verhulst, An, Ilse Depraetere & Liesbet Heyvaert. 2013. Source and strength of modality: An empirical study of root *should, ought to* and *be supposed to* in present-day British English. *Journal of Pragmatics* 55. 210–225.

Westney, Paul. 1995. *Modals and periphrastics in English: An investigation into the semantic correspondence between certain English modal verbs and their periphrastic equivalents*. Tübingen: Max Niemeyer Verlag.

Weskott, Thomas & Gisbert Fanselow. 2011. On the informativity of different measures of linguistic acceptability. *Language* 87(2). 249–273.

Zehr, Jeremy & Florian Schwarz. 2018. *PennController for Internet Based Experiments (IBEX)*.

Ziegeler, Debra P. 2010. Semantic determinism and the grammaticalisation of *have to* in English: a reassessment. *Journal of Historical Pragmatics* 11(1). 32–66.

Ziegeler, Debra. 2014. On the generic argument for the modality of *will*. In Juana I. Marín-Arrese, Marta Carretero, Jorge Arús Hita & Johan van der Auwera (eds.), *English Modality*, 221–250. Berlin: De Gruyter Mouton.

6 Does the intersubjectivity of modal verbs boost inter-individual differences?

Clemens Hufeld and Hans-Jörg Schmid

1 Introduction

Modal verbs encode meanings and functions with a strong intersubjective load. Likelihood and certainty, obligation, permission, ability – all these notions connect speakers and hearers in a triadic relation vis-à-vis some idea, state of affairs or action (Du Bois 2007, van Duijn and Verhagen 2018). Given the intersubjective potential inherent in modal verbs, it is not surprising that modal verbs have proven to be a particularly dynamic area of English grammar. Modal verbs are known to be subject to language change as well as regional and social variation (Nagle 1989, Leech et al. 2009, Siemund 2013). And, as other chapters in the present book show in great detail (see in particular discussion in Chapter 1), it is difficult to pin down the ranges of meanings and functions of modal verbs, from a systematic perspective as well as in actual usage (Divjak, Szymor and Socha-Michalik 2015).

In short, modal verbs are marked by a high degree of intersubjectivity, context-dependence and potential for change as well as situational and social variation. A growing body of research suggests that the dynamicity and flexibility of such linguistic domains may ultimately be due to a high degree of inter-individual variation. Recent studies taking a usage-based perspective on language change demonstrate that there is considerable variation among speakers regarding the extent to which they participate in and contribute to ongoing change, see e.g. Gries and Hilpert (2010), Schmid and Mantlik (2015), Baxter and Croft (2016), Petré and Van de Velde (2018), Schmid (2020), Anthonissen (2020a, 2020b), Petré and Anthonissen (2020). At the same time, more and more researchers in variationist sociolinguistics emphasize the importance of taking inter-individual differences into account when interpreting findings on situational and social variation (e.g. MacKenzie 2019, Tagliamonte and Baayen 2012, van de Velde and van Hout 1998). In a recent publication, Schmid et al. (2021) showed that inter-individual differences accounted for a surprisingly large proportion of the overall variance observed in the use of the lexico-grammatical pattern THAT'S ADJ (e.g. *that's right, that's true, that's nice, that's great*). For the choice of the pattern *that's right* in comparison with quasi-synonymous patterns such as *that's true* and *that's correct*, inter-speaker variation accounted for a much larger proportion of the overall variance than systematic social variation conditioned by age, gender, education and social class. Schmid et al. (2021) argue that this inter-speaker variation is largely the result of the routines and habits of individual speakers who solve recurrent communicative tasks in consistent, but inter-individually different ways. For example, one speaker in the British National Corpus 2014 used the pattern *that's right* with a stunning frequency of 2,400 instances per million words, while another speaker, who contributed a comparable number of words to the corpus, produced no more than 8 per million words. The average normalized frequency of the phrase in the whole corpus was 297 instances per million words.

The pattern THAT'S ADJ investigated by Schmid et al. (2021) has a strong intersubjective component. It is used to express epistemic stance (*that's right, that's true*) and attitudinal stance (*that's lovely, that's nice*) and to realize interpersonal discourse moves such as signalling uptake (*that's alright, that's fine*). Modal verbs share this intersubjective potential with the pattern THAT'S ADJ. However, there is a crucial difference. Though grammatically more or less compositional, the pattern THAT'S ADJ tends to produce stand-alone discourse moves comparable in function to backchannel items and discourse markers such as *mhm* ('I have heard what you said and am paying attention'), *yeah* ('I have heard what you said and agree') or *my goodness/gosh* ('I have heard what you said and find it irritating'). In contrast, modal verbs are firmly embedded in the syntactic structure of larger units and make up a core part of grammar proper. This invites testing the hypothesis whether intersubjectivity fosters inter-individual variation, not only at the interface of grammar, lexicon and discourse, as in the case of the pattern THAT'S ADJ, but also in pure grammar, so to speak.

In order to test this hypothesis, we extracted data from the spoken component of the British National Corpus 2014 (BNC2014) and compared the cross-speaker frequency distribution of selected uni-grams, bi-grams and tri-grams containing modals with that of comparably frequent uni-grams, bi-grams and tri-grams not containing modal verbs. The available metadata were used to gauge potential effects of the social variables GENDER, AGE, EDUCATION and SOCIAL CLASS. Regression models were fitted to estimate the effect of these variables and the contribution of differences between individual speakers to the overall variance found.

2 Research question and hypothesis

While our study is generally of an exploratory nature, we have framed it in confirmatory terms to increase objectivity and systematicity. Our research question is as follows:

> Do speakers differ more and have more pronounced individual routines and habits in the domain of modal verbs than in other domains of grammar and lexis?

We assume that individual linguistic routines and habits contribute to the overall variance observed in the frequency distribution of linguistic elements in corpora (Schmid 2020, Stefanowitsch and Flach 2017). Based on this assumption, we operationalize our research question in the form of the following 0-hypothesis and alternative hypothesis:

H_0: The contribution of inter-individual differences to the overall variance observed in the frequency distribution of modal uni-grams, bi-grams and tri-grams in BNC2014 does not differ significantly from the contribution of inter-individual differences to the overall variance observed in the frequency distribution of other comparable uni-grams, bi-grams and tri-grams.

H_1: The contribution of inter-individual differences to the overall variance observed in the frequency distribution of modal uni-grams, bi-grams and tri-grams in BNC2014 is significantly higher than the contribution of inter-individual differences to the overall variance observed in the frequency distribution of other comparable uni-grams, bi-grams and tri-grams.

Our investigation is designed in a maximally data-driven manner. This has the obvious advantages that the effect of subjective decisions is reduced and that – within the limitations of corpus linguistics, e.g. corpora being representative of themselves rather than real-life language – the methodology of our study is transferrable to any corpus or data source, ensuring replicability. On the downside, the bag of words model used for this study means that we cannot take semantic and pragmatic aspects into consideration, as the larger conversational context is ignored. In addition, the manual annotation of several hundred thousand examples is not feasible. We are aware that it is likely that speakers not only differ with regard to the sheer frequency with which they use modal verbs, but also with regard to the meanings and functions in the service of which they use them. However, this perspective will have to await further studies.

3 Data source and retrieval

The data used in this chapter is taken from the spoken component of the British National Corpus 2014 (Love et al. 2017, Brezina, Hawtin and McEnery 2021). This 11.5-million-word subcorpus contains conversation between friends and family from the United Kingdom collected between 2012 and 2016. It has been compiled by the Centre for Corpus Approaches to Social Science (CASS) at Lancaster University and Cambridge University Press as a successor to the 1994 version of the BNC. The spoken component of the BNC2014 offers a synchronic, closed, single medium resource, representing 668 speakers who contributed to 1,251 conversations.

The BNC2014 is available online for free as a collection of XML files. The files contain metadata on all speakers and conversations. Each conversation is available in tagged and untagged form. In the tagged documents, each word is annotated with regard to lemma, word class (on two levels of specificity) as well as meaning, using the UCREL Semantic Analysis System (USAS) developed at Lancaster University (Wilson and Rayson 1993).

This data was processed using the Python programming language, in particular the pandas library.[1] First, all tagged documents were parsed to transfer the entire BNC2014 into a pandas dataframe, using the etree ElementTree XML API. The dataframe format greatly facilitated initial filtering and data retrieval while extracting modal verbs and their contexts. Because of the size of the BNC2014 dataframe, the operations were performed using multiprocessing in the form of the concurrent.futures module and the inbuilt ProcessPoolExecutor to parallelize the tasks.

A list of all modal verbs with their respective context of four words to either side was extracted, using the part of speech tag "VM" ('modal verb') as a target. After dropping insignificant modal verb occurrences (these were historical uses in sayings, e.g. *shalt*, *wilt* or words erroneously tagged as modals), we were left with a list of 206,000 tokens of modal verbs embedded in a small context window of four words to the left and right. This list was further refined to exclude sequences straddling the boundaries of sentence units and speakers' utterances, so that each chunk only contained one speaker's utterance within one sentence unit as indicated in the corpus. For example, a 9-word chunk might be reduced to a two-word chunk in the following example: Speaker 1: *to town tomorrow* Speaker 2: *I can* Speaker 1: *well then let's*" → "I can". Whereas the original dataframe contained only one spoken word per line, in the resulting list the context words and the modal verb were combined, so that each line shows at least one word – the modal verb – and at most nine words if there is a context of up to four words on either side of the modal verb, similar to the KWIC concordance view (Luhn 1960).

The items in the resulting list of n-grams were then merged with speakers' metadata. This metadata is freely available in the BNC2014 data and contains

---

1 For the full code, see the book's companion website (https://www.degruyter.com/document/isbn/9783110734157/html), or go directly to the chapter's Github repository found at https://github.com/chufeld/moutonModelsOfModalsHufeldSchmid.

information on the variables AGE, GENDER, SOCIAL CLASS, EDUCATION LEVEL, DIALECT, PLACE OF BIRTH and PLACE OF RESIDENCE. The combination of the modal verb n-grams with the metadata produces a dataframe that allows for frequency-based analyses of the usage of n-grams containing modal verbs.

Our research question and hypotheses require comparable data on n-grams that do not contain modal verbs. These n-grams were extracted in essentially the same way. The next section describes the selection of the modal and non-modal items investigated.

4 Selection of modal target and non-modal control n-grams

4.1 Data sampling

The modal target n-grams and their non-modal counterparts to be used for the analysis were selected in a multi-step procedure. The main goal of this procedure was to choose modal and non-modal items which are comparable with regard to their frequency of occurrence and frequent enough to lend themselves to an analysis of inter-speaker variation in usage frequency. Additional considerations – to be explained below – served as further inclusion and exclusion criteria.

In the first step, frequency lists of uni-grams, bi-grams and tri-grams containing a modal verb were compiled. Uni-grams were the 11 modal verb forms *can*, *would*, *will*, *could*, *should*, *might*, *must*, *shall*, *may*, *dare* and *need* (including the cliticized forms *'ll* and *'d*). Bi-grams included two-word combinations with the modal verb either on the left (as in *can you* and *would be*) or on the right (e.g. *you can* or *I will*). In the tri-grams, we allowed all three positions of the modal verb, i.e. as the first (*would like to*), second *(it can be)* or third word *(and you can)* of a three-word sequence.

In the second step, all n-grams were rank-listed in terms of their frequency of occurrence. Since the goal of this study is to investigate inter-individual variation, it was important to test at this early stage whether and to what extent the frequency counts would allow this type of investigation. If the data volume had been too low or if it had turned out that speakers do not differ in terms of their usage frequencies, all our efforts would have been doomed to fail right from the start. A suitable way of testing the degree of variance was to calculate the coefficient of variation for the 100 most frequent n-grams by dividing the standard deviation by the arithmetic mean ($CV=\frac{\sigma}{\mu}$) of the usage frequency of all speakers in the corpus (see also Section 5.1). The coefficient of variation shows the extent of variation in relation to the mean. The advantage of including this relation is that we can compare different sets of data. For example, comparing the modal verbs *can* and *might*, with a relative frequency of 3,274 and 898 instances per million words respectively, one would intuitively expect to find more variance for *can* than for *might*, simply because there seems to be more room for variation in the former case. Linking the degree of variation expressed by the standard deviation to the mean promises to reduce this difference, thus allowing the comparison of standard deviation between measurements with different means (Brown 1998: 155). As regards its interpretation, if the coefficient is above 1, there is greater dispersion in the data than the statistical assumption of equal distribution would suggest. Larger coefficients indicate greater dispersion and hence variation, which may be indicative of more pronounced differences between speakers.

Applying this procedure, we were able to confirm that all items were subject to inter-speaker variation, allowing us to base our choice of target items on additional criteria, in particular the goal to include a range of different modal verbs, subject pronouns and main verbs. Overall, however, the range of eligible items was severely restricted by the low frequency of occurrence of many n-grams, especially bi-grams and of course tri-grams.

Balancing these criteria, the following eleven modal target items were chosen for investigation:
- the uni-grams *can* and *might*,
- the bi-grams *you can*, *I'll*, *we'll* and *it would* as examples of context to the left of the modal verb, and *would be*, *can you*, *'ll have* and *might be* as examples of context to the right of the modal verb,
- and the tri-gram *'ll have to*.

The non-modal control items were selected in an opportunistic manner to match the frequency of the modal items (see Table 1). In addition, we selected items in such a way that they did not share any lexical or morphological material such as the occurrence of *a* or *of* in several controls. Another consideration was to select both purely grammatical control items such as *of them* and *on a* as well as items that included lexical material, e.g. *look at* and *you think*.

Data for all 22 n-grams were extracted from the BNC2014, combined with speaker metadata and stored as dataframes. This dataset underwent further pruning described in the next section.

4.2 Data pruning

More than 660 speakers are recorded in the BNC2014. Their respective contributions to the corpus differ greatly, ranging from not more than 28 to as many as 362,107 words. Among the speakers, 68 contribute fewer than 1,000 words, 433

4 Selection of modal target and non-modal control n-grams

Table 1: Modal target and non-modal control items and their comparable frequencies of occurrence.

Type	Modal target items	Frequency per million words in BNC2014	Non-modal control items	Frequency per million words in BNC2014
uni-grams	can	3274	get	3612
	might	898	take	847
frequent bi-grams	you can	1197	and it	1298
	I'll	1129	to be	1276
less frequent bi-grams	would be	489	of them	434
	we'll	432	on a	385
	it would	329	it does	475
	can you	337	they have	347
	'll have	291	look at	361
	might be	235	you think	394
tri-grams	'll have to	125	I went to	107

fewer than 10,000 words, and only 23 more than 100,000 words. It is important to be aware of these numbers, because the likelihood that a given speaker uses any given modal or non-modal n-gram depends on the number of words they contribute. Table 1 indicates, for instance, that the tri-gram *'ll have to* occurs 125 times per million words in the whole corpus. If we use the overall frequency as a benchmark for individual speakers, the expected frequency of this tri-gram in the data of a speaker who contributes 10,000 words is 1.25. With an expected frequency of 0.13, speakers who contribute less than 1,000 words are in fact extremely unlikely to have delivered this sequence. Therefore, if it is found that such speakers do not produce a given target item, it is impossible to decide whether the zero-score is due to the fact that they do not use this sequence frequently enough, or whether it is caused by data scarcity and is an artefact of the corpus data.

In order to do justice to this observation, we did not use the full BNC2014 data for each of our analyses. Instead, for each of the 22 target and control items, we calculated the number of words statistically required for them to be expected to occur at all. This was done by dividing the overall number of words in the corpus (11,422,617) by the raw number of occurrences of a given n-gram in the corpus. For example, the tri-gram *'ll have to* occurs 1,423 times in the whole corpus. If the tri-gram was distributed perfectly evenly across the corpus, we would expect to see it once in 8,027 words – a figure that we get by dividing 11,422,617 (all words in the corpus) by 1,423 (number of instances of the tri-gram in the corpus). Statistically speaking, a corpus extract of 8,027 would be expected to contain one instance of the tri-gram *'ll have to*. Therefore, if a speaker contributed less than

8,027 words to the corpus, it could simply be due to data scarcity if we found no example of *'ll have to*. Using this threshold as an exclusion criterion, 392 speakers who contributed fewer than 8,027 words were excluded from the dataset for the analysis of *'ll have to*. In contrast, since *can* boasts a raw frequency of 37,398 occurrences, the corresponding threshold lies at 305 words, within which the word *can* can be expected to occur. Applying this much lower threshold, we excluded only 7 speakers who contributed a smaller number of words. Note that this does not rule out the possibility that speakers score 0 for a given item, since even if their contribution is well above the threshold, they still may not have used the item in question. However, in these cases we can be more confident that the zero-score is not due to data scarcity relating to this particular speaker. Table 2 reports the speakers and zero-values for all n-grams: the second and the fifth columns list the number of speakers above the threshold whose data were included in the analyses, the third and sixth columns report the number of speakers who did not use a given item although their contribution exceeded the threshold.

Table 2: Data report related to data pruning.

Modal target items	Number of speakers after pruning	Remaining number of 'valid' zero observations	Non-modal control items	Number of speakers after pruning	Remaining number of 'valid' zero observations
can	654	17	get	654	18
might	587	59	take	580	53
you can	608	41	and it	619	41
I'll	605	56	to be	618	39
would be	513	59	of them	499	53
we'll	499	118	on a	481	63
it would	448	63	it does	495	67
can you	454	70	they have	459	66
'll have	425	79	look at	468	76
might be	390	83	you think	484	99
'll have to	269	72	I went to	238	50

5 Results

Next, we report the results of our analysis, starting with descriptive and then moving on to inferential statistics. Throughout, we focus on the usage frequencies of individual speakers.

5.1 Descriptive statistics

5.1.1 Five-number summaries

To provide a first idea of the frequencies with which speakers used the selected n-grams, Figures 1 to 3 provide visualized five-number summaries of the data, showing the minimum frequency per speaker, the maximum, the median and the upper and lower quartiles of the data. These are rendered in the form of boxplots for the two pairs of uni-grams (Figure 1), the eight pairs of bi-grams (Figure 2) and the two tri-grams (Figure 3). In all figures, non-modal controls are in blue, modals in red, as well as in green in Figure 2 (in order to distinguish left-context and right-context bi-grams). All boxplots provide information about the extent to which usage frequency varies across speakers, with the boxes indicating the second and third quartiles (encompassing those speakers found in the frequency range between 25% and 75% of the range), whiskers indicating the first and fourth quartiles and dots outliers.

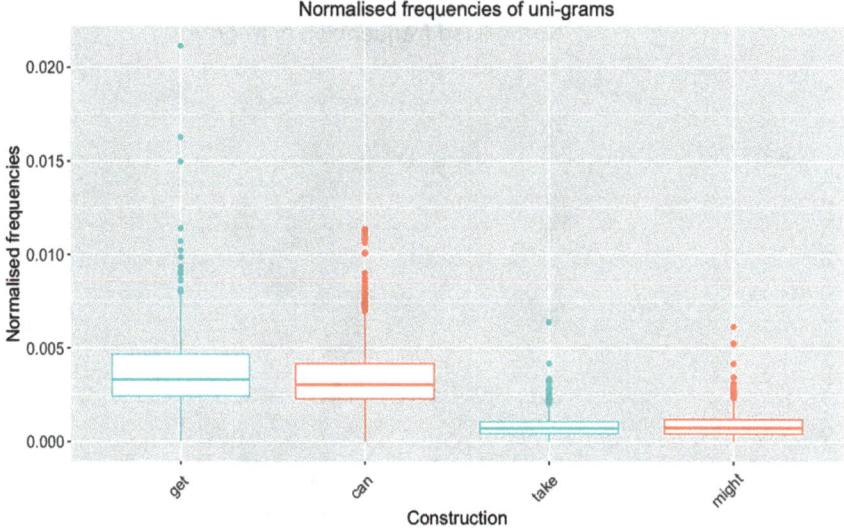

Figure 1: Five-number summary for uni-grams.

The visual inspection of the three figures yields the following observations: in general, there is a large dispersion over speakers, with long upwards whiskers indicating a large top quartile, accompanied by a considerable number of outliers. All boxplots display this situation, regardless of the relative frequencies of n-grams. Since the datasets include some zero-values for each n-gram, all boxplots start at zero and display shorter lower quantiles than upper ones, but the

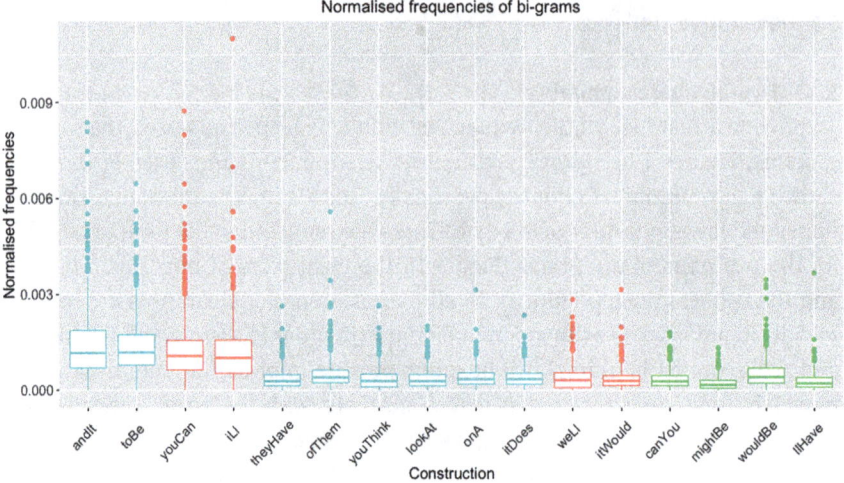

Figure 2: Five-number summary for bi-grams.

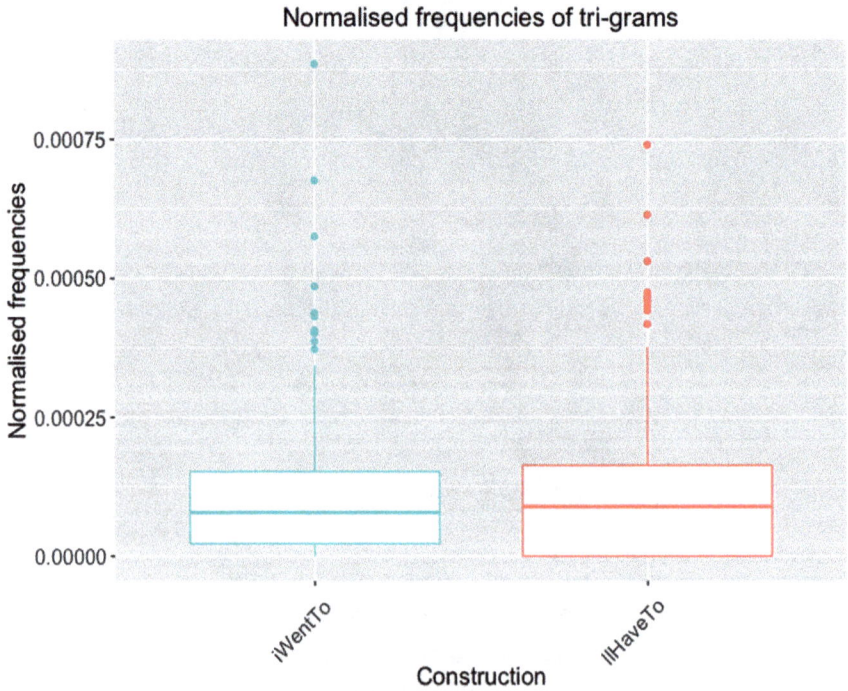

Figure 3: Five-number summary for tri-grams.

amount of variation towards the high frequencies differs considerably and does not seem predictable. As the datasets get larger in terms of n-gram frequency, they also tend to include more of the 680 speakers in the BNC2014, have higher means and span a greater range of frequencies.

Notably, there is no immediately visible difference in the profiles of modal n-grams and non-modal n-grams with matching frequencies (e.g. *to be* and *you can*). This means that modal n-grams and non-modal n-grams with similar frequencies appear to be subject to individual preferences in the same way. A precise assessment of differences between boxplots of two n-grams is made more difficult by the large number of outliers in each plot and by unresolved questions of the effect of an n-gram's frequency on the distribution. Therefore, further analysis of the difference in variation is required.

5.1.2 Coefficients of variation

To make the n-grams more comparable to each other, a normalized value is needed. As explained in Section 4.1 above, the coefficient of variation, also known as relative standard deviation, can be used for this. The formula $c_v = \frac{\sigma}{\mu}$ takes the standard deviation σ and divides it by the population mean μ, which promises to neutralize the effect of variation in the differences in frequency (Bindu et al. 2019: 3). Figure 4 reports the coefficients of variation for all n-grams.

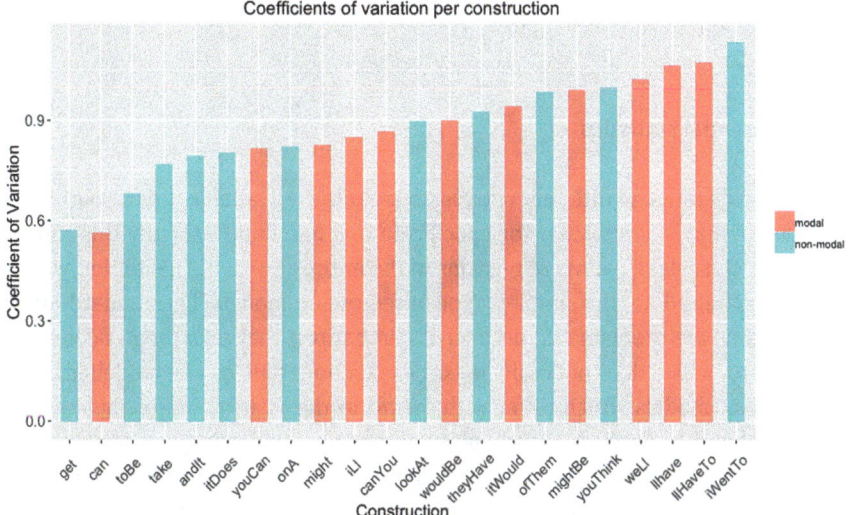

Figure 4: Coefficients of variation for each n-gram.

Inspecting Figure 4, we can see that the effect of overall or mean frequency is only reduced, but not completely excluded, since the two most frequent unigrams and the least frequent tri-grams cluster on opposing ends of the graph. Examining the difference between modal and non-modal n-grams, we see that modal and non-modal items do not cluster together. The figure does not provide information indicating that there is a general difference between comparably frequent modal and non-modal n-grams. This is true in spite of the fact that the lower half (up to *can you*) includes one more non-modal n-gram and the upper half one more modal n-gram.

However, it is still possible that differences between modal and non-modal n-grams are not revealed by the coefficient of variation, which is a fairly simple measure after all. Thus, further analysis of the data is needed in the form of regression models. Such models estimate the relation between a response or dependent variable, here the frequency distribution of n-grams, and one or more independent variables, for example, the gender and age of the speaker. The advantage of such models is that they reduce the effect of differences in numbers of speakers and usage frequencies, as the regression model produces its estimate on the basis of the available data, regardless of the number of speakers or frequency of the n-gram. In addition, the effects of systematic sociolinguistic predictor variables as sources of variation can be measured. In the case of BNC2014 data, these are AGE RANGE, GENDER, SOCIAL GRADE and EDUCATION QUALITY. Fitting a regression model thus allows for a more robust assessment of inter-speaker variation than the coefficient of variation alone.

5.2 Inferential statistics

Since a wide range of different regression models are available, it is important to select one that is suitable for the specific data at hand and to justify this choice. The data consists of counts of n-grams in the entire corpus of 11.5 million words. For such count data, the simplest type of regression models, i.e. standard linear regressions, are problematic, because it can happen that they predict counts of below zero, which does not really make sense. Count data can be modelled using a variety of models which differ with regard to the distribution of the dependent variable they assume, mainly poisson models, quasipoisson models or negative binomial models. The poisson model is inappropriate, as it is based on the assumption that mean and variance are equal, i.e. $(Y_i|\eta_i) = (Y_i|\eta_i) = \mu_i$. This model assumes a constant dispersion value of 1, which is not what we have in our data, as we have shown in Section 4.1. In such cases, quasipoisson models tend to be chosen for count data, because here the dispersion value is not assumed a priori but instead included in the model as a parameter (ø), as in the case of the negative binomial model (Ver Hoef and Boveng 2007: 2767). To make a choice between the negative binomial and the quasipoisson model, the relationship between the variance and the mean was inspected visually. In the negative binomial distribution, the variance is quadratic in the mean, whereas it is linear for the quasipoisson distribution (Ver Hoef and Boveng 2007: 2767). The visual inspection of a variance-mean plot of normalized frequencies of several n-grams suggested that the quasipoisson model was the better choice for the regression.

As far as the main target of our study, i.e. inter-speaker variation, is concerned, the so-called *dispersion parameter* reported in the quasipoisson model summaries can be taken as a relevant measure. Dispersion parameters above 1 indicate overdispersion, meaning that the variance increases more than the mean. The higher the dispersion parameter, the stronger the effect of individual differences in the model.

The systematic sociolinguistic predictors included in the model were the AGE RANGE, SOCIAL GRADE, GENDER and EDUCATIONAL QUALITY as provided in the BNC2014 data. Where categories of the predictors were underrepresented in terms of raw counts by at least a factor of eight when compared to the most frequent category, they were combined with other categories of the same predictor, to create a balance between the categories. For example, while GENDER is a uniformly binary category in the data, for AGE RANGES all categories above 50-year-olds were severely underrepresented. These categories were collapsed into a 50- to 99-year-old category, to balance the frequencies somewhat. For EDUCATIONAL QUALITY, the categories primary education, secondary education and unknown level were combined. The categories were then relevelled, so that the most frequent category is taken as the standard for comparison of significant deviance, rather than the first category alphabetically.

In line with the assumptions of variationist sociolinguistics (Eckert 2000, 2018, Labov 1972), our expectation is that the models will find significant relationships between the sociolinguistic factors and the variation observed (e.g. in the boxplots), to help explain the observed variation. Additionally, the dispersion values might give further insights into the amount of inter-speaker variation of modal and non-modal n-grams.

5.2.1 Results regarding sociolinguistic predictors

For each n-gram, we fitted a quasipoisson model with GENDER, AGE RANGE, SOCIAL CLASS and EDUCATIONAL QUALITY as covariables. Since the number of words each speaker contributes to the corpus differs vastly, we used the decimal logarithm of the number of words each speaker contributed to the corpus as an offset, rather than dividing the occurrences by the number of words. The reason is that while both methods have the same effect on the mean, they differ in their effect on the variance. Dividing by number of words reduces the variance in proportion to the mean squared. The offset reduces the variance according to the model, i.e. proportional to the change in mean. Out of all models fitted, a selection of significant effects are reported in the model summaries available in the github repository referenced in footnote 1. A subset is presented in Table 3, ignoring significant effects of the value 'unknown'.

Table 3: Quasipoisson model results with indications of significance; the levels are '***' < 0.001; '**' < 0.01; '*' < 0.1.

N-gram	Significant Covariable	Estimate	Standard Error	T value	Pr(>|t|)	Level of Signif.
can	genderM	0.16896	0.03236	5.222	2.40e-07	***
	agerange0_18	0.29073	0.06527	4.454	9.95e-06	***
	agerange30_49	0.20438	0.03896	5.246	2.12e-07	***
get	genderM	0.13902	0.02955	4.705	3.12e-06	***
I went to	agerange30_49	−0.37820	0.16045	−2.357	0.01927	*
can you	agerange30_49	0.348993	0.081357	4.290	2.2e-05	***
you can	genderM	0.313504	0.043847	7.150	2.56e-12	
	agerange30_49	0.254816	0.053509	4.762	2.41e-06	***
	agerange50_99	0.176579	0.055996	3.153	0.0017	**
	socgradeB	0.128440	0.060101	2.137	0.0330	*
I' ll	edqual5_postgrad	−0.307535	0.059233	−5.192	2.87e-07	***
we' ll	edqual5_postgrad	−0.21182	0.07794	−2.718	0.00681	**

Overall, the model results do not yield a coherent picture, neither of the difference between modal and non-modal n-grams, on the one hand, nor of the effects of sociolinguistic variables, on the other. It is true that five out of the seven items listed in Table 3 are modals, leaving only two non-modals, which points in the direction that social variables have stronger effects on the use of modal than on non-modal n-grams. But this trend should be interpreted with utmost caution, because the results regarding the effects of sociolinguistic variables themselves are not coherent. For example, the model for *can* reports positive effects for the AGE RANGES 0–18 and 30–49 when compared to the group of 19- to 29-year-olds. This is difficult to interpret, as there is no linear development with increasing AGE, but rather a jump between the groups. The model further indicates that speakers in the age range of 30–49 tend to use the n-gram *I went to* less often than their younger counterparts. However, the lower number of occurrences is reflected in the larger standard errors and the lower significance thresholds, when compared to other, more frequent n-grams. For *can you* and *you can*, the model predicts that people above the age of 29 tend to use both n-grams more often, and males favour *you can* when compared to female speakers. The clitic n-grams *I'll* and *we'll* show an effect with regard to the educational level of the speaker. In both n-grams, the model's results indicated that speakers with a postgraduate degree use the clitic n-grams less often than students, i.e. speakers still enrolled in tertiary education.

Overall, the insights to be gained regarding the effects of social variables on the distinction between modals and non-modals remain limited. Since we are mainly interested in effects of individual variation, this is not problematic. On the contrary, it increases the importance of looking at the dispersion values of the models which are indicative of individual variation.

5.2.2 Results regarding inter-speaker variation

The dispersion scores estimated in the quasipoisson models are reported in Figure 5. The higher the score, the stronger the overdispersion and the more pronounced the effect of individual variation.

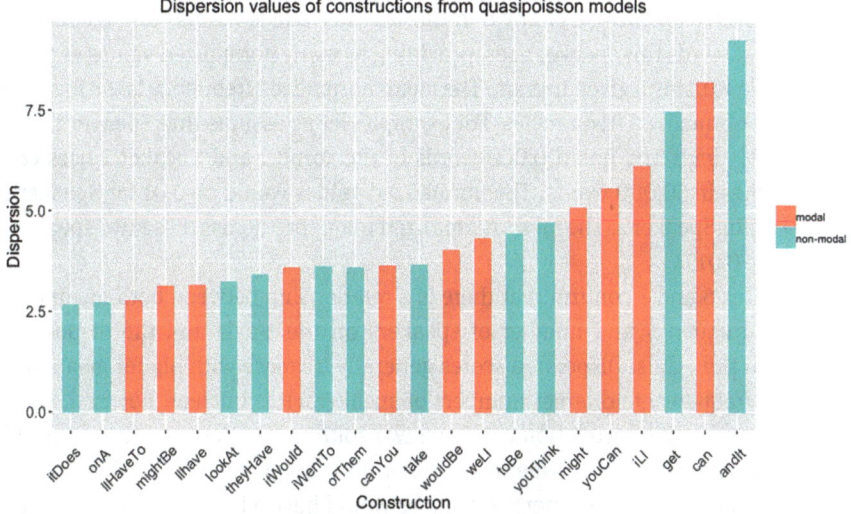

Figure 5: Dispersion values from quasipoisson models of all n-grams.

Like Figure 4 reporting coefficients of variation, Figure 5 does not show a clear division between modal and non-modal n-grams. The dispersion values seem to be independent of the presence of a modal verb. Dispersion parameters range from 2.65 to 9.21, indicating strong individual preferences even for the least overdispersed n-grams and extreme preferences for the most overdispersed ones. However, the modal n-grams are not remarkable in the overdispersion they display.

There also appears to be a weaker correlation between the raw frequencies and the dispersion values, as the tri-grams are not clustered at the lower end, as with the coefficients of variation, but are rather in the middle of the range. At the same time, *get* and *can* both display large dispersion values, indicating that their use is clustered in the data, in the sense that some individuals tend to use them disproportionately often. *And it* and *to be* appear similarly frequently in the corpus but display very different dispersion values, which speaks against a correlation of frequency and dispersion value.

These inconclusive findings call for a closer look at how dispersion scores are related to frequency of occurrence and also to the number of speakers whose data go into the various models. Are dispersion scores sensitive to, or even mainly determined by, frequency and/or number of speakers providing data? To answer this question, Figure 6 plots the dispersion values against the mean normalized frequencies of the n-grams, allowing a vizualization of this relationship. Figure 7 does the same for numbers of speakers. The mean normalized frequency used in these figures is a combination of two measures. Each speaker has a different raw frequency for the use of any n-gram. This raw use is normalized against the number of words this speaker uses, providing as many normalized values as there are speakers using a given n-gram. The mean normalized frequency is the mean of all these normalized frequencies. For example, let us assume that Speaker 1 uses *can* 4,000 times and has 100,000 words in the corpus, and Speaker 2 uses *can* 1,000 times in 50,000 words. The normalized values would be 0.01 for Speaker 1 and 0.02 for Speaker 2. The mean normalized frequency across these two speakers would be 0.015.

Figures 6 and 7 confirm that there is a relationship between both mean normalized frequency and number of speakers on the x-axis and the dispersion scores on the y-axis. Dispersion scores generally increase with higher mean normalized frequency and larger numbers of speakers. It is unclear, however, what this means, as this correlation can have two sources. On the one hand, it could mean that more frequent elements are generally more prone to be subject to individual variation. From this perspective, we would have a finding regarding a fact of language. On the other hand, the correlation could be an artefact of the limitations of the corpus. Low-frequency items might simply lack the volume and diversity of data required to reveal overdispersion on the same scale as high-frequency items. To adjudicate between these two scenarios, we extracted several smaller samples of high-frequency elements which were comparable in size and number of speakers with the samples available for less frequent items, e.g. several 5,000-token samples of the uni-grams *get* and *can*. It turned out that these subsets of

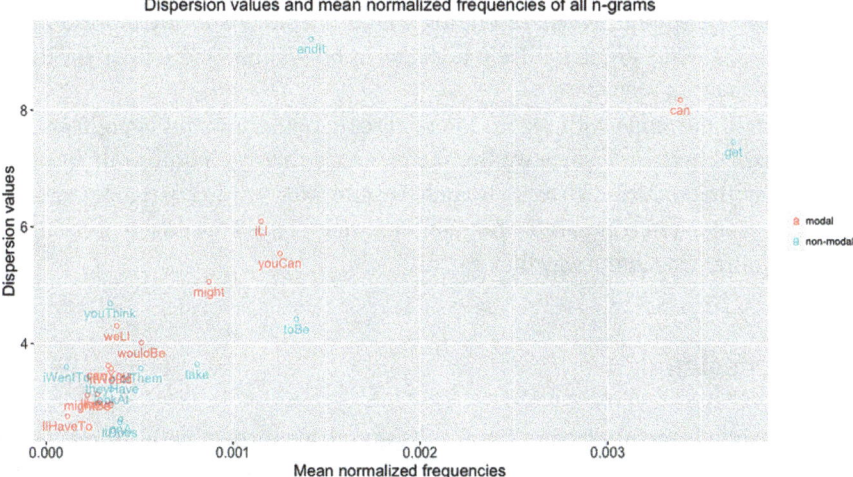

Figure 6: Relationship between dispersion values and mean normalized frequencies of all n-grams.

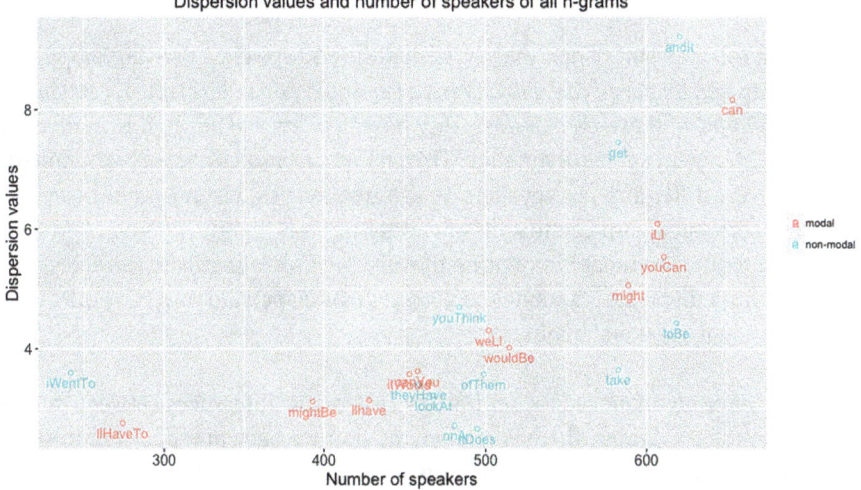

Figure 7: Relationship between dispersion values and number of speakers per n-gram.

data of more frequent items had smaller dispersion scores than n-grams with comparable frequencies. This result suggests that the overdispersion observed for high-frequency items might be an artefact of the higher number of attestations in the corpus. As regards findings on language as such, it also indicates that individual variation may actually be lower (rather than higher) for more frequent items than for less frequent items – a finding which is in line with the intuition that less frequent items are more likely to occur in bursts than more frequent items expected to occur anywhere.

Overall, our hope with regard to our research question and hypothesis has been dashed here, too, since we find no evidence that would allow us to reject the 0-hypothesis. Although there is considerable inter-speaker variation for each n-gram, modal and comparably frequent non-modal n-grams do not show a significant difference in the way they vary.

6 Discussion

In this section, we summarize the results and discuss them with regard to the hypothesis and their relevance for the field of quantitative analysis of inter-speaker variation.

6.1 Summary of results

The most robust result of our analysis is that the 660 speakers use the 22 n-grams *can, might, get, take, you can, I'll, and it, to be, would be, we'll, it would, can you, 'll have, might be, of them, on a, it does, they have, look at, you think, 'll have to* and *I went to* with a great degree of variation. This emerged from all measures we reported:
- from the differences in speakers' usage frequencies, visualized in box plots and correlated with coefficients of variation,
- from regression models exploring the effects of sociolinguistic variables,
- and from dispersion parameters gauging overdispersion and thus effects of individual speakers' habits.

Since we have not managed to identify any systematic differences between modal and non-modal n-grams, there is no denying that we have to report a null-result for our hypothesis. While the boxplots display a large degree of variation between speakers, they do not show any differences between modal and non-modal n-grams. The coefficients of variation and the dispersion values, while both high, are not sensitive to the modal quality of the n-gram. The regression models do not provide any indication either that the social variables condition the use of modal n-grams differently from non-modal n-grams, insofar as the model estimates are interpretable at all. Dispersion scores indicating overdispersion are not sensitive to the difference between modal and non-modal n-grams, but rather to the frequency of n-grams and the number of speakers included in the respective analyses.

6.2 Discussion of findings

How can the null-result be explained? The most obvious answer to this question would be that our initial expectation and hypothesis were wrong. To be sure, these were not built out of thin air, but derived from established theoretical considerations and empirical observations: the well-known attitudinal quality of modals and the tendency of attitudinally loaded elements to vary and change, on the one hand (see e.g. Chapter 1, Section 3.4), and the findings of Schmid et al. (2021) indicating that individual variation is an important factor for the use of the stance-marking pattern THAT'S ADJ, on the other. However, our results suggest that simple modal verbs as well as bi-grams and tri-grams containing modal verbs do not seem to have any inherent quality that increases the likelihood that speakers develop individual habits. Further research will have to be conducted to find out whether our failure to reject the 0-hypothesis lies in incorrect assumptions about the nature of modals.

This research will have to take into consideration other possible explanations for the null-result. Firstly, it could be due to our decision to ignore semantic and pragmatic aspects. After all, our initial assumption was based on semantic considerations, so it would definitely be promising to integrate at least a crude and easily applicable semantic analysis, e.g. by cross-tabulating epistemic vs. root and possibility vs. necessity, in future studies.

Secondly, one big elephant in the room is of course situational and topical variation. There can be no doubt that any type of linguistic choice is at least partly determined by context and topic. In Schmid et al.'s (2021) study, the conversations in BNC2014 also had a very strong effect on the frequency distribution of some lexically filled patterns (e.g. *that's right*). The fundamental question here is to what extent the observed inter-individual differences and hypothesized speaker habits are conditioned by situations and topics. All conversations in BNC2014 belong to the register of casual spoken conversation, but they cover a wide range of topics, e.g. filthy flatmates, vaping, dog attacks, queuing, Alzheimer's, proofreading, and South Park, to name but a few. It cannot be ruled out that the observed speaker-related variation is no more than a side-effect of topic-related variation. Preliminary analyses of our data for this study confirm such effects, but these, too, do not seem to be affected by the contrast between modals and non-modals.

Thirdly, the somewhat mechanical, almost entirely frequency-driven choice of target items could play a role. While there is nothing wrong with the choice of the simple forms *can* and *might* vs. *get* and *take*, bi-grams such as *we'll* or *of them* do not seem to have a place as elements in the linguistic system or speakers' repertoires other than by virtue of the sheer fact that their parts frequently co-occur.

However, we assume that this is not a fundamental problem contributing to the null-result, because less arbitrary and semantically and pragmatically more intuitive bi-grams like *can you, you can* or *you think* did not emerge from our study in any special way.

Fourthly, the uneven distribution of data across sociolinguistic variables and missing metadata contribute to difficulties in the analysis, especially when the overall data volume for a given item is low. This has a strong effect on the investigation of the sociolinguistic variables and is one reason why we have decided against working with mixed-effects regression models in this study. Given this highly skewed distribution, we think that a more detailed investigation of the data structure of the BNC2014 is definitely in order because we can put more trust in the application of such models. This includes the internal cross-validation of the corpus regarding the effect different slices of the BNC2014 have on the results and is a way of assessing skewed representations of the covariables in the corpus. This would not only enhance the reliability of the results, but could be taken as an important contribution to corpus building. The situation for Schmid et al. (2021) was different in this respect, because they applied binomial regression models to investigate the use of near-synonymous variants of only one pattern.

Lastly, the different usage frequencies could have a confounding effect on our study, though again perhaps not so much on the hypothesized difference between modal and non-modal n-grams. As we saw, differences in absolute frequencies in the corpus and in number of speakers included in the analysis affected both coefficients of variation and dispersion scores. This raises an important question relevant for all investigations of individual-speaker corpus data relying on closed corpora: would less frequent items behave in a similar way to more frequent ones if a larger corpus were available in which the less frequent items reached higher frequencies of occurrence? The preliminary tests that we ran suggest that the observed difference between the frequent items *can* and *get*, on the one hand, and much less frequent items such as *'ll have* and *look at* is due to the lower data volume (and resulting lower number of observations and speakers). Yet there seems to be a difference between high- and low-frequency linguistic items which is linguistically relevant regardless of the data volume, but this difference points in the opposite direction, indicating that higher frequency correlates with lower dispersion. Future research is required to investigate how the corpus architecture relates to the frequency distribution of n-grams and how different frequency distributions impact on the comparability of n-grams.

7 Conclusion

Reporting a null-result is not what one aims for when one embarks on a confirmatory study like the present one. The results simply do not suggest a special status for modal n-grams regarding inter-individual differences in usage frequencies, as compared to similarly frequent non-modal grammatical and lexico-grammatical n-grams. And given the multitude of uncertainties in the present research, we are not able to consider our study as support for the 0-hypothesis and conclude that modal verbs do not differ from other elements with regard to effects of inter-individual variation. Nevertheless, our results are an important step in the direction of understanding individual variation in modal verbs. We do think that our findings robustly reveal a surprising, perhaps even stunning degree of inter-individual differences. This insight, too, serves as an invitation for further research in two distinct areas. Firstly, whether the differences found in the data are systematic across different corpora compiled from the spoken or written medium, and secondly, to what extent the individual influences modal usage in isolation from other confounding factors. We therefore take the results of our study as an important step on the road to a more robust quantitative understanding of modality and an incentive to renew efforts and redress methodological issues.

References

Anthonissen, Lynn. 2020a. Cognition in construction grammar: Connecting individual and community grammars. *Cognitive Linguistics* 31(2). 309–337.

Anthonissen, Lynn. 2020b. *Special Passives across the Life Span. Cognitive and Social Mechanisms*. Antwerp: Antwerp University.

Baxter, Gareth & William Croft. 2016. Modeling language change across the lifespan: Individual trajectories in community change. *Language Variation and Change* 28(2). 129–173.

Bindu, Hima K., M Raghava, Nilanjan Dey & C. Raghavendra Rao. 2019. *Coefficient of variation and machine learning applications*. New York: Routledge.

Brezina, Vaclav, Abi Hawtin, & Tony McEnery. 2021. The Written British National Corpus 2014 – design and comparability. *Text & Talk* 41(5–6). 595–615.

Brown, Charles E. 1998. Applied Multivariate Statistics in Geohydrology and Related Sciences. Berlin, Heidelberg: Springer.

Divjak, Dagmar, Nina Szymor and Anna Socha-Michalik. 2015. Less is more: possibility as centres of gravity in a usage-based classification of core modals in Polish. *Russian Linguistics* 39(3). 327–349.

Du Bois, John. 2007. The stance triangle. In Robert Englebretson (ed.), *Stancetaking in Discourse: Subjectivity, Evaluation, Interaction*, 139–182. Amsterdam/Philadelphia: PA: Benjamins.

Eckert, Penelope. 2000. *Linguistic Variation as Social Practice: The Linguistic Construction of Identity in Belten High*. Malden, MA: Blackwell Publishers.

Eckert, Penelope. 2018. *Meaning and Linguistic Variation: The Third Wave in Sociolinguistics*. Cambridge: Cambridge University Press.

Gries, Stefan Th. & Martin Hilpert. 2010. Modeling diachronic change in the third person singular: A multifactorial, verb- and author-specific exploratory approach. *English Language and Linguistics* 14(3). 293–320.

Labov, William. 1972. *Sociolinguistic Patterns*. Philadelphia, PA: University of Pennsylvania Press.

Leech, Geoffrey, Marianne Hundt, Christian Mair & Nicolas Smith. 2009. *Change in Contemporary English: A Grammatical Study*. Cambridge: Cambridge University Press.

Love, Robbie, Claire Dembry, Andrew Hardie, Vaclav Brezin, & Tony McEnery. 2017. The Spoken Bnc2014. Designing and building a spoken corpus of everyday conversations. *International Journal of Corpus Linguistics* 22(3). 319–344.

Luhn, Hans Peter. 1960. Key word-in-context index for technical literature (kwic index). *American Documentation*, 11(4). 288–295.

Nagle, Stephen J. 1989. Quasi-modals, marginal modals, and the diachrony of the English modal auxiliaries. *Folia Linguistica Historica* 22. 93–104.

Petré, Peter & Lynn Anthonissen. 2020. Individuality in complex systems: A constructionist approach. *Cognitive Linguistics* 31(2). 185–212.

Petré, Peter & Freek Van de Velde. 2018. The real-time dynamics of the individual and the community in grammaticalization. *Language* 84(4). 867–901.

Schmid, Hans-Jörg. 2020. *The Dynamics of the Linguistic System. Usage, Conventionalization, and Entrenchment*. Oxford: Oxford University Press.

Schmid, Hans-Jörg & Annette Mantlik. 2015. Entrenchment in historical corpora? Reconstructing dead authors' minds from their usage profiles. *Anglia* 133(4). 583–623.

Schmid, Hans-Jörg, Quirin Würschinger, Sebastian Fischer & Helmut Küchenhoff. 2021. *That's cool*. Computational sociolinguistic methods for investigating individual lexico-grammatical variation. *Frontiers in Artificial Intelligence* 3(89).

Siemund, Peter. 2013. *Varieties of English: A Typological Approach*. Cambridge: Cambridge University Press.

Stefanowitsch, Anatol & Susanne Flach. 2017. The corpus-based perspective on entrenchment. In Hans-Jörg Schmid (ed.), *Entrenchment and the Psychology of Language Learning: How We Reorganize and Adapt Linguistic Knowledge*, 101–127. Boston, MA/Berlin: APA and Walter de Gruyter.

van Duijn, Max & Arie Verhagen. 2018. Beyond triadic communication: A three-dimensional conceptual space for modelling intersubjectivity. *Pragmatics & Cognition* 25(2). 384–416.

ver Hoef, Jay M. & Peter L. Boveng. 2007. Quasi-poisson vs. negative binomial regression: How should we model overdispersed count data?. *Ecology* 88(11). 2766–2772.

Wilson, Andrew & Paul Rayson. 1993. Automatic content analysis of spoken discourse. In Clive Souter & Eric Atwell (eds.), *Corpus Based Computational Linguistics*, 215–226. Amsterdam: Rodopi.

7 Modals as a predictive factor for L2 proficiency level

Natalia Grabar, Thierry Hamon and Benoît Leclercq

1 Background and aim

This chapter now turns to the acquisition of modality by non-native speakers of English. For indeed, to ask about how modals are used exactly is really to ask about speakers' linguistic skills. While typical (adult) native speakers will show no difficulty in mastering those skills, this is not necessarily the case of non-native speakers, whose command of modals will vary depending on their level of proficiency. Here, the aim is to apply techniques from NLP (*Natural Language Processing*) research and to pin down the extent to which modality alone can be used to predict accurately the proficiency level of non-native speakers.

Modality is a universal linguistic category that represents a central aspect of human experience. This is why it is such an interesting topic of study (e.g. Nuyts and van der Auwera 2016). At the same time, analyzing modals and modal meaning can be a real challenge since, as the previous chapters have shown, there are many (syntactic, semantic and pragmatic) factors involved in using and understanding modals (see also Abraham 2020). This complexity is directly reflected in the acquisition process, which is not straightforward but rather involves incremental steps: different modal expressions and different modal meanings are acquired at distinct stages throughout childhood (cf. Choi 2006, Hickman and Bassano 2016, Cournane 2020). In English, "the pathway of emergence is roughly from bouletic verbs denoting desires (e.g., *want*) and ability modals (e.g., *can*; typically negated at first), to deontic modals (e.g., *have to, must*), and finally to epistemic modals (e.g., *must, might*)" (Cournane 2015: 51; see also overviews in Shatz and Wilcox 1991, Papafragou 1998). A child's modal system develops mainly between the ages of 2 and 6, but it does not become completely adult-like until the age of 12 (Papafragou 1998: 392). Part of this gradual acquisition process is due to the necessity for the child to develop in parallel a number of social and cognitive skills including theory of mind abilities, i.e. the ability to attribute mental states and intentions to other individuals (Papafragou 1998; see also Choi 2006: 151–157). In the case of second language (L2) acquisition, especially for adults, those basic social and cognitive skills are well developed, and the learner already possesses a complete modal system. One could therefore assume, in spite of the many factors that play a role in the acquisition of a second language (Ortega 2009, Ellis 2015), that learners of English probably do not need to go through similar sequential stages. Previous research has clearly established however that, although L2 English learners do use both deontic and epistemic modality early on compared to native speakers, their command of English modals shows similar developmental patterns. Low proficiency learners, for instance, tend to prefer deontic modality, overuse certain modal forms (highly frequent ones, e.g. *can*) at the expense of already marginalized modal expressions, and use modals in morpho-syntactic contexts that are not typical of native speakers (Gibbs 1990, Stephany 1995, Dutra 1998, Moloi 1998, Chen 2010, Biewer 2011, Oh and Kang 2013, Mitkovska, Bužarovska and Kusevska 2014, Elturky and Salsbury 2016, Leclercq and Edmonds 2017, Seog and Choi 2018). It is only as they become more advanced learners of English that near-native command of modals starts to show in terms of the modal verb used, meaning expressed, as well as morpho-syntactic contexts.[1] This observation is interesting as it exposes disparity between L2 English learners, especially across proficiency levels, which suggests that the category of modality alone might provide a strong indication of a learner's general linguistic abilities. As mentioned at the beginning of this section, it is the aim of this chapter to test this hypothesis and to identify the extent to which modal markers alone can predict L2 English learners' overall proficiency.

This hypothesis can be found in previous research. Altman (1984) for instance was interested in issues that concern proficiency assessment and created a test (the *Special English Test*) that targeted English modal expressions. The aim was to see how accurately modal verbs could be used to measure a learner's level. She administered the test and managed to distinguish between native speakers and three levels of non-native speakers at 70% accuracy (compared to other placement tests). One of the main issues with direct testing however, as pointed out by the author, is how to be sure – in spite of all the care given – that the test is sufficiently well-designed to achieve an accurate assessment of the learner's level. Altman (1984: 66) acknowledges that spontaneous productions would be preferable to elicited responses, but she points out that elicitation considerably reduces the amount of data that has to be collected and analyzed, and it therefore constitutes "the best approach to data collection". With the advent of digital computing and the develop-

---

[1] Note that the research on L2 English modality is often not developmental. Most papers rather focus on the use of epistemic modality by advanced learners in academic writing (student essays) and try to pin down the factors that explain the differences between learners and native speakers (e.g. cultural or social factors, transfer from L1, register variation, gender-related preferences, teaching methods, etc.). Here is a small list of references: Hinkel (1995, 2009), Hyland and Milton (1997), Aijmer (2002), Hunston (2002), Neff et al (2003), Gabrielatos and McEnery (2005), Oh (2007), Saeed (2009), Jaroszek (2013), Deshors (2014a, 2014b), Hu and Li (2015), Torabiardakani, Khojasteh and Shokrpour (2015), Mifka-Profozik (2017), Hatipoğlu and Algı (2018), Btoosh (2019).

ment of new methods in corpus linguistics, this issue can now be dealth with more easily however. The field of 'learner corpus research' has in fact precisely grown out of a necessity to manage larger amounts of data and to deal with more representative uses of the language by non-native speakers (see Granger, Gilquin and Meunier 2015, Gilquin 2020, Meunier 2020). Recently, Maden-Weinberger (2008) used a learner corpus to test a hypothesis similar to ours, namely whether modals can be used to establish L2 proficiency in German. Using standard methods from learner corpus research (cf. Granger 1996), she shows that modality in German provides strong clues about a learner's proficiency, even at advanced levels of acquisition. The present chapter aims to verify this observation with learners of English. To do so, like Maden-Weinberger, we will use data from a learner corpus. In English, a large number of learner corpora are now available, including: the *Longitudinal Database of Learner English* (LONGDALE) (Meunier 2016), the *EF-Cambridge Open Language Database* (EFCAMDAT) (Geertzen, Alexopoulou and Korhonen 2013; Huang et al 2018), the *International Corpus of Learner English* (ICLE) (Granger et al 2020), the *Corpus of English as a Foreign Language* (COREFL) (Lozano, Díaz-Negrillo and Callies 2021), the *Multilingual Traditional Immersion and Native Corpus* (MulT-INCo) (Meunier et al 2020), the *Interphonology of Contemporary English corpus* (IPCE-IPAC) (Herry-Bénit et al 2021).[2] In this chapter, we will use EFCAMDAT (see Section 2) to determine whether modality is a strong predictor of English learners' overall abilities, and we will apply methods from NLP (*Natural language Processing*)* to analyze the data.[3] We use the EFCAMDAT for a number of reasons: it is free, it is a large corpus that contains real productions of L2 English learners, and it associates each production with a specific proficiency level.

NLP methods have been applied to a variety of issues in the domain of learner corpus research (see discussion in Meurers 2015), including automated scoring of learner productions (cf. Higgins, Ramineni and Zechner 2015), native language identification (e.g. Koppel, Schler and Zigdon 2005; Tetreault, Blanchard and Cahill 2013; Tsvetkov et al 2013; Jiang et al 2014; Nisioi 2015; Malmasi and Dras 2017; Malmasi et al 2017), automatic error detection (cf. Leacock, Chodorow and Tetreault 2015), and prediction of learner proficiency (e.g. Granfeldt and Nugues 2007; Pilán, Volodina and Zesch 2016; Arnold et al 2018; Balikas 2018; Bailler et al

---

2 The *Centre for English Corpus Linguistics* has compiled a rather exhaustive list of learner corpora at the following address (last accessed: March 8th, 2022): https://uclouvain.be/en/research-institutes/ilc/cecl/learner-corpora-around-the-world.html.
3 The field of NLP uses a specific terminology that all readers of this book may not be familiar with. For that reason, a number of terms are listed in Appendix A with simple definitions. In the text, these terms will be followed by an asterix, such as is the case here for 'natural language processing'.

2020). The advantage of NLP over more traditional corpus methods is the possibility to manage vast amounts of data since most annotations that would traditionally have to be added manually can instead be taken care of automatically (cf. Van Rooy 2015). In our study, for instance, we can exploit the entire EFCAMDAT corpus (over 70M words), and not only a selected subset. Another advantage is that NLP methods enable us to analyse the data on its own, without necessarily comparing the learner's production to a native speaker standard (which is one of the potential limits recently identified by Gilquin 2022 regarding more standard methods in learner corpus research).

The chapter is organised as follows. In Section 2, we introduce the EFCAMDAT corpus. Section 3 then provides statistical information about 17 modal verbs within the corpus. The methodological approach for the prediction of proficiency levels is explained in Section 4. The features exploited relate to 17 modal verbs and 38 modal markers (e.g. adjectives, nouns), n-grams, readability indexes and information. The results of this set of experiments are presented in Section 5. Finally, Section 6 discusses these results and provides a conclusion.

2 The EFCAMDAT corpus

The analysis presented in this chapter uses data from the open-access corpus EFCAMDAT (Geertzen, Alexopoulou and Korhonen 2013; Huang et al 2018), which was developed at the University of Cambridge (Department of Theoretical and Applied Linguistics) on the basis of data made available by the international teaching school *EF Education First*. The corpus consists of written compositions produced by 174,732 adult learners across 198 different countries.[4] These productions were initially submitted to EnglishTown (EF's online school) by the learners. Upon registration to EnglishTown, students take a placement test that puts them into one of the 16 EF teaching levels, which are aligned with the six levels of the CEFR (*Common European Framework of Reference for languages*, see North 2014): A1 *beginner* (Englishtown levels 1–3), A2 *elementary* (levels 4–6), B1 *intermediate* (levels 7–9), B2 *upper intermediate* (levels 10–12), C1 *advanced* (levels 13–15), and C2 *proficiency* (level 16).[5] At each EF level, students need to respond to eight prompts. As a consequence, a student who started at level 1 and completed the entire course

---

[4] Note that EFCAMDAT only gives the country of origin of each learner but does not specify the L1, which in some cases thus makes for only a partial evaluation of the learner's linguistic background.
[5] Murakami (2014) provides empirical evidence that the mapping between EF's 16 levels and the CEFR is reliable.

will have submitted a total of 128 written productions. Table 1 provides general statistics about EFCAMDAT. For each CEFR level (first column), we find the total number of written productions (column 2), the total number of word tokens (column 3), and the average number of word tokens per production (column 4).

Table 1: Production statistics for each CEFR level.

Level	# productions	# word tokens	Average number of word tokens per production
A1	625,904	23,177,587	37
A2	307,971	20,298,823	66
B1	168,350	15,954,602	95
B2	61,326	8,155,783	133
C1	14,697	2,436,694	166
C2	1,940	329,802	170
Total	1,180,188	70,353,290	60

Table 1 shows that the corpus is not fully balanced and that lower proficiency levels (A1 to B1) contain a much bigger number of productions than higher levels (C1 and C2). The data provided by the corpus is therefore not perfectly longitudinal (indeed, although some students follow the entire course, some start at more advanced levels and others drop out before the end) but it is as close as we can get, which is what we need for our study.

A crucial advantage of EFCAMDAT is that the prompts students respond to are sufficiently varied (especially in terms of topics covered) that it does not restrict our analysis to only one specific text type or register (e.g. essays). For instance, learners are asked to write a letter or an email, to summarize information provided in a text, or to compose a short argumentative text (see Alexopoulou et al 2015). Here are examples of prompts given to the students at each CEFR level: *Describing their favorite day* (A1), *Complaining about a meal* (A2), *Making a business proposal* (B1), *Describing a terrifying experience* (B2), *Covering a news story* (C1), *Attending a robotics conference* (C2). The written productions are also heterogeneous in terms of form (see Alexopoulou et al 2017 for discussion). Depending on the level of the student, each production can contain one or several sentences and convey more or less complex ideas. Table 2 provides examples of productions for each proficiency level.[6]

---

6 Note that some A1 productions are not written in English (e.g. *eu prefiro usar roupas despojadas para o dia a dia. Minha preferida jeans e blusa. para algum casamento ou evento, eu uso*

Table 2: Examples of written productions for each proficiency level.

A1	Hi Sue, Sorry, I'm busy. Right now I'm working in my office. Then, I have to clean my house. And after, cook for my parents. See you another day. xoxo.
A2	Dear friends, excuse me but I couldn't come to a mariage. I feel awful and I think that I'm sick. I have a cold, a headache and a fever. I went to the doctor and I should stay in bed a few days. The pharmacist gave me some medecine. I'm sorry, let' go and have fun.
B1	I saw this girl at the swimming pool. I found her very attractive. She had a necklace with her first name. I introduced me and I asked her few questions to know her better. After we met, I invited her for a date the next day. Unfortunately, I was late. She left when I arrived. The next day, I tried my luck again and we had a new date for a tennis party. Of course I was careful to be on time. We played tennis but the next time she left on holiday for a week. We phoned us during this week and I welcomed her for her back at the station. It was 27 years ago. We got married since.
B2	I don't practise any extreme sport. I am definitely not a thrill-seeker. I'm scared of deep water, I have the vertigo . . . However, I am awestruck by people who pratise this kind of activities. They still search to overtook their limits. I can understand them. When I was younger, I was passionate about pacey carousels. It was fantastic to fly in the air even though I was just in a seat with a harness. I always got in them alone because my friends were so afraid. I could feel such a rush. One time, I tried one carousel who was going very fast. I felt like I was going to pass out. Now I always wimp out.
C1	In general I admire succesfull persons who keep their humility and stay simple. This kind of person are not self oriented, they have all they could wish and they are not selfish. Being focused on the others and attentive to his/her friends, relatives and colleagues give to succesful something more, making them more human and noble.
C2	In France, robots are commonly used in industrial fields. They replace humans for heavy duties, dangerous or repetitive tasks. Also, we find more and more robots in houses, like vacums that move by themselves, same idea for lawn mawers. But in my opinion, these kind of robots are making people lazy. I admit that we can save time by using them, but on the other hand, do we really use this spare time doing good stuff? I am not sure.

In previous research (Grabar et al 2020), we used a subset of EFCAMDAT (which was provided to us during the CAP challenge in 2018, see Bailler et al 2020). This is not the case in the study presented here, in which we analysed all of the data contained in EFCAMDAT. Only empty productions (or productions that contained less than 5 words) were excluded from the analysis.

---

vestido) or involves code-mixing (e.g. *So Paulo is do carmo, sabawey bat is basy*). All of them were kept for the analysis.

3 Modal verbs in EFCAMDAT

Our analysis of EFCAMDAT focuses on the same 10 modal verbs, complemented with *will*, *would*, *shall*, and 3 further modal idioms and semi-auxiliaries (see Section 1.1): *may, might, can* and *cannot, could, shall, should, will, would, must, have to, got to, need to, be supposed to, had better, be allowed to, be able to*. As shown in Table 3, within the whole set of productions (n=1,180,188), 434,411 productions (36.81%) contain at least one of these modals, while 745,777 productions do not contain any of them. This constitutes a rather high number of productions with modals as the set of items studied here is relatively small.

Table 3: Use of modals in EFCAMDAT.

Level	Productions with modals	Productions without modals	Token frequency of modals
A1	114,089 (18.23 %)	511,815 (81.77 %)	191,899
A2	127,976 (41.55 %)	179,995 (58.45 %)	257,547
B1	126,553 (75.17%)	41,797 (24.83 %)	338,600
B2	51,325 (83.70%)	10,001 (16.3 %)	154,114
C1	12,853 (87.45%)	1,844 (12.55 %)	53,604
C2	1,615 (83,25 %)	325 (16.75 %)	5,848
Total	434,411 (36,81 %)	745,777 (63.19 %)	1,001,612

Table 3 reveals an important difference between the learners, which is that the more proficient they become, the more modals they use. Only 18.23% of beginner productions contain at least one modal verb, while it exceeds 80% in the case of advanced learners. These numbers are consistent with observations made in the existing literature (cf. references in Section 1) whereby modality is said to be acquired progressively. Nevertheless, we tested whether the use of modals presents a statistical difference across levels. A chi-square test (performed with the Statistics::ChisqIndep perl module[7]) indicates that the use of modals is indeed statistically different across levels (p-value < 0.00001).

Table 4 indicates the frequency of the main modals within those productions: global frequency and frequency normalized by the size of productions. Focusing on global frequencies, we can see that the verb *can* is the most frequent modal found in the learners' productions. It is quickly followed by the verb *will*, which, as mentioned in Chapter 1, is most often used as a temporal marker and not with a modal value. The remaining modal verbs show more moderate frequencies. The

---

7 https://metacpan.org/pod/Statistics::ChisqIndep.

same observation can be made on the basis of normalized frequencies. These observations are consonant with previous findings (cf. introductory section).

Table 4: Frequency of the main modals in language productions of L2 English learners.

Modal	Frequency	Normalized frequency	Modal	Frequency	Normalized frequency
can	342,094	5,284.82	be able to	7,594	71.91
will	272,381	3,587.93	might	5,705	50.31
should	87,307	1,321.51	cannot	2,986	29.92
would	75,933	816.12	got to	1,153	14.95
have to	56,470	637.27	shall	979	11.41
could	47,337	500.93	had better	335	3.57
need to	39,095	472.85	be allowed to	249	2.57
must	35,272	414.91	be supposed to	14	0.13
may	26,708	407.25			

Finally, Table 5 contains information about the use of modals in terms of the learner's nationality. It includes figures for the top 20 nationalities represented in the corpus for which at least 2,000 productions have been recorded. (Productions from the United States and the United Kingdom were omitted, as no metadata is available about the learners' mother tongue.) For each nationality, the table gives the number of productions that contain at least one modal verb, the number of productions without modals, and the total number of modal verb tokens found.

Table 5: Use of modals per nationality of learners.

Nationality of learners	# productions with modals	# productions without modals	Token frequency of modals
Brazil	149,786 (31.42%)	326,998 (68.58%)	320,348
China	66,825 (40.46%)	98,324 (59.54%)	155,936
Mexico	27,866 (31.94%)	59,383 (68.06%)	60,503
Russia	28,257 (40.25%)	41,941 (59.75%)	70,574
Germany	27,881 (51.07%)	26,715 (49.93%)	71,188
Saudi Arabia	13,055 (27.59%)	34,261 (72.41%)	28,056
Italy	20,072 (44.37%)	25,170 (55.63%)	49,024
France	18,538 (44.54%)	23,086 (55.46%)	45,305
Taiwan	15,162 (51.28%)	14,407 (48.72%)	36,957
Japan	9,918 (46.40%)	11,456 (53.30%)	22,598
Turkey	5,066 (35.69%)	9,130 (64.31%)	12,758
Colombia	3,488 (34.99%)	6,480 (65.01%)	7,792
Spain	4,257 (52.02%)	3,927 (47.98%)	11,385

Table 5 (continued)

Nationality of learners	# productions with modals	# productions without modals	Token frequency of modals
South Korea	2,664 (49.03%)	2,769 (50.97%)	6,397
Switzerland	2,187 (48.84%)	2,291 (51.16%)	5,681
Arab Emirates	1,443 (40.51%)	2,119 (59.49%)	3,479
Indonesia	1,701 (57.60%)	1,252 (42.40%)	4,656
Thailand	790 (34.08%)	1,528 (65.92%)	1,799
Egypt	1,012 (44.38%)	1,271 (55.62%)	2,554
Austria	1,157 (51.74%)	1,079 (48.26%)	3,164

The share of productions with modals varies between 27.59% (Saudi Arabia) and 57.60% (Indonesia). On average, for the 20 countries considered together, 42.91% of productions contain modal verbs. It is striking that little regularity can be found in the use of modals according to nationality, especially when the L1 is supposedly the same or very similar. There is, for instance, great variability between spanish-speaking countries (compare Spain vs Mexico and Columbia) as well as between arab-speaking countries (compare Saudi Arabia vs. Arab Emirates and Egypt). The data suggest (Table 3) that the use of modal verbs can be established more accurately when taking into account the proficiency level of the learners more than their nationality.

4 Methodology for the prediction of proficiency levels

Having introduced the data, this section now presents the method used in this study. Our goal is to pin down the extent to which modality can be used to predict (automatically) the proficiency level of L2 English learners. To do so, we used supervised learning algorithms* from the Scikit-learn library[8] (Pedregosa et al 2011). These algorithms use a representative subset of data (one tenth) from the EFCAMDAT corpus and a number of features were specifically selected to train the predictive model and then test the rest of the corpus. These features are described in the following paragraphs.

The first set of features that were taken into account by the model were the modals themselves. The learning algorithm was instructed to focus on the 17 modal verbs mentioned above (*may, might, can* and *cannot, could, shall, should, will, would, must, have to, got to, need to, be supposed to, had better, be allowed to, be*

---

[8] Available from: https://scikit-learn.org/.

able to) as well as an additional set of 38 modal markers (e.g. *believe, likely, possible, seem*; cf. complete list in Appendix B).[9] These markers were included in the analysis since modal meaning can be expressed not only by means of modal verbs but also by other lexical units. In this way, we hope to obtain an accurate view of modality in L2 English and especially to highlight the importance of modal verbs in establishing L2 proficiency in comparison to other modal markers. It is especially the frequency of these modal forms that was computed here. For each level of proficiency, the training model takes into account both the overall frequency of all the modal forms (i.e. of the 17 modal verbs and the 38 modal markers) as well as the individual frequency of each of these forms.

Another set of features that was taken into account are 'readability indicators'. Readability indicators give more or less general information on the content of the productions that relate to formal aspects and the easiness of their reading. This includes:
- Sentence length (i.e. number of words, syllables, and characters) and average length of sentences (longer sentences imply higher proficiency);
- Average length of words (i.e. number of syllables and characters), number and percentage of short and long words (longer words also imply higher proficiency);
- Number and percentage of simple words from the Dale and Chall list. This list contains 3,000 words reliably understood by fourth-grade American children (see Dale and Chall 1948). It is considered that any word not on that list is difficult (Dale and Chall 1948).
- Lexical diversity, number and percentage of prepositions and conjunctions. The size of vocabulary, its richness and diversity correspond to a major predictor of proficiency.

There are in total 29 such indicators, all of which have been listed and defined in Appendix C. On the basis of these indicators, we computed 36 readability indexes (i.e. scores) which enable us to measure the complexity of the productions analyzed. Some of these indexes rely on the length of words and sentences, and on derived indicators (Flesch 1948, McLaughlin 1969, Gunning 1973, Kincaid et al 1975, Björnsson and Hård af Segerstad 1979); other indexes rely on the presence or absence of simple words, such as those listed by Dale and Chall (Dale and Chall 1948, Spache 1953, Bormuth 1966, Colleman and Liau 1975). Three indexes (Flesch 1948; Gunning 1973; Kincaid et al 1975), based on length of words and sen-

---

[9] This additional set of markers issues from previous studies (Grabar and Hamon, 2009) and corresponds to markers of modal meaning that are frequently used in English.

tences, have been implemented in the Fathom Perl module.[10] We implemented the readability formulas for the remaining 33 indexes. The scores obtained were taken to reflect the learners' proficiency, with more proficient learners showing higher scores of complexity. This was important for us, as it makes it possible to test and compare the predictive power of modal features alone and in combination with other textual aspects of the productions analyzed.

A final set of features taken into account relates to the use of n-grams. The focus on n-grams is motivated by the observation that collocational (i.e. lexical) and collostructional (i.e. grammatical) preferences are other strong indicators of L2 proficiency (Ellis 2003). Advanced learners of English, for instance, tend to use more idiomatic sequences (e.g. *to commit atrocities*), while beginners more openly choose between different lexical items (e.g. *do atrocities, perform atrocities*, etc). With a specifically created perl program, we thus collected n-grams (2-grams, 3-grams, and 4-grams) from COCA (Corpus of Contemporary American English) and the BNC (British National Corpus), two reference corpora (Davies 2004, 2008-). This enabled us to establish a reference list of n-grams typically used by native speakers. We then applied the same perl program with the data from EFCAMDAT and, for each production, computed the number and percentage of n-grams that was common with the reference list to establish the degree of overlap between native and non-native speakers for each production. Among all the n-grams, we have given special attention to those n-grams containing the 17 modal verbs studied here.

The trained models were then put to the test on the rest of the corpus. First, separate tests were performed to establish the predictive power of each individual set of features (e.g. modality, readability information, n-grams). Combinations of sets of features (modality and readability, modality and n-grams, etc.) were then tested to identify significant differences from individual patterns. Specifically, these tests consist in the automatic prediction of proficiency levels (i.e. each production is to be classified into one of the six proficiency levels from CEFR) via multi-class classification*. We use several learning algorithms with their default parameters in a 10-fold cross-validation* and the results are evaluated in their micro and macro versions according to three standard measures: Precision* P (whether the assignments are correct), Recall* R (whether the assignments are complete), and F-measure* F (harmonic mean of precision and recall). We tested several algorithms (called 'classifiers'): Decision Trees (Quinlan 1993), Random Forest (Breiman 2001), linear SVM (Platt 1998), Gradient Boosting (Friedman 2001), SGDC (Zadrozny and Elkan 2002), and Logistic Regression (Yu, Huang and

---

10 See https://metacpan.org/pod/Lingua::EN::Fathom.

Lin 2011). It turns out that Random Forest provides the best results for this task, which we now turn to.

5 Results

This section presents the results obtained when automatically classifying the productions into the CEFR levels using Random Forest. We present the classification results according to the sets of features described in the previous section and their combinations.

Table 6 provides general information about micro and macro evaluation measures according to the sets of features used, either individually or in combination. Micro version corresponds to the capacity of the system to assign each entity (language production) correctly, while macro version corresponds to the capacity of the system to recognize correctly each class (CEFR level). The table shows that the results are higher at the micro level of productions than at the macro level. This can be easily explained. At the micro level, a great number of productions are assigned to the correct CEFR level, which thus leads to high global performance. At the macro level, however, some CEFR levels may be predicted better than other levels and, since the global evaluation with macro values depends on the evaluation of each CEFR level, the average values become lower.

Table 6: Classification results with Random Forest according to features used.

Features	Micro			Macro		
	P	R	F	P	R	F
Readability (indicators and indexes)	0.80	0.80	0.80	0.72	0.55	0.57
BNC n-grams	0.78	0.78	0.78	0.69	0.52	0.54
COCA n-grams	0.78	0.78	0.78	0.70	0.51	0.54
17 modal verbs	0.61	0.61	0.61	0.45	0.29	0.31
38 modality markers	0.55	0.55	0.55	0.38	0.19	0.16
Readability + 17 modals	0.81	0.81	0.81	0.74	0.57	0.59
Readability + 38 markers	0.80	0.80	0.80	0.72	0.55	0.57
Readability + 17 modals+38 markers	0.81	0.81	0.81	0.74	0.57	0.59
Readability + 17 modals+38 markers + BNC n-grams	**0.83**	**0.83**	**0.83**	**0.76**	**0.58**	**0.60**
Readability + 17 modals+38 markers + COCA n-grams	0.79	0.79	0.79	0.64	0.55	0.57

The overall performance obtained can be considered as good: our best results reach up to 0.83 F-measure which means that the correct CEFR level can be predicted for over 80% of productions. This table shows though that the best results are obtained when *all* the features are exploited together, with BNC n-grams slightly surpassing COCA n-grams. Readability features are especially efficient and permit to reach up to 0.80 micro F-measure and 0.57 macro F-measure. This indicates that, as learners become more proficient, the composition of sentences and their overall structure become sufficiently more complex and sophisticated that the distinct proficiency levels can be automatically identified. By contrast, Table 6 shows that, even though they outperform the additional modal markers, the 17 modal verbs alone permit to correctly classify only two thirds of the productions (micro F-measure 0.61). The relative importance of modals in the classification of these productions is further emphasized by the observation that, when modals are combined with readability factors, the F-measure hardly increases (+0.01) compared to when readability features alone are taken into account.

Given the numbers just presented, it could of course be argued that modals alone are therefore not a good (or rather, not the best) indicator of L2 proficiency, but here are some counter-arguments to this claim. First of all, the small addition that modals make to readability factors might simply reveal a natural correlation between the use of modal verbs and the evolution of readability indicators and indexes. If modals truly were weaker predictors, one would have expected the value to remain the same as when readability factors are used alone (i.e. 0.80), which is not the case here. More importantly, it is crucial to take into account size-effect for each of these features. Indeed, the number of readability indicators and n-grams is much bigger than the number of modal verbs, which therefore provide more solid ground for testing. Besides, modals are spread in a smaller number of sentences. It is therefore difficult to compare the score obtained with huge sets of features (like those with n-grams or readability indicators and indexes) from that obtained with a small set containing only 17 modal verbs. In fact, for such a small set of features, we can consider that the cues provided by the 17 modals to the learning algorithm are quite high and, in ratio, constitute stronger indicators than the readability features and n-grams.

Attention now needs to be given to the predictive power of our model for each individual proficiency level. We will start with the predictive power of the algorithm when all the features (i.e. readability factors, 17 modals, 38 markers, BNC n-grams) are taken together, the result of which is given in Table 7.

Table 7: Classification results per proficiency level (all features and BNC n-grams).

Level	P	R	F
A1	0.91	0.92	0.91
A2	0.76	0.74	0.75
B1	0.71	0.74	0.73
B2	0.65	0.62	0.63
C1	0.58	0.38	0.46
C2	0.96	0.07	0.12

Table 7 shows that the A1 level is by far the easiest to predict (F-measure 0.91). This can be explained in terms of two specific factors: a quantitative factor (as mentioned in Table 1, this level contains the highest number of productions, and the learning algorithm could thus receive better training) and a qualitative factor (beginners provide productions that are very distant from the native standard and from productions from other levels). In opposition, the C2 level shows very poor performance (F-measure 0.12). This is certainly due to the small number of productions available. The C1 level, which contains a higher number of productions, reaches 0.46 F-measure. Overall, except for the C levels, the performance obtained can be considered as good, with precision and recall values that are very similar. Figure 1 presents the confusion matrix for this test. The diagonal corresponds to the number of productions which are correctly classified. Other numbers indicate erroneous classification of productions. Figure 1 shows, for instance, that 40,670 A1 productions are classified as A2 productions, and 52,598 A2 productions are classified as A1 productions. Overall, we can see that the highest number of errors occurs between neighbor levels and that errors decrease as the levels become more distant. Only in the case of C2, certainly because of the limited number of examples available, do we find an important confusion with several other levels (B2, C1, and B1).

A similar test was then conducted to establish the predictive power of the algorithm for each of the different levels when only the 17 modal verbs are taken into account. The results are reported in Table 8 and Figure 2. Only the recognition of the A1 level can be considered as good. For all the other levels, a small portion of the productions can be assigned correctly. More precisely, the values of recall fall. Modals therefore permit to classify correctly two thirds of productions but seems to be insufficient for a more efficient differentiation between the CEFR levels at advanced levels.

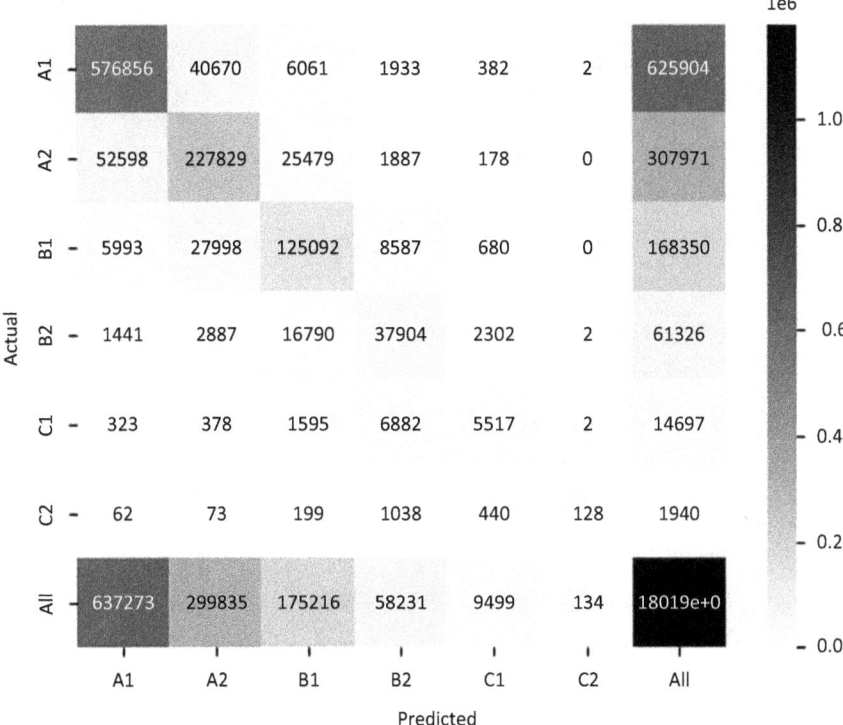

Figure 1: Confusion matrix (all features).

Table 8: Classification results per proficiency level (17 modal verbs).

Level	P	R	F
A1	0.66	0.94	0.78
A2	0.45	0.20	0.28
B1	0.47	0.35	0.40
B2	0.44	0.17	0.24
C1	0.36	0.07	0.12
C2	0.30	0.02	0.04

In Table 3, we saw that the percentage of productions with modals increases importantly as speakers become more proficient, and that levels B2, C1 and C2 provide comparable percentage of productions with modal verbs. This may be the confusing factor during the classification of productions into CEFR levels. Indeed, these three levels show the lowest performance. The other three levels (A1, A2 and B1), in which the percentage of modals is different, get better predictions. For this

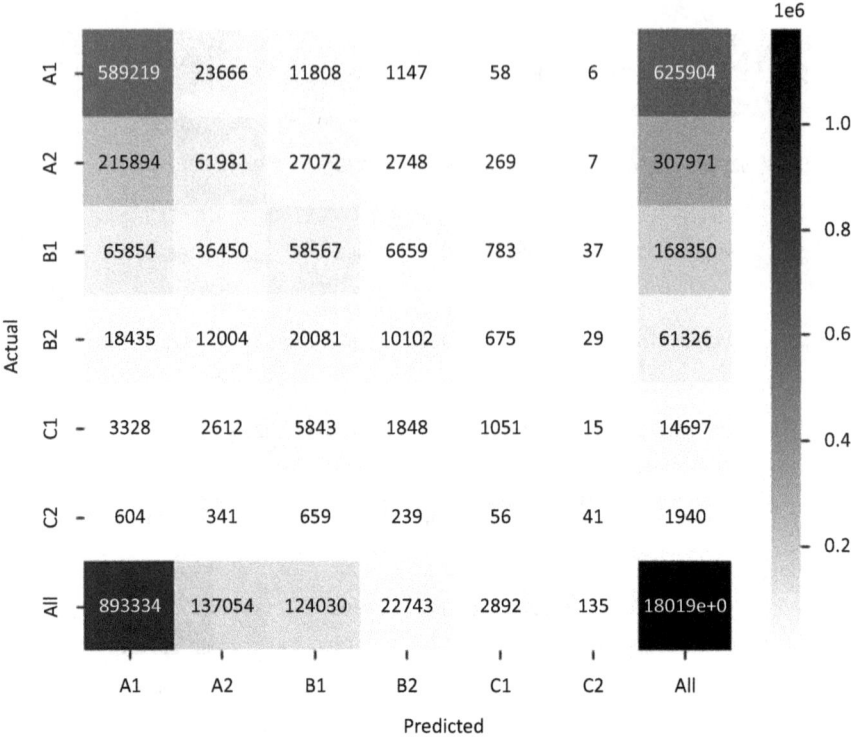

Figure 2: Confusion matrix (RandomForest and 17 modal verbs).

reason, we performed the same test but with randomly under-sampled data, so that the size of each level be no more than the mean of all levels. Figure 3 presents the size of classes with original and under-sampled distributions. Table 9 presents the results of this test. We can see that the results are generally poorer (which confirms that the larger the set of training data, the better the results). N-grams from BNC and COCA now achieve similar results, and modal verbs permit to classify correctly 44% of productions. As per level, there is an increase for three levels (B1, B2 and C1) and a decrease for the three other levels (A1, A2, C2).

In future work, we shall test other approaches to overcome the imbalance of the data, like the weighting of productions or their over-sampling. In addition, semantic disambiguation of the modal verbs should also be performed to provide additional insights into their acquisition. Another final issue relates to the combination of all n-grams (from BNC and COCA), thus providing a more complete view of this aspect.

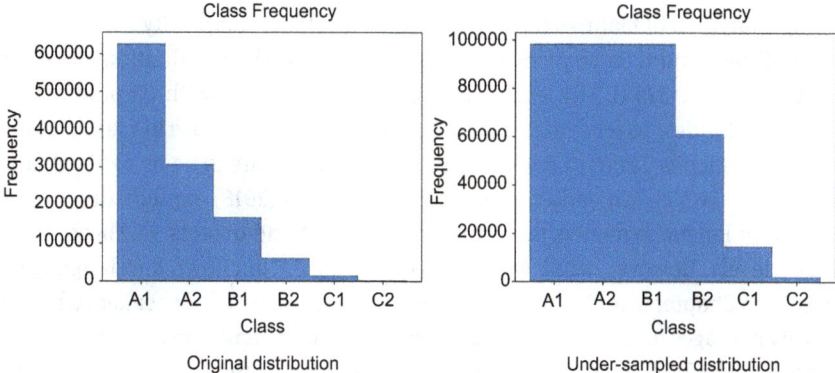

Figure 3: Size of classes in original and under-sampled distributions.

Table 9: Classification results with under-sampled dataset.

Features	Micro			Macro		
	P	R	F	P	R	F
Readability (indicators and indexes)	0.72	0.72	0.72	0.72	0.56	0.58
BNC n-grams	0.70	0.70	0.70	0.69	0.53	0.55
COCA n-grams	0.70	0.70	0.70	0.70	0.53	0.55
17 modal verbs	0.44	0.44	0.44	0.41	0.32	0.29
38 modality markers	0.30	0.30	0.30	0.30	0.20	0.14
Readability + 17 modals	0.74	0.74	0.74	0.74	0.58	0.60
Readability + 38 markers	0.73	0.73	0.73	0.72	0.56	0.58
Readability + 17 modals+38 markers	0.74	0.74	0.74	0.75	0.58	0.60
Readability + 17 modals+38 markers + BNC n-grams	**0.76**	**0.76**	**0.76**	**0.76**	**0.59**	**0.61**
Readability + 17 modals+38 markers + COCA n-grams	**0.76**	**0.76**	**0.76**	**0.77**	**0.59**	**0.61**

6 Discussion and conclusions

It is difficult to compare our results with previous work. This chapter is, to our knowledge, the first attempt to classify proficiency levels in L2 English on the basis of modal verbs alone. And even when considering all the other features, NLP researchers often use methods whose results need to be interpreted carefully. We will consider two experiments conducted in the context of the recent CAp challenge, a machine learning competition for classifying CEFR levels (cf. description in Bailler et al 2020). For instance, Arnold et al (2018) find results similar to ours, using a large set of features (metrics of lexical diversity, complexity and readability, POS-tags and their sequences, word frequencies). Their evaluation measures vary between 0.525 (B2-C1 levels) and 0.916 (A1-A2 levels), with C2 productions being the hardest to recognize. However, Arnold et al (2018) use bi-class classification* (which is easier to perform as only two classes are to be recognized) and not multi-class classification. In opposition, Balikas (2018) exploits descriptors related to language models and word embeddings* and obtains 98.2% accuracy for all levels. However, while word embeddings nicely pin down *how* language is used (see Chapter 6, for instance), it is not clear in the case of L2 speakers whether it truly manages to assess their proficiency level. For instance, to take an example discussed before, word embeddings may cluster together verbs like *commit*, *perform*, and *do*, which can then be found in expressions like *commit atrocities*, *perform atrocities* and *do atrocities*. Yet, among these expressions, only *commit atrocities* corresponds to the idiomatic expression that native speakers would use. All this naturally depends on what the learners' goals are (i.e. to sound native-like or not), but it seems to us that, for instance, n-grams are more reliable to represent the proficiency level for a given learner than word embeddings. Regarding the use of modal verbs to perform this task, we have no similar points of comparison. We have shown that the results are good, except when it comes to more advanced levels of proficiency. The question then is to know how our results might be improved. In the study conducted by Maden-Weinberger (2008) with German modals, the meaning of the verbs is taken into account, and the author manages to establish fine distinctions even at advanced levels of proficiency. This might be what is crucially missing here. While the entire analysis was performed automatically, and no annotation was added to the data, it appears that accurate evaluation of the learners' level might also require more attention to the semantic and pragmatic features that are present in the learners' productions of modal verbs (as is shown to be important in Chapters 2, 3 and 4 of this book). At the same time, it appears that advanced levels are generally difficult to assess, not only when modal verbs are the focus (cf. previous discussion). From the point of view of the NLP domain, the efficacy of the models is evaluated according to the quality of the reference data and our capacity to describe these data through the features. Both requirements were met here. The EFCAMDAT corpus provides a large and representative set of learner data, and we have made sure that the features exploited reflect correctly the different aspects of the productions. As the results indicate, this combination makes it possible to make the best prediction of the proficiency of L2 English learners.

Appendix A. Terminology

10-fold cross-validation is an evaluation set-up in which the corpus is segmented into 10 sets. Nine sets are used for the training of supervised learning algorithms and one set for their testing and evaluation. The operation is repeated 10 times, and each time the test and evaluation set is different. The final evaluation value corresponds to the average of the evaluation values obtained at each of the 10 iterations. It is also possible to segment the whole dataset into a different number of susbsets : 4 for 4-fold cross-validation, 5 for 5-fold cross-validation, etc.

Assignment is the result of the classification or categorization. For instance, when a given production is classified as level A1, it is also possible to say that this production is 'assigned' to level A1.

Bi-class classification is an NLP task during which two classes (or groups) must be predicted at the same time, such as assignment of language productions to CEFR levels A1 or A2.

Categorization and classification are spans of data organized within homogeneous groups according to the learning methods used. These groups can be created on the basis of the reference annotations and/or inner nature of the data.

Multi-class classification is an NLP task during which several classes must be predicted at the same time, such as assignment of language productions to one of the six CEFR levels (A1, A2, B1, B2, C1, C2).

NLP or Natural Language Processing is an experimental research domain whose purpose is to automatically perform tasks related to building, organizing, annotating and analyzing textual corpora. The tasks in question are often those done by human users (information retrieval and extraction, translation, indexing, question-answering, etc.). NLP is thus aimed at helping human users perform tedious and time-consuming tasks, and execute them more systematically.

Precision, recall, F-measure and accuracy are examples of evaluation measures of automatic learning algorithms. Accuracy indicates the fraction of predictions the model gets right; precision (P) measures whether the assignments of productions to a given class are correct; recall (R) measures whether the assignments of productions to a given class are complete; F-measure (F) is the harmonic mean of precision and recall. The evaluation measures P, R and F can be computed in their micro and macro versions.

Supervised learning algorithms or methods are used with the purpose to learn models of language on the basis of reference annotations, which are usually done by human experts. Hence, these algorithms are trained on annotation examples and learn language models, which can be applied (or tested) to new unknown data of a comparable type and content.

Unsupervised learning algorithms or methods are used to explore the data and organize them on the basis of the inner nature of these data, such as co-occurrences of words. These algorithms do not require to have reference annotated data. Yet, they require that the results provided are interpreted by human experts.

Word embedding is a method used for the creation of vector representation of words. The method is based upon the distributional hypothesis (Harris 1968) according to which words which occur in similar contexts are semantically close. Hence, word embeddings represent words by vectors of their contexts. Accordingly, words that are semantically similar have similar vectors.

Appendix B. Complete list of modal markers

apparently	hypothesizes	presumptive
assume	hypothesis	probable
assumes	hypothesized	probably
assumed	likely	putative
assumption	plausible	putatively
believe	plausibly	seem
believes	possible	seems
believed	possibly	speculate
eventual	potential	speculates
expect	potentially	speculative
expects	presumable	suggestive
expected	presumably	unlikely
hypothesize	presumed	

Appendix C. Readability indicators used in the study

Feature	Definition (for each production)
nb_sent	number of sentences
nb_words	number of words
nb_syll	number of syllables
nb_chars	number of characters
nb_blanks	number of blanks
nb_1syll_words	number of words with 1 syllable
p_1syll_words	percentage of words with 1 syllable
nb_1_2syll_words	number of words with 1 and 2 syllables
p_1_2syll_words	percentage of words with 1 and 2 syllables
nb_2syllormore_words	number of words with 2 syllables
p_2syllormore_words	percentage of words with 2 syllables
nb_3syllormore_words	number of words with 3 syllables or more
p_3syllormore_words	percentage of words with 3 syllables or more
nb_6charormore_words	number of words with 6 syllables or more
p_6charormore_words	percentage of words with 6 syllables or more
nb_simple	number of simple words (from the Ogden list)
nb_diff	number of difficult words
nb_uniquew	number of unique words
nb_conj	number of conjunctions
nb_prep	number of prepositions
afw	average of simple words
psw	percentage of simple words
adw	average of difficult words
pdw	percentage of difficult words
a_words_per_sent	average of words per sentences
a_syll_per_word	average of syllables per word
a_char_per_word	average of characters per word
ttr	Type-Token Ratio

References

Abraham, Werner. 2020. *Modality in Syntax, Semantics, and Pragmatics*. Cambridge: Cambridge University Press.

Aijmer, Karin. 2002. Modality in advanced Swedish learners' written interlanguage. In Sylviane Granger, Joseph Hung & Stephanie Petch-Tyson (eds.), *Computer Learner Corpora, Second Language Acquisition and Foreign Language Teaching*, 55–76. Amsterdam: John Benjamins.

Alexopoulou Theodora, Jeroen Geertzen, Anna Korhonen & Detmar Meurers. 2015. Exploring big educational learner corpora for SLA research: Perspectives on relative clauses. *International Journal of Learner Corpus Research* 1(1). 96–129.

Alexopoulou, Theodora, Marije Michel, Akira Murakami & Detmar Meurers. 2017. Task effects on linguistic complexity and accuracy: A large-scale learner corpus analysis employing natural language processing techniques. *Language Learning* 67. 180–208.

Altman, Rick. 1984. *Assessing Modal Proficiency in English as a Second Language*. Phd dissertation, University of Southern California, California, USA.

Arnold, Taylor, Nicolas Ballier, Thomas Gaillat & Paula Lissòn. 2018. Predicting CEFR levels in learner English on the basis of metrics and full texts. *Proceedings of the 20th Conférence Sur l'Apprentissage Automatique*. 31–38.

Balikas, Georgios. 2018. Lexical bias in essay level prediction. *Proceedings of the 20th Conférence Sur l'Apprentissage Automatique*. 1–5.

Ballier, Nicolas, Stéphane Canu, Caroline Petitjean, Gilles Gasso, Carlos Balhana, Theodora Alexopoulou & Thomas Gaillat. 2020. Machine learning for learner English: A plea for creating learner data challenges. *International Journal of Learner Corpus Research* 6(1). 72–103.

Biewer, Carolin. 2011. Modal auxiliaries in second language varieties of English: A learner's perspective. In Joybrato Mukherjee & Marianne Hundt (eds.), *Exploring Second-Language Varieties of English and Learner Englishes: Bridging a Paradigm Gap*, 7–33. Amsterdam: John Benjamins.

Björnsson, Carl Hugo & Birgit Hård af Segerstad. 1979. *Lix på Franska och tio Andra Språk*. Stockholm: Pedagogiskt centrum, Stockholms skolförvaltning.

Bormuth, John R. 1966. Readability: A new approach. *Reading Research Quarterly* 1(3). 79–132.

Breiman, Leo. 2001. Random forests. *Machine Learning* 45(1). 5–32.

Btoosh, Mousa A. 2019. Modals in Arab EFL learners' composition: A corpus-based approach. *Linguistics and Literature Studies* 7(3). 100–109.

Chen, Hsin I. 2010. Contrastive Learner Corpus Analysis of Epistemic Modality and Interlanguage Pragmatic Competence in L2 Writing. *Arizona Working Papers in SLA & Teaching* 17. 27–51.

Choi, Soonja. 2006. Acquisition of modality. In William Frawley (ed.), *The Expression of Modality*, 141–172. Berlin/New York: Mouton de Gruyter.

Coleman, Meri & T. Liau. 1975. A computer readability formula designed for machine scoring. *Journal of Applied Psychology* 60. 283–284.

Cournane, Ailís. 2015. *Modal Development: Input-Divergent L1 Acquisition in the Direction of Diachronic Reanalysis*. PhD Thesis, University of Toronto, Toronto, Canada.

Cournane, Ailís. 2020. Learning modals: A grammatical perspective. *Language and Linguistics Compass* 14(10). 1–22.

Dale, Edgar & Jeanne Chall. 1948. A formula for predicting readability. *Educational Research Bulletin* 27. 11–20.

Davies, Mark. 2004. *British National Corpus* (from Oxford University Press). Available online at https://www.english-corpora.org/bnc/.

Davies, Mark. 2008–. *The Corpus of Contemporary American English (COCA)*. Available online at https://www.e/nglish-corpora.org/coca/.

Deshors, Sandra C. 2014a. Constructing meaning in L2 discourse: The case of modal verbs and sequential dependencies. In Dylan Glynn & Mette Sjölin (eds.), *Subjectivity and Epistemicity: Stance Strategies in Discourse and Narration*, 329–348. Lund: Lund University Press.

Deshors, Sandra C. 2014b. Towards an identification of prototypical non-native modal constructions in EFL: A corpus-based approach. *Corpus Linguistics and Linguistic Theory* 11(1). 19–50.

Dutra, Deise Prina. 1998. *The Acquisition of English Root Modality by Non-Native Speakers*. PhD thesis. Gainesville: University of Florida.

Ellis, Nick. 2003. Constructions, chunking, and connectionism: The emergence of second language structure. In Catherine Doughty and Michael Long (eds.), *The Handbook of Second Language Acquisition*, 62–103. Oxford: Blackwell.

Ellis, Rod. 2015. *Understanding Second Language Acquisition*. 2nd edn. Oxford: Oxford University Press.

Elturki, Eman & Tom Salsbury. 2016. A cross-sectional investigation of the development of modality in English language learners' writing: A corpus-driven study. *Issues in Applied Linguistics* 20.

Flesch, Rudolph. 1948. A new readability yardstick. *Journal of Applied Psychology* 23. 221–233.

Friedman, Jerome. 2001. Greedy function approximation: A gradient boosting machine. *The Annals of Statistics* 29(5). 1189–1232.

Gabrielatos, Costas & Tony McEnery. 2005. Epistemic modality in MA dissertations. In Pedro A Fuertes Olivera (ed.), *Lengua y Sociedad: Investigaciones Recientes en Lingüística Aplicada*, 311–331. Valladolid: Universidad de Valladolid.

Geertzen, Jeroen, Teodora Alexopoulou & Anna Korhonen. 2013. Automatic linguistic annotation of large scale L2 databases: The EF-Cambridge Open Language Database (EFCAMDAT). *Proceedings of the 31st Second Language Research Forum* (SLRF). Cascadilla Press.

Gibbs, Dorothy A. 1990. Second language acquisition of the English modal auxiliaries *can, could, may,* and *might*. *Applied Linguistics* 11(3). 297–314.

Gilquin, Gaëtanelle. 2020. Learner corpora. In Magali Paquot & Stefan Gries (Eds.), *A Practical Handbook of Corpus Linguistics*, 283–303. Berlin: Springer.

Gilquin, Gaëtanelle. 2022. One norm to rule them all? Corpus-derived norms in learner corpus research and foreign language teaching. *Language Teaching* 55(1). 87–99.

Grabar, Natalia & Thierry Hamon. 2009. Exploitation of speculation markers to identify the structure of biomedical scientific writing. *Ann Symp Am Med Inform Assoc (AMIA) 2009*. 203–207.

Grabar, Natalia, Thierry Hamon, Bert Cappelle, Cyril Grandin, Benoît Leclercq & Ilse Depraetere. 2020. Prédire le niveau de langue d'apprenants d'anglais. *Traitement Automatique des Langues Naturelles (TALN)*. 1–9.

Granfeldt Jonas & Pierre Nugues. 2007. Évaluation des stades de développement en français langue étrangère. *Traitement Automatique des Langues Naturelles (TALN)*. 1–10.

Granger, Sylviane. 1996. From CA to CIA and Back: An Integrated Approach to Computerized Bilingual and Learner Corpora. In Karin Aijmer, Bengt Altenberg & Mats Johansson (eds.), *Languages in Contrast. Text-based Cross-Linguistic Studies*, 37–51. Lund: Lund University Press.

Granger, Sylviane, Maïté Dupont, Fanny Meunier, Hubert Naets & Magali Paquot. 2020. International corpus of learner English. *Version 3* (Handbook + web interface). Louvain-la-Neuve: Presses Universitaires de Louvain.

Granger, Sylviane, Gaëtanelle Gilquin & Fanny Meunier. 2015. *The Cambridge Handbook of Learner Corpus Research*. Cambridge: Cambridge University Press.

Gunning, Robert. 1973. *The Art of Clear Writing*. New York: McGraw Hill.

Harris, Zellig S. 1968. *Mathematical Structures of Language*. New York: Wiley.

Hatipoğlu, Çiler & Sedef Algi. 2018. Catch a tiger by the toe: Modal hedges in EFL argumentative paragraphs. *Educational Sciences: Theory & Practice* 18. 957–982.

Herry-Bénit, Nadine, Stéphanie Lopez, Takeki Kamiyama & Jeff Tennant. 2021. The interphonology of contemporary English corpus (IPCE-IPAC). *International Journal of Learner Corpus Research* 7(2). 275–289.

Hickmann, Maya & D. Bassano. 2016. Modality and mood in first language acquisition. In Jan Nuyts & Johan van der Auwera (eds.), *The Oxford Handbook of Modality and Mood*, 430–447. Oxford: Oxford University Press.

Higgins, Derrick, Chaitanya Ramineni & Klaus Zechner. 2015. Learner corpora and automated scoring. In Sylviane Granger, Gaëtanelle Gilquin & Fanny Meunier (eds.), *The Cambridge Handbook of Learner Corpus Research*, 587–604. Cambridge: Cambridge University Press.

Hinkel, Eli. 1995. The use of modal verbs as a reflection of cultural values. *TESOL Quarterly* 29. 325–341.

Hinkel, Eli. 2009. The effect of essay prompts and topics on the uses of modal verbs in L1 and L2 academic writing. *Journal of Pragmatics* 41(4). 667–683.

Hu, Chunyu & Xuyan Li. 2015. Epistemic modality in the argumentative essays of Chinese EFL learners. *English Language Teaching* 8(6). 20–31.

Huang Yan, Akira Murakami, Teodora Alexopoulou & Anna Korhonen. 2018. Dependency parsing of learner English. *International Journal of Corpus Linguistics* 23(1). 28–54.

Hunston, Susan. 2002. *Corpora in Applied Linguistics*. Cambridge: Cambridge University Press.

Hyland, Ken & John Milton. 1997. Qualification and certainty in L1 and L2 students' writing. *Journal of Second Language Writing* 6(2). 183–205.

Jaroszek, Marcin. 2013. L1 vs L2 spoken modality use–results of a study. *Studia Linguistica Universitatis Iagellonicae Cracoviensis* 130. 139–152.

Jiang, Xiao, Yufan Guo, Jeroen Geertzen, Teodora Alexopoulou, Lin Sun & Anna Korhonen. 2014. Native language identification using large, longitudinal data. *Proceedings of the Ninth International Conference on Language Resources and Evaluation* (LREC '14). 3309–3312.

Kincaid, J Peter, Robert Fishburne, Richard Rogers & Brad Chissom. 1975. *Derivation of New Readability Formulas (Automated Readability Index, Fog Count and Flesch Reading Ease Formula) for Navy Enlisted Personnel*. Navy research branch report (8–75), Memphis, TN.

Koppel, Moshe, Jonathan Schler & Kfir Zigdon. 2005. Determining an author's native language by mining a text for errors. *Proceedings of KDD 2005*. 624–628.

Leacock, Claudia, Martin Chodorow & Joel Tetreault. 2015. Automatic grammar- and spellchecking for language learners. In Sylviane Granger, Gaëtanelle Gilquin & Fanny Meunier (eds.), *The Cambridge Handbook of Learner Corpus Research*, 567–586. Cambridge: Cambridge University Press.

Leclercq, Pascale & Amanda Edmonds. 2017. How L2 learners of French and English express modality using verbal means: A crosslinguistic and developmental study. *International Review of Applied Linguistics in Language Teaching* 55 (3). 265–282.

Lozano, Cristóbal, Ana Díaz-Negrillo and Marcus Callies. 2021. Designing and compiling a learner corpus of written and spoken narratives: COREFL. In Christiane Maria Bongartz & Jacopo Torregrossa (eds.), *What's in a Narrative? Variation in Story-Telling at the Interface between Language and Literacy*, 21–46. Bern: Peter Lang.

Maden-Weinberger, Ursula. 2008. Modality as indicator of L2 proficiency? A corpus-based investigation into advanced German interlanguage. In Maik Walter & Patrick Grommes (eds.), *Fortgeschrittene Lernervarietäten: Korpuslinguistik und Zweitspracherwerbsforschung*, 141–164. Tübingen: Niemeyer.

Malmasi, Shervin & Mark Dras. 2017. Multilingual native language identification. *Natural Language Engineering* 23(2). 163–215.

Malmasi, Shervin, Keelan Evanini, Aoife Cahill, Joel Tetreault, Robert Pugh, Christopher Hamill, Diane Napolitano & Yao Qian. 2017. A Report on the 2017 Native Language Identification Shared Task. *Proceedings of the 12th Workshop on Innovative Use of NLP for Building Educational Applications*. 62–75.

McLaughlin, G. Harry. 1969. SMOG grading – a new readability formula. *Journal of Reading* 12(8). 639–646.

Meunier, Fanny. 2016. Introduction to the LONGDALE project. In Erik Castello, Katherine Ackerley & Francesca Coccetta (eds.), *Studies in learner corpus linguistics: Research and applications for foreign language teaching and assessment*, 123–126. Berlin: Peter Lang Publishing.

Meunier, Fanny. 2020. Introduction to learner corpus research. In Nicole Tracy-Ventura & Magali Paquot (Eds.), *The Routledge Handbook of Second Language Acquisition and Corpora*, 23–36. New-York: Routledge.

Meunier, Fanny, Isa Hendrikx, Amélie Bulon, Kristel Van Goethem & Hubert Naets. 2020. MulTINCo: multilingual traditional immersion and native corpus. Better-documented multiliteracy practices for more refined SLA studies. *International Journal of Bilingual Education and Bilingualism*. 1–18. https://doi.org/10.1080/13670050.2020.1786494

Meurers, Detman. 2015. Learner corpora and natural language processing. In Sylviane Granger, Gaëtanelle Gilquin & Fanny Meunier (eds.), *The Cambridge Handbook of Learner Corpus Research*, 537–566. Cambridge: Cambridge University Press

Mifka-Profozic, Nadia. 2017. Processing epistemic modality in a second language: A self paced reading study. *International Review of Applied Linguistics and Language Teaching* 55(3). 245–264.

Mitkovska, Liljana, Eleni Bužarovska & Marija Kusevska. 2014. Corpus evidence for the acquisition of modal verbs of obligation by Macedonian learners of English. *Continual professional development – opportunities and challenges* 1. 55–63.

Moloi, Francina. 1998. Acquisition of modal auxiliaries in English L2. *Southern African Journal of Applied Language Studies* 6(2). 1–22.

Murakami Akira. 2014. *Individual Variation and the Role of L1 in the L2 Development of English Grammatical Morphemes: Insights from Learner Corpora*. Phd thesis, University of Cambridge, Cambridge, United Kingdom.

Neff, JoAnne, Emma Dafouz, Honesto Herrera, Francisco Martínez, Juan Pedro Rica, Mercedes Diez, Rosa Prieto & Carmen Sancho. 2003. Contrasting learner corpora: the use of modal and reporting verbs in the expression of writer stance. In Sylviane Granger & Stephanie Petch-Tyson (eds.), *Extending the Scope of Corpus-Based Research. New Applications, New Challenges*, 211–230. Amsterdam and New York: Rodopi.

Nisioi, Sergiu. 2015. Feature analysis for native language identification. In Alexander Gelbukh (ed.), *Computational Linguistics and Intelligent Text Processing* (CICLing 2015), 644–657. Cham: Springer.

North, Brian. 2014. *The CEFR in Practice*. Cambridge: Cambridge University Press.

Nuyts, Jan & Johan van der Auwera (eds). 2016. *The Oxford Handbook of Modality and Mood*. Oxford: Oxford University Press.

Oh, Sun-Young. 2007. A corpus-based study of epistemic modality in Korean college students' writings in English. *English Teaching* 62 (2). 147–175.

Oh, Sun-Young & Suk-Jin Kang. 2013. The effect of English proficiency on Korean undergraduates' expression of epistemic modality in English argumentative writing. *The Journal of Asia TEFL* 10 (4). 97–132.

Ortega, Lourdes. 2009. *Understanding Second Language Acquisition*. London: Hodder Education.
Papafragou, Anna. 1998. The acquisition of modality: Implications for theories of semantic representation. *Mind and Language* 13(3). 370–399.
Pedregosa, Fabian, Gaël Varoquaux, Alexandre Gramfort, Vincent Michel, Bertrand Thirion, Olivier Grisel, Mathieu Blondel, Peter Prettenhofer, Ron Weiss, Vincent Dubourg, Jake Vanderplas, Alexandre Passos, David Cournapeau, Matthieu Brucher, Matthieu Perrot & Edouard Duchesnay. 2011. Scikit-learn: Machine learning in Python. *Journal of Machine Learning Research* 12. 2825–2830.
Pilán, Idliko, Elena Volodina & Torsten Zesch. 2016. Predicting proficiency levels in learner writings by transferring a linguistic complexity model from expert-written coursebooks. *Proceedings of the 26th International Conference on Computational Linguistics: Technical Papers*. 2101–2111.
Platt, John C. 1998. Fast training of support vector machines using sequential minimal optimization. In Christopher Burges, Alexander Smola & Bernard Schölkopf (eds.), *Advances in Kernel Methods – Support Vector Learning*, 185–208. Cambridge: MIT Press.
Quinlan, J Ross. 1993. *C4.5 Programs for machine learning*. San Mateo, CA: Morgan Kaufmann.
Saeed, Aziz. 2009. Arab EFL learners' acquisition of modals. *Research in Language* 7. 75–98.
Seog, Daria Soon-Young & Incheol Choi. 2018. Interlanguage development of young Korean EFL learners' modal usage: A learner corpus study. *Linguistic Research* 35. 83–103.
Shatz, Marilyn & Sharon Wilcox. 1991. Constraints on the acquisition of English modal. In Susan A. Gelman & James Byrnes (eds.), *Perspectives on Language and Thought*, 319–353. Cambridge: Cambridge University Press.
Spache, George. 1953. A new readability formula for primary grade reading materials. *The Elementary School Journal* 53. 410–413.
Stephany, Ursula. 1995. Function and form of modality in first and second language acquisition. In Anna G. Ramat & Grazia C. Galeas (eds.), *From Pragmatics to Syntax: Modality in Second Language Acquisition*, 105–120. Tübingen: Gunter Narr Verlag.
Tetreault, Joel, Daniel Blanchard & Aoife Cahill. 2013. A Report on the First Native Language Identification Shared Task. *Proceedings of the Workshop on Innovative Use of NLP for Building Educational Applications*. 48–57.
Torabiardakani, Najmeh, Laleh Khojasteh & Nasrin Shokrpour. 2015. Modal auxiliaries and their semantic functions used by advanced EFL learners. *Acta Didactica Napocensia* 8(2). 51–60.
Tsvetkov, Yulia, Naama Twitto, Nathan Schneider, Noam Ordan, Manaal Faruqui, Victor Chahuneau, Shuly Wintner & Chris Dyer. 2013. Identifying the L1 of non-native writers: the CMU-Haifa system. *Proceedings of the Eighth Workshop on Innovative Use of NLP for Building Educational Applications*. 279–287.
van Rooy, Bertus. 2015. Annotating learner corpora. In Sylviane Granger, Gaëtanelle Gilquin and Fanny Meunier (eds.), *The Cambridge Handbook of Learner Corpus Research*, 79–105. Cambridge: Cambridge University Press.
Yu, Hsiang-Fu, Fang-Lan Huang & Chih-Jen Lin. 2011. Dual coordinate descent methods for logistic regression and maximum entropy models. *Machine Learning* 85(1–2). 41–75.
Zadrozny, Bianca & Charles Elkan. 2002. Transforming classifier scores into multiclass probability estimates. *Proceedings of the International Conference on Knowledge Discovery and Data Mining (KDD)*. 694–699.

8 Revisiting modal sense classification with contextual word embeddings

Mathieu Dehouck and Pascal Denis

1 Introduction

Modal verbs can take on different interpretations or senses (e.g., epistemic vs. deontic vs. dynamic) depending on the context in which they appear (Kratzer, 1991). Below are a few illustrative examples for the verb *can*, along with its realized senses, from the MPQA dataset annotated for modality by Ruppenhofer and Rehbein (2012):

(1) That contract, extended indefinitely in 1934, **can** be broken only by mutual agreement. (deontic)

(2) By all conservative estimates, there are scores of other countries which **can** easily qualify as repressive and violating human rights. (epistemic)

(3) I hope that this **can** alert the Brazilian Government to revise its relationship with the IMF. (dynamic)

In this chapter, we are interested in the problem of automatically assigning a modal meaning to a modal verb in context, also known as Modal Sense Classification (or MSC for short). Being able to disambiguate modal verbs in context is an important part of natural language understanding, and it has implications for many other NLP problems, including factuality recognition (Saurí and Pustejovsky, 2012), sentiment analysis (Liu, Yu, Chen and Liu, 2013), or hedge detection (Morante and Daelemans, 2009).

Modality is a complex linguistic phenomenon that requires a deep understanding of the full context, including being able to access many different factors, from syntax to lexical and propositional semantics to discourse and pragmatics. As a result, previous approaches have attempted to tap into these different sources of knowledge, either through hand-crafted features (Ruppenhofer and Rehbein, 2012; Zhou, Frank, Friedrich and Palmer, 2015), static word representations (Marasović and Frank, 2016), or a mix of the two (Li, Dehouck and Denis, 2019). Due to the apparent similarity of MSC with the more general problem of word-sense disambiguation, previous works have consistently cast the problem of MSC as training a set of independent classifiers, learning one classification model for each modal verb. In the case of MSC, this seems like a strong, and probably simplistic, modelling assumption, as modal verbs share the same sense inventory (in most taxonomies modal verbs' senses come from a shared, restricted set of possible senses). Another trademark of earlier work is that, despite reported high accuracy figures, existing modal classifiers rarely outperform the strong majority sense baseline for certain modal verbs. This comes from the fact that sense distribution is very skewed for most modal verbs, which has led previous authors to work on artificially re-balanced datasets.

This chapter breaks away from previous work in at least two main respects. First, and foremost, we propose to use recent contextualised word representation models, namely BERT (Devlin, Chang, Lee and Toutanova, 2019), instead of hand-crafted or static word embeddings for encoding the linguistic inputs. Based on their successes on other semantic tasks (e.g. WSD, named entity recognition (NER), textual entailment), we hypothesize that these representations are a good candidate to represent arbitrary contexts and complex relationships between the context and the word of interest (in our case, modal verbs). As far as we know, this is the first attempt at using BERT for MSC. Like previous, static word embeddings (e.g., Word2Vec), these representations are fully automatic and require no feature engineering, but they are also more expressive in incorporating contextual information, and in effect perform some form of on-the-fly sense disambiguation. Our experiments show that BERT-based classification models indeed deliver substantial and consistent performance improvements over previously reported results. We also carry out a couple of probing experiments in order to better understand where the relevant linguistic information is located by comparing performance obtained with different layers of the BERT representations. Second, we also hypothesize that sharing information across modal verbs is beneficial for modals with similar usage; hence, we propose to train (or learn) a single model for the different modal verbs. Comparative experiments reveal that allowing for parameter sharing indeed yields accuracy improvements over separately trained models especially for verbs that are less represented in the training corpus and to the extent that their sense distribution is not so different from the overall sense distribution.

This chapter is organized as follows. In Section 2, we briefly review previous works on the task of modal sense classification. Section 3 presents the existing datasets for MSC. Next, Section 4 describes our approach based on contextualized word representations. Our experimental settings and our empirical results are then reported in Section 5. In Section 6, we propose a deeper analysis of the kind of information stored in contextual word representations in the context of modal sense classification. Finally, in Section 7, we summarize our findings and propose some directions for future research.

2 Related work

Work on modality annotation goes back at least to the work of Baker et al. (2010), who propose a modality annotation scheme (using 13 modal categories), a modality lexicon, and two derived heuristic-based automatic taggers. The first work fully devoted to MSC is that of Ruppenhofer and Rehbein (2012), who were also the first to publicly release a hand-annotated corpus of modal verbs using a 6-way sense inventory[1]. In their study, individual logistic regression models are trained for five distinct modal lemmas to assign one of the six modal senses. Input representations for the modal verb and its context consist of hand-crafted syntactic and lexical features. These include the form, lemma and part-of-speech of the target modal and a number of words to the left and to the right, but also information about the grammatical categories of parent and grandparent nodes in a constituency tree and other similar features.

Next, Zhou, Frank, Friedrich and Palmer (2015) propose to use multilingual sense projection from German data in order to increase the number of training sentences. They follow Ruppenhofer and Rehbein in training separate models for each verb, but they reduce the sense inventory to three classes. They also propose to add semantic features to the set of lexical and syntactic features used by Ruppenhofer and Rehbein (2012). These features refer both to the embedded verb and subject noun phrase. For the embedded verb, semantic features encode information about its tense, aspect and voice. For the subject noun phrase, semantic features include the noun type (common, proper or pronoun), the number and the person. Top senses from the WordNet hierarchy are also included for both the embedded verb and the head of the subject noun phrase.

In a follow-up paper, Marasović, Zhou, Palmer and Frank (2016) delve deeper into the question of modality classification, notably by studying the role of genre in modal use. The work of Marasović and Frank (2016) is the first to use dense word vectors (aka word embeddings) only as input to the classifiers. In their case, they use a convolutional neural network in order to extract the relevant features from a series of vectors representing the words of the sentence.

Finally, the work of Li, Dehouck and Denis (2019) investigates the use of automatically learned word representations that are combined with hand-crafted features. Specifically, they compare various weighting schemes used to combine pre-trained word representations that are then used alongside hand-crafted features as input to their classifier.

---

[1] See Section 3 for a more detailed description of the corpora used for MSC.

3 Data

Previous work on MSC heavily relied on two main publicly available datasets, namely the MPQA dataset and the EPOS dataset. The first dataset was released by Ruppenhofer and Rehbein (2012), who annotated modality in 535 documents of the first MPQA Opinion corpus release (Wilson, Wiebe and Hoffmann, 2005) [2]. It therefore consists of sentences extracted from news articles only. Their annotation scheme contains 8 different modal verbs (i.e., *can*, *could*, *may*, *might*, *must*, *ought*, *shall*, and *should*), which are labelled with one of six possible senses (i.e., epistemic, deontic, dynamic, concessive, optative and conditional). This initial sense inventory was then reduced to three classes by Zhou, Frank, Friedrich and Palmer (2015) by merging the three latter senses with two of the three former ones, which are more frequent (concessive and conditional with epistemic, and optative with deontic).

The second corpus used for MSC is the EPOS dataset, also released by Frank, Friedrich and Palmer (2015). Whereas MPQA was hand-annotated, EPOS was constructed automatically via paraphrase-driven modal sense projection on Europarl and OpenSubtitles (European politics and movies). As such, it is often used as an additional (possibly noisy) training data and not for the evaluation of MSC systems. Modal and sense distributions for these two datasets are reported in Table 1 for MPQA and Table 2 for EPOS, and they are shown side-by-side using a log-scale in Figure 2. As shown in these tables, the existing datasets are very small by current NLP standards, comprising only a few thousand examples. Also note that the modal and sense distributions are rather different. For instance, *may* and *must* are over-represented in EPOS compared to MPQA, making up more than 60% of the annotations. The sense distribution for the latter is very different, as most instances of *must* are deontic in EPOS, as compared to a more balanced distribution between deontic and epistemic in MPQA, which even leans towards the latter sense. These datasets will be used in our experiments (see Section 5) to maintain a form of comparability with previous works on modal sense classification.

We will also use a third, newer, manually annotated dataset derived from COCA and representing its five main genres (academic, fiction, magazines, news and spoken), which was presented in Chapter 1 of this volume. In what follows, we refer to this dataset as REM. This corpus differs from MPQA and EPOS in

---

[2] https://mpqa.cs.pitt.edu/

various respects. First, the modal taxonomy is different from that of Ruppenhofer and Rehbein (2012) or Zhou, Frank, Friedrich and Palmer (2015), relying on a two-level sense inventory. The first level simply distinguishes between two categories: epistemic and root meanings, thus collapsing both dynamic and deontic meanings of previous works, while the second level further refines root meanings into a number of new sub-categories (e.g., ability, opportunity, general situation necessity/possibility, subject external/internal necessity) [3]. The distribution of these categories is given in Table 4. Another important difference is the definition of the context around the modal verb. While in MPQA and EPOS, modals appear in a context that comprises a single sentence, in REM the context is broader than a single sentence with surrounding sentences sometimes cut in the middle so that the modal is roughly in the middle of its context. This makes for both longer contexts on average and a very different distribution of the relative position of modal verbs within their respective contexts. This is shown in Figure 4 where we represent the distribution of the relative positions of the modal verbs within their contexts. We already see a clear difference in modal position between EPOS and MPQA, with EPOS modals occurring slightly earlier in their contexts than those of MPQA, which are more evenly distributed. But the difference is really marked with REM, where modals overwhelmingly appear in the middle of their contexts by design.

Table 1: Original MPQA data distribution. For the three last senses we have indicated the merger proposed by Zhou et al.

Modal	Deontic (de)	Dynamic (dy)	Epistemic (ep)	Conditional > ep	Concessive > ep	Optative > de
Can	116	273	2			
Could	17	67	158			
May	8		114		19	2
Might	1		60		1	
Must	184		11			
Ought	4					
Shall	11	2				
Should	258		14	12		
Total	599	342	359	12	20	2

---

[3] Definitions associated with this taxonomy are discussed in detail in Chapter 1.

Table 2: EPOS data distribution.

Modal	Deontic (de)	Dynamic (dy)	Epistemic (ep)
Can	9	130	15
Could	22	38	28
May	134		875
Must	417		637
Shall	4	5	
Should	131		8
Total	717	173	1563

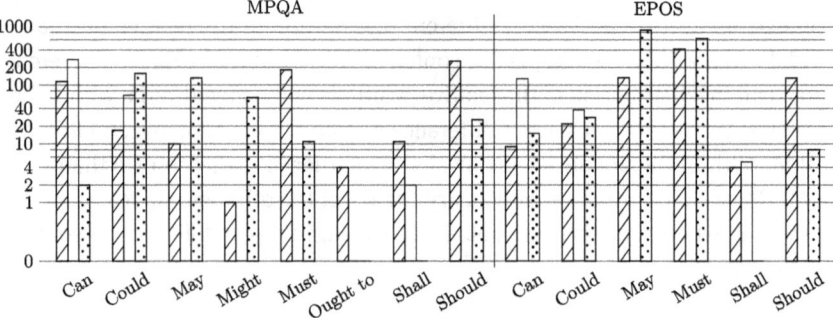

Figure 1: Modal sense distributions for MPQA and EPOS modals. The vertical axis in logarithmic scale to accomodate for the wide range of values. Deontic is represented by slanted lines, epistemic by dots and dynamic is left blank.

Table 3: REM data distribution.

Modal	Root (rt)	Epistemic (ep)	Indeterminate (?)
Be able to	500		
Can	492	8	
Could	378	121	1
Have to	469	19	
May	47	453	
Might	62	435	
Must	358	140	1
Need to	488	6	
Ought to	462	37	
Should	457	30	
Total	3713	1249	2

4 Our approach

Our approach to MSC differs from previous work in two main respects. First, our input representations are contextualized word representations extracted from the BERT neural languages models. Second, we propose to model MSC as a single classification problem, thus allowing for parameter sharing across different modal verbs. These two aspects are further developed in the rest of this section.

4.1 Contextualized representations

Contextualized word representations have allowed researchers to push the state of the art in many areas of NLP, including long-standing syntactic and semantic problems. While both static and contextualized word embeddings can be viewed in terms of mutual information maximization between a word and its context words, the latter differ in being tailored to its immediate context, thus each occurrence has its own vector representation encoding information about its neighbouring words. Among contextual models, transformer-based models and BERT (Devlin, Chang, Lee and Toutanova, 2019) specifically have arguably been the most successful, outperforming static and other contextual models alike.

More technically, BERT (Bidirectional Encoder Representations from Transformers) is a stack of transformer encoder layers consisting of multiple self-attention heads (Devlin, Chang, Lee and Toutanova, 2019; Vaswani et al., 2017). A self-attention head is a mechanism to compare the representation of a token with that of all the other tokens in the context in order to find relations between them, and to update the token's representation accordingly. Using multiple self-attention heads allows the model to consider different types of relation between tokens (verbs with their subject pronoun/noun, nouns with their determiner, etc). This constitutes a so-called transformer layer. BERT is made of a stack of these transformer layers, in which each subsequent layer infuses information from the context into each token's representation from the previous layer. The main effect is that representations become more contextualized the higher up in the stack they are found.

BERT is trained using two self-supervised tasks: masked language modeling (MLM) and next sentence prediction (NSP). In MLM, the model encounters sentences from which some tokens have been masked; its parameters are tuned in such a way that the contextualised representation of the mask best match the

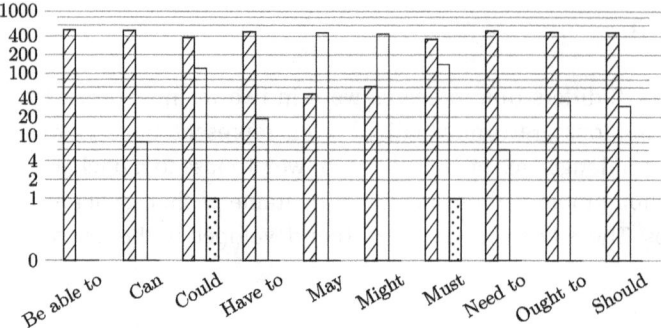

Figure 2: Coarse-grained modal sense distributions for REM modals. The vertical axis in logarithmic scale to accomodate for the wide range of values. Root meaning is represented by slanted lines, epistemic is left blank. There are only two modals whose meaning is indeterminate represented with dots.

actual hidden word. For the following sequence, the MLM task is to predict the verb *sleep*:

(4) *The cat sleeps on the mat.*

(5) *The cat < MASK > on the mat.*

In NSP, the objective is to be able to predict whether two sentences are indeed adjacent to each other. This dual training procedure has been shown to capture a number of linguistic factors necessary to predict hidden words and sentence adjacency. Input representations for this training procedure are obtained by combining token, segment and position embeddings into fixed-length vectors. For token embedding, the input sequence is tokenized and embedded in a special way called WordPiece embedding. Special dummy tokens [CLS] and [SEP] are inserted, respectively at the beginning of the sequence and to separate pairs of segments. They are handled as plain words by the encoder but are used to store information about the whole sentence.

Once trained using masked language modeling and next sentence prediction, BERT can be fine-tuned for a downstream application, by simply adding one or more fully-connected layers to the final encoder layer. Depending on the task at hand, different hidden layers are used for predictions, the vector associated with the [CLS] token having a special –yet still not fully understood– status as it is assumed to capture information about the whole sentence. Of course, BERT can also be used as an extractor of feature vectors that are fed into classical, non-neural machine learning algorithms. In this case, BERT's parameters are frozen

Table 4: REM fine-grained modal sense categories distribution.

Modal	Ambiguous (?)	Ability (ab)	Epistemic (ep)	General Situation Necessity (gsn)	General Situation Possibility (gsp)	NA (na)	Opportunity (op)	Permission (perm)	Root (root)	Situation Permissibility (sitperm)	Subject External Necessity (subjextn)	Subject Internal Necessity (subjintn)
be able to		182			72		226	12		8		
can		85	8		256		112	29		10		
could		97	121		169	1	100	9		3		
have to			11	91					1		377	8
may		1	453		20		8	10		8		
might			435		40		19			3		
must	1		140	123							234	1
need to			6	120							361	7
ought to			37	145							317	
should			30	199							258	
Total	1	365	1241	678	557	1	465	60	1	32	1547	16

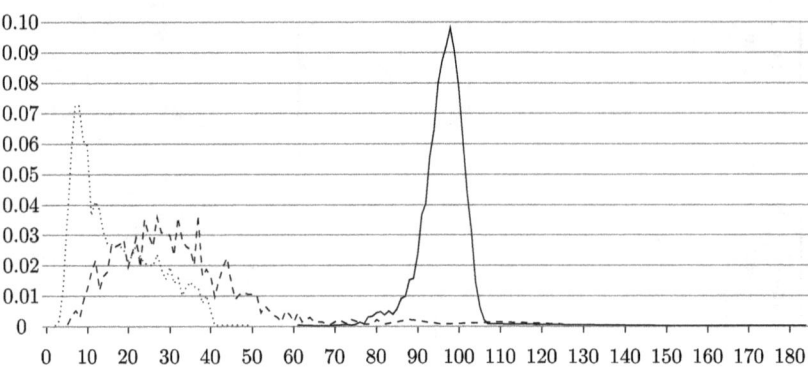

Figure 3: Context length distribution for EPOS, MPQA and REM.

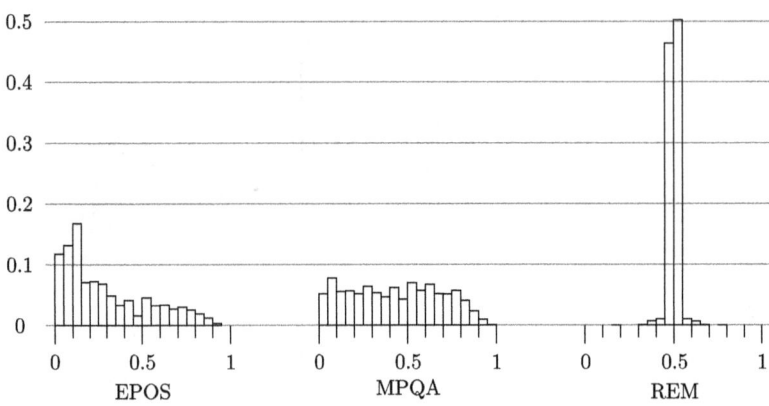

Figure 4: Distribution of the relative position of the modals within their contexts for each dataset. The relative position of a modal verb is computed as $\frac{position\ of\ the\ modal}{length\ of\ the\ context-1}$. Thus, the context starts at 0 (first word) and ends at 1 (last word), 0.5 being the middle. The relative positions are then grouped in 20 bins of width 0.05.

and word representations from the last layer are used as input features to some learning algorithm. For more detailed explanations on BERT we refer the reader to the tutorial presented by Hang Dong[4].

---

[4] https://cgi.csc.liv.ac.uk/~hang/ppt/BERT%20and%20Transformer.pdf

4.2 Classification models

In the present work we take the latter route, namely : using BERT as a feature extractor for the token associated with the modal verb. This is motivated by two main reasons. On the one hand, available datasets for MSC only have very few data points, and are therefore not well suited for training neural models with large numbers of parameters. On the other hand, we are interested in using "simple" models that get us better insight as to whether the relevant information is directly accessible from BERT.

Specifically, we consider two classification algorithms for MSC : namely k nearest neighbours (k-NN) and logistic regression (Hastie, Tibshirani and Friedman, 2001). The idea behind k-NN classification is to predict the class of a new data point through a vote over the k closest labeled data points, based on some distance (typically, the Euclidean distance) in the space of features (in this case, the space induced by the BERT word representations). Tunable hyper-parameters include the size of the neighbourhood (k) and the weighting of the vote of the neighbours (identical or proportional to their distance). More formally, if we note $l(x)$ the class of a data point $x \in \mathbb{R}^d$, $\mathcal{L}$ the set of possible classes, $\mathcal{N}(x)$ the neighbourhood of x and $w(x, x')$ the weight of a neighbour x' with respect to x, the predicted label of a data point is given by:

$$\tilde{l}(x) = \operatorname*{argmax}_{y \in \mathcal{L}} \sum_{x' \in \mathcal{N}(x)} w(x,x') \mathbf{1}_{l(x')=y}.$$

Note that k-NN is one of the simplest classification algorithms there is, as it does its predictions by memorizing the entire training data and performs no learning per se. It is nevertheless a powerful model in the sense that it can learn non-linear decision boundaries.

The second classification model, logistic regression, is different in both respects. It has internal parameters that need to be tuned to the task and data at hand, and it is a linear model. The idea is to assign a class label to a datapoint, based only on the feature representation of that datapoint. Since each feature can have a different attraction toward each class, we need an independent weight for each feature/class pair. These weights are learnt by optimizing the following objective:

$$\min_{w,c} \frac{1}{2} w^T w + \alpha \sum_{i=0}^{n} \log\left(1 - \frac{\exp(w_{y_i}^T x_i + c_{y_i})}{\sum_k \exp(w_k^T x_i + c_k)}\right),$$

where $\{(x_i, y_i)\}_{i=0}^n$ is the training set with y_i the class of vector x_i. The right part of the objective tries to maximize the relative score of the actual class of each datapoint with respect to the score of the other classes, while the left part prevents w from taking arbitrarily large values.

The hyper-parameter α is used to control the relative strength of the learning objective with respect to the L_2 regularization over the weights w (left part). The bias vector c is trained to offset the score of each label class irrespective of the input vector x.

4.3 Shared vs. independent models

As discussed in Section 2, previous approaches have all treated MSC through the use of independently trained classifiers, with one classifier for each modal verb.[5] This is actually also standard practice in the related task of word-sense disambiguation (WSD). Treating WSD as a set of unrelated classification problems does make sense to the extent that sense inventories (typically expressed as WordNet synsets) are very specific to each word form, and they rarely overlap. Things are very different in MSC, however. Modal senses are indeed more abstract and independent from the lexical items and are thus shared more widely between them. Training independent models in this case seems much less natural, as these would miss important commonalities between the different modal verbs. By training a unique shared model for all modals (or a model for necessity modals and another for possibility modals), one could benefit from information sharing between the different modals. We will investigate this hypothesis by running experiments with both independent models trained for each modal verb separately, and with single models trained on the whole set of modal verbs at once.

5 Experiments

In order to test our main hypotheses, we carry out different sets of experiments. On the one hand, we want to assess whether BERT word representations are indeed useful for MSC and are able to outperform state-of-the-art systems for this task. In order to train and evaluate our models, as well as to allow comparability with previous work, we first run a first set of experiments on the MPQA dataset, using this dataset in standalone fashion or using EPOS as auxiliary training data.

---

[5] We should note that in this respect, Ruppenhofer and Rehbein (2012) in fact use a less extreme setting, as they handled the historical pairs *may/might*, *can/could* and *shall/should* as paradigmatic variants, and thus trained only one model per pair.

In addition, we run another set of experiments on the new REM dataset. On the other hand, we would like to establish to what extent training a single classification model for all modal verbs, thus allowing for parameter sharing, can indeed improve sense prediction. We therefore perform comparative experiments, in which we use the traditional approach of training an independent model for each modal verb (we label it *Ind* in the tables) and the other corresponds to a single model trained on all the modals at the same time (we label it *One**). We do this both for k-NN and logistic regression (or logit, for short) models.

5.1 Settings

5.1.1 BERT features

The feature extraction from BERT works as follows. Using the bert-base-uncased release of BERT available from Huggingface, we first encode each modal verb and in its co-occurrence context. We then extract the last (i.e. 12th) hidden layer word vector corresponding to the modal verb, and use this 768-dimensional vector alone as input representation to our k-NN and logistic regression models. Using other layers yields worst accuracy performance on initial development experiments. See Section 6 for a more detailed comparison of using different layers.

5.1.2 Training and tuning of the models

k-NN and logistic models are trained using the implementations provided by scikit-learn (Pedregosa et al., 2011). For k-NN, we tune the number k of neighbours from the {1, 2, 5, 10, 20} and for logistic regression, we tuned the weighting between the prediction loss and the regularization from {0.01, 0.1, 1, 10, 100} as well as a class weight (inversely proportional to class frequency) to handle label imbalance.

5.1.3 Nested cross-validation

We estimate the test accuracy of our different models via nested cross validation, aka two-level cross-validation (Cawley and Talbot, 2010), over the dataset. This evaluation protocol indeed provides more realistic estimates of model performance than standard (one-level) cross-validation, as it reduces its bias due to combined hyperparameter tuning and model selection. It does so by using an outer K-fold cross-validation loop for hyper-parameter tuning along with an inner K-fold cross-validation loop for parameter fitting. In this case, we set K and K to 10 and 5, respectively, for each model. That is, the dataset is first divided into 10 outer sections. Then we keep each of the 10 outer sections in turn aside as a test set while recombining the 9 others. The combined 9 outer sections are further split into 5 new inner sections. For each of the 5 inner sections, the other 4 inner sections are recombined to form a training set. Then for each combination of hyper-parameters, a model is trained on the training set and tested on the remaining inner section. The best combination of hyper-parameters is chosen based on the results achieved for each of the inner sections. Eventually, the 5 inner sections are recombined and a model is trained on them using the best combination of hyper-parameters, which is then applied to the outer section that had been left out. By repeating this process for the 10 outer sections, we have a prediction for each modal in context, from which we can compute test accuracy figures.

5.1.4 Dealing with data imbalance

Due the very skewed sense distributions, studies starting from Zhou, Frank, Friedrich and Palmer (2015) onward have considered two training and evaluation regimes: an unbalanced setting and a balanced one. In the unbalanced case, the training set is taken directly from the set of annotated data, but in the balanced case, the sentences from the training set are duplicated in order to balance the number of examples in each class. This comes with a number of problems, the first being that the test set itself is not balanced, but rather follows the original distribution of the annotated dataset, which means that comparing its results to a random baseline may not be very meaningful. Another problem comes from the fact that the sense distributions are highly skewed. For example, *can* has 17 epistemic examples in MPQA and EPOS combined for 303 dynamic ones, which means that each epistemic sentence in the training set needs to be repeated about 20 times. At this level of imbalance and sentence repetition, it is not clear if the model learns to be balanced or if it actually learns to recognise the most frequent sentences as independent entities. This is really obvious for models such as k-NN, which do not actually learn classification parameters but rather rely on the geometry of the feature space to classify data points. Multiplying a point over and over again at the very same spatial position does not change the overall space, but merely adds weights to these duplicated points. Finally, if the data to be annotated have been sample randomly, the considerable sense imbalance ought to reflect an actual imbalance in the way modal verbs are used. Therefore, balancing the data makes the task more artificial and more remote from what a deployed model would actually face with real data. For these different reasons, we decided to stick to the original unbalanced setting.

5.2 Results

5.2.1 MPQA

Table 5: Results for the MPQA dataset in comparison to previous studies. Note that Scikit's logistic regression refuses to learn a model on only one class, which is very common for *might* due to its very skewed distribution, so we assumed a frequency baseline instead for computing averages. Freq stands for most frequent sense baseline. Are also reported, the results of Ruppenhofer and Rehbein (2012) ('RR'), Zhou, Frank, Friedrich and Palmer (2015) ('ZH') and Li, Dehouck and Denis (2019) ('LI').

Modal	Freq	RR	ZH	LI	k-NN		Logit	
		Syn	Sem	Vec	One*	Ind	One*	Ind
Can	69.9	66.6	66.0	70.1	68.4	**70.3**	69.9	66.7
Could	65.0	62.5	67.9	70.5	72.6	**72.9**	72.5	72.5
May	93.6	93.6	93.6	93.6	**94.4**	93.6	93.7	92.9
Might	98.4	**100.0**	**100.0**	–	98.4	98.4	98.4	(98.4)
Must	94.3	94.3	94.3	94.3	95.4	98.4	**98.5**	97.9
Shall	**84.6**	83.3	83.3	83.3	**84.6**	80.0	**84.6**	80.0
Should	90.8	90.8	92.9	90.8	94.7	**96.1**	95.8	**96.1**
Macro Avg	85.2	84.4	85.4	83.8	86.9	87.1	**87.6**	86.3
Micro Avg	81.1	78.7	80.0	81.3	83.1	**84.2**	**84.2**	82.9

Table 5 reports the prediction accuracies for the MPQA dataset for our different models alongside results reported in previous studies.

The first thing to note from these results is that both k-NN-based and logistic-regression-based classifiers achieve higher accuracy scores for most modals than both the frequency baseline and results published previously. This is interesting in two regards. First, since nominal increases are seen for both types of models, it seems that the results are due to the use of contextual word representations from BERT rather than to the learning algorithms themselves. Second, it shows that even with such skewed distributions, it is possible to learn to classify with success beyond the majority baseline. Recall from Section 3 that the MPQA dataset indeed has important class imbalance. The first column gives the score of the majority baseline, and we see that it achieves 94.3% accuracy for *must* for example, and even 98.4% (61/62) for *might*. That was one of the reason for Zhou, Frank, Friedrich and Palmer (2015) to balance the training data in order to render the effect of their new semantic features noticeable.

The results for *might* and *shall* are not really significant, with such skewed distributions and small sample sizes, random fluctuations can have great effects on the score. But this applies more broadly and should be kept in mind. Any analysis based on such small samples and skewed distributions must be taken with necessary caution.

Comparing accuracy numbers for *Ind* and *One** for different modals, we see that *can, could* and *should* reach higher results with independent models while *may, must* and *shall* have higher results with a single model trained on all the modals at the same time. The score difference between independent models and single models is most likely due to the difference in modal sense distributions between the various modals, as can be seen from Table 1. While most modals have either mostly epistemic or deontic uses, *can* has a mostly dynamic use in this corpus, which could easily explain why it works better on its own. However, we also see that while, one average, independent models seem to work better, the single model performs slightly better for Logistic regression. If this is meaningful, it could be due to the fact that k-NN is not actually learning, but rather uses the given features to classify data points, which again can be difficult when the various distributions are very different. The logit model, on the contrary, does learn a set of parameters, and can therefore make better use of the input features space even in the face of very divergent distributions.

Beside the majority baseline, human level performance is also a good point of comparison. While we do not know human performance on the task of modal sense classification, Ruppenhofer and Rehbein (2012) report the agreement rate between the two annotators that labelled their MPQA dataset, which can be viewed as a surrogate of the former. While they report 98% agreement for *must*, the inter-annotator agreement is only at 77% for *can/could*. This means that *can* and *could* are genuinely harder to analyse (at least for humans, but as we see, for machines too). Our results are still below inter-annotator agreement for both *can* and *could*, but since we do not have more information about the annotation process, we cannot rule out happy accidents where both annotators agree on the same mistake. This is all the more likely as we have a small number of classes (virtually two for *can*) and a low level of agreement. Furthermore, *can* is easily ambiguous given a single sentence of context. For example, in the sentence '*You can run fast, now*', *can* can be both deontic and dynamic (i.e., expressing either permission or ability). In a situation where person A was pretending not to be able to run fast because of an injury, and then ran fast for some reason, person B could say the above sentence with an intended dynamic meaning ('So you are in fact capable of running fast.'). In another situation where person A was first warming up and not running at full capacity, person B could then say the above sentence with an intended deontic meaning ('*Warm-up is over. It is now time to run fast.*', with the permission meaning here pragmatically strengthened to convey something close to an order). Such sentences occur in MPQA. The modal in the sentence '*If a country fails to use up its quota, it can sell the "surplus"'* is annotated as deontic ('countries are allowed by international laws to sell their unused quotas') but an independent k-NN model classified it as dynamic, which is not wrong ('countries have the capacity to sell things they possess and they do not use, regardless of international laws'). So, given the low inter-annotator agreement and the related inherent ambiguity of modals such as *can* and *could*, it is hard to know if it is really possible to do much better with the current annotation scheme and data.

Table 6 reports the prediction accuracies of our MSC models for the MPQA dataset but this time using the EPOS dataset as additional training data; specifically, we used the original unbalanced version of this dataset. Our BERT-based systems are compared to another system that was trained under the same regime, namely: Marasović and Frank (2016) noted as 'MF'. Before comparing the systems themselves, note that the most frequent sense baseline scores have changed slightly in relation to the addition of EPOS data; as noted in Section 6, modal sense distributions differ between MPQA and EPOS most substantially for the verb *must*, whose most frequent sense across both MPQA and EPOS is now epistemic, while this sense is in fact very marginal in MPQA on its own.

As in the previous experiment, we see that BERT-based models are able to deliver important performance gains over the frequency baseline and previous work. Interestingly, these are obtained with single (i.e., One*) models, irrespective of the learning algorithm; we suspect that the important performance losses observed for the individual models (e.g., for the model of *may*) come from the important distribution changes from MPQA to EPOS, hence between test and train data. Overall, the only system that is able to fully take advantage of the extra training data without being negatively impacted by these distribution differences is the single k-NN model. Specifically, this model achieves micro- and macro-average accuracies of 84.2 and 88.2, respectively, which are the best overall performances on MPQA. This lends strong support to our initial hypothesis that sense predictions for different modal verbs are indeed strongly related tasks and that it is beneficial to handle them together as a single task.

5.2.2 REM

Table 7 reports prediction scores for the coarse epistemic/root modal sense classification of the REM dataset. Because of the different annotation choices and the differences in contexts (see Section 3), the performances reported for REM cannot be compared with those reported for MPQA/EPOS but should rather be interpreted on their own.

Table 6: Results for the MPQA dataset using EPOS as additional training data. The model used by Marasović and Frank (2016) is a neural network called a convolutionnal neural network or CNN.

Modal	Freq	MF	k-NN		Logit	
		CNN	One*	Ind	One*	Ind
Can	69.9	**70.9**	70.2	68.0	67.9	69.5
Could	65.0	66.6	**73.8**	72.9	70.4	71.7
May	93.6	93.5	**93.7**	28.6	93.0	67.9
Might	**98.4**	–	**98.4**	73.3	**98.4**	88.3
Must	5.6	95.0	98.5	94.2	**99.0**	94.8
Shall	**84.6**	–	76.9	80.0	61.5	70.0
Should	90.8	90.6	94.7	95.7	94.7	**96.8**
Macro Avg	72.5	83.3	**88.2**	73.2	85.6	79.8
Micro Avg	68.1	80.0	**84.2**	74.7	82.8	80.1

Table 7: Prediction accuracy of the coarse-grained epistemic/root distinction for REM. For the same reason as in Table 5, we assume frequency-baseline-level prediction for *be able to*.

Modal	Freq	k-NN		Logit	
		One*	Ind	One*	Ind
Be able to	100,00	100,00	100,00	100,00	(100,00)
Can	98,40	98,20	**98.40**	96,40	97,60
Could	75,60	**89.40**	87.40	87,11	86.40
Have to	96,11	97.95	97,71	98.36	**98,75**
May	90,60	**94,20**	93,20	**94,20**	93,60
Might	87,53	89.13	**89.18**	88.73	86.53
Must	71,74	**95.19**	94,69	94.79	94.90
Need to	98,79	98,78	98,57	**98,99**	97.96
Ought to	92,59	92,57	**92,65**	91.97	92,45
Should	93,84	**95.05**	94.79	94,64	94.58
Macro Avg	90.52	**95.05**	94.78	94.55	94.28
Micro Avg	90.49	**95.04**	94.78	94.54	94.27

This being said, the results for the REM dataset support our analysis of the results on MPQA. Beside *can*, which has with *need to* the most skewed coarse sense distribution (*be able to* is not relevant since it has virtually one sense only), each modal has scores above the frequency baseline in Table 7. This means that

Table 8: Prediction accuracy of the fine-grained modal categorization for REM.

Modal	Freq	k-NN		Logit	
		One*	Ind	One*	Ind
Be able to	45,20	54.80	58.40	**61.00**	60.20
Can	51,20	58.60	58,80	**63.40**	58.80
Could	33,80	58.80	58.40	64.60	**65.60**
Have to	77,25	79.71	80.21	83,61	**85.42**
May	90,60	91,60	91.40	91.40	**92.60**
Might	87,53	87,53	**89.18**	85.31	85.10
Must	46,89	84.77	84.49	87.17	**87,96**
Need to	73,08	82.76	82,86	**89,05**	88,16
Ought to	63,53	81.12	80,41	**86.35**	85.71
Should	52,98	78.76	78.33	85.98	**87,71**
Macro Avg	62.21	75.85	76.25	**79.79**	79.73
Micro Avg	62.17	75.81	76.16	**79.74**	79.61

even with very skewed distributions, contextual representations are able to distinguish between broad modal senses.

However, this time the single models work best for both k-NN and logistic regression, with k-NN actually beating logistic regression. This is likely because contrary to MPQA, there is no real outlier in REM. While not all modals follow the same sense distribution, there is always another modal with a very similar sense distribution, and there are enough data to learn them.

Table 8 reports prediction scores for the fine-grained modal sense categorisation of Table 4. Again, each modal has scores above the (much lower) frequency baseline. And in the face of much less skewed distributions we can see that there is still room for improvement.

Note that there is now a much stronger asymmetry between k-NN and logit results in favour of logit. When k-NN models perform best, logit models are usually not far behind (at most 4 points for *might*). However, when logit models score better, the difference is much more pronounced, with up to 9 points for *should*, and 3.5 points on average. But remember that while logit is an actual learning algorithm with learnable parameters, k-NN can only be tuned to some extent and it does not learn to use the data representations, relying instead on the dataset geometry in order to classify the data points. This seems to imply that while contextual word representations already capture a lot of information, with k-NN beating the frequency baseline by 14 points on average, it is still necessary to actually learn to classify modal meanings to achieve an average 17.5-point improvement.

This is also supported by the fact that the independent k-NN models again fare better than the single ones (+0.40 macro average points, +0.35 micro average points). This is likely due to the fact that the fine-grained modal sense distributions are much more diverse than the coarse-grained ones, therefore hindering the ability to share information between modals through data space geometry alone. In comparison, logit models have much more balanced results, with roughly half of the modals faring better with independent models and half faring better with the single model, for +0.06 macro-average points and +0.13 micro-average points in favour of the single model.

6 Dissecting contextual representations

One of the main limitations of neural network-based representations is their lack of interpretability and their black-box-like nature. While hand-crafted features are readily interpretable, and can easily be analysed and modified for the sake of experimentation, dense contextual representations based on deep neural architectures are much harder to understand.

However, a number of approaches have been proposed to understand what is learned by neural models and how exactly they represent information. One such method, known as probing (Alain and Bengio, 2016; Vulić et al., 2020; Chronis and Erk, 2020; Mickus, Paperno, Constant and van Deemter, 2020; Karidi et al., 2021; Yenicelik, Schmidt and Kilcher, 2020), consists in feeding representations from intermediary layers to simple classifiers, typically linear ones, in order to measure the extent to which a given phenomenon is readily exposed at that layer. The classifiers should remain simple enough and are usually under-trained so as to prevent them from learning to perform the task at hand, but only train them to pick readily available clues.

In our case, since we are interested in modal sense classification, we use the same classification task as in the experiment section. Next, while hyper-parameters can be fine-tuned in k-NN, there are no internal parameters to be trained, so k-NN is a great candidate for probing, since it relies only on the quality of the input features. So we propose a variant of the above k-NN classification experiment where we change the layer from which the contextual word representations are extracted in order to investigate the impact of the representation layer.

The probing procedure we propose works as follows. We split a dataset into a test set consisting of 20% of the data and a training set consisting of the remaining 80%. Then we apply Sci-kit's k-NN to this 80/20 split, setting $k = 5$ and using the euclidean distance for weighting contributions from neighbours. Again, we do not tune hyper-parameters since we are not interested in optimizing performance on the task, rather we aim to find out how much of the information necessary to resolve the sense of modal verbs is readily accessible. We repeat this process 25 times for each layer shuffling the data between each run.

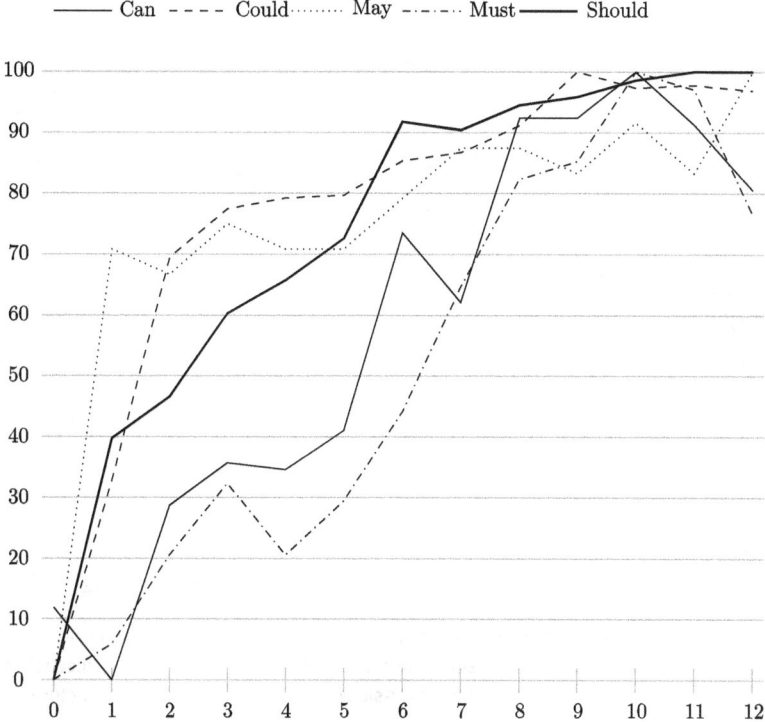

Figure 5: Scaled averaged accuracy of k-NN prediction with respect to representation layer for the MPQA dataset.

Since it is very easy to learn the majority baseline with very skewed distributions, as we have here, and since we are not interested in comparability with other models for this specific experiment, we have decided to scale the accuracy values to make them more readable. We thus proceed as follows. For each layer l from 0 to 12, we extract the representations of the modals in context. Then, we perform 25 runs of k-NN classification, with different train and test sentences, and compute the average accuracy $\bar{s}_{lm}$ for each modal m over those 25 runs. Then for each modal, we set $b_m = \min_{l \in 0..12} \bar{s}_{lm}$ the minimum average accuracy and $a_m = \max_{l \in 0..12} \bar{s}_{lm}$ the maximum average accuracy, and we set the new scaled accu-

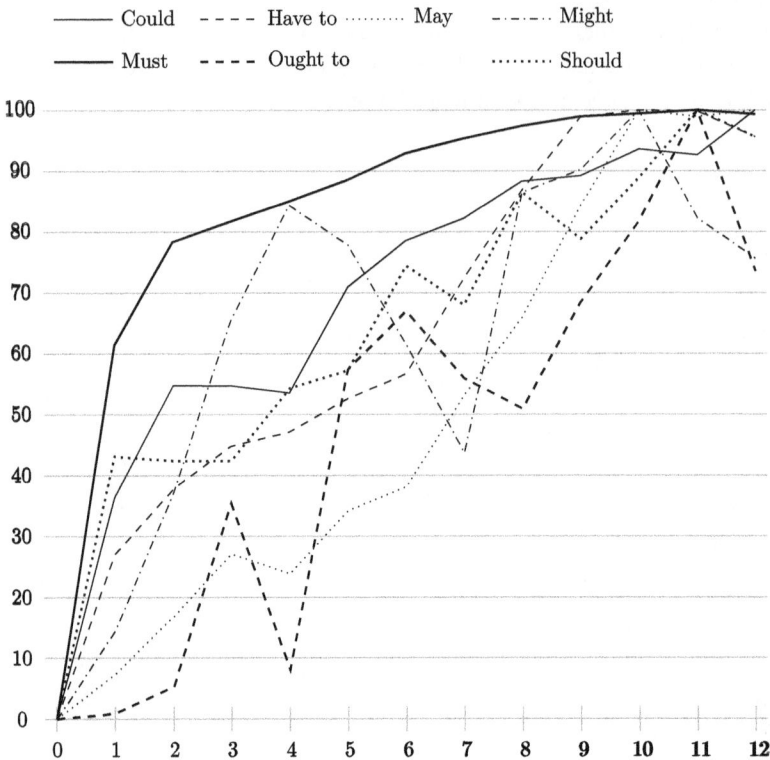

Figure 6: Scaled averaged accuracy of k-NN prediction with respect to representation layer for REM data. We have omitted *be able to* since the accuracy of its predictions always reaches 100% as well as *can* and *need to* because their over-skewed distributions blurred the picture.

racy $\tilde{s}_{lm} = 100 \frac{\bar{s}_{lm} - b_m}{a_m - b_m}$. This way, the scaled accuracies of each modal fully span the range [0, 100] in spite of their respective distributions' imbalance.

The scaled results for MPQA are plotted in Figure 5 and the maximum and minimum scores are reported in Table 9. We see that in spite of great variation in extremum values, all the curves follow the same upward trend. The modality sense prediction accuracy increases as representations are taken from layers higher up in the encoder. Even though this is not strictly monotonic, this behaviour is well marked.

Figure 6 represents the same operation performed on the REM dataset for the coarse-grained epistemic/root distinction. It shows the same upward trend, with prediction scores increasing as we use word representations coming from higher and higher layers.

Table 9: Minimum and maximum values of the average accuracy for each modal in the MPQA dataset.

Modal	Min b_m	Max a_m	Δ $a_m - b_m$
Can	64.20	73.57	9.37
Could	55.43	73.88	18.45
May	91.45	94.76	3.31
Must	94.87	98.36	3.49
Should	88.14	93.26	5.12

Table 10: Minimum and maximum values of the average accuracy per layer for each modals in the REM dataset.

Modal	Min b_m	Max a_m	Δ $a_m - b_m$
Be able to	100,00	100,00	0,00
Can	97,38	98,78	1,40
Could	69,21	88,45	19,24
Have to	95,06	98,15	3,09
May	89,60	94,69	5,09
Might	87,01	89,06	2,05
Must	63,11	94,73	31,62
Need to	98,46	98,78	0,32
Ought to	91,40	92,71	1,31
Should	92,63	95,38	2,75

Other studies on the internal representations of transformer networks (Jawahar, Sagot and Seddah, 2019) have linked lower layers to surface-level phenomena (e.g. sentence length, presence of certain words in the sentence) and higher layers to more complex phenomena (e.g. tense, subject-verb agreement). Thus, the fact that representations taken from higher layers are better suited for modal sense classification seems to support the idea that modality is a high-level phenomenon that requires machines to finely model, and humans to fully comprehend, the whole context.

Figures 7 and 8 represent the first two dimensions of a principle components analysis (PCA) of the contextual representations of modal verbs from MPQA and REM, respectively, in function of the layer. The shape of the points represents the modal verb and the colour the sense of the verb in context. Since we only

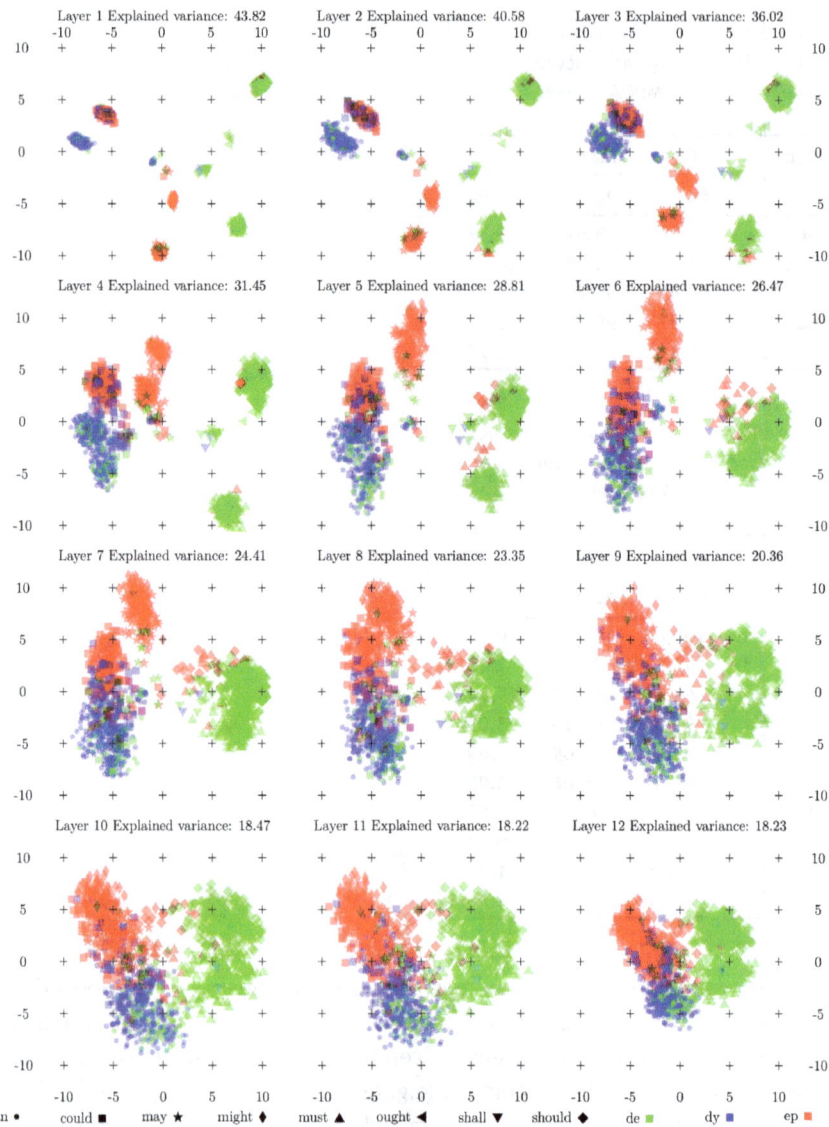

Figure 7: 2-dimensional PCA of MPQA data.

6 Dissecting contextual representations — 249

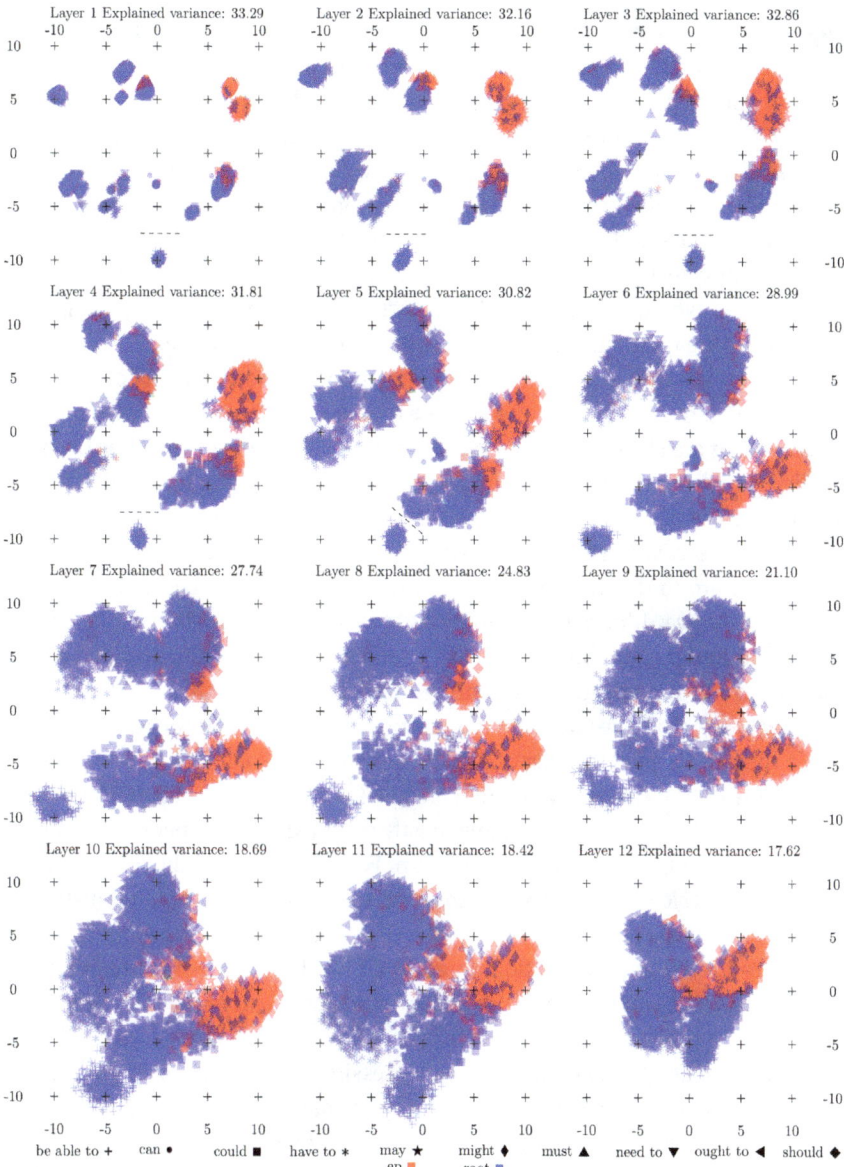

Figure 8: 2-dimensional PCA of REM data. For space reasons, we have brought the *be able to* cluster closer to the rest of the plot for layer 1 to 5. This is marked by a dashed line, representing an actual vertical translation of 4 to 10 units.

represent the two main dimensions amongst 768 dimensions, we also report the percentage variance explained by these two dimensions.

For both datasets on the first layer (upper left), data points are well clustered by modals since their representations are still mostly made of the basic embedding and position embedding, with very little contextualisation. From here, the higher up we move in the layers, the more contextualised the representations become and the more spread-out the modal clusters get. Note that this coincides with a steady decrease of the percentage of variance explained by the two main dimensions, which means that all the available dimensions (not just the two main ones) are used more evenly to encode contextual information.

We can see that there is indeed some notion of modality being captured by BERT. In Figure 7, if we look at *should* (♦), in the first layer, both epistemic and deontic uses are clustered together around (10, 6). But slowly – and this becomes really visible after the sixth layer – deontic *should*s move down toward the deontic cluster, while epistemic *should*s move leftward to the rest of the epistemic cluster. Similarly, the *could* (■) cluster is slowly sorted, with dynamic *could*s migrating downward to the dynamic cluster. However, the deontic *could*s tend to also migrate downward, rather than to the right, and end up in the dynamic cluster. We face a similar situation with *can* (●). It seems that deontic and dynamic uses of *can* and *could* are indeed easily confused (at least in two dimensions). Note that since we only show the two main dimensions, any conclusion can only be partial since there are a great number of dimensions we cannot explore.

Figure 8 shows a slightly different picture. On top of the general root/epistemic clustering, with epistemic uses being mostly confined to the upper right quadrant in the last layers, we have a second pattern. We obtain a possibility cluster on the right with *be able to* (+), *can* (●) and *could* (■) toward the bottom of the cluster and *may* (★) and *might* (♦) toward the top of it, the whole cloud being globally sorted for the root/epistemic distinction. In addition, we have three necessity clusters: a 'mild'-necessity cluster on the top left comprising *ought to* (◄) and *should* (♦), a 'stronger'-necessity cluster on the bottom left with *have to* (∗), *need to* (▼) and root uses of *must* (▲), and an epistemic-necessity cluster made mostly of *must* in the centre, between necessity modals and epistemic-possibility modals.

This seems to show that BERT is not only sensitive to general modality sense, but also captures the difference between necessity and possibility, as well as more subtle trends in necessity modals. This is not only supported by the classification performance increase as representations are taken from higher layers, but it can also be seen directly from a projection of the representation space on the main dimensions.

7 Conclusions and perspectives

In summary, this chapter has first confirmed that the contextual word representations provided by BERT indeed provide substantial accuracy performance compared to previously used representations, whether they relied on hand-engineered features or on static word embeddings, or on both. Performance improvements were consistent with the two classification algorithms we used, namely k-NN and logistic regression. Second, this work has also shown that, under certain circumstances, allowing for parameter sharing across classification models for different modal verbs can further increase accuracy performance.

These results open up different directions for future work. First, note that completely independent models and a unique model for all the modals are two extremes on a spectrum of model interaction. It would be interesting to see if we could find a middle ground using multi-task learning algorithms. Indeed, in multi-task learning, each task has its own model, although it is not trained independently from the others; rather, information is let free to flow from model to model. We could learn the relationships between the different tasks in order to share more between similar modals and less between more distant modals.

Our investigation into the BERT layers showed that understanding modality seems to be a high-level task in the sense that purely syntactic and lexical clues from a narrow context are not enough to get a reasonable analysis of modality, at least from the perspective of an automated system. But it also seems to be corroborated by linguists' findings, as previous chapters of this book have shown. Furthermore, the fact that transformer networks trained on huge amounts of data show a significant increase in modal sense classification accuracy, seems to indicate that a lot can be learned about modality from raw text alone (albeit from a huge quantity of raw text). It would be interesting to assess to which extent modality is also a discourse phenomenon by analysing modality with larger, more complete context (whole books or conversations at a time), and whether it also depends on knowledge of human interactions, which is arguably less accessible from text alone.

References

Alain, Guillaume & Yoshua Bengio, 2016. Understanding intermediate layers using linear classifier probes. doi:10.48550/ARXIV.1610.01644. URL https://arxiv.org/abs/1610.01644.
Baker, Kathrin, Michael Bloodgood, Bonnie Dorr, Nathaniel W. Filardo, Lori Levin & Christine Piatko, 2010. A modality lexicon and its use in automatic tagging. In Nicoletta Calzolari (Conference Chair), Khalid Choukri, Bente Maegaard, Joseph Mariani, Jan Odijk, Stelios

Piperidis, Mike Rosner & Daniel Tapias, editors, *Proceedings of the Seventh International Conference on Language Resources and Evaluation (LREC'10)*. European Language Resources Association (ELRA), Valletta, Malta. ISBN 2-9517408-6-7.

Cawley, Gavin C. & Nicola L. C. Talbot, 2010. On over-fitting in model selection and subsequent selection bias in performance evaluation. *Journal of Machine Learning Research*, 11(70):2079–2107. URL http://jmlr.org/papers/v11/cawley10a.html.

Chronis, Gabriella & Katrin Erk, 2020. When is a bishop not like a rook? When it's like a rabbi! multi-prototype BERT embeddings for estimating semantic relationships. In *Proceedings of the 24th Conference on Computational Natural Language Learning*, pages 227–244. Association for Computational Linguistics, Online. doi:10.18653/v1/2020.conll-1.17. URL https://aclanthology.org/2020.conll-1.17.

Devlin, Jacob, Ming-Wei Chang, Kenton Lee & Kristina Toutanova, 2019. BERT: Pre-training of deep bidirectional transformers for language understanding. In *Proceedings of NAACL-HLT*, pages 4171–4186.

Hastie, Trevor, Robert Tibshirani & Jerome Friedman, 2001. *The Elements of Statistical Learning*. Springer Series in Statistics. Springer New York Inc., New York, NY, USA.

Jawahar, Ganesh, Benoît Sagot & Djamé Seddah, 2019. What does BERT learn about the structure of language? In *Proceedings of the 57th Annual Meeting of the Association for Computational Linguistics*, pages 3651–3657. Association for Computational Linguistics, Florence, Italy. doi:10.18653/v1/P19-1356. URL https://aclanthology.org/P19-1356.

Karidi, Taelin, Yichu Zhou, Nathan Schneider, Omri Abend & Vivek Srikumar, 2021. Putting words in BERT's mouth: Navigating contextualized vector spaces with pseudowords. In *Proceedings of the 2021 Conference on Empirical Methods in Natural Language Processing*, pages 10300–10313. Association for Computational Linguistics, Online and Punta Cana, Dominican Republic. doi:10.18653/v1/2021.emnlp-main.806. URL https://aclanthology.org/2021.emnlp-main.806.

Kratzer, Angelika, 1991. *Modality*, pages 639–650. De Gruyter Mouton, Berlin • New York. doi:doi:10.1515/9783110126969.7.639. URL https://doi.org/10.1515/9783110126969.7.639.

Li, Bo, Mathieu Dehouck & Pascal Denis, 2019. Modal sense classification with task-specific context embeddings. In *ESANN 2019 – 27th European Symposium on Artificial Neural Networks, Computational Intelligence and Machine Learning*. Bruges, Belgium. URL https://hal.archives-ouvertes.fr/hal-02143762.

Liu, Yang, Xiaohui Yu, Zhongshuai Chen & Bing Liu, 2013. Sentiment analysis of sentences with modalities. In *Proceedings of the 2013 International Workshop on Mining Unstructured Big Data Using Natural Language Processing*, UnstructureNLP '13, page 39–44. Association for Computing Machinery, New York, NY, USA. ISBN 9781450324151. doi:10.1145/2513549.2513556. URL https://doi.org/10.1145/2513549.2513556.

Marasović, Ana & Anette Frank, 2016. Multilingual modal sense classification using a convolutional neural network. In *Proceedings of the 1st Workshop on Representation Learning for NLP*, pages 111–120. Association for Computational Linguistics, Berlin, Germany. doi:10.18653/v1/W16-1613. URL https://www.aclweb.org/anthology/W16-1613.

Marasović, Ana, Mengfei Zhou, Alexis Palmer & Anette Frank, 2016. Modal sense classification at large: Paraphrase-driven sense projection, semantically enriched classification models and cross-genre evaluations. In *Linguistic Issues in Language Technology, Volume 14, 2016 – Modality: Logic, Semantics, Annotation, and Machine Learning*. CSLI Publications. URL https://www.aclweb.org/anthology/2016.lilt-14.3.

Mickus, Timothee, Denis Paperno, Mathieu Constant & Kees van Deemter, 2020. What do you mean, BERT? In *Proceedings of the Society for Computation in Linguistics 2020*, pages 279–290. Association for Computational Linguistics, New York, New York. URL https://aclanthology.org/2020.scil-1.35.

Morante, Roser & Walter Daelemans, 2009. Learning the scope of hedge cues in biomedical texts. In *Proceedings of the BioNLP 2009 Workshop*, pages 28–36. Association for Computational Linguistics, Boulder, Colorado. URL https://aclanthology.org/W09-1304.

Pedregosa, F., G. Varoquaux, A. Gramfort, V. Michel, B. Thirion, O. Grisel, M. Blondel, P. Prettenhofer, R. Weiss, V. Dubourg, J. Vanderplas, A. Passos, D. Cournapeau, M. Brucher, M. Perrot & E. Duchesnay, 2011. Scikit-learn: Machine learning in Python. *Journal of Machine Learning Research*, 12:2825–2830.

Ruppenhofer, Josef & Ines Rehbein, 2012. Yes we can!? annotating English modal verbs. In *Proceedings of the Eighth International Conference on Language Resources and Evaluation (LREC'12)*, pages 1538–1545. European Language Resources Association (ELRA), Istanbul, Turkey. URL http://www.lrec-conf.org/proceedings/lrec2012/pdf/778_Paper.pdf.

Saurí, Roser & James Pustejovsky, 2012. Are you sure that this happened? assessing the factuality degree of events in text. *Computational Linguistics*, 38(2):261–299. doi:10.1162/COLI_a_00096. URL https://aclanthology.org/J12-2002.

Vaswani, Ashish, Noam Shazeer, Niki Parmar, Jakob Uszkoreit, Llion Jones, Aidan N Gomez, Ł ukasz Kaiser & Illia Polosukhin, 2017. Attention is all you need. In I. Guyon, U. V. Luxburg, S. Bengio, H. Wallach, R. Fergus, S. Vishwanathan & R. Garnett, editors, *Advances in Neural Information Processing Systems*, volume 30. Curran Associates, Inc. URL https://proceedings.neurips.cc/paper/2017/file/3f5ee243547dee91fbd053c1c4a845aa-Paper.pdf.

Vulić, Ivan, Edoardo Maria Ponti, Robert Litschko, Goran Glavaš & Anna Korhonen, 2020. Probing pretrained language models for lexical semantics. In *Proceedings of the 2020 Conference on Empirical Methods in Natural Language Processing (EMNLP)*, pages 7222–7240. Association for Computational Linguistics, Online. doi:10.18653/v1/2020.emnlp-main.586. URL https://aclanthology.org/2020.emnlp-main.586.

Wilson, Theresa, Janyce Wiebe & Paul Hoffmann, 2005. Recognizing contextual polarity in phrase-level sentiment analysis. In *Proceedings of Human Language Technology Conference and Conference on Empirical Methods in Natural Language Processing*, pages 347–354. Association for Computational Linguistics, Vancouver, British Columbia, Canada. URL https://aclanthology.org/H05-1044.

Yenicelik, David, Florian Schmidt & Yannic Kilcher, 2020. How does BERT capture semantics? a closer look at polysemous words. In *Proceedings of the Third BlackboxNLP Workshop on Analyzing and Interpreting Neural Networks for NLP*, pages 156–162. Association for Computational Linguistics, Online. doi:10.18653/v1/2020.blackboxnlp-1.15. URL https://aclanthology.org/2020.blackboxnlp-1.15.

Zhou, Mengfei, Anette Frank, Annemarie Friedrich & Alexis Palmer, 2015. Semantically enriched models for modal sense classification. In *Proceedings of the First Workshop on Linking Computational Models of Lexical, Sentential and Discourse-level Semantics*, pages 44–53. Association for Computational Linguistics, Lisbon, Portugal. doi:10.18653/v1/W15-2705. URL https://www.aclweb.org/anthology/W15-2705.

9 Modals in the network model of Construction Grammar

Martin Hilpert and Susanne Flach

1 English modal auxiliaries and Construction Grammar

Construction Grammar (Goldberg 1995, 2006, Hilpert 2019) aims to provide a theoretical model of what speakers know when they know a language. That model is commonly presented as a network of form-meaning pairings (Langacker 2013: 24). Foundational studies in Construction Grammar (Fillmore, Kay and O'Connor 1988, Kay and Fillmore 1999, inter alia) have shown that the form-meaning pairings in that network commonly exhibit either non-compositional meanings or non-predictable formal characteristics, so that they cannot be explained in terms of a small set of general rules. Documenting such idiosyncratic patterns and analyzing their conditions of use has been an important aspect of constructional work that continues to yield new insights, as illustrated by recent studies on forms such as the *way*-construction (Fanego 2019), the comparative correlative construction (Hoffmann 2019), or insubordination constructions (Kaltenböck 2021). By comparison, canonical syntactic patterns and constructions that encode basic grammatical distinctions have received less attention. There is thus relatively little discussion on constructions that appear not particularly unruly or that do not seem to convey non-compositional meaning. As a result, substantial areas of grammatical description are currently underserved by Construction Grammar. We argue that modality, despite efforts to the contrary (cf. Boogart and Fortuin 2016 and references therein), remains one such area.

This chapter tries to address this issue. It takes a programmatic stance and aims to make a theoretical point. It uses the phenomenon that lies at the center of this volume, English modal auxiliary constructions, as a case study that allows us to examine how the grammatical category of modality can be understood in terms of the network model of Construction Grammar. On the basis of the example of English modal auxiliaries, we argue that grammatical constructions can be fruitfully understood as networks of associative connections. Following recent work in Construction Grammar that places a major emphasis on the role of links in the organization of linguistic knowledge and that examines the division of labor between different types of connection (Diessel 2019, Schmid 2020, Sommerer and Smirnova 2020), we examine how these ideas can be applied to the analysis of modal constructions. We adopt a typology of connections that has been developed by Schmid (2020), who distinguishes between four different types. Symbolic associations connect form and meaning. Paradigmatic associations obtain between constructions that constitute mutual alternatives and thus stand in a relation of competition for activation. Syntagmatic associations obtain between constructions that follow each other in a temporal sequence. Pragmatic associations link constructions to situational contexts and to discourse-functional meanings. The central argument presented in this chapter is that speakers' knowledge of modal constructions can be exhaustively represented in terms of these links. This constitutes a re-conceptualization of how knowledge of modal constructions, and in fact linguistic knowledge more generally, is modeled in the network of constructions. We review psycholinguistic work and corpus studies that allow us to assess this view on the basis of empirical evidence.

The remainder of this paper is structured as follows. Section 2 will present our theoretical point of departure, which concerns the way in which many approaches in Construction Grammar have modeled knowledge of idiosyncratic constructional characteristics. Aspects of form and meaning that are judged as not being predictable from more abstract generalizations have been inscribed in the nodes of the network, which are viewed as symbolic units with a formal pole and a meaning pole (Fillmore, Kay and O'Connor 1988, Kay and Fillmore 1999). We will spell out the implications of this practice and examine if and how a view that strengthens the relative importance of connections can be developed. Section 3 addresses an important tool that we adopt for that task, namely Schmid's (2020) Entrenchment-and-Conventionalization model. Schmid presents a usage-based theory of linguistic knowledge that shares a lot of its basic assumptions with Construction Grammar as conceived of by Goldberg (1995, 2006) and others (cf. also Chapter 2, Section 2.2 in this volume), but that also goes beyond these approaches in important respects. With the theoretical foundations in place, Section 4 presents a discussion of empirical studies, both based on psycholinguistic experimentation and corpus-based analysis, that allow us to spell out how knowledge of modal constructions can be re-thought as a network of connections. The studies address in turn the syntagmatic, paradigmatic, symbolic, and pragmatic aspects that characterize English modal constructions. We conclude this chapter with a set of open questions for further investigations.

2 The fat node problem

This section discusses a feature of constructional approaches that, on closer inspection, raises a number of theoretical questions. As will be further explained below, we will refer to this feature as *the fat node problem*. What is that problem? A cornerstone of constructional approaches to language has been the tenet that speakers' knowledge of language contains a multitude of form-meaning pairs whose idiosyncratic traits require them to be represented in their own right. In the words of Goldberg (2003: 219), Construction Grammar "allows observations about constructions to be stated directly, providing long-standing traditions with a framework that allows both broad generalizations and more limited patterns to be analyzed and accounted for fully". To illustrate this point, we can take the English ditransitive construction as an example. The construction conveys the frame-semantic meaning of an intended transfer of a theme from an agent to a recipient. A semantic constraint of this construction is that it only allows for recipients that can be conceptualized as animate, thus ruling out examples such as *?Liza sent storage a book* (Goldberg 2003: 221). The ditransitive construction further has the pragmatic characteristic that it is preferably used with recipients that are given information, rather than new information (Bresnan et al. 2007). These aspects of meaning and use are directly associated with the syntactic form of the construction and would hence be inscribed directly into the node that represents the ditransitive construction in the network of constructions. Often this is done in terms of attribute-value matrices, as for example in the formalism adopted by Kay and Fillmore (1999: 14). This practice provides constructional research with a powerful descriptive tool. If a construction deviates in its meaning or form from broader generalizations that exist in the network of constructions, these differences can be stated as such at the level of the construction. By contrast, formal and functional features that are shared across a wider set of constructions are represented as a more schematic generalization, from which they are passed down to its more specific instantiations. This organization principle is known as inheritance in the Construction Grammar literature (Kay and Fillmore 1999: 7). While a construction such as the ditransitive construction thus inherits several basic characteristics from more general clause-level constructions, its specific features are represented as a separate generalization. This allows for a very elegant representation of linguistic knowledge that is characterized both by broad generalizations and specific idiosyncrasies, but it also comes at a price. It means that the nodes that represent the constructions in the network have complex internal structure that comprises features of meaning, constraints on usage, as well as formal characteristics. This has been pointed out by Hudson (2015: 692), who argues that the assumption of complex internal node structure hollows out the claim that constructional approaches aim to model language purely in terms of a network structure:

> I believe that language is, indeed, a network, and that this network is, indeed, a structure. Many other readers may protest that they too see language as a network; after all, cognitive linguists envisage 'an elaborate network comprising any number of conventional units linked by categorizing relationships' (Langacker 2000: 12) or a 'network of constructions

[which] captures our grammatical knowledge of language in toto, i.e. it's constructions all the way down' (Goldberg 2006: 18). But notice that in these cases the complex units which the network connects have their own internal stucture which is not part of the network. [...] [N]etwork theory goes further by claiming that 'it's networks all the way down'.

The issue identified by Hudson, which we refer to as "the fat node problem" from here on, is thus the analytical practice of enriching the nodes in the constructional network with different pieces of linguistic information that are merely stated as such. The more idiosyncratic information is stated at the level of a particular construction, the fatter the node that represents that construction. This can be contrasted for example with neural networks in which nodes only serve to pass on activation or inhibition to other nodes. In order to satisfy the vision that Hudson expresses, any and all construction-specific characteristics would have to come in the shape of networks themselves, thereby replacing fat nodes with networks that comprise different types of connections. Schmid (2017: 25) argues for precisely this kind of perspective, defending the assumption that "linguistic knowledge is available in one format only, namely associations". It is worth pointing out that this suggestion has far-reaching consequences. In Schmid's model, a construction would no longer be a node that is qualitatively separate from links connecting the nodes, but instead a set of associations that processes the information that current approaches assign to nodes. We can illustrate the contrast between these alternative approaches with the example of English modal auxiliaries. On the node-centered approach, any and all idiosyncratic and non-predictable aspects of their form and meaning would be inscribed in nodes that capture for example the syntactic behavior of a modal such as *might*, its various meanings, and its typicality for specific text types. An association-centered approach would re-conceptualize these pieces of information in terms of connections. Section 4 will offer a detailed discussion of how this could be achieved.

At this point, it is a legitimate question to ask why the current, node-based approach should be a problem to begin with. Is this merely a terminological issue, or a question of notational variants, where the same linguistic phenomena are captured by different descriptive instruments? We believe that there is more to it. Among the arguments that can be made for a view that prioritizes connections, a particularly strong one is that it accommodates the dynamic nature of language use and language change much more easily than a representation that works with static features (Budts and Petré 2020: 320). Of course, any proposal to alter a descriptive apparatus that has acquired a near-consensual status in constructional research is in need of a solid proof of concept. Is it feasible to take the information that current approaches store in the nodes and to model it in terms of connections? What would be the basic conceptual notions that are needed? The next section will lay out several ideas from Schmid's (2020) Entrenchment-and-Conventionalization model, which we will then adopt for our discussion of English modal constructions.

3 Association types in Schmid's Entrenchment-and-Conventionalization model

As the name of Schmid's model suggests, its two major elements are entrenchment on the one hand and conventionalization on the other (2020: 4). These elements have been central to discussions in usage-based linguistics (Bybee 2010, Langacker 2017). Entrenchment, understood in general terms as the organization of knowledge in response to experience, applies to the mind of the individual speaker. As such, it is subject to forces such as priming, iconicity, or salience. Conventionalization, which is the process of establishing regular patterns of behavior in a community, accounts for the social nature of language. Conventionalization thus applies to the speech community, where it is shaped by factors that include for example prestige and stigma. Entrenchment and conventionalization overlap in the area of usage, which is going to be in the focus of our discussion here. The specific aspect of Schmid's model that is crucial for our purposes is his typology of patterns of associations that characterize entrenched, conventionalized constructions. Schmid (2020: 5) identifies four association types, namely symbolic associations, paradigmatic associations, syntagmatic associations, and pragmatic associations. Each of the four will be briefly discussed below.

Symbolic associations concern relations between form and meaning. In language use, they do their work when a speaker has a communicative intention and mentally activates linguistic units that may serve to express that intention. Symbolic associations are central to the theoretical framework of Construction Grammar due to the fact that linguistic knowledge is assumed to be an inventory of symbolic units in which form and meaning are connected through a symbolic link (Goldberg 2006: 5). Schmid (2020: 46) emphasizes that his view of symbolic associations is dynamic, not static. Instead of viewing constructions as stored form-meaning pairs that can be accessed and retrieved when they are needed, we are to understand constructions as cognitive routines that unfold through time. In other words, a construction is a process that is triggered when speakers intend to verbalize a concept. For example, what we refer to as the ditransitive construction is a routine that allows a speaker to observe a scene of a transfer and describe it as *The receptionist handed her the key card*. Symbolic associations dynamically connect meaning and form in that routine, and they are also active in the mirror image of that routine, as a hearer processes that utterance and forms a corresponding idea.

Paradigmatic associations are found wherever elements in speakers' knowledge of language constitute mutual alternatives and thus compete for activation (Schmid 2020: 47). This is the case for grammatical paradigms in the traditional structuralist sense of the term. In English, linguistic forms with procedural meaning that encode oppositions include for example the contrast between singular and plural, present and past tense, or the well-known dative alternation. A speaker who wishes to verbalize the situation of a transfer of an object needs to make a paradigmatic choice in which the ditransitive construction and the prepositional dative construction compete for activation. The decision to use one option rather than another involves a reasoning process that draws on paradigmatic associations. Similarly, languages commonly provide several alternative lexical forms for the expression of an idea, so that speakers have to make a choice and pick the one that best matches their communicative intentions. A plate of spaghetti, served around noon, can be labeled as *lunch*, *pasta*, or simply *food*. All of these labels are conceivable candidates and stand in a relation of competition through which they are mutually associated. In the domain of grammar, alternative constructions such as the active and the passive, or the ditransitive and the prepositional dative trigger similar decision processes. In all of these scenarios, speakers and hearers reason in terms of relations of similarity, mutual contrast and competition.

Syntagmatic associations (Schmid 2020: 47), which are also referred to as sequential relations (Diessel 2019: 63), obtain between elements that follow each other in a temporal sequence. In language use, syntagmatic associations allow hearers to anticipate sounds, words, and structures that the speaker has not uttered yet, but that are very likely to come up, given the prior context. Syntagmatic associations can manifest themselves in idiomatic expressions and semi-fixed collocations. If a speaker begins an utterance with the words *let's take a little . . .* , the hearer can predict with a high degree of certainty that the following word will be *break*. By the same token, hearing the initial phonemes of a word, for example the first two phonemes of the word *hotel*, will provide a strong cue for the entire word, leading the hearer to anticipate the remaining phonemes, especially when the word resonates semantically with the prior context. At a more abstract level, grammatical constructions may foreshadow the structures with which they will be eventually completed. These cues may be more or less specific. For example, an utterance beginning in *The more I think about it* serves as a cue for the comparative correlative construction, so that hearers will expect the speaker to go on with a word sequence such as *the less convinced I am*. Syntagmatic associations may vary in strength. While some cues point to a single continuation that is possible, others allow only probabilistic predictions. A string such as *I expect* can be followed by a *that*-clause, a *to*-infinitive, or a noun phrase. The verb *expect* entertains syntagmatic associations with all of these structures. In general terms, the greater the strength of a syntagmatic association, the easier it will be for a hearer to process the following element. As with symbolic and paradigmatic associations, it is important to emphasize the dynamic character of syntagmatic associations. At any moment during language use, the set of ideas that are currently active in the speaker's mind will lead to patterns of syntagmatic associations that will influence the selection of linguistic elements with which an utterance will be continued.

The fourth type of association that Schmid discusses is the type of pragmatic associations (2020: 48). These associations relate linguistic utterances to the extralinguistic context in which they occur. A single speaker's language use will vary considerably across contextual situations, along dimensions such as formality, politeness, orientation towards a standard variety, or the use of multi-lingual resources such as code-switching. By adopting a certain level of formality, the speaker conveys an assessment of the situational context and its requirements that will be interpreted as such by the hearer. Other ways in which pragmatic associations influence language use concern the extent of common ground that is shared between speaker and hearer in a given situation, which impacts the interlocutors' reliance on deictic elements such as pronouns and demonstratives, as well as the use of implicature in indirect speech acts. Similarly, the use of technical terms and professional jargon presumes a dense network of pragmatic associations that is only accessible to certain speakers in certain situational contexts. For example, the text on this page presupposes not only a general understanding of linguistic concepts but also familiarity with the kinds of question that are raised in discussions of Construction Grammar as a linguistic theory.

Schmid (2020: 45) assumes that these four association types are both necessary and sufficient for language production and comprehension. The next section will examine how the ideas that have been discussed up to this point can be applied to an analysis of English modal constructions.

4 Re-thinking English modal constructions in terms of associative links

To what extent can knowledge of English modal constructions be modeled in terms of symbolic, paradigmatic, syntagmatic, and pragmatic associations? This section reviews the respective roles of each type and discusses empirical, corpus-based and experimental studies that shed light on the issue.

4.1 Syntagmatic associations

It is well-documented that English modal auxiliaries have idiosyncratic collocational preferences that can be usefully understood as syntagmatic associations in the entrenchment-and-conventionalization model. Among the contextual elements that have received particular attention, adverbs stand out as an important category (Hoye 1997, Celle 2009, cf. also Chapter 8 in this volume). Flach (2021) uses collostructional analysis (Stefanowitsch and Gries 2003) to investigate what has been described in the literature as modal harmony, that is, the combination of elements that converge with regard to their respective meanings. Her study yields the result that there is a continuum of modal idiomaticity that goes beyond modal harmony. Certain combinations, such as *may well* or *could possibly*, occur much more often than expected and exhibit a more unit-like behavior, while the reverse is true for sequences such as *can rather* or *may probably*. Between the two poles, there are combinations that exhibit neither attraction nor repulsion and in which the adverb commonly relates semantically to the context that follows the sequence of modal auxiliary and adverb. In other words, the usage of modal auxiliaries and accompanying adverbs is shaped by a gradient of syntagmatic associations of different strengths.

While the fact that modal auxiliaries exhibit collocational preferences of this kind already illustrates the importance of syntagmatic associations, the concept actually has implications that go a lot further. The general idea can be applied not only to lexical contextual elements, but also to grammatical structures. Hohaus (2020) uses corpus data and multivariate statistics in order to study dependencies between English modal auxiliaries and the syntactic contexts in which they are used. The analysis distinguishes between modals in independent clauses, adverbial clauses, relative clauses, and complement clauses. Several control variables are taken into account, including the animacy of the subject, grammatical aspect, and the meaning of the lexical verb. The results indicate that the English modal auxiliaries are not distributed randomly across syntactic contexts. For example, the auxiliary *could* is overrepresented in adverbial clauses, whereas *must* is underrepresented in relative clauses. What this indicates is that speakers' choices between alternative modal expressions is not only dependent on the lexical elements that appear in the immediate context, but also influenced by associations with more abstract linguistic units, including syntactic patterns.

The observations made by Hohaus (2020) concern probabilistic tendencies, that is, speakers' preferences to use modal auxiliaries in specific contexts. It was discussed in the previous section that associations can vary in strength. Syntagmatic associations that are maximally strong can be invoked to describe hard constraints in the use of grammatical structures. The conventionalized morpho-syntactic characteristics of modal auxiliaries, often labeled as the so-called NICE properties (Huddleston and Pullum et al. 2002: 1209, cf. also Chapter 1 in this volume), can thus be re-conceptualized as a network of syntagmatic associations. The morpho-syntactic behavior of English modal auxiliaries reflected in the NICE properties pertains to negation, inversion, code (i.e. the use as a pro-verb in tag questions and ellipsis constructions), and emphasis. The examples below illustrate the respective constructions.

(1) a. I can't do that. (negation)
    b. Can you do that? (inversion)
    c. I can't do it, but he can. (code)
    d. That CAN be a problem. (emphasis)

The NICE properties distinguish modal auxiliaries from lexical verbs, which means that they would have to be inscribed into the fat node of a modal auxiliary construction that inherits only some of its characteristics from a more general verbal construction. An alternative perspective is possible, and in fact plausible. Analog to the results obtained by Hohaus (2020), it can be maintained that English modal auxiliaries entertain syntagmatic associations with syntactic constructions such as the sentence-level negation construction, the polar interrogative construction, tag question constructions, and information structure constructions that encode emphasis. To give a concrete example, if a speaker of English hears the string *I would*, a possible continuation of that string is the negative particle *not*, which in turn can be followed by a verb in the infinitive. Together, these elements constitute a negative declarative sentence. The constructional network, as it is conceived of in standard accounts such as that of Fillmore, Kay and O'Connor (1988) or Goldberg (2006), already contains links between modal auxiliaries and constructions such as the sentence-level negation construction, because they can be combined syntactically. This would suggest that collocational preferences and morphosyntactic characteristics of constructions can be reduced to the same underlying phenomenon, namely syntagmatic associations. Instead of inscribing these characteristics into the nodes that represent modal auxiliaries in the constructional network, they can be modeled in terms of syntagmatic associations of varying strengths.

4.2 Paradigmatic associations

The paradigmatic organization of the English modal auxiliaries is one central indicator of their status as grammatical elements. This organization manifests itself in terms of both meaning and function. As members of a paradigm, modal auxiliaries encode semantic oppositions, as for example the difference between possibility and necessity. At the level of linguistic form, they exhibit shared distributional behaviors such as the ability to appear before the grammatical subject in questions or exclamatives. Arguing for the psychological reality of paradigms, Diewald (2020: 278) states that they are important generalizations that are part of speakers' knowledge and that are motivating forces in language change. This section explores if that kind of knowledge can be understood in terms of associations.

The fact that speakers access paradigmatic associations in language processing has been documented in different ways. Perek (2012) has devised an experiment in which participants were given the opportunity to sort different English sentences into categories of their own choosing. Working with a design developed by Bencini and Goldberg (2000), which showed that speakers are sensitive to the meaning of argument structure constructions, Perek adapted his stimuli and gathered evidence for the view that participants spontaneously form categories that are based not just on a single argument structure pattern, but instead on sets of semantically related constructions, that is constructional paradigms. Further psycholinguistic evidence comes from priming studies. Lester, Feldman and Moscoso del Prado Martín (2017) analyzed response time data from a large-scale project on semantic priming (Hutchison et al. 2013), focusing on pairs of nouns that served as primes and targets respectively. Lester and colleagues determined how similar the noun pairs were in terms of their syntactic behavior. For this, they devised a corpus-based measure of syntactic similarity that was based on the relative frequency of syntactic elements in the immediate context of the nouns. This measure took into account, amongst other things, the relative frequency of determiners, verb phrases and prepositional phrases that stood in a dependency relation with the noun. A statistical analysis determined that syntactic similarity yields a priming effect. Response times are faster if prime and target have similar syntactic profiles (Lester, Feldman and Moscoso del Prado Martín 2017: 2540). This finding suggests that elements with similar morphosyntactic distributional profiles are mutually associated. This concerns not only the member elements of grammatical paradigms. Even members of more loosely organized linguistic sets, such as nouns with similar syntactic properties, are linked to one another.

An important conclusion that can be drawn from these findings is that paradigmatic organization can be seen as the outcome of a set of associative connections in which not only links between mutual alternatives play a role. The members of linguistic paradigms compete for attention and convey semantic contrasts, but they are also characterized by similarity with regard to their syntagmatic associations. Paradigmatic associations and syntagmatic associations thus jointly contribute to the psychological reality of paradigms.

4.3 Symbolic associations

Symbolic associations, conceived of as links between a linguistic form and an idea that a speaker wishes to express, connect modal auxiliaries to categories of meaning. Depraetere and Cappelle (this volume) offer an overview of semantic and pragmatic categories that have been proposed for the analysis of modal meanings. Importantly, the interpretation of a given modal auxiliary in a given utterance also depends on its context, which means that syntagmatic associations have a central role to play as well. As Cappelle and Depraetere (2016) point out, the utterance *I can't complain* is a fully conventionalized symbolic unit with non-compositional meaning, so that the meaning of the individual words, including that of the modal auxiliary, is overridden by the meaning that is conveyed holistically by the utterance (cf. also Section 3.4 in Chapter 1 of this volume). Among the symbolic associations that are relevant for the analysis of modal auxiliaries, we thus have to count also the symbolic associations that connect multi-word units containing modal auxiliaries with their respective meanings.

Between utterances with fully transparent, compositional meanings and utterances that have conventionalized, non-compositional meanings, there is a continuum. There are utterances that merely allow for a non-compositional interpretation, but that do not enforce it. For example, the question *Why would he do that?* can be understood fully compositionally ('What are his reasons for doing that?'), while also allowing for the interpretation of an implicit criticism ('I do not approve of him doing that'). In such a case, symbolic links are in place both at the level of the individual words and at the level of the multi-word unit, and their relative strengths determine which interpretation is favored by the hearer (cf. the discussion of 'lexically regulated saturation' in Chapter 2). If a hearer is repeatedly exposed to a multi-word unit with an intended non-compositional meaning, this leads to what Schmid (2020: 236) calls syntagmatic strengthening: "As the syntagmatic links within a sequence are strengthened by repetition, symbolic, paradigmatic, and pragmatic connections associated with the component parts are weakened, while symbolic, paradigmatic, and pragmatic associations of the sequence become stronger". In other words, shifts in the context in which a linguistic unit is commonly experienced leads to shifts in meaning. With regard to modal auxiliaries, this phenomenon has been addressed empirically. For example, Hilpert (2013b, 2016) shows that the English modal auxiliaries exhibit clear collocational profiles with regard to their co-occurring lexical verbs in the infinitive, and that these profiles are subject to diachronic change, reflecting semantic developments. To illustrate that idea, the English modal auxiliary *may* has undergone a semantic development from permissive to epistemic meaning between the 19th and the late 20th century (Millar 2009). This change in symbolic associations manifests itself in a changing pattern of syntagmatic associations, so that for example the collocation *may say*, which is associated with permissive meaning, decreases in frequency over time, whereas frequency increases are observed for collocations such as *may help* or *may need*, which are more likely to be interpreted in terms of deontic meaning (Hilpert 2013b: 76). The network architecture of Construction Grammar, and the interplay of syntagmatic and symbolic links, as envisioned by Schmid (2020), thus offer a theoretical framework for the analysis of modal meanings that is well-equipped to deal with the analytical challenges that characterize this area of study (cf. Depraetere and Cappelle, this volume).

4.4 Pragmatic associations

The previous sections have addressed the respective roles of symbolic, syntagmatic, and paradigmatic associations in the network of form-meaning pairings that is posited in Construction Grammar. Pragmatic (in the sense of linguistic co-text, see Chapter 1, Section 3.4) associations connect linguistic units with the situational context (Schmid 2020: 48), and as such, they go beyond what would be conceived of as linguistic knowledge in the narrow sense of the term. That being said, it is still possible to investigate the pragmatic associations of English modal auxiliaries on the basis of language data.

Hilpert and Flach (2021) apply token-based semantic vector space modeling (Heylen et al. 2015, Hilpert and Correia Saavedra 2020) in order to study how pairs of modal constructions can be distinguished in terms of their respective collocational profiles. Token-based semantic vector space modeling differs in its approach from type-based techniques. The latter are designed to determine the collocational profile of a linguistic unit based on large concordances of that unit. For example, a large concordance of the word *breakfast* will yield the result that words such as *morning* or *eat* appear more frequently than expected in the context of that word. Token-based semantic vector space modeling can be used to analyze meaning differences between concordance lines of the same linguistic unit, which can provide insights into the meaning spectrum of that unit. The method relies on the analysis of second-order collocates, that is, method not only considers the elements that appear to the left and right of a key word, but it also takes into account the collocates of those elements. This makes it possible to determine degrees of semantic similarity even between concordance lines that convey similar meanings but that do not have any overlap in the actual words they contain (Hilpert and Correia Saavedra 2020: 10). Hilpert and Flach (2021) used the British National Corpus to retrieve concordance lines of two pairs of modal constructions, namely *may* and *might* as well as *must* and *have to*. For each concordance line, they constructed context vectors based on second-order collocates and tested how accurately those vectors distinguish between uses of *may* and *might*, and *must* and *have to* respectively. The results indicate that second-order collocates do contain information that significantly improves classification accuracy.

What is more decisive with regard to pragmatic associations is the result that second-order collocates commonly reflect broader text topics, such as for example a medical context. The statistical models can be seen to make predictions on the basis of such categories, so that for example a concordance line that contains medical terms such as *placental* or *atrophic* will lead the modal to predict that the used modal auxiliary will be *may* rather than *might*. By the same token, the model is sensitive to elements that are typical of conversational contexts, that is, elements such as the pronouns *I* and *you* and forms such as *gonna* and *wanna*, and assigns higher likelihoods of *might* rather than *may* to concordance lines that contain those forms. With regard to *must* and *have to*, similar contrasts can be observed. Concordance lines that contain computational terminology or legal language exhibit a relatively stronger association with *must*. Conversely, concordance lines with conversational elements such as *oh* or *alright* are associated with *have to*.

The idea that constructions are endowed with meaning that relates to issues of genre, interactional contexts, and discourse pragmatics has been formulated already in Östman (2005: 136), who points to examples such as newspaper headlines (e.g. *Mother drowns baby*) as a genre-specific construction in which the omission of articles is possible. In his analysis, Östman actually anticipates an analysis in terms of pragmatic associations of the kind that Schmid (2020) argues for. Instead of describing the discourse properties of a construction as part of its semantic pole, Östman prefers to capture these properties in terms of a link that connects the headline construction to a discourse pattern, that is, the textual genre in which it is likely to appear. We argue that the observations made in Hilpert and Flach (2021) support a parallel argument for English modal auxiliaries. A rich network of associations ties each of the modal auxiliaries to the contexts in which they are preferably used. This conclusion is further supported by the results obtained by Flach, Hilpert and Cappelle (this volume). A particular context will make the activation of one choice more likely, and this effect persists even when other potentially intervening factors are properly controlled for.

5 Concluding remarks

The main aim of this chapter has been to examine whether speakers' knowledge of English modal constructions can be usefully described and captured in terms of associations. We have adopted ideas from Schmid (2020), who distinguishes between four different kinds of association that cover different aspects of linguistic knowledge. We have argued that all four kinds are relevant to the analysis of modal constructions, and we have illustrated their respective roles on the basis of results from corpus-based and experimental studies. We believe that the findings that have been discussed can address what we described as the fat node problem, that is, the tendency to inscribe the rich and idiosyncratic information that speakers associate with constructions into the nodes of the network. If knowledge of language is conceived of as a network, as put forward by Goldberg (2006) and Langacker (2013), among many others, it would appear useful to make the most of that assumption and to prioritize explanations in terms of associations. We would argue that analyses that draw on symbolic, syntagmatic, paradigmatic, and pragmatic associations can indeed accomplish a re-conceptualization of constructional knowledge that yields substantially leaner nodes, but an important question does of course remain: Can our model of modals live up to the challenge set up by Schmid (2017: 25), which aims to reduce linguistic knowledge to associations and nothing else in addition? Are nodes still a necessary part of the constructional network, or should they be abandoned entirely? We cannot claim to resolve this issue here, and we would submit that the answer to that question would partly depend on the level of granularity at which language is studied. The notion of constructions, understood as form-meaning pairs that represent nodes in a network, has led to important insights that retain their value even as our understanding of constructions progresses. In this paper, we have offered illustrations of how some aspects of linguistic knowledge can be re-thought in terms of associations, but we concede that more evidence is needed. We believe Schmid's model to be viable, and we hope to inspire further discussions that will allow us to assess it critically and to identify open questions.

References

Bencini, Giulia M. L. & Adele E. Goldberg. 2000. The contribution of argument structure constructions to sentence meaning. *Journal of Memory and Language* 43(4). 640–51.
Boogaart, Ronny & Egbert Fortuin. 2016. Modality and mood in cognitive linguistics and construction grammars. In Johan van der Auwera & Jan Nuyts (eds.), *The Oxford handbook of mood and modality*, 514–533. Oxford: Oxford University Press.
Bresnan, Joan, Anna Cueni, Tatiana Nikitina & Harald R. Baayen. 2007. Predicting the dative alternation. In Gerlof Boume, Irene Kraemer & Joost Zwarts (eds.), *Cognitive Foundations of Interpretation*, 69–94. Amsterdam: Royal Netherlands Academy of Science.
Budts, Sara & Peter Petré. 2020. Putting connections centre stage in Diachronic Construction Grammar. In Sommerer, Lotte, & Elena Smirnova (eds.), *Nodes and Networks in Diachronic Construction Grammar*, 317–352. Amsterdam: John Benjamins.

Bybee, Joan L. 2010. *Language, Usage, and Cognition*. Cambridge: Cambridge University Press.
Cappelle, Bert & Ilse Depraetere. 2016. Short-circuited interpretations of modal verb constructions. Some evidence from The Simpsons. *Constructions and Frames* 8(1). 7–39.
Celle, Agnès. 2009. Hearsay adverbs and modality. In Raphael Salkie, Pierre Busuttil & Johan van der Auwera (eds.), *Modality in English: Theory and description*, 269–93. Berlin: Mouton de Gruyter.
Diessel, Holger. 2019. *The Grammar Network: How Linguistic Structure Is Shaped by Language Use*. Cambridge: Cambridge University Press.
Diewald, Gabriele. 2020. Paradigms lost – paradigms regained: Paradigms as hyper-constructions. In Lotte Sommerer & Elena Smirnova (eds.), *Nodes and Networks in Diachronic Construction Grammar*, 277–315. Amsterdam: John Benjamins.
Fanego, Teresa. 2019. A construction of independent means: The history of the Way construction revisited. *English Language and Linguistics* 23(3). 671–699.
Fillmore, Charles J., Paul Kay & Mary Catherine O'Connor. 1988. Regularity and idiomaticity in grammatical constructions: The case of let alone. *Language* 64(3). 501–38.
Flach, Susanne. 2021. Beyond modal idioms and modal harmony: A corpus-based analysis of gradient idiomaticity in modal-adverb collocations. *English Language and Linguistics* 25(4). 743–765.
Goldberg, Adele E. 1995. *Constructions: A Construction Grammar Approach to Argument Structure*. Chicago: University of Chicago Press.
Goldberg, Adele E. 2003. Constructions: A new theoretical approach to language, *Trends in Cognitive Sciences* 7/5, 219–24.
Goldberg, Adele E. 2006. *Constructions at Work: The Nature of Generalization in Language*. Oxford: Oxford University Press.
Heylen, Kris, Thomas Wielfaert, Dirk Speelman & Dirk Geeraerts. 2015. Monitoring Polysemy. Word Space Models as a Tool for Large-Scale Lexical Semantic Analysis. *Lingua* 157. 153–172.
Hilpert, Martin. 2013a. *Constructional Change in English: Developments in Allomorphy, Word-formation and Syntax*. Cambridge: Cambridge University Press.
Hilpert, Martin. 2013b. Die englischen Modalverben im Daumenkino: Zur dynamischen Visualisierung von Phänomenen des Sprachwandels. *Zeitschrift für Literaturwissenschaft und Linguistik* 42. 67–82.
Hilpert, Martin. 2016. Change in modal meanings: Another look at the shifting collocates of may. *Constructions and Frames* 8(1). 66–85.
Hilpert, Martin. 2018. Three open questions in Diachronic Construction Grammar. In Evie Coussé, Peter Andersson & Joel Olofsson (eds.), *Grammaticalization meets Construction Grammar*, 21–39. Amsterdam: John Benjamins.
Hilpert, Martin. 2019. *Construction Grammar and its Application to English*. 2nd edition. Edinburgh: Edinburgh University Press.
Hilpert, Martin. 2021. *Ten Lectures on Diachronic Construction Grammar*. Leiden: Brill.
Hilpert, Martin & David Correia Saavedra. 2020. Using token-based semantic vector spaces for corpus-linguistic analyses: From practical applications to tests of theoretical claims. *Corpus Linguistics and Linguistic Theory* 16(2). 393–424.
Hilpert, Martin & Susanne Flach. 2021. Disentangling modal meanings with distributional semantics. *Digital Scholarship in the Humanities* 36(2), 307–321.

Hohaus, Pascal. 2020. *Subordinating Modalities. A Quantitative Analysis of Syntactically Dependent Modal Verb Constructions*. Heidelberg: Metzler.
Hoye, Leo. 1997. *Adverbs and modality in English*. London: Longman.
Hoffmann, Thomas. 2019. *Comparative Correlatives: Diachronic and Synchronic Variation at the Lexicon-Syntax Interface*. Cambridge: Cambridge University Press.
Hudson, Richard. 2015. Review of Rolf Kreyer, The nature of rules, regularities and units in language: A network model of the language system and of language use. *Journal of Linguistics* 51(3). 692–696.
Hutchison, Keith A., David A. Balota, James H. Neely, Michael J. Cortese, Emily R. Cohen-Shikora, Chi-Shing Tse, Melvin J. Yap, Jesse J. Bengson, Dale Niemeyer & Erin Buchanan. 2013. The Semantic Priming Project. *Behavior Research Methods* 45. 1099–1114.
Huddleston, Rodney and Geoffrey K. Pullum. 2002. *The Cambridge Grammar of the English Language*. Cambridge: Cambridge University Press.
Kaltenböck, Gunther. 2021. Funny you should say that: On the use of semi-insubordination in English. *Constructions and Frames* 13(1). 126–159.
Kay, Paul & Charles J. Fillmore. 1999. Grammatical constructions and linguistic generalizations: The What's X Doing Y? construction. *Language* 75(1). 1–33.
Langacker, Ronald W. 2013. *Essentials of Cognitive Grammar*. Oxford: Oxford University Press.
Langacker, Ronald W. 2017. Entrenchment in cognitive grammar. In Hans-Jörg Schmid (ed.), *Entrenchment and the psychology of language learning: How we reorganize and adapt linguistic knowledge*, 39–56. Boston: De Gruyter.
Langacker, Ronald W. 2000. A Dynamic Usage-Based Model. In Michael Barlow and Suzanne Kemmer (eds.), *Usage-Based Models of Language*. Stanford: CSLI Publications, 1–63.
Lester, Nicholas A., Laurie B. Feldman & Fermín Moscoso del Prado Martín. 2017. You can take a noun out of syntax . . . : Syntactic similarity effects in lexical priming. In Glenn Gunzelmann, Andrew Howes, Thora Tenbrink & Eddy J. Davelaar (eds.), *Proceedings of the Thirty-ninth Annual Meeting of the Cognitive Science Society*, 2537–2542. Austin, TX: Cognitive Science Society.
Millar, Neil. 2009. Modal verbs in TIME. Frequency changes 1923-2006. *International Journal of Corpus Linguistics* 14(2). 191–220.
Östman, Jan-Ola. 2005. Construction discourse: A prolegomenon. In Jan-Ola Östman & Mirjam Fried (eds.), *Construction grammars. Cognitive grounding and theoretical extensions*, 121–144. Amsterdam: John Benjamins.
Perek, Florent. 2012. Alternation-based generalizations are stored in the mental grammar: Evidence from a sorting task experiment. *Cognitive Linguistics* 23(3). 601–635.
Schmid, Hans-Jörg (ed.). 2017. *Entrenchment and the psychology of language learning: how we reorganize and adapt linguistic knowledge*. Boston: De Gruyter.
Schmid, Hans-Jörg. 2020. *The dynamics of the linguistic system. Usage, conventionalization, and entrenchment*. Oxford: Oxford University Press.
Sommerer, Lotte & Elena Smirnova (eds.). 2020. *Nodes and Networks in Diachronic Construction Grammar*. Amsterdam: John Benjamins.
Stefanowitsch, Anatol & Stefan T. Gries. 2003. Collostructions: Investigating the interaction of words and constructions. *International Journal of Corpus Linguistics* 8(2). 209–43.

Index

ability 4, 21–35, 39, 43–45, 49–51, 65, 78, 83, 94, 97, 102, 103, 107, 109, 113–122, 177, 199, 229, 233, 240, 244, 263
acceptability 52, 156, 162, 166, 175, 176
acquisition 4, 12, 56, 80, 88, 199, 201, 214, 219, 220–224
actualization 2, 12, 18, 20, 31, 33, 57, 75–78, 82, 97, 101, 102, 109, 114–117, 126, 128, 131, 141, 153
agentivity 9, 99–109, 116, 122, 145, 152–164, 169–175
agreement 18, 22, 35, 130, 132, 139, 146, 225, 240, 241, 247
algorithm 95, 105, 107, 207, 211, 212, 234, 241, 243
alternation 149, 150, 157, 164–168, 173, 175, 259, 267, 269
ambiguity 37, 38, 40, 41, 42, 43, 51, 56, 57, 58, 59, 241
American English 8, 11, 55, 56, 57, 63, 88, 156, 166, 175, 176, 209, 220
animacy 99, 103, 107, 109, 112, 116, 156, 261
applied linguistics 56, 202, 221, 222, 223
association 9, 13, 58, 96, 105, 133–136, 144, 145, 155–161, 168, 169, 170, 171, 173, 252–260, 266, 267

barrier 30, 31, 32, 33, 54, 81
British National Corpus 9, 53, 178, 179, 197, 209, 220, 265

categorization 55, 68, 146, 217, 243
circumstantial source 8, 121, 125, 136, 137, 142
classification 10, 12, 15, 18, 59, 95, 96, 103, 105, 106, 109, 111, 114, 117, 120, 122, 124, 131, 141, 159, 197, 209–217, 225–253, 266
cluster 113, 114, 168, 188, 216, 249, 250
COCA corpus 10, 11, 20, 53, 55, 63, 67, 68, 73–75, 84, 88, 94, 115, 119, 131, 150–161, 175, 209, 210, 211, 214, 215, 220, 228

cognition 1, 5, 13, 47, 62, 87, 91, 141, 197, 198, 268
Cognitive Linguistics 4, 11, 12, 56, 58, 88, 90, 91, 92, 147, 175, 197, 198, 267, 269
collexeme analysis 155, 158, 160, 168
collocation 71, 72, 151, 158, 160, 164, 168, 175, 209, 259–265, 268
collostructional analysis 165, 175, 176, 209, 261
communication 2, 13, 62, 63, 76, 77, 83–87, 91, 153, 198
complexity 7, 61, 66, 67, 71, 73, 79, 85, 155, 158, 199, 208, 209, 216, 220, 224
computational linguistics 10, 198, 223, 224, 252, 253
concordance 180, 265, 266
conditional random forest 105–113
configural frequency analysis 120, 134, 143, 148
Construction Grammar 4–7, 10, 11, 12, 13, 45, 52, 55, 57, 60–62, 67, 71, 85–91, 197, 254–269
context-dependent semantics 81, 82
contextual representations 243, 244, 245, 247, 249
contextual word embeddings 10, 225–252
conventionalization 13, 176, 198, 255, 258, 259, 261, 269
corpus linguistics 6, 8, 12, 13, 52, 56, 89, 137, 149, 175, 176, 198, 220–223, 255, 260–268

Dative alternation 164, 165, 166, 168, 175, 259, 267
deontic modality 13, 21–29, 33, 35, 44, 54, 57, 58, 72, 118, 120, 138, 140, 147, 152, 199, 200, 225, 228, 229, 230, 240, 241, 250, 265
diachrony 13, 55, 57, 90, 198, 220, 264–269
Diachronic Construction Grammar 13, 55, 57, 267–269
disambiguation 10, 43, 50, 65, 83, 214, 225, 226

Index

discourse 2, 8, 31, 49, 51, 55, 59, 67, 77, 86, 87, 97, 115, 121–146, 152, 161, 178, 197, 198, 220, 225, 251–255, 266, 269
discourse-internal source 121, 123, 130, 131, 137, 138, 139, 141, 142, 161
dispersion 9, 182, 185, 188–196
distribution 9, 102, 103, 114, 132, 133, 142, 152, 154, 162, 167, 168, 169, 175, 178, 179, 182, 187, 188, 189, 195, 196, 215, 226–234, 238–243
ditransitive 256, 258, 259
dynamic modality 25, 26, 27, 28, 35, 44, 56, 118, 120

education 9, 189, 191, 219, 220, 221, 223, 224
entrenchment 13, 176, 198, 255, 258, 259, 261, 269
epistemic modality 2, 3, 7, 12, 18–48, 54, 57, 58, 60, 68–89, 93, 94, 97, 102, 103, 107, 109, 113–120, 131, 132, 146–149, 156, 157, 178, 195, 199, 200, 220–233, 238–246, 250, 264
experiment 52, 149, 155, 156, 159–174, 241, 244, 245, 269
explicature 63, 77, 78, 79, 87

factuality 14, 16, 17, 75, 76, 225, 253
features 6, 9, 10, 14, 15, 16, 17, 23, 25, 26, 30, 34, 51, 53, 54, 61, 62, 66, 70, 76, 80, 83, 101, 118, 120, 121, 125, 140, 202, 207–216, 225, 227, 234, 235, 237, 239, 240, 244, 251, 256, 257
frames 11, 12, 55, 87, 89, 90, 92, 175, 176, 268, 269
frequency 9, 57, 67, 88, 120, 134, 143, 148, 175–196, 205–208, 215, 237–243, 263, 265, 269
future 12, 17, 18, 19, 23, 32, 55, 59, 89, 93, 96, 98, 103, 109, 113–116, 135, 139, 157, 195, 196, 214, 226, 251

gender 5, 9, 169, 177–181, 188, 189, 200
general situation necessity 30, 33, 34, 38, 229
general situation possibility 30, 32, 33, 34, 39, 41, 94, 103, 109, 113, 115, 116

generalization 12, 68, 89, 256, 268
genericity 8, 123, 153, 154, 158, 160, 161, 162, 163, 176
genre 96, 97, 100, 103, 107, 109, 112, 113, 115, 132, 158, 159, 160, 161, 170, 227, 252, 266
German 21, 58, 120, 146, 201, 216, 222, 227
gradience 28, 40, 41, 42, 43, 54, 67
grammatical subject 22, 121, 122, 139, 152, 153, 263
grammaticalization 12, 56, 57, 79, 89, 90, 198, 268
n-grams 9, 10, 55, 87, 175, 178–197, 202, 209–216

hearer 2, 37, 40, 45–51, 63, 69, 77, 78, 79, 82, 83, 84, 85, 121, 123, 124, 258–260, 264
homonymy 36, 37, 38, 40, 84

idiomaticity 73, 74, 151, 157, 209, 216, 259
idiosyncraticity 254, 255, 256, 257, 261, 267
illocutionary act 44, 46, 47, 81, 82
implicit meanings 77, 78, 87, 126, 264
indeterminacy 40, 42, 54, 56, 57, 91
individual differences 9, 10, 114, 177, 178, 179, 180–198
individual variation 9, 10, 17, 178, 181, 191, 195, 197, 223
infinitive 9, 15, 71, 93, 96, 112, 116, 127, 141, 155, 158, 159, 168, 171, 259, 262, 264
intersubjectivity 9, 177–198
inversion 8, 14, 141, 151, 262

language acquisition 4, 56, 88, 219–224
language learning 12, 115, 198, 220, 252, 269
language processing 4, 10, 201, 217, 220, 223, 252, 253
language teaching 219, 221, 222, 223
learner corpora 201, 219, 221, 222, 223, 224
learner corpus research 201, 202, 219, 220, 221, 222, 223, 224
learner English 56, 201, 220, 221, 222
learning algorithms 10, 95, 207, 209, 217, 218, 232, 239, 251
lemma 96, 102, 180, 227
lexical semantics 36, 37, 38, 57, 86, 89, 253

Index

lexically regulated saturation 8, 52, 61, 80, 81, 82, 83, 84, 85, 86, 264
linguistic knowledge 5, 11, 62, 67–75, 198, 254, 255, 257, 258, 265, 267, 269
logistic regression 8, 159, 160, 169, 209, 224, 227, 235, 237, 239, 240, 243, 251

machine learning 6, 53, 197, 215, 220, 224, 232, 252, 253
metadata 96, 102, 178, 180, 181, 182, 196, 206
modal sense classification 10, 12, 59, 225–253
monosemy 7, 35, 36, 37, 38, 39, 41, 43, 45, 47, 49, 51, 60, 61, 64, 65, 70, 81, 90
mood 11, 13, 14, 27, 56, 57, 58, 88, 90, 91, 117, 146, 147, 148, 222, 223, 267
multivariate analysis 94, 95, 101, 175, 197, 261

narrow scope 30, 32, 33, 34
native language identification 201, 222, 223
natural language processing 4, 10, 201, 217, 220, 223, 252, 253
necessity verbs 16, 119, 131, 138, 141
negation 8, 14, 39, 99, 101, 102, 112, 116, 141, 151, 156, 164, 262
network model 6, 9, 10, 11, 52, 173, 254, 256, 258, 260–269
node 47, 48, 51, 103, 104, 105, 109, 110, 112, 173, 255, 256, 257, 262, 267
non-native speakers 199, 200, 201, 209, 221

obligation 13, 23, 29, 41, 42, 65, 78, 118, 123, 138, 139, 147, 150, 176, 177, 223
overdispersion 189, 191, 192, 193, 194

paradigm 2, 16, 79, 162, 165, 168, 172, 220, 262
participant 25, 27, 29, 31, 122, 156, 164–173
passive 98, 153, 155, 158, 259
performance 210, 211, 212, 213, 226, 237, 240, 241, 250, 251, 252
performative 22, 24, 25, 26, 118, 123, 124
permissibility 26, 32, 33, 34, 39, 42, 81, 102, 233

permission 2, 4, 21–34, 38, 39, 42, 45, 49, 50, 51, 58, 81, 94, 97, 102, 103, 109, 113–118, 148, 177, 233, 240
person 8, 9, 15, 17, 68, 94, 99, 103, 107, 109, 112, 115, 116, 120, 137, 152, 153, 154, 155, 158, 159, 160, 161, 162, 163, 169, 170, 198, 204, 227, 240
polysemy 7, 14, 35–51, 54, 56, 58, 60, 61, 64, 65, 70, 80–88, 253, 268
possibility 1–8, 16, 17, 20–44, 51–58, 65, 66, 69, 70, 75–98, 100–124, 129, 130, 146, 162, 175, 184, 195, 197, 229, 233, 236, 250, 263
pragmatic associations 11, 173, 174, 255, 260, 264, 265, 266, 267
priming 258, 263, 269
procedural meaning 6, 7, 11, 52, 62, 66, 75–92, 259
proficiency 5, 6, 10, 148, 167, 199–224
pronouns 77, 80, 91, 182, 260, 266
proposition 2, 20, 21, 30, 31, 33, 39, 47, 48, 50, 66, 75–79, 85, 99, 128, 130, 141, 149, 153
prototypicality 16, 18, 27, 42, 220
psycholinguistics 5, 6, 11, 52, 173, 255, 263

random forest 95, 105, 106, 108, 109, 111, 113, 117, 209, 210
referent 22, 30, 31, 33, 43, 46, 50, 64, 80, 119, 122, 152, 153, 154, 160
regression analysis 8, 9, 95, 117, 149, 158–161, 169, 170, 188, 189, 194, 196, 198, 209, 224, 227, 235–243, 251
Relevance Theory 4–8, 11, 12, 45, 52, 54, 58–64, 76, 83, 85–92
REM dataset 8, 9, 10, 53, 94, 119, 120, 121, 131, 132, 155, 237, 241, 242, 246, 247
representations 8, 10, 62, 77, 78, 176, 196, 225–227, 231–236, 243–251
residuals 120, 133, 136, 144, 145, 169
root modality 20, 21, 26, 28, 38, 39, 41, 60, 76–79, 82, 114, 115, 131, 221
root necessity 19, 23, 25, 30, 33, 41, 42, 45, 47, 48, 118, 119, 120, 122, 123, 125, 131, 132, 141, 150, 151, 173

root possibility 21, 22, 23, 28, 30, 35, 38, 39, 41, 42, 56, 88, 103, 118, 119, 121, 146, 175
rules and regulations 8, 24, 31, 121, 126, 129, 131, 135, 136, 137, 138, 140, 142, 151, 152

salience 46, 76, 79, 164, 171, 172, 173
schematic modal constructions 69, 70
scope 20, 21, 25, 26, 30–34, 39, 41, 42, 48, 54, 57, 81, 82, 97, 99, 101, 102, 112, 116, 128, 156, 223, 253
second language acquisition 56, 219, 221, 223, 224
semantics-pragmatics interface 5, 6, 12, 58, 85, 88, 90, 91
sense classification 10, 12, 59, 225, 226, 228, 230, 232, 234, 236, 238, 240, 242, 244, 246, 247, 248, 250, 251, 252, 253
sense distributions 228, 230, 232, 238, 240, 241
short-circuited interpretations` 11, 45, 46, 47, 50, 55, 87, 89, 268
significance 6, 34, 100, 133, 134, 143, 144, 190
situation possibility 30, 32, 33, 34, 39, 41, 94, 103, 109, 113, 115, 116
sociolinguistics 4, 13, 147, 188, 189, 190, 194, 196, 198
source of modality 95, 123, 146, 149, 156, 175
speaker variation 10, 177, 181, 182, 188, 189, 191, 194
speech 5, 8, 20, 21, 24, 25, 26, 27, 45, 49, 50, 57, 58, 77, 81, 82, 94, 95, 100, 103, 107, 109, 112, 116, 156, 180, 227, 258, 260
subclause 96–103, 109, 115, 116, 126, 128, 130
subject-external source 31–34
subject-internal source 8, 31, 32, 121, 122, 132, 142, 152, 157
subjectivity 12, 23, 24, 25, 57, 123, 147, 172, 197, 220
suppletion 135, 136, 143, 144, 145
syllables 208, 219

symbolic associations 255, 258, 264
synonymy 9, 25, 119, 149, 156, 162, 165, 173, 177, 196
syntagmatic associations 255, 258, 259, 260, 261, 262, 263, 265
syntax 12, 59, 86, 89, 175, 219, 224, 225, 268, 269

taxonomy 7, 16, 19–22, 25, 28–34, 42, 44, 54, 56, 61, 83, 88, 137, 146, 175, 229
temporal location 93, 98, 101, 103, 106, 107, 109, 112, 113, 114, 115, 116
tense 12, 17, 19, 54, 58, 87, 88, 90, 93, 103, 112, 116, 135, 145, 151, 175, 227, 247, 259
MPQA dataset 225, 228, 236, 239, 240, 241, 242, 245, 247
truth-conditional content 45, 49, 50, 51, 54, 86

usage 6, 8, 9, 12, 13, 18, 40, 47, 49, 53, 56, 67, 87, 88, 89, 147, 149, 154, 155, 171, 175–177, 181, 184, 185, 188, 194–198, 224, 226, 255, 256, 258, 261, 268, 269
usage-based models of language 6, 8, 12, 47, 56, 67, 88, 89, 176, 177, 197, 255, 258, 269
utterance 21, 42, 46, 47, 49, 50, 51, 57, 61, 63, 68, 75, 84, 86, 89, 94, 172, 180, 258, 259, 260, 264

vagueness 36, 37, 40, 56, 57, 58
variables 8, 9, 80, 83, 95–115, 121, 151, 152, 156–164, 169, 170, 172, 173, 178, 181, 188–196
variation 3–6, 9, 10, 17, 78, 82, 85, 86, 103, 106, 147, 164, 176–182, 187–200, 222, 223, 246, 269
vector 218, 224, 231–237, 252, 265, 268

wide-scope possibility 30–32
word embeddings 10, 216, 225–252
word representations 10, 225, 226, 227, 231, 234, 235, 236, 243, 244, 246

www.ingramcontent.com/pod-product-compliance
Lightning Source LLC
Chambersburg PA
CBHW050554170426
43201CB00011B/1686